Financing Economic Development
in the
21st Century

Financing
Economic
Development
in the
21st Century

Edited by
Sammis B. White, Richard D. Bingham,
and Edward W. Hill

M.E. Sharpe
Armonk, New York
London, England

Library of Congress Cataloging-in-Publication Data

Financing economic development in the 21st century / edited by Sammis B. White,
Richard D. Bingham, and Edward W. Hill.
   p. cm.
Includes bibliographical references and index.
ISBN 0-7656-0830-8 (cloth: alk. paper) — ISBN 0-7656-0831-6 (pbk.: alk. paper)
   1. United States—Economic conditions—2001– 2. Venture capital—United States.
3. Finance, Public—United States. 4. New business enterprises—United States—
Finance. I. White, Sammis B. II. Bingham, Richard D. III. Hill, Edward W.

HC106.83 .F557 2003
338.973—dc21   2002030895

Printed in the United States of America

The paper used in this publication meets the minimum requirements of
American National Standard for Information Sciences
Permanence of Paper for Printed Library Materials,
ANSI Z 39.48-1984.

BM (c)	10	9	8	7	6	5	4	3	2	1
BM (p)	10	9	8	7	6	5	4	3	2	1

Contents

List of Tables and Figures

Tables

Figures

Overview

Communities across the country seek secure financial futures. But seeking and achieving may be two different things. The national and international economies march to their own drummers. Local municipal entities do not have control over their own economic fates. They must adjust to the changing larger economies. Sometimes areas win big, as did Pittsburgh with the growth of steel or the Silicon Valley with the growth of computers. But as Pittsburgh has also shown, there are downturns as well. Economies that had been growing begin shrinking. Such communities are challenged to find ways to strengthen themselves. Other communities may be slow to grow, and they also must find ways to ensure a more secure future.

A critical ingredient for economic growth is capital. That is the central point of a capitalist economy. Fortunately, in the United States, we have developed a wide variety of tools to fund business activity. We rely heavily on such traditional financial institutions as banks. But we have also developed many innovative ways to reach portions of the market that are not served well by traditional financial institutions. New firms, for example, are not as likely to receive loans from banks as are established businesses. Businesses in specific areas, such as inner cities or rural communities, have a more difficult time convincing traditional sources that they are reasonable firms to which to make loans.

Additionally, communities compete with one another for development. Unless they have revenue sharing agreements, neighboring communities seek to enlarge their own economic base. They want to do so with the least possible expenditure on their part. So they develop tools that appear to have little or no cost to their community, tools such as tax incremental finance districts, impact fees, developer donations, and the like. The idea is to promote development, but not at the expense of existing residents and businesses.

The federal government also has a hand in this. A periodic federal government goal is to improve equity in the nation by increasing the employment opportunities for those with few opportunities. The federal government for the past forty years has tried several initiatives to expand job opportunities in low-income areas. In recent years, the federal government has created special zones in which employers are offered incentives to locate and to hire workers who have few opportunities.

Communities also face a number of special situations in which they might have to provide capital in order to stimulate development. For example, communities may have previously used land that is environmentally contaminated. With current laws placing financial responsibility on any owner, such lands are difficult to get developed. But for communities with little open space, such lands are the future. Creative mechanisms need to be developed to attract investments. Similarly, communities are being pressed to enhance themselves with sports stadiums of various sorts. Not all communities do so, but the pressure is there to put public dollars into such developments, even in communities that have resisted subsidizing other forms of economic development.

Public subsidies are not the only solution. In fact, subsidies are but a small part of the solution. The answer in most situations is private capital. More and more communities are realizing the important role that "risk capital," as opposed to the more conservative bank capital, plays in developing new businesses. The more of such risk capital that can be attracted to ventures in a community, the greater the community's chances of generating viable new businesses that will grow in the future. Communities need to learn about "angel financing" and "venture capital." Communities must do what they can to ensure that such sources are available locally and that there is a demand for such moneys (i.e., businesses are being started and grown).

For individuals who are interested in economic development and what makes it work, knowledge of alternative means of financing is critical. This volume is intended as an introduction to many of the more viable forms of finance available for economic development. The chapters cover a wide range, from angel finance to revolving loan funds to tax incentives to various developer payment schemes. The methods cover public, private, and combined techniques. The options vary from ways to force developers to pay to methods to publicly underwrite new economic activity. The alternatives may be utilized by municipalities, the state, or even the federal government, but most are local. The alternatives covered are those that we think are most likely to be employed in the foreseeable future. These are the techniques that have stood the test of time or have a history that should be recognized.

Economic development finance has become much more sophisticated than it was fifteen years ago. Many of the methods that were tried then have been refined or eliminated. A few, such as tax increment finance, venture capital, and business angels, have been expanded upon and used even more widely. Others such as industrial revenue bonds and export financing have largely disappeared from the landscape. This new volume introduces readers to a number of finance techniques and to some of the formal assessments of the variety of alternatives that have been employed to promote economic development. The featured techniques are likely to be in use for the foreseeable future, given their success to date.

The book may be read cover to cover, or individual chapters can be used in any order desired. The intent is to inform the reader of the basics of the options and to review what is known about how well many of the financing options work.

Introduction

Before looking at alternative ways to fund development, it is important to obtain an understanding of what it is that communities are seeking to achieve and how legally they are able to operate. The first chapter, by Stephen Malpezzi, starts by defining economic development. He goes on to discuss various goals of economic development that communities might seek. Examples include more employment, higher property values, and higher per capita income. Fortunately, these often occur together. But they are not exclusive, and they imply somewhat different paths of development.

Malpezzi then takes a cursory look at what factors are thought to be responsible for development, in addition to capital and public incentives. But his real focus is the special role of finance in the economy. He discusses many forms of finance. He talks of numerous efforts by the public sector to supplement the forms available in the private sector. He introduces the many topics that are covered by the subsequent chapters.

Ferdinand (Andy) Schoettle sets the legal stage for public intervention in financing economic development. Government involvement came early in the United States. Opened in 1825, the Erie Canal was dug with money from bonds floated by the state of New York. The effort was so successful that other states and municipalities decided it was an approach they should also try. Unfortunately, few enterprises were as successful as the Erie Canal. Municipal and state budgets were greatly strained by their ill-conceived investments. The result was the enactment of strict limits on such endeavors.

But those limits did not stop communities from creating alternative ways to attempt to stimulate development. The issue is what is legal and why. This chapter discusses some of the enabling laws and some of the limits that have developed over time and sets the stage for many of the subsequent chapters.

The Developer Pays

Communities want development to occur. In the middle of the twentieth century there were many examples of communities that generated development by investing their own money in such development stimulants as infra-structure. If a developer would propose building a 200-unit residential sub-division or an industrial park, the community would commit to building the streets and supplying the water and sewer infrastructure. Such an aggressive approach has largely been abandoned because it proved to be too expensive to the community. In fact, the tables have almost completely turned—developers must now agree to pave the streets and put in the local infrastructure for sewer and water before they even begin to get approval for a proposed project.

The next three chapters discuss various elements of economic develop-ment finance in the new world for developers. The chapter by Rachel Weber discusses a very popular technique for funding the construction of infra-structure for development. The technique is called tax incremental financing (TIF). It is a technique that involves the individual municipality putting in some or all of the infrastructure for a development, as an incentive to attract that development. Although the municipality pays for the development up front through the sale of bonds, it is the purchasers of the parcels that pay in the long run. All of the increment in property taxes above and beyond what was paid before development occurs is channeled to pay off the bonds for the infrastructure. Once the bonds are paid off, then the additional tax rev-enue goes into the community's general fund. The community does not pay directly, nor does the developer. But by putting in the infrastructure up front, the community is able to stimulate development that might not have other-wise occurred. That is its appeal. TIFs are not without flaws; Weber dis-cusses some of these and suggests improvements that might help them to be even more successful as an economic development technique.

The chapter by Larry Ledebur and Douglas Woodward talks of modifica-tion to public funding techniques that can be employed to the benefit of a community. In some cases, communities decide that they must invest some of their own money to stimulate development. Each time a community does so, it is taking a chance that such development might not repay the community what it has invested, much less pay a return on that investment. After several high visibility situations in which companies received financial inducements to lo-cate to specific communities and then left after having accepted the money, communities began to wise up. Communities still offer financial incentives, but instead of just suffering if the company does not stay or does not create as many jobs as promised, communities can get tough. They can create what have come to be known as "recapture agreements," ways to retrieve money from companies that have not kept their promises. Recapture agreements are prevalent in Europe and just beginning to gain acceptance here.

These recapture agreements cover a range of situations. Sometimes com-panies do not get a free ride; they get a repayable inducement to do business in a given community. Such inducements are termed "clawbacks." Another term is a "recision" agreement, one that allows for cancellation of a subsidy agreement, should certain specific conditions not be met. In other instances penalties can be charged to firms for not performing in the manner specified or for moving before an agreement expires. Yet another modification is termed a "recalibration." This applies in situations where a subsidy agreement is adjusted over time in response to changing business conditions. In each situation communities are not committed to a certain subsidy and then left out to dry. This chapter discusses the many issues related to such recapture agreements. The various agreements have yet to be universally used. But the case is made that they should be to better protect the communities offering subsidies.

The third chapter in this section is about another way to extract concessions from developers that want to develop in a given community. Unlike the recapture agreements that apply to communities that have given subsidies to attract development, development exactions apply to developers that want entrée to a community and the community wants to avoid some of the costs associated with that development. Michael Peddle and Roger Dahlstrom discuss many alternative ways to get the developer and ultimately the developed property owner to pay for some of the costs that development generates for a community. Examples include such techniques as impact fees; developer donations; in-kind developer provision of services; and developer-constructed, off-site infrastructure. The chapter explores these options and discusses some of the places where each might be more appropriate. In addition, it looks at what might be the costs of attempting to use such techniques on developers.

Public Financing

For at least the past thirty years in the United States, communities, sometimes with the help of the federal government, have developed various ways to try to induce new development to occur within their boundaries. Several of the methods employed have involved subsidies. Subsidies have sometimes been direct cash grants. Other times they have involved the government provision of services that otherwise would have cost the developer additional money. In still other instances, they have involved property tax reductions or income tax reductions or credits. Subsidies may also involve reduced fees, free employee training, or several other ways to reduce the private sector costs of locating in a specific community.

The big question for all communities and for the U.S. government is to what degree these various forms of subsidization have actually helped to bring about the desired development. Several chapters in this section explore specific types of subsidy programs and assess the degree to which the subsidies have succeeded in stimulating the types and scale of development intended.

Alan Peters and Peter Fisher are experts on a federally led program known as enterprise zones. These are specially designated geographic areas in which firms can earn tax credits or other forms of tax reductions for locating and adding specified types of employees. The idea behind them is the inducement of new development in a specified territory and the hiring of specific, low-income employees. The federal zones have been duplicated by many states and even some cities. The big question is whether this approach actually works. Peters and Fisher review the fairly extensive literature on that issue and report on their own extensive efforts to answer the question.

Rod Hissong goes even further to review a number of different approaches to inducing economic development. He discusses enterprise zones, but he goes beyond to explore the literature on several alternatives. He criticizes not only the specific mechanisms, but also the means of evaluating the mechanisms. He suggests alternative means of evaluation and discusses some superior examples.

Donald Schunk and Douglas Woodward report on their recent assessment of state incentives in the context of overall state economic development, using BMW's location in South Carolina as a case study. It is the first published, comprehensive case study of the impact of industrial incentives. The authors make the explicit attempt to link economic development incentives and a variety of outcomes. They make the case that, when properly designed and executed, economic development incentives can attract significant capital investment, create jobs, and promote regional restructuring. They also suggest that these aims are not always, nor necessarily often, achieved.

The next two chapters take a different tack. They explore in some detail two public means of stimulating development. Kelly Robinson examines publicly funded revolving loan funds. These are entities that take the original capital, lend it out, and then make additional loans to new firms as the original set of loans is repaid. The appeal is that loans can be targeted to firms with specific characteristics and that the money continues to circulate among those types of firms. Such loans are usually made to firms that may not be able to get bank financing or as much bank financing as they think they need to succeed. Thus, the public sector is helping to meet a need and bring about additional development.

Beverly McLean and James Bates explore an approach to development that is the result of years of learning from mistakes. They examine a refined way of collaborating to finance neighborhood business revitalization. They review the many barriers to neighborhood business development, examine the strengths and weaknesses of private sector financing tools for this purpose, and then provide some examples of successful collaborative efforts to revitalize neighborhood businesses. They see a role for public sector financial involvement.

Special Situations

General finance techniques can work in many situations to promote economic development. But in some instances the usual may not be enough or it may not be appropriate. The chapters in this section examine what we think are special situations, instances in which the more common forms of economic development finance might not be sufficient.

The first chapter of the section deals with a very high visibility mechanism that many communities have selected as a means of economic development—sports facilities. Ziona Austrian and Mark Rosentraub review the recent wave of largely public investment in sports facilities. Communities look to this investment to generate construction jobs, skyline enhancement, entertainment employment, and a psyche boost for the community. Sports franchise owners often convince local politicians that they will betray the public trust if they do not commit public financing to keep the "symbol" of being a "major league city" in the community by constructing a new facility. But is this a wise public investment? Austrian and Rosentraub review the expanding literature that assesses the evidence on this question. They cite the few instances in which private owners have stepped up and made the investment themselves, as they did before the latest round of facility construction. And they explore the many, and sometimes unique, ways that communities have employed to come up with the dollars needed to pay for these expensive facilities.

The second chapter of special situations is quite different. The topic is brownfields—environmentally contaminated land or buildings that have proved to be difficult to reuse because of the liability for cleanup involved. These sites have economic potential from the private perspective because some exceptional profits can be made if the sites can be reused. From the public sector viewpoint, the sites hold potential as an additional tax base and as the location of many new jobs. The difficulty is that reclamation is thought to be very expensive and the results are not assured. Private developers have been slow to step into these situations, preferring to put their money and time into safer "greenfield" development.

To stimulate brownfield redevelopment, the public sector often has to step forward in order to reduce perceived risk. Local, state, and federal governments have created a variety of techniques, often financial subsidies, to convince private investors to get involved with brownfields. Peter Meyer and Kristen Yount review the problems and many of the finance schemes that have been created to address brownfield redevelopment. Progress has been made on this topic, but much remains to be done.

The third chapter in this section covers a quite different situation, that of retail. Unlike help for manufacturing, which can be easily justified because manufacturing is thought to be a "base" industry that brings in money from outside the local economy, retail seldom plays this role. The Mall of America in Bloomington, Minnesota, is an exception. Most retail serves a largely local audience. Providing a public subsidy to encourage most forms of retail development is harder, because what a subsidy does is modestly change the location of that activity. William Bowen, Kimberly Winson-Geideman, and Robert Simons explore the difficult subject of public investment in retail development.

The authors explore the rationale for public involvement. They try to find situations in which public investment can be justified. That is not an easy task. Having explored possible situations, they go on to examine the variety of tools available for the task and discuss several examples where each has been used. They finish by exploring a special situation in which public investment might be justified more easily—the assisting of retail for equity reasons, mainly attempts to serve underserved, low-income neighborhoods.

The fourth chapter in the section is also quite different. It focuses on rural development. Rural development is very different from urban development because the scale of development and densities are much smaller. Rural areas have been declining for over a century, yet almost one-quarter of all Americans live in places designated as rural by the Census Bureau. The difficulty is that this 25 percent of the population is spread over the vast majority of the landscape. Most rural areas are limited in terms of financial capital, human capital, and natural resources beyond vast acreage. Development does not occur as naturally as in urban areas.

Rural economic development is more likely than urban development to need partnerships. The risk is greater, as are the hurdles, such as lack of capital, absence of economies of scale, few entrepreneurial networks, and an independent spirit among rural populations. These hurdles can be lowered through policy and effort. That is the charge. Economic development finance has a role, and John Magill reviews many of the ways in which economic development is being undertaken. Readers will find many acronyms for government programs that have been used in rural economic development. These programs appear to be the needed ingredient to stimulate more rural development.

Private Finance

In a variety of situations public finance in different guises is used to stimulate private investment. But what is clear is that it is private finance that drives development. Certainly, in specific situations a good case has been made for various forms of public intervention. However, most of the investment in local economies comes from private sources of capital, especially for new business formation. The last section of the book contains three chapters that cover three of the most important sources of private capital for new business formation and growth.

Timothy Bates examines the use of bank credit for small businesses. A common misperception is that new business owners do not have access to bank loans. Bates contradicts this "myth" and contends that over 50 percent of the startup funding to launch new businesses comes from borrowings, mainly from banks. As the new firms mature, they rely increasingly on banks for financing. This is not to say that assembling sufficient capital is easy; it is not. The chapter explores the degree to which barriers to funding small businesses exist and for whom the barriers are larger. Bates also explores some means of overcoming those barriers.

For some new businesses, those thought to have high-growth potential, a highly sought source of capital is the "business angel." Business angels are individuals with substantial net worth who invest in startup and early stage businesses. These wealthy individuals have the wherewithal to absorb losses if a firm does not succeed to the degree initially imagined. The angels can and often do invest in several new startups concurrently, hoping that at least one will "hit the home run" and return many times the original investment. The firms they choose to support are thought to have the potential to grow much more rapidly than the norm. Such firms are often called "gazelles" because they jump so far into the lead. Angels commonly provide not just capital but seasoned business advice to help the firms succeed. Fortunately for the U.S. economy, the number of business angels grew rapidly in the 1990s as numerous business enterprises flourished.

Adam Bock discusses many aspects of angel finance, from the perspectives of both the angel and the individual seeking angel finance. This chapter is a comprehensive look at angel financing, and it contains a wealth of information for all who may be involved in the activity. Bock actually runs two angel-finance networks, organizations that pool business angel money and interests. Angel networks are a recent development that has added efficiency to the search for angel money. New firm owners can now reach thirty or more potential investors by making a pitch to one network, and angels can listen to a limited number of prescreened pitches to seek the firms in which they care to invest. The chapter is a mini-handbook on the subject of business angels.

The final chapter is a similar handbook, but it covers a more specialized commodity, venture capital. Venture capital is invested in even fewer firms than angel finance. At its high point in 2001, venture capitalists invested over $210 billion in new enterprises. That is a staggering figure and speaks to its importance. But venture capital is reserved for those firms that appear to have the best chance of succeeding past the initial business angel or other informal financing rounds. In recent years the bulk of these venture capital funds has gone to high-tech firms. But that pattern is likely to change a bit as the high-tech sector loses its luster and enormous expectations.

David Arnstein, a venture capitalist, gives the reader a host of insights into this oft-mentioned form of capital. The chapter explores just what venture capital is, to whom it is most likely to go, and the various stages of firm growth and finance needs. He goes on to discuss current industry preferences and the history of venture capital. He then explores the details of how one goes about obtaining venture capital and how venture capitalists operate. The details offer insights to anyone who wants to be involved in any role in the venture capital process.

Part 1
Introduction

1

Local Economic Development and Its Finance

An Introduction

Stephen Malpezzi

Introduction

The title of this volume fairly reflects its contents: *Financing Economic Development in the 21st Century*. In this chapter we have two objectives. First, we briefly discuss what is meant by economic development. Second, we provide a short overview of the general role finance plays in economic development. Third, we briefly introduce some of the particular ways local economic development is financed in the United States.

What Is Economic Development?

Economic development is surprisingly difficult to define precisely. What is our goal, and how can we measure our progress to it? Is it the number of jobs, income or wages, wealth, an improved distribution of income, education, health, structural change, or a better environment? Or is it the "quality of life," measured in some broad way incorporating noneconomic as well as economic factors? All these elements are valid components of the multidimensional thing we call development. As we will see below, it is fortunate that many positive measures are at least roughly correlated, so that, for example, actions that increase employment also tend to increase wages and income, and even to some extent improve the distribution of income.[1]

If you meet an economist in the street and ask her what the best measure of development is, she will probably reply "welfare" or "well-being." Since we cannot easily measure welfare directly, at least in a reliable fashion, we can think of things like income and employment as intervening variables that enable one to attain a higher degree of well-being. Generally, a person's welfare is greater if their income rises; and generally, a person is better off with a job than if unemployed.[2]

The use of measures like income or gross domestic product is hardly surprising; despite criticism, and greater availability of alternatives, these indicators remain the most popular kinds of summary measures of development. Over the long run and in the aggregate, of course, income and gross product or output are closely linked. In the short run, and from person to person and from place to place, these can diverge. For example, localities with large numbers of retirees will have a larger gap between output and income than localities with few retirees.

Many local economic development "practitioners" (local politicians, policy wonks, and applied academics) focus on employment. Employment matters, of course, but income is probably more directly related to well-being, and hence a better summary measure. If we look at differences from one metropolitan area to another, there is substantial correlation between employment and income. So, fortunately, it is not often that development practitioners have to make a choice to improve one at the expense of the other, at least in the long run.

Other development practitioners focus on the value of local real estate. This is particularly true of local government officials concerned with increasing the size of their tax base, especially in states like Wisconsin, New Hampshire, and New Jersey that rely heavily on the taxation of real property.

Malpezzi (2002) presents empirical tests of the relationships between and among seven candidate measures of development, including income, employment, the size of the real estate stock, and the distribution of income. The results of a detailed statistical analysis show that in most respects the most common "usual suspects," namely, per capita income or output, and measures of employment, are well correlated with each other and with other potential measures. The most important exception is that income and employment measures are not strongly correlated with a more even distribution of income. However, even in this respect, it appears that faster growing metropolitan areas are usually seeing some improvement in their income distribution. Furthermore, there is even stronger evidence that higher incomes and growth are correlated with lower poverty rates (which is related to but different from the distribution of income per se).[3] In the rest of this chapter, we will focus on income and employment, though we will say a little more about distribution as well.

U.S. Growth and Distribution: A Few Stylized Facts

In order to present some basic underpinnings for the discussion below, we need to present some stylized facts. In this chapter, we will focus on state level data; more detailed comparisons, including metropolitan level comparison, can be found in Malpezzi (2002). Tables 1.1 through 1.3 present some basic data on population, employment, and real income per capita, and these data are for the fifty states, the District of Columbia, and the United States as a whole.[4]

From Table 1.1 we see that U.S. *population* grew more or less steadily over the past thirty years, from about 201 million in 1969 to an estimated 276 million in 2000, or an annual compounded growth rate of about 1.0 percent.[5] Generally, the Midwest has been growing more slowly than the country as a whole, and a number of states in the South and West, such as Arizona, California, Colorado, Georgia, and Texas are growing faster. The fastest growing state, Nevada, racked up an impressive 4.5 percent annual rate of population growth.

Table 1.2 shows that U.S. *employment* also grew steadily over the past thirty years, from about 91 million to about 167 million, or an annual compounded growth rate of 2.0 percent. Employment has grown twice as fast as population for several reasons, mainly that much of the "baby boom" and "baby boomlet" entered the workforce during this period, and workforce participation by women increased. However, demographic forecasts tell us this pattern is not likely to hold over the next few decades.[6] The rise in female labor force participation has tapered off, and the baby boom is retiring, while the "baby bustlet" is entering the labor force.

Notice that states with fast rates of employment growth (Table 1.2) are the states with high rates of population growth (Table 1.1). In fact, the correlation between population growth and employment growth is about 0.97, as strong as any correlation one would observe across states. With only a few exceptions (New York and Hawaii), state employment growth was about one percentage point higher than the state's corresponding population growth over the 1969–98 period. Of course, by itself, this correlation begs the question of causality.[7] Regional economists have long studied the question, do people follow jobs, or do jobs follow people? The consensus view after many studies is that both effects can be found, but, in the long run, the latter dominates.[8] That is, the effect of an increase in population on future job growth is considerably stronger than the effect of an increase in employment on future population growth.

While population and employment are important, in many respects *income per capita* is an even better summary measure of local economic performance, in that it is most closely tied to standards of living.[9] As Table 1.3 shows, in 1969, average income per capita was about $14,800 for the United States as a whole in today's dollars.[10] Over the next thirty years, U.S. per capita income grew at about 2.1 percent to $29,600. Broadly speaking, we

Table 1.1

U.S. Population by State

State	Population 1969	Population 1998	Annual growth rate of population 1969–1998 (%)	Trend forecast of population 2000
Alabama	3,440,000	4,351,037	0.8	4,576,201
Alaska	296,000	615,205	2.6	658,604
Arizona	1,737,000	4,667,277	3.5	4,759,193
Arkansas	1,913,000	2,538,202	1.0	2,628,281
California	19,711,000	32,682,794	1.8	34,076,770
Colorado	2,166,000	3,968,967	2.1	3,992,842
Connecticut	3,000,000	3,272,563	0.3	3,345,717
Delaware	540,000	744,066	1.1	724,851
District of Columbia	762,000	521,426	−1.3	551,332
Florida	6,641,000	14,908,230	2.8	15,450,010
Georgia	4,551,000	7,636,522	1.8	7,888,873
Hawaii	743,000	1,190,472	1.6	1,236,878
Idaho	707,000	1,230,923	1.9	1,238,525
Illinois	11,039,000	12,069,774	0.3	12,185,703
Indiana	5,143,000	5,907,617	0.5	5,915,680
Iowa	2,805,000	2,861,025	0.1	2,893,884
Kansas	2,236,000	2,638,667	0.6	2,676,645
Kentucky	3,198,000	3,934,310	0.7	3,985,352
Louisiana	3,619,000	4,362,758	0.6	4,432,273
Maine	992,000	1,247,554	0.8	1,272,088
Maryland	3,868,000	5,130,072	1.0	5,159,837
Massachusetts	5,650,000	6,144,407	0.3	6,191,989
Michigan	8,781,000	9,820,231	0.4	9,976,746
Minnesota	3,758,000	4,726,411	0.8	4,796,875
Mississippi	2,220,000	2,751,335	0.7	2,781,597
Missouri	4,640,000	5,437,562	0.5	5,527,137
Montana	694,000	879,533	0.8	886,799
Nebraska	1,474,000	1,660,772	0.4	1,815,298
Nevada	480,000	1,743,772	4.5	1,804,130
New Hampshire	724,000	1,185,823	1.7	1,196,661
New Jersey	7,095,000	8,095,542	0.5	8,402,265
New Mexico	1,011,000	1,733,535	1.9	1,733,892
New York	18,105,000	18,159,175	0.0	18,674,014
North Carolina	5,031,000	7,545,828	1.4	7,559,739
North Dakota	621,000	637,808	0.1	640,538
Ohio	10,563,000	11,237,752	0.2	11,453,406
Oklahoma	2,535,000	3,339,478	1.0	3,448,258
Oregon	2,062,000	3,282,055	1.6	3,287,042
Pennsylvania	11,741,000	12,002,329	0.1	12,050,476
Rhode Island	932,000	987,704	0.2	1,015,432
South Carolina	2,570,000	3,839,578	1.4	3,863,440
South Dakota	668,000	730,789	0.3	747,726
Tennessee	3,897,000	5,432,679	1.2	5,654,106

Texas	11,045,000	19,712,389	2.0	20,682,054
Utah	1,047,000	2,100,562	2.4	2,144,648
Vermont	437,000	590,579	1.0	606,522
Virginia	4,614,000	6,789,225	1.3	7,042,683
Washington	3,343,000	5,687,832	1.8	5,702,337
West Virginia	1,746,000	1,811,688	0.1	1,833,852
Wisconsin	4,378,000	5,222,124	0.6	5,359,984
Wyoming	329,000	480,045	1.3	480,045
United States	201,298,000	270,248,003	1.0	275,793,973

found that income per capita roughly doubled over the period. Such performance is quite stunning when we think of it this way: It took us about 10,000 years to get from (at best!) subsistence level living to $14,000 per capita in the late 1960s. Then it took us only thirty years to double that amount!

Distributional Considerations

Despite the impressive performance of the U.S. economy in the aggregate, all citizens have not shared in these economic gains equally. After adjusting for inflation, income per capita within the five income quintiles of the United States shows that median household incomes have barely budged for those in the bottom 20 percent of the U.S. income distribution.[11] On the other hand, those in the top 20 percent saw a real growth of about 1.4 percent per annum over the period.[12]

Although national data show that in the aggregate the distribution of income is worsening over time while the overall economy has been growing, two important points need to be put on the table. First, a world in which the distribution is becoming more unequal because *top incomes are growing fast while the incomes of the poor are stagnant or growing slowly* is unquestionably cause for serious concern. However, while such a divergence is, in my view, a bad thing, such an outcome is still a better situation than an alternative world where an equivalent increase in inequality is driven by *modest increases in income at the high end and falling incomes at the low end*. In other words, it matters *not only* whether the spread is getting wider, but also *why it is doing so*.

Second, the fact that we happen to have increasing income inequality at the same time our economy is growing does not necessarily imply one always accompanies the other. In fact, careful studies of U.S. metropolitan areas such as those by Bartik (1994) and Madden (2000), for example, show that in a broad range of metropolitan areas (with some exceptions), faster economic growth, as usually measured, improves the economic conditions of the poor even more than it does those of the rich.

Table 1.2

U.S. Employment by State

State	Employment 1969	Employment 1998	Annual growth rate of employment 1969–1998 (%)	Trend forecast of employment 2000
Alabama	1,411,229	2,386,331	1.8	2,474,366
Alaska	143,815	384,853	3.5	411,886
Arizona	711,345	2,613,862	4.6	2,859,316
Arkansas	799,913	1,463,142	2.1	1,525,360
California	9,032,879	18,534,120	2.5	19,475,978
Colorado	1,001,382	2,738,645	3.5	2,935,413
Connecticut	1,417,072	2,067,414	1.3	2,121,975
Delaware	270,578	483,264	2.0	502,986
District of Columbia	678,131	720,591	0.2	723,615
Florida	2,856,903	8,348,688	3.8	8,989,531
Georgia	2,119,102	4,624,248	2.7	4,879,921
Hawaii	415,913	746,150	2.0	776,839
Idaho	315,334	737,116	3.0	781,570
Illinois	5,179,183	7,212,394	1.1	7,379,007
Indiana	2,326,790	3,576,683	1.5	3,684,325
Iowa	1,289,309	1,900,182	1.3	1,951,694
Kansas	1,029,010	1,743,012	1.8	1,807,529
Kentucky	1,331,867	2,252,227	1.8	2,335,322
Louisiana	1,440,229	2,362,004	1.7	2,443,981
Maine	443,445	752,597	1.8	780,558
Maryland	1,679,356	2,971,500	2.0	3,090,777
Massachussets	2,678,963	3,935,507	1.3	4,041,292
Michigan	3,639,948	5,458,174	1.4	5,612,832
Minnesota	1,690,875	3,232,307	2.3	3,380,022
Mississippi	908,671	1,462,732	1.7	1,511,555
Missouri	2,215,956	3,420,531	1.5	3,524,486
Montana	297,952	543,333	2.1	566,318
Nebraska	703,748	1,151,260	1.7	1,191,009
Nevada	243,701	1,135,380	5.4	1,262,495
New Hampshire	334,070	743,600	2.8	785,787
New Jersey	3,061,498	4,623,071	1.4	4,756,365
New Mexico	394,799	945,953	3.1	1,004,712
New York	8,495,813	10,087,855	0.6	10,208,061
North Carolina	2,457,991	4,732,896	2.3	4,951,661
North Dakota	273,930	441,719	1.7	456,517
Ohio	4,695,425	6,696,762	1.2	6,862,758
Oklahoma	1,107,253	1,969,570	2.0	2,049,375
Oregon	920,165	2,030,583	2.8	2,144,510
Pennsylvania	5,249,958	6,799,335	0.9	6,921,688
Rhode Island	440,081	562,836	0.9	572,467
South Carolina	1,170,439	2,220,403	2.2	2,320,652
South Dakota	303,106	499,978	1.7	517,537
Tennessee	1,788,719	3,357,985	2.2	3,507,061

Texas	5,005,236	11,678,353	3.0	12,381,063
Utah	443,666	1,313,022	3.8	1,415,043
Vermont	202,578	384,047	2.2	401,368
Virginia	2,147,847	4,208,607	2.3	4,408,447
Washington	1,538,772	3,419,408	2.8	3,612,988
West Virginia	651,781	877,900	1.0	896,118
Wisconsin	1,943,519	3,330,028	1.9	3,456,019
Wyoming	157,955	316,542	2.4	332,087
United States	91,057,200	160,198,700	2.0	166,563,298

These distributional considerations are of interest first on their own account, because most American citizens care about the well-being of their neighbors. But they also have implications for state and local fiscal conditions. For example, Gyourko (1998) has estimated that a city with a poverty rate one percentage point higher than average spends an extra $2.20 per capita on police services after controlling for other determinants of such spending. And, unsurprisingly, poorer localities have weaker tax bases.

Why Do Regions Grow and Develop?

Our work above suggests that the "usual suspects," especially income, are reasonable summary measures of development. But our results also suggest that there is much to be gained from considering several indicators at once, when feasible, notably those related to income distribution and poverty. But ultimately, of course, the most interesting questions involve *how* to grow and develop. That is the focus of the rest of this volume. For manageability, most of the discussion in this volume focuses on a range of programs and policies usually within the purview of local officials charged with economic development, and, even more particularly, on programs affecting how we finance local development. Topics covered include various tax and subsidy mechanisms, for example, tax incremental financing (TIF), enterprise and empowerment zones, various lending instruments including government loan pools and venture capital as well as "traditional" bank lending. But this is a good place to remind ourselves that successful development requires many other things besides finance, like well-functioning schools, a solid infrastructure, and a high-performance public sector. In addition to the financial capital and public incentives that are the focus of this volume, a partial list of the things that matter most in the long run might include:

- Physical capital including equipment as well as real estate (Jorgenson 1998)
- Infrastructure (Gramlich 1994; Hulten and Schwab 1995)

Table 1.3

U.S. Per Capita Income by State

State	Per capita income year 2000 U.S. dollars 1969	Per capita income 1998	Annual growth rate of per capita income 1969–1998 (%)	Trend forecast of per capita income 2000
Alabama	10,575	22,945	2.7	24,204
Alaska	18,275	28,960	1.6	29,894
Arizona	13,426	25,184	2.2	26,300
Arkansas	10,078	22,022	2.7	23,242
California	17,470	29,301	1.8	30,365
Colorado	14,184	31,206	2.8	32,950
Connecticut	18,652	38,846	2.6	40,863
Delaware	17,012	30,570	2.0	31,831
District of Columbia	17,424	37,886	2.7	39,971
Florida	14,080	27,930	2.4	29,280
Georgia	12,168	26,883	2.8	28,393
Hawaii	17,501	27,840	1.6	28,746
Idaho	12,579	22,971	2.1	23,945
Illinois	16,755	31,059	2.2	32,410
Indiana	14,292	26,180	2.1	27,296
Iowa	14,053	25,745	2.1	26,842
Kansas	13,653	26,569	2.3	27,817
Kentucky	11,433	23,079	2.5	24,225
Louisiana	11,163	23,103	2.5	24,292
Maine	12,083	24,448	2.5	25,666
Maryland	16,197	31,792	2.4	33,305
Massachussets	16,189	34,849	2.7	36,742
Michigan	15,950	27,971	2.0	29,076
Minnesota	14,542	30,445	2.6	32,037
Mississippi	9,266	20,575	2.8	21,739
Missouri	13,703	26,166	2.3	27,360
Montana	12,637	22,087	1.9	22,954
Nebraska	13,745	26,971	2.4	28,255
Nevada	17,393	30,380	1.9	31,571
New Hampshire	14,407	30,671	2.6	32,312
New Jersey	17,413	35,772	2.5	37,593
New Mexico	11,240	22,019	2.3	23,064
New York	17,713	33,405	2.2	34,899
North Carolina	11,741	26,198	2.8	27,689
North Dakota	11,744	23,817	2.5	25,007
Ohio	15,138	27,126	2.0	28,240
Oklahoma	12,306	22,851	2.2	23,848
Oregon	14,149	26,959	2.2	28,184
Pennsylvania	14,680	28,579	2.3	29,922
Rhode Island	14,873	29,404	2.4	30,819
South Carolina	10,879	23,276	2.7	24,529
South Dakota	11,525	24,673	2.7	26,003

Tennessee	11,417	25,424	2.8	26,867
Texas	12,980	26,394	2.5	27,718
Utah	11,941	23,138	2.3	24,219
Vermont	13,037	25,596	2.4	26,815
Virginia	13,692	29,197	2.6	30,762
Washington	15,766	29,879	2.2	31,226
West Virginia	10,767	21,000	2.3	21,991
Wisconsin	14,434	27,346	2.2	28,578
Wyoming	13,792	25,294	2.1	26,375
United States	14,800	28,302	230.0	29,596

- Human capital, education, and training (Black and Lynch 1996; Psacharopoulos 1994; Hanushek and Kim 1995)
- Trade (Hewings et al. 1997; Dollar 1992)
- Economies of scale, especially those from well-functioning cities (Glaeser, Scheinkman, and Shleifer 1995; Henderson 1988)
- The structure of our local economy, appropriate to our resources, skill set, and market opportunities (Ó hUallcháin 1992)
- Environment, climate, and amenities (Kusmin 1994)
- Business management (Baily and Blair 1988)
- Culture and entrepreneurial spirit (Saxenian 1994)
- A well-functioning public sector, including cost-effective delivery of essential public services, and appropriate incentives and a balanced regulatory environment (Malpezzi 2001)

However, no single volume can do justice to all these important topics. The focus of this volume is finance, and it is to that subject that we now turn.

The Special Role of Finance in the Economy

Every modern economy has real assets and financial assets.[13] Let us remind ourselves of the distinction, of the differences and similarities, and how the two sides of the economy fit together. Real assets (or capital) are the things we use to make other things. They comprise tangible capital (equipment and machinery, infrastructure, and real estate), and human capital.

Financial assets (or capital) assign claims on the output of the tangible and human capital. The assets of a firm comprise primarily its real estate, other tangible capital like equipment, and, of course, its people and the knowledge they embody. The stocks and bonds of a firm assign the cash flows from the firm's operations, that is, from its tangible/human capital, as revenues, and these are used to make loan or bond payments and to pay dividends. Analogously, on the household side, household assets, including their human capital, furniture, clothing, vehicles, owned real estate, and the like, produce income. Most income is used to trade for goods and services, although some household capital produces consumption goods (notably housing) directly.

Financial systems comprise many elements. There are banks, bond and other capital markets, markets for trading equity, and so on. In addition to these public markets, there is a wide range of important private markets, from the corner moneylender to venture capitalists and large institutional investors. Why is financial capital important? Is it *only* about claims, that is, about how the pie is divided up? No, well-functioning financial markets are also directly productive. Consider a world *without* financial intermediation. The investors must *first* defer sufficient consumption from today's output long enough to save the necessary resources *before* they make the investment. This implies that investments will come later than they otherwise would. It also implies that investments will be made only if the same people who have the investment idea or opportunity can save sufficiently to finance the investment.

Thus, in a world *with* a well-developed financial system, it is no longer necessary that the same people who are investors be the savers. No longer is it necessary that savers figure out how to invest each dollar of their savings productively. A well-running financial system does it for them and better than they could on their own.

A large literature notes the central role financial intermediation plays in economic development. Much of this literature is international in character, for example, Fry (1988) and the works cited therein. But it certainly matters within a country and across small units as well. Studies such as those by Brito and Mello (1995), Fazzari, Hubbard, and Peterson (1988), and Mayer (1990) illustrate the point using a variety of data sources and methodologies.

Sources and Types of Finance

Before we discuss examples of specific development finance mechanisms, it is useful briefly to discuss some general categories. The first important distinction is that between *debt* and *equity*. Debt finance is characterized by an investment of a predetermined amount, either a single up-front loan, for example, as with a typical home first mortgage, or a line of credit that can be drawn down over some specific period of time. Debt is usually repaid according to some predetermined schedule, and these payments have priority over payments to equity investors.[14]

Equity investments, on the other hand, are those that have claims on the residual cash flows, after debt has been serviced. Some equity investments are characterized by a more or less regular payment of dividends, but unlike debt, the size of the payments will usually vary with the fortunes of the firm or project, and may be at the discretion of the entity's management. In case of default, equity investors will be repaid only after debt claims are paid. Thus, equity is generally riskier than debt, but, of course, there is a corresponding upside; if a project goes well, debt holders' return will be limited to their contracted payments, with equity investors sharing the higher returns.

The second, major, general distinction in types of finance is between *public* and *private*. Confusingly, there are two very different ways in which the terms public and private are used. Investment professions also use the terms quite differently from planners and public policy wonks. Both distinctions are important. Public markets, to an investment professional, are markets that offer investments that can be (more or less) freely bought and sold on recognized markets. Offerings of public shares are subject to legal requirements that accounts and certain other information about the enterprise are public information. Private markets, on the other hand, are those where such information is more closely held by the investors and is not in the public domain. Securities traded on recognized exchanges like the NYSE or NASDAQ are well-known examples of public investments, in this sense. Family-held firms or investments in projects by institutional investors or wealthy individuals are examples of private investments, in this sense.

The other way we use the terms public and private corresponds more closely to common usage. Public in this sense refers to activities of government, and private to those of individuals and firms. But in today's world, especially in the context of this volume, the public-private distinction is more of a spectrum. Many forms of nongovernmental organizations (NGOs) exist that are relevant to local economic development, such as community development corporations, and local business and social groups. Many of these NGOs would also be characterized as not-for-profit, but it can be argued that NGOs are better characterized by their objective functions than their profit/nonprofit status, insofar as the latter can be largely an accounting/tax-rule decision, while the former captures whether the entity's objective is to maximize some financial surplus (whether or not that surplus is considered "profit" by the IRS), or some broader set of social objectives.

These issues suffuse the rest of the volume. For example, contributions by Timothy Bates and by Kelly Robinson yield particularly important insights about the roles of public and private actors regarding "traditional" bank finance and variants on the theme such as revolving loan funds. Chapters by Adam Bock and by David Arnstein explain the role played by (largely private) venture capital and "angel" investors. Public finance is further represented by Alan Peters's and Peter Fisher's treatment of enterprise zones, Rod Hissong's analysis of public subsidies, and Donald Schunk's and Douglas

Woodward's discussion of BMW's use of local tax incentives. William Bowen, Kimberly Winson-Geideman, and Robert Simons examine the special problems of financing retail development; John Magill explains the challenges of financing economic development in rural areas.

Public Interventions in the Local Economic Development Process

To put development finance in context, especially targeted financial instruments with implicit or explicit public support, we need briefly to discuss the wider range of public interventions that affect development. To encourage or otherwise influence local economic development (or, for that matter, any activity), governments may avail themselves of one or more of the following policy instruments. First, and most fundamental, government plays a central role in defining and enforcing property rights and security, and in enforcing contracts. This includes, but is not limited to, government's central role in providing a legal system. Furthermore, a well-functioning local criminal law enforcement system could improve basic safety and security, which could certainly affect the attractiveness of a location to firms and workers. At a different level, state laws that affect the cost of enforcing contracts (e.g., bankruptcy law) could easily affect business activity. By global standards, virtually all locations in the United States provide basic property rights and a broadly similar and reasonably functioning judicial system; these are essential for the development of a good economic development climate. In general, see, for example, Furubotn and Pejovich (1972), Jaffe and Louziotis (1996), and North (1990); but for a more focused discussion of the legal underpinnings of local economic development finance, see chapter 2, by Ferdinand Schoettle, on the constitutional framework for local economic development finance.

Malpezzi (2000) presents more discussion of these instruments, and, more fundamentally, principles to help decide when activities should be undertaken by the public sector (through these instruments), rather than the private sector. Briefly, these rationales include the existence of significant economies of scale, monopoly or other market power by firms, real costs or benefits that are somehow omitted from market prices, and information or coordination failures.

Another important class of intervention is direct public provision of a good or service. Many kinds of infrastructure fit this mold. Roads and other transportation systems are classic examples that also have important local economic development effects. The classic rationale for direct public provision of roads hinges on the economies of scale in their provision and their resultant character as natural local monopolies. Of course, sometimes the line between public and private provision is blurred, as is often the case with major sports stadiums; see the chapter by Ziona Austrian and Mark Rosentraub.

The third major category of public intervention is taxation. One important reason to tax is, of course, to finance expenditures (see above). At the local level, taxes pay for some fraction of local services, though in the United States most local governments also receive significant transfers from higher level taxing authorities (state and national governments). In addition to the obvious need to tax in order to finance government's activities, taxation can also be used to shape behavior. Consider a simple example. Suppose a developer is contemplating building a new subdivision, of some standard size and quality, in a particular location. In simple terms, the developer will consider the costs (land, construction costs, onsite infrastructure, marketing costs, and others, including a sufficient level of profit to make the project worthwhile), and compare this to the expected market value of the units. If value equals or exceeds cost, the developer will go ahead. In a competitive market with many developers, costs and values will generally be in line.

But suppose further that there are other costs of the proposed subdivision that are not included in the developer's calculation. For example, suppose the development requires additional offsite infrastructure, or suppose the development greatly increases local traffic congestion. Alternately, suppose that the particular development is expected to generate more local service costs (schools) than it will generate in revenues. Under any or all of these scenarios, if the additional costs are large enough, we could easily obtain a socially undesirable result. Suppose, for example, that private value exceeded the developer's private costs and he or she would proceed with the project, even if in actual point of fact, full social costs (i.e., private costs plus external costs such as offsite infrastructure, congestion, and fiscal costs) exceeded social benefit (private benefit plus external benefit).

How can we avoid building such socially inefficient projects? If local planners have a good idea of the size of these external costs, and a tax is placed on development of approximately that amount, the tax would have the effect of "internalizing the externality," in the felicitous phrase of economists. Hence, the newly calculated private costs (initial private costs, plus tax) would roughly equal the true social cost of the project. Only projects where value exceeded social cost—efficient projects—would therefore proceed. Impact fees and other development charges are examples of real-world taxes that, if correctly set, can solve these externality problems.

Of course, there are other externalities that can exist on the benefit side. Studies like those of Green and White (1997) and Haurin, Parcel, and Haurin

(2000) have documented the existence of external benefits to housing as well as costs, but, of special interest to readers of this volume, are the external benefits (and costs) that occur with the development or expansion of particular business establishments. Such developments could also generate external benefits, such as forward and backward linkages in the local economy, including developing local supplier networks. Other potential external benefits might be fiscal benefits (if the proposed project is expected to add more to local tax revenues than what it will require in public services), or the attraction of a critical mass of workers with particularly desirable skills. External benefits such as these are the classic rationales for subsidies to establishment openings or relocations. (Note that, analytically, a subsidy is the same as a tax, except for the fact that a subsidy gives money to someone and a tax takes it away.)

Some such subsidies make the national news, such as Alabama's 1993 subsidy package granted to a new Mercedes assembly plant (with subsidies reported to cost roughly $150,000 per worker), or Chicago's 2001 wooing of Boeing's corporate headquarters (reported to cost roughly $63 million, for a headquarters employing about 500).[15] In fact, proponents of such large and visible subsidies sometimes argue that their very newsworthiness generates another externality, namely a signal that their locality is "open for business" and has been judged desirable by a discerning world-class corporation with many locational alternatives.

Others, of course, have argued that the signal offered is quite different, that a locality is ready to tax their existing firms and residents to attract a small number of new jobs that might have arrived anyway. These controversies will be revisited in some detail elsewhere in this volume. Here we merely note that the question is, just how large *are* these external benefits, how much do we pay for them, and who ultimately bears the cost? Several chapters address these questions, such as Rod Hissong's on public subsidies, and Donald Schunk's and Douglas Woodward's on local incentives.

Our fifth major class of public intervention is regulation. Often local governments can achieve a given objective through different instruments; and, in particular, governments often have a choice among taxes, regulations, and subsidies. For example, it is readily shown that if we chose to forgo impact fees (taxes) as a way to solve the external costs of the housing development that we posited above, we could reach the same general outcome (number of units built, housing price, level of external costs borne by society) by simply restricting the number of units built to some number. In a similar fashion, we could subsidize a relocating firm by writing them a check, or by reducing their local tax liability, or by granting them an exemption or forbearance from some environmental or labor regulation. Regulation can be used even to forestall competition for early entrants to a market, for example, "fair trade" regulations restricting retail trade, or (now defunct) early city charters granting local monopolies to favored cable companies.[16] Sometimes targeted finance is used to ameliorate unintended consequences of regulations, such as the costs environmental regulations impose on real estate development; the chapter by Peter Meyer and Kristen Yount discusses this important example in some detail.

There are many ways to skin cats, and there are many kinds of government interventions that can be adapted to deal with externalities and other kinds of market failure. But while taxes, subsidies, regulations, property rights assignments, and direct public provision can, under the right conditions, substitute for each other, that does not mean they are identical in all respects. For instance, in our previous example we can, with sufficient information, reach the same level of external costs either with impact fees (taxes) or with growth management regulations. In the former case, consumers ultimately pay the external cost to the developer, who in turn pays a tax to the local government treasury; in the latter case, consumers will pay a higher price to developers (since with fewer units on the market, price will rise), who will then retain the increase as excess profits.[17] Among the contributions below that address how interventions affect a developer's bottom line, see especially Rachel Weber's chapter on TIF, Larry Ledebur's and Douglas Woodward's assessment of recapture agreements, and Mike Peddle's and Roger Dahlstrom's analysis of impact fees and other development exactions.

Each of these major classes of public intervention plays some role in local economic development finance. Most fundamentally, without clear assignment of property rights, including rights to claim repayment, and bankruptcy and foreclosure laws to help manage project risks, there would be little finance of any kind. Local economic development finance often incorporates some significant subsidy, implicit if not explicit. And local governments are often, in effect, direct providers of at least some financial backing for development projects.

Specific Sources of Finances for Local Economic Development: Two Examples

Armed with the general concepts above, next we proceed to describe and categorize several kinds of local economic development (LED) finance commonly used in the United States. As will become clear, most LED finance techniques are hybrids, not always fitting neatly into the debt/equity or public/private boxes. And once again, we will greatly simplify our discussion of these techniques; more detailed explanations can be found in the chapters on specific techniques elsewhere in this volume. In this chapter, we will briefly discuss two of the most widely discussed mechanisms, enterprise or empowerment zones, and tax incremental financing.

Example 1: Enterprise/Empowerment Zones

Enterprise/empowerment zones are complex, highly localized development tools that have been debated and tried in several forms for about the past twenty years. While there are certainly earlier precursors, most trace the focus to very small area financing and subsidies, and the term "enterprise zones," to British policy experiments under the conservative governments, inspired by the writings of the English planner Sir Peter Hall.[18] For reasons that are apparently partly substantive and partly political, in the United States, Republicans tend to put forward specific program proposals under the rubric "enterprise zones," while Democrats have more often preferred the term "empowerment zones." While there are some substantive differences between proposals specifically put forward by Democrats and Republicans, these differences need not concern us here, and we will simply refer to these programs collectively as EZs.

The basic idea behind an EZ is to select a small area—usually something along the lines of a census tract—and to apply a series of localized subsidies, planning initiatives, and other economic development activities. EZs are thus an attempt to respond to the observed highly localized pattern of economic development—and, unfortunately, lack of development—that is observed in U.S. cities. Not only have central cities tended to fare worse than the suburbs economically in the United States over the past several decades, but even within central cities it is very common to have a more or less vibrant downtown surrounded by some upscale neighborhoods, some doing moderately well, and some deteriorating. The EZ concept is an attempt to focus economic development efforts on the places that most require assistance.

The most important feature of a typical EZ program, in addition to its attempt to localize its efforts, is its complexity. No two EZ programs are identical. But generally, they bring to bear a package of policy changes, including localized finance, tax incentives, regulatory relief, social services, and new infrastructure. For example, the current empowerment zone programs begun in 1994 by the U.S. Department of Housing and Urban Development incorporate six major categories of targeted assistance.[19] Title XX Social Service Block Grants are one integral part of the current EZ program. These can be used for many purposes such as education and training, housing, and social services. These EZs also provide employment credits, a tax credit subsidy for the wages of employees drawn from the local area. These empowerment zones also grant accelerated depreciation of certain business property and can also provide tax exempt loan financing to subsidize investment in additional commercial real estate. Furthermore, economic development initiative grants can be used for a wide range of local purposes.

As will be detailed below in the contribution by Fisher and Peters, as well as elsewhere in the volume, the efficacy of EZs is still hotly debated. Carefully evaluating EZs is difficult for a number of reasons, including the most difficult problem usually faced in such program evaluation: knowing what the counterfactual would be, that is, what would happen to this particular localized area in the absence of the program. An EZ that experiences a decline in, say, employment of 10 percent over some period would truly be a success if, in the absence of the program, the observed decline would have been, say, 25 percent. On the other hand, if the EZ locality grows, it is always tempting to attribute the growth to the EZ itself, though this is difficult to demonstrate rigorously. Evaluation is also made difficult by the fact that there have been so many different program designs, and the current program has been in place for less than a decade. Given inevitable lags in data collection and research, the most current published evaluations of these EZs are based primarily on the first five years of the program, which is probably not enough data to be authoritative either way.[20]

Example 2: Tax Incremental Financing

Tax incremental financing has become increasingly popular as an economic development tool in most U.S. states over the past twenty years. The initial idea behind TIF is a simple one: to use the incremental tax revenue from a revitalized area to finance the infrastructure or other investments that made the revitalization possible; hence the "increment."

Consider a localized "blighted" area, that is, an area where economic activity is low, residents have low incomes, and, in particular, the value of local real estate—the property tax base—is also low. Assume that in the absence of some intervention, this state of affairs would more or less continue. The idea behind TIF is to generate finance for infrastructure and possibly other investment in the local area that will not only boost the local economy but also increase the tax base by raising property values. If property values rise due to the provision of, say, new infrastructure, then proponents of TIF argue that it is reasonable to earmark the incremental tax revenues, that is, the revenues due to the intervention, to finance the intervention.

20

Figure 1.1 **Stylized Example of Tax Incremental Financing (TIF)**

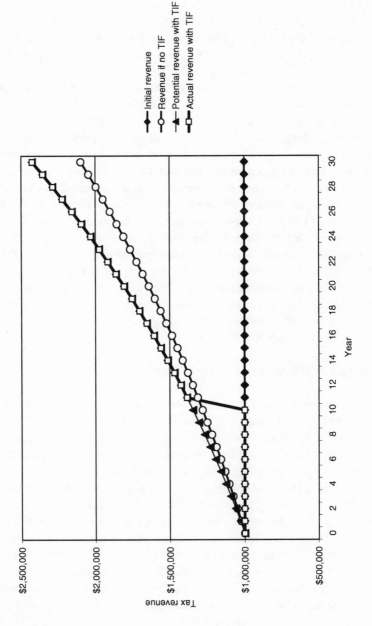

Tax revenue

- Initial revenue
- Revenue if no TIF
- Potential revenue with TIF
- Actual revenue with TIF

A simplified example will help make this clear (Figure 1.1). Assume for simplicity that tax rates remain identical over some specified period, say a decade. Let us adopt a thirty-year overall time horizon, and suppose our local government has a discount rate of 10 percent. Suppose an area is currently blighted but still has a tax base that generates initial tax revenue of $1 million in property tax revenues every year. Suppose that if financing were available for provision of, let us say, improved infrastructure, then in fact the tax base would rise steadily at a rate of 3 percent per year. The tax incremental financing idea is to earmark this additional revenue to financing bonds that were used to make the investment that returns the increment in the future. Thus, in a typical TIF district, at least the stylized version, the municipality or other controlling authority issues bonds to be paid off with the incremental financing. The general municipal fund and local school districts continue to get the tax revenue as in the initial period ($1 million in our example), but instead of growing with the tax base, this portion of revenue is frozen for the duration of the bonds. The idea is that over the period the bonds are paid off, the schools and general municipal fund are no worse off than before because their revenues would not have risen in the absence of the TIF activity. Furthermore, once the bonds are paid off, the schools and the localities are better off because they are now enjoying the fruits of the higher tax base. With our assumptions, Figure 1.1 shows that in the absence of a TIF, revenue rises slowly over time, and is only about $1.3 million per year at the end of thirty years. Under our assumptions with a TIF, revenue grows faster, to almost $2.5 million after thirty years. Thus, municipalities give up some revenue today, in return for the promise of higher revenue in the future. With our particular assumptions—including the municipality's discount rate of 10 percent—the present value of tax receipts is about $11.4 million with no TIF; and the present value of tax receipts with the TIF, after netting out the increment devoted to debt service, is $12.7 million. Thus, in this particular example, the value of the TIF is the $1.3 million difference.[21]

While an extremely ingenious idea in theory, of course, the devil is in the details. For example, what exactly is the counterfactual? Would the tax base have risen as slowly as assumed over the period in question in the absence of the TIF investment? If we make a change in our example so that no-TIF tax revenues rise by 2.5 percent (closer to the TIF of 3 percent), the present value of TIF-enhanced revenues is about $300,000 *less* than without a TIF. Which areas are to be determined as blighted, or will there be other rationales for the use of TIF financing? Perhaps most important, are the specific investments undertaken with the TIF well-chosen investments of sufficient scale, so that, in fact, the projected increases in tax base are realized? In our simple example, for instance, the cash flows from the TIF are sufficient to finance a bond of about $1.3 million—hardly a huge investment likely to triple the rate of growth of property prices!

In chapter 3, by Rachel Weber, these issues are investigated in some detail. Here we simply point out that over time in many states the eligibility and uses of TIF have greatly expanded, often incorporating subsidies to areas that are not blighted. In fact, in some states, most TIF districts are undertaken in higher-income locations. Furthermore, the purposes of TIF financing have expanded to include not only basic infrastructure but other expenditures, including reducing the investment costs of private real estate developers. As TIF has become more widespread, local school districts and other recipients of property tax funds in some states have begun to take issue with the growth of TIF investments. This occurs especially because these local development actors often have little say in whether a TIF is approved or not, even though they bear part of the cost.

Conclusion

Local economic development is complicated, and it is important. Many elements contribute to an area's development, but little happens without finance. In this chapter, we have provided a general discussion of finance, and an introduction to two important mechanisms—enterprise zones and tax incremental financing. The following chapters elaborate on these examples, but also discuss many other issues, such as venture capital, the role of banks and revolving loan pools, impact fees, and many other approaches to finance and to the public-private partnerships that, if done well, can enhance development. The ultimate objective of this volume is to improve our understanding of some of the special methods by which local economic development can be strengthened and facilitated.

Notes

1. By an "improved" distribution of income, I mean one where employment, income, or some other measure of well-being increases as much or more at the bottom end of the distribution as at the top. Such a definition implies a value judgment, but one that I suspect is shared by many readers.

2. "Generally" is an important qualifier. For example, many students and retired people, among others, are presumably better off not employed, at least for the time being; and many of us have occasionally considered how winning a really big lottery jackpot might ruin our lives.

3. For example, it is possible for one metropolitan area to have an even distribution of income because everyone is poor, while a metro area like Stamford, CT, has little poverty but an unequal distribution of income because of its substantial population of rich households. However, in general, metropolitan areas with a more equal distribution of income tend to have less poverty.

4. Data are from the Bureau of Economic Analysis (BEA) of the U.S. Department of Commerce. Population is self-evident; employment includes public and private, and full and part-time. Per capita incomes are in constant year 2000 dollars, adjusted using the GDP price deflator.

5. BEA data are available from 1969 to 1998; we computed a very simple trend forecast of each variable in 2000 using each location's average 1969–98 growth rate for each variable.

6. These employment figures include both full-time and part-time employment, and another broad pattern on the period was an increase in part-time employment. See the BEA Web site at http://www.bea.doc.gov, and see Kruse and Blasi (2000).

7. And as noted above, demographic shifts may well lead to a changing aggregate relationship between population growth and employment growth in future.

8. See Steinnes (1977), Thurston and Yezer (1994) and Mills and Lubuele (1995), for example.

9. Of course, some income is derived from transfers outside the state; not least of which are government transfer payments such as Social Security. I should also mention that many alternative statistics of income, broadly construed, are available. For example, we could examine GDP per capita, median family income, median household income, or average/median wages. Each measure has its pros and cons. One key advantage of our current measure is that these BEA data are available on a consistent basis for about thirty years for the United States as a whole, states, metro areas, and counties. Also, *per capita* measures roughly abstract from changes in family/household composition over the period. The flip side is that our measure does not pick up changes in well-being from economies of scale in producing welfare from households of different size and composition. For example, two one-person households making $20,000 each are equivalent to a two-person household with a total income of $40,000 using our per capita measure; but the two-person household is probably better off due to economies of scale. Another disadvantage is that BEA data go back only to 1969; it would be desirable to go back earlier than 1969 in our analysis, if BEA data permitted.

10. Again, income figures are presented in constant 2000 dollars.

11. See Malpezzi (2002) and especially U.S. Census Bureau (2000) for data and additional discussion. It is well known that the individuals comprising the bottom 20 percent, or any other quintile, change markedly from year to year. In this respect, the United States has one of the more dynamic income distributions in the world.

12. Note that household income growth is usually significantly lower than per capita income growth because typical household sizes are shrinking.

13. This section draws on Malpezzi (forthcoming).

14. There are, in turn, often clearly defined priorities for the repayment of different classes of debt. For example, consider the familiar home mortgage. In case of default, the first mortgage must be entirely repaid before claims are paid on second mortgages or equity lines of credit.

15. Details of these and other incentives payments can be found in various issues of Site Selection, or at their Web site http://www.conway.com/ssinsider/incentive/.

16. In this industry, economies of scale have turned out to be a sufficient natural guarantor of monopoly. Most existing cable companies retain their monopoly position without such sole-source agreements.

17. See Landis (1986) and Malpezzi (1996).

18. See Hall (1981) and Butler (1981).

19. See Hebert et al. (2001).

20. Ibid.

21. In reality, growth rates of revenue may well vary over time. In Figure 1.1 we've assumed two different, constant rates for simplicity. Other, more realistic assumptions could be readily incorporated into our calculations.

References

Baily, Martin Neil, and Margaret M. Blair. 1988. "Productivity and American Management." In *American Living Standards: Threats and Challenges*, ed. Robert E. Litan, Robert Z. Lawrence, and Charles L. Schultze, 178–214. Washington, DC: Brookings Institution.

Bartik, Timothy J. 1994. "The Effects of Metropolitan Job Growth on the Size Distribution of Family Income." *Journal of Regional Science* (November): 483–501.

Black, Sandra, and Lisa Lynch. 1996. "Human Capital Investments and Productivity." *American Economic Review* 86 (May): 263–68.

Brito, Paulo, and Antonio S. Mello. 1995. "Financial Constraints and Firm Post-Entry Performance." *International Journal of Industrial Organization* 13: 543–65.

Butler, Stuart. 1981. *Enterprise Zones: Pioneering in the Inner City*. Washington, DC: Heritage Foundation.

Dollar, David. 1992. "Outward-Oriented Developing Economies Really Do Grow More Rapidly: Evidence from 95 LDCs, 1976–85." *Economic Development and Cultural Change* 40: 523–44.

Fazzari, Steven M.; R. Glenn Hubbard; and Bruce C. Petersen. 1988. "Financing Constraints and Corporate Investment." *Brookings Papers on Economic Activity*, no. 1: 141–206.

Fry, Maxwell. 1988. *Money, Interest and Banking in Economic Development*. Baltimore, MD: Johns Hopkins University Press.

Furubotn, Eirik G., and Svetozar Pejovich. 1972. "Property Rights and Economic Theory: A Survey of Recent Literature." *Journal of Economic Literature* 10, no. 4: 1137–62.

Glaeser, Edward L.; Jose A. Scheinkman; and Andrei Shleifer. 1995. "Economic Growth in a Cross Section of Cities." *Journal of Monetary Economics* 36, no. 1: 117–43.

Glaeser, Edward L.; Hedi D. Kallal; Jose A. Scheinkman; and Andrei Shleifer. 1992. "Growth in Cities." *Journal of Political Economy* 100, no. 6: 1126–52.

Gramlich, Edward M. 1994. "Infrastructure Investment: A Review." *Journal of Economic Literature* 32, no. 3: 1176–96.

Green, Richard K., and Michelle J. White. 1997. "Measuring the Benefits of Homeowning: Benefits to Children." *Journal of Urban Economics* 41: 441–61.

Gyourko, Joseph. 1998. "Regionalism: The Feasible Options." *Wharton Real Estate Review* 11, no. 2: 7–14.

Hall, Peter. 1981. "The Enterprise Zone Concept: British Origins, American Adaptations." University of California Working Paper.

Hanushek, Eric A., and Dongwook Kim. 1995. "Schooling, Labor Force Quality and Economic Growth." NBER Working Paper 5399 (December).

Haurin, Donald R.; Toby L. Parcel; and R. Jean Haurin. 2000. "The Impact of Home Ownership on Child Outcomes." Ohio State University Department of Economics.

Hebert, Scott; Avis Vidal; Greg Mills; Franklin James; and Debbie Gruenstein. 2001. *Interim Assessment of the Empowerment Zones and Enterprise Communities (EZ/ EC) Program: A Progress Report.* Washington, DC: U.S. Department of Housing and Urban Development.

Henderson, J. Vernon. 1988. *Urban Development: Theory, Fact and Illusion.* New York: Oxford University Press.

Hewings, Geoffrey J.D.; Philip R. Israilevich; Yasuhide Okuyama; Darla K. Anderson; Graham R. Schindler; Matthew Foulkes; and Michael Sonis. 1997. "Returns to Scope, Returns to Trade and the Structure of Spatial Interaction in the U.S. Midwest." University of Illinois Regional Economics Applications Laboratory Discussion Paper.

Hulten, Charles R., and Robert M. Schwab. 1995. "Infrastructure and the Economy." In *Readings in Public Policy*, ed. J.M. Pogodzinski, 213–34. Cambridge, MA: Blackwell.

Jaffe, Austin J., and Demetrios Louziotis, Jr. 1996. "Property Rights and Economic Efficiency: A Survey of Institutional Factors." *Journal of Real Estate Literature* 4: 137–59.

Jorgenson, Dale W. 1998. "Investment and Growth." In *Econometrics and Economic Theory in the 20th Century*, ed. S. Strom, 204–37. New York: Cambridge University Press.

Kruse, Douglas, and Joseph Blasi. 2000. "The New Employee-Employer Relationship." In *A Working Nation: Workers, Work and Government in the New Economy*, ed. David T. Ellwood et al., 42–91. New York: Russell Sage.

Kusmin, Lorin. 1994. *Factors Associated with the Growth of Local and Regional Economies: A Review of Selected Empirical Literature.* Washington, DC: U.S. Department of Agriculture, Economic Research Service.

Landis, John. 1986. "Land Regulation and the Price of New Housing: Lessons from Three California Cities." *Journal of the American Institute of Planners* (Winter): 9–21.

Madden, Janice F. 2000. *Changes in Income Inequality within U.S. Metropolitan Areas.* Kalamazoo: W.E. Upjohn Institute.

Malpezzi, Stephen. 1996. "Housing Prices, Externalities, and Regulation in U.S. Metropolitan Areas." *Journal of Housing Research* 7, no. 2: 209–41.

———. 2000. "What Should State and Local Governments Do? A Few Principles." University of Wisconsin, Center for Urban Land Economics Research Working Paper.

———. 2001. What Do We Know About Economic Development? What Does It Mean for State and Local Governments? Unpublished manuscript.

———. 2002. "What Is Economic Development?" University of Wisconsin, Center for Urban Land Economics Research Working Paper.

———. Forthcoming. *Tales from the Real Side: Lessons of Urban Research for Housing Finance in Developing and Transition Economies.* Washington, DC: U.S. Department of Housing and Urban Development.

Mayer, Colin. 1990. "Financial Systems, Corporate Finance and Economic Development." In *Asymmetric Information, Corporate Finance, and Investment*, ed. R. Glenn Hubbard. Chicago: University of Chicago Press.

Mills, Edwin S., and Luan Sende Lubuele. 1995. "Projecting Growth of Metropolitan Areas." *Journal of Urban Economics* 37, no. 3: 344–60.

North, Douglass C. 1990. *Institutions, Institutional Change and Economic Performance.* New York: Cambridge University Press.

Ó hUallacháin, Breandán. 1992. "Economic Structure and Growth of Metropolitan Areas." In *Sources of Metropolitan Growth*, ed. Edwin S. Mills and John F. McDonald, 510–85. New Brunswick, NJ: Rutgers University Press.

Psacharopoulos, George. 1994. "Returns to Investment in Education: A Global Update." *World Development* 22, no. 9: 1325–43.

Saxenian, Annalee. 1994. *Regional Advantage: Culture and Competition in Silicon Valley and Route 128*. Cambridge, MA: Harvard University Press.

Steinnes, Donald. 1977. "Causality and Intraurban Location." *Journal of Urban Economics* (January).

Thurston, Lawrence, and Anthony M.J. Yezer. 1994. "Causality in the Suburbanization of Population and Employment." *Journal of Urban Economics* 35, no. 1: 105–18.

2

What Public Finance Do State Constitutions Allow?

Ferdinand P. Schoettle

Overview

This chapter introduces readers to the role of law in guiding, empowering, and constraining state and local governments' decisions concerning revenues and expenditures. Some of the provisions discussed are uniquely related to finances while others, such as Dillon's rule, not only relate to public finance decisions but also apply generally to all local government decisions. The chapter explains the active role played by courts, as assigned by state constitutions and judicial precedent, in monitoring the decisions of state and local governments.

The judiciary review both the substance of state and local government decisions and the question of which level of government can decide a particular matter. Governmental power in the United States is divided both by area of jurisdiction and by function. The general-purpose governments, such as the federal, state, county, municipal, and township governments, have particular areal jurisdictions. Other governments, such as school districts, sewer districts, and airport commissions are limited both by function and by area. The proliferation of local units of government has·necessitated judicial activism to control local power as well as to mediate between governments.

The powers of local units of government spring from their parent states. The states are natural sovereigns, not governments of ceded power like the federal government. State legislatures possess all powers not ceded to the federal government or prohibited by the state constitution (Grad 1970: 27–58; Hurst 1950: 242). Local governments are strictly subject to the state's control. Local authorities, nevertheless, often enjoy protections granted by state constitutions from state interference in their affairs. In general, however, in the absence of state constitutional provisions, the local units of government are units of the state. The state may legislate about their affairs, abolish them, and do as the state and its legislature may wish (McBain 1916: 300–303; *Hunter v. Pittsburgh* 1907).

This chapter begins with an introduction to general legal doctrines and state constitutional provisions that limit the exercise of power by state governments. The chapter first introduces the reader to debt limits, to prohibitions against the lending of credit, and to the public purpose doctrine. Next, the chapter looks at Dillon's rule, at home rule, at the requirement of uniformity and equality in state taxation, and at prohibitions against enacting local or special laws. Finally, the last section of the chapter examines how various state courts have interpreted and applied state constitutional mandates in litigation involving school finance.

Checks on the Authority of State Governments

General Limitations

The three doctrines we investigate below, the public purpose doctrine, debt limits, and prohibitions against lending of credit share a common function and history (Amdursky and Gillette 1992: 84). Each of these doctrines aims at restricting public funding to activities that serve the interests of the public at large and precluding governmental participation in activities that serve only a small group of individuals within the community (Ibid.). These doctrines had their development, if not their genesis, in the second half of the nineteenth century when the public became concerned about the activities of governments in financing internal improvements (Pinsky 1963: 277–82). As the nation's population expanded westward between 1820 and 1840, the need for transportation and transcontinental communication increased (Amdursky and Gillette 1992: 13). The capital necessary for making these internal improvements exceeded the resources of private enterprise. The anticipated rewards from such improvements led to partnerships between states and private enterprise through which the states financed the construction of privately or jointly owned canals, railroads, turnpikes, and toll roads (Amdursky and Gillette 1992: 13).

The drive to make internal improvements and benefit from the resulting revenues inspired many state officials to incur public debt for making these improvements. The benefits in all likelihood went both to the public fisc and to state officials, such as legislators, individually. State officials were particularly inspired by the great success of New York's Erie Canal. The Erie Canal, which was America's first major public works project, was financed by a public credit (Amdursky and Gillette 1992: 13). New York derived enormous revenues from the canal, which enabled the state to pay back within ten years the debt incurred to build it. Other states followed New York's lead in incurring large debts in order to grant aid to private corporations to build projects like the Erie Canal. However, other state projects were not as successful as the Erie Canal. By 1837, some internal improvement projects lacked funds to complete their projects. In addition, the states were short on revenues to finance debt service on securities. State residents then began to show displeasure at the state's mismanagement of internal commerce, which led to the adoption of provisions in numerous state constitutions limiting the state's capacity to incur debt. These provisions were known as debt limits.

The constitutional debt limits generally applied to states, but not to state measures authorizing local governments to incur debt. Consequently, municipalities in the 1840s and 1850s issued large amounts of debt to aid railroad entrepreneurs. States and their municipal subdivisions invested over $1.25 billion in the railroad industry between 1830 and 1860 (Amdursky and Gillette 1992: 18). Competition or fraud in the 1860s produced numerous defaults on railroad bonds as entrepreneurs became bankrupt or simply abandoned lines. Once again the public called for restrictions on government debt, thus encompassing local authorities. States adopted constitutional and statutory measures prohibiting the state and its municipal subdivisions from lending public credit to or investing in private business corporations. These measures were known as prohibitions against lending of credit.

The judiciary also took note of popular discontent with governmental assistance to private industry and formulated the public purpose doctrine as a new constraint on public debt. Under the public purpose doctrine, governmental entities could exercise their spending power only for projects that promised to return some benefit to the general public. We now turn to an examination of each of the above doctrines in their current embodiment.

Debt Limits

Debt limits apply to bonds that obligate the state to use its taxing power to satisfy the debt. The specific type of debt limit that a state employs varies from jurisdiction to jurisdiction depending on the state constitutional provision. Currently, only five states have no constitutional limitations on long-term borrowing.

Subject to the debt limit are general obligation bonds, which are bonds backed by the taxing power, or full faith and credit of the issuing governmental entity (Gelfand et al. 2000: 171). Not normally subject to the debt limit are revenue bonds. Revenue bonds are not secured by a pledge from the issuer's taxing power but are payable from the income of the projects that are built using the bond proceeds.[1] Holders of revenue bonds can look only to the revenues from underlying assets to pay the bonds and may not look for payment to the state. In the event of a default on a revenue bond the bondholders cannot look to the state for repayment but must enforce their rights against the underlying assets whose revenues were pledged to pay the principal and interest of the bonds. In addition to normal revenue bonds, such as turnpike bonds that might be used to fund a toll road, non-general-obligation bonds include moral obligation bonds and industrial development bonds (IDBs)/private activity bonds. Moral obligation bonds are a form of revenue bonds where the issuer does not specifically pledge taxes for their repayment, but promises that consideration will be given to using tax revenues to cure deficiencies in the principal or interest accounts (Gelfand et al. 2000: 182). IDBs/private activity bonds are a form of revenue bonds issued by a municipality to fund a private project. The private corporation or charitable organization using the facility makes lease payments that match the payments due under the bonds issued to fund the project.

First in importance of the mechanisms for circumventing debt limits are standard revenue bonds payable from a dedicated nontax source of revenue. According to settled doctrine, revenue bonds payable from a "special fund" do not pledge the credit of the issuing government and therefore are not "debt" subject to a mandated debt limit.[2] The states are split on whether the special fund need be newly generated. The majority view seems to be that revenues from unrelated projects can be paid into the special fund and be payable to bondholders regardless of the status of the underlying project (Amdursky and Gillette 1992: 177). South Dakota and a few other states take a different view. In those states, the revenues that are placed within the special fund are limited to those derived from or otherwise payable as a result of operation of the project financed with the bond proceeds (Amdursky and Gillette 1992: 177).

A 1987 Kentucky case extends the reach of these holdings and also provides an example of how constitutional provisions can limit public alternatives. At issue in *Hayes v. State Property and Building Commission* (1987) was the validity of some of the enticements that the commonwealth of Kentucky offered to induce Toyota to locate an automotive assembly plant in the state. Among other things, Kentucky offered to obtain and convey to Toyota a parcel of land on which Toyota was to construct a plant for the production of automobiles. The parcel was to be paid for by the issuance of $35 million in revenue bonds. Pledged for payment of the bonds were incremental tax revenues arising from the presence of the project in the state. The court held, with strong dissents, that the bonds were valid "revenue bonds" not subject to the debt provisions contained in sections 49 and 50 of the Kentucky Constitution, which would have required, had the bonds not been revenue bonds, that the debt to be created by the bonds be "submitted to the people at a general election" and be approved by a majority of those voting on the issue. Presumably, most states would not follow the Supreme Court of Kentucky in such a holding. For instance, in four states, tax increment financing bonds have been held to be subject to the debt limit. The additional property taxes generated by the projects financed by the proceeds of the bonds were not regarded as a special fund (*University of Missouri at Kansas City Law Review* 1985).

Prohibitions Against Lending of Credit

Prohibitions against public lending of credit were added to many state constitutions in the late nineteenth century, chiefly to end the practice by state municipalities of guaranteeing revenue bonds sold by private railroad companies (Gelfand et al. 2000: 205). States were concerned about state funds being used to benefit private interests where the public interest was not primarily served. When the private companies defaulted on such bonds, state and local governments were forced to honor the debtor railroad's obligations (Ibid.). Currently, nearly all states have constitutional provisions prohibiting the state and its political subdivisions from "giving or lending its credit in the aid of any individual, association, or corporation" (Ibid.: 116). For instance, the Washington Constitution reads,

> No county, city, town or other municipal corporation shall hereafter give any money, or property, or loan its money, or credit to or in aid of any individual, association, company or corporation, except for the necessary support of the poor and infirm, or become directly or indirectly the owner of any stock in or bonds of any association, company or corporation.[3]

Courts in various states have differing interpretations with respect to the kinds of political entities prohibited from expending loans of credit, the kinds of entities to whom an extension of credit is prohibited, and the definition of a gift or loan of credit (Amdursky and Gillette 1992: 140). In some jurisdictions, the list of prohibited lenders runs from a general reference to "political subdivisions"[4] to specific listings of any "county, city, town, township, board of education, or school district."[5] Typically, the issues presented to the courts concern whether the constitutional prohibition runs against a political entity not expressly mentioned in the provision and what counts as a public gift or loan of credit. For instance, in Minnesota, Maryland, and Wisconsin, the constitutional text refers only to the state itself, and the courts have refused to extend the prohibitions against state lending of credit to municipalities or other subdivisions (Amdursky and Gillette 1992: 142).

A 1996 Washington case, *CLEAN* [Citizens for Leaders with Ethics and Accountability Now!] *v. State,* provides an example of how courts deal with lending of credit cases. In *CLEAN*, the Washington state legislature adopted the Stadium Act, which provided a means by which the state could generate additional revenue for constructing a new baseball stadium (Amdursky and Gillette 1992: 790). The baseball stadium would then be leased to the Seattle Mariners (Ibid.). In upholding the Stadium Act, the court developed a two-pronged analysis to determine whether a gift of state funds to a private entity had occurred (Ibid.: 797–98). First, the court asked if the funds were being expended to carry out a fundamental purpose of government (Ibid.). If yes, then no gift of public funds had occurred. If no, then the court focused on the consideration or benefit received by the public and the donative intent of the appropriating body (Ibid.).

In some states a lending-of-credit analysis differs little, if at all, from a public-purpose analysis. In *State ex rel. Tomino v. Brown,* for instance, the Ohio Supreme Court held that credit given to ultimate purchasers of housing units was for a public welfare purpose, and thus was not in violation of Ohio's constitutional prohibition against lending of credit in aid of private interests. Like many state courts, the Ohio Supreme Court viewed the lending of credit limitation as simply an extension of the public purpose doctrine (Gelfand et al. 2000: 205).

Public Purpose Doctrine

The Public Purpose Doctrine is a judicially created rule, which states typically, that public money can be expended only for public purposes (Rubin 1999: 417). For instance, in 1853, when taxpayers complained about the validity of the city of Philadelphia's subscribing to stock in specific railroads, Mr. Chief Justice Black of the Supreme Court of Pennsylvania in *Sharpless v. Mayor of Philadelphia* (1853), although upholding the challenged actions, used the occasion to enunciate a public purpose doctrine. According to the court:

> Neither has the legislature any constitutional right to create a public debt, or to levy a tax, or to authorize any municipal corporation to do it, in order to raise funds for a mere private purpose. No such authority passed to the Assembly by the general grant of legislative powers. This would not be legislation. Taxation is a mode of raising revenue for public purposes.

The doctrine, which had its genesis in judicial pronouncement, now appears in state constitutional provisions requiring that taxes be levied and collected for public purposes only (Gelfand et al. 2000: 8). For instance, the Wyoming Constitution states, "no . . . debts [shall be] contracted by municipal corporations except in pursuance of law for public purposes specified by law."[6] The Illinois Constitution states, "public funds, property or credit shall be used only for public purposes."[7] But even if a state constitution does not expressly require that taxes be levied and collected for public purposes only, courts will generally find the public purpose doctrine implicit either in other constitutional provisions[8] or in general doctrines and principles.[9]

Public purpose is not, however, a static concept and takes its meaning from an ever-changing economic and social context.[10] Beginning with *Sharpless*, courts have always grappled with the issue of what constitutes a valid public purpose. A major principle that guides state courts in dealing with such cases is the requirement that the courts not debate the wisdom of a particular legislative policy (Gelfand et al. 2000: 203). This does not mean that a legislative declaration of public purpose will end the inquiry, but that the burden of proof on that question will be a heavy one for a challenger to such a determination. Typically, a legislative determination of public purpose will be upheld because of a presumption of validity unless "manifestly and palpably incorrect."

Courts have generally interpreted the phrase "public purpose" in two ways. On the one hand, courts have held that public monies are spent for a public purpose if the public derives a benefit, even though the object of the expenditure remains under private ownership and control (Rubin 1993: 154). This "public benefit" interpretation was derived from the realization that governmental entities could not provide all of the services needed or demanded by the public sector (Ibid.). Other courts have held that public monies spent for public purposes are monies spent for those functions that government has traditionally performed for its populace. This strict "public use" interpretation signifies public ownership, use, and control, even if a private entity is paid to perform the activity in question (Ibid.).

In recent years, the "public benefit" interpretation has frequently been evoked in cases involving public aid to professional sports teams. The typical case involves a state's attempt to use public funds in constructing a sports stadium later to be leased to professional sports teams. The issue is usually whether the construction of a publicly owned stadium to be leased to professional sports teams serves a public purpose. In *CLEAN v. State* (1996), the Supreme Court of Washington held that the construction of a major league baseball stadium in King County satisfied the public purpose doctrine. The court held that public expenditures need only confer a benefit of reasonably general character to a significant part of the public to satisfy the public benefit test. The court cited cases from other states that also had adopted this broad view of public purpose. Some older cases come out the other way.

The Florida and the Massachusetts Supreme Courts held in 1966 and 1969, respectively, that public funding for facilities for professional sports teams did not satisfy the public benefit test.[11] These jurisdictions are in the minority, and their opinions were distinguished in *CLEAN*.

Other Constitutional and Statutory Limitations

Dillon's Rule

Dillon's rule mandates strict construction of statutes that grant authority to local governments. The rule is named after former Iowa Supreme Court Judge John Forest Dillon, who in 1872 published his influential *Treatise on the Law of Municipal Corporations*. As first announced by Judge Dillon in an 1868 case, the rule reads as follows:

> It is a general and undisputed proposition of law that a municipal corporation possesses, and can exercise, the following powers, and not others: first, those granted in express words; second, those necessarily or fairly implied in, or incident to, the powers expressly granted; third, those essential to the declared objects and purposes of the corporation—not simply convenient, but indispensable. Any fair, reasonable doubt concerning the existence of power is resolved by the courts against the corporation, and the power is denied. (Dillon 1872: 101–2)

Judge Dillon announced the rule in an 1868 case, *Merriam v. Moodys Executors*.

Note first that the rule applies only to ambiguous grants of authority. If authority is clearly, unambiguously granted, courts usually give municipal authorities latitude in the exercise of that authority.[12] Second, note exactly what the rule says: If a power is not expressly granted, it must be necessarily implied or essential to the exercise of powers that are expressly granted. The rule thereby creates a presumption against all nonexpressed powers. As such, it is a limit on the powers of local governments.

According to Dillon's rule, local authorities within the state can derive power only from the state itself. Historically, however, the opposite may have been the case. Municipal corporations, exemplified by the medieval town, were regarded as autonomous corporations for the exercise of self-determination (Frug 1994: 23). As corporations, their powers were stated in their charters. Initially, there was no distinction between public and private corporations. However, in the 1800s, widespread corruption within municipal authorities, particularly with respect to financing railroad construction, caused a shift in the relationship between municipal authorities and state legislatures.

In "The City as a Legal Concept" (1980), Frug notes that municipalities seemed to operate as miniature republics, impervious to state power. There was a need to allow the legislature to control local governments (Ibid.: 25). To solve the dilemma, early nineteenth century legal doctrine divided the law concerning the powers of corporations into two different bodies of law. Public corporations no longer were viewed in the same way as private corporations. Public corporations were subject to state authority while private corporations were more autonomous units.

Judge Dillon believed the dilemma facing municipal corporations could be solved by legislative oversight and strict judicial construction of legislative grants of power that would limit the power of municipalities (Williams 1986: 94). Dillon emphasized state control of cities, restriction of cities to "public" functions, and strict construction of city powers (Ibid.). There were other commentators who argued that municipal corporations had an inherent right to self-government. Notable supporters of this view were Thomas M. Cooley,[13] a Michigan Supreme Court justice, Amasa Eaton,[14] and treatise-writer Eugene McQuillin. McQuillin even suggested that "all grants [of municipal authority should be construed] in light of the maxims of the Magna Carta" (Frug 1994: 58).

Dillon's rule, however, became the dominant rule of judicial construction of statutory and constitutional grants of power to municipal authorities (Sebree 1989: 157). Between 1868 and 1971, the majority of jurisdictions adopted Dillon's rule, and many state legislatures directed state courts to strictly construe the scope of local authority (Owens 2000: 679). From about 1971 to the present, legislatures have passed statutes calling for a broad interpretation of the scope of local authority, thus implicitly abandoning Dillon's rule of strict construction (Ibid.). The rule has also been criticized (*Virginia Law Review* 1982; *Missouri Law Review* 1976), and more than twenty state constitutions have limited its use (Hirshman 1985: 1370). Dillon's rule, nonetheless, has been mentioned in hundreds and hundreds of cases, the majority of which were in the period after 1972, especially between 1972 and 1992, a period when the legislatures are purported to have abandoned the rule.

Some states, like Virginia and Tennessee, still adhere to the Dillon rule of strict construction concerning the powers of local governing bodies.[15] In such states, municipal cases that apply Dillon's rule typically involve the issue of whether the proposed measure is within the municipality's grant of authority or is *ultra vires*. For instance, in *Chattanooga Area Regional Transportation Authority* (CARTA) *v. T.U. Parks Construction Company* (1999), the principal issue was whether CARTA had authority to enter into a contract providing for arbitration. Applying Dillon's rule, the Court of Appeals of Tennessee held that the action of CARTA in executing the contract providing for arbitration was *ultra vires*.

The state supreme courts that have abandoned Dillon's rule, however, do not give local governments carte blanche to do as they will. For instance, the Supreme Court of Utah rejected the Dillon approach in *State v. Hutchinson* (1980), but in *Price Development Company v. Orem City* (2000), the court stated, "Local governments must abide by the explicit limitations the constitution and statutes place on their financing schemes, but if they can find an alternative permissible way to achieve the same end, we will not stand in their way." Like Utah, a majority of jurisdictions that purport to have abandoned the Dillon rule have not resorted to the "inherent right to self-government" theory, but merely to giving local authorities wider latitude in the exercise of their delegated powers.

So important that it deserves special mention is the controversy surrounding the Washington Public Power Supply System (WPPSS). WPPSS, an association of nineteen Washington public utility districts and four Washington cities, was formed as part of an effort to add nuclear power to the hydroelectric power distributed by the Bonneville Power Administration. WPPSS was to supply the power needs of the Northwest and service, among other states, Oregon, Idaho, and Washington. Organized in 1957, WPPSS first built a nuclear generating plant at Hanford, Washington, which was completed in 1966. In 1976, WPPSS entered into agreements with eighty-eight governmental entities in six states pursuant to which it was to construct and operate Washington nuclear projects 4 and 5. Each participant was to be entitled to a fraction of the power generated by the new power plants. The participants' agreements contained a "dry hole provision" pursuant to which the participants were financially responsible, even if the project should result in creating no power. To gain funds, WPPSS issued revenue bonds, pledging the revenues it would receive from the participants as security for payment of the bonds. After spending several billion dollars, WPPSS abandoned projects 4 and 5; the hole was quite dry. The issue of the validity of the agreements by the participating governmental agencies became a trapdoor through which some of the participants might escape.

Escape was possible because the standard rule of law provides that an unauthorized agreement by a governmental agency is void and provides no grounds for liability. Thus, if the original agreements were not authorized, the loss of several billion dollars could be shifted from the participating governments to the bondholders. The supreme courts of Idaho, Oregon, and Washington each considered suits in which it was alleged that the participating units of government did not have authority to enter into the agreement with WPPSS. The pressures to decide that the agreements were *ultra vires*—that is, beyond the authority of the governmental units making the agreements—must have been substantial (Wohabe 1984).

The state supreme courts of Idaho and Washington both found the agreements unauthorized. In *Asson v. City of Burley* (1983), the Supreme Court of Idaho found that the authority of municipalities to acquire, own, maintain, and operate power plants did not authorize the cities to purchase "project capability" but permitted them only to purchase power. The cities acted *ultra vires*. The debt to WPPSS was void. Similarly in *Chemical Bank v. Washington Public Power Supply System* (1983), the Supreme Court of Washington, quoting part of Dillon's rule, held that even the powers of home rule cities should be narrowly construed, and, like Idaho, found no authority to purchase project capability. Arguably, the Washington court was merely seeking a result that would be favorable to the citizens of Washington (Shattuck 1984). However, the two supreme court opinions that found the WPPSS agreements unauthorized are excellent illustrations of the view that municipalities should be subject to the legislative oversight and strict judicial construction of delegated powers that was advocated by Judge Dillon.

Only Oregon held that the agreement was authorized. The state supreme court in *DeFazio v. Washington Public Power Supply System* (1984) held that the agreements by Oregon governments were authorized. Under Oregon's constitutional home rule provisions, cities had wide latitude to adopt charters granting power. The authority in a home rule charter to supply power to its citizens included in its ambit the right to purchase project capability, as well as power. We turn now to home rule.

Home Rule

The doctrine of municipal home rule is a constitutional or statutory grant of power that gives municipalities independence and control as to their own local affairs (Reynolds 1982: 95). In "Inherent Tensions Between Home Rule and Regional Planning," Frank Alexander notes that home rule powers exist in three basic forms across the United States (Alexander 2000: 543). The first, and predominant form, is "legislative home rule" in which the state legislature has delegated to various classes of local governments general powers of self-rule (Ibid.). The second form, which is far less common, is "constitutional home rule" in which the state constitution grants certain powers directly to cities or counties (Ibid.). The third form takes place when the state legislature grants a charter authorizing the creation of a specific municipality, district, or county commission, and specifies in the charter the scope of powers delegated (Ibid.). An example of a constitutional home rule provision is the state of Washington's constitution, which reads, "Any county, city, town or township may make and enforce within its limits all such local police, sanitary and other regulations as are not in conflict with general laws."[16]

The origins of the doctrine of municipal home rule can be traced to the same debates on the relationship between municipal authorities and state legislatures that led to the development of Dillon's rule. As noted earlier, around the time Dillon's rule was being developed in the late nineteenth century and early twentieth century, there was a movement that endorsed an extra-constitutional doctrine known as "inherent home rule." The inherent home rule principle supported the theory that quite apart from any constitutional or statutory provisions, municipal authorities had a natural "inherent" right to govern their own affairs where purely local matters were concerned (Reynolds 1982: 66). Thomas M. Cooley, a supporter of this theory, in "Treatise on Constitutional Limitations," which was first published in 1868 and went through seven editions, gave voice to the theory not only that the state legislatures should not meddle in local affairs, but also that the local governments had a legal right to the absence of such interference. The theory was particularly attractive during the period following the Civil War when state legislatures were generally viewed as corrupt. Other notable supporters of the theory included Howard Lee McBain (1916) and Judge McQuillin (1911).

The doctrine of inherent home rule has now been clearly rejected in almost all U.S. jurisdictions (Reynolds 1982: 68). However, central to the debate over the relationship between municipal authorities and state legislatures has been the recognition that municipalities need the ability to control their own local affairs (*Rutgers Law Journal* 1999). As noted by the Court of Appeals of New York in *City of New York v. State of New York* (2000), "there are some affairs intimately connected with the exercise by the city of its corporate functions, which are city affairs only; there are other affairs exclusively those of the state; and there is a zone where state and city concerns overlap and intermingle." To address this need for municipal autonomy, most states, beginning with Missouri in 1875,[17] have adopted constitutional or statutory methods through which certain qualifying municipalities may obtain a home rule charter. These constitutional or statutory methods, known as the doctrine of municipal home rule, have greatly reduced the need for the inherent home rule principle. Currently, the doctrine of municipal home rule is granted by constitution and/or statute in well over half the states (Reynolds 1982: 95).

Most of these constitutional and/or statutory grants of municipal home rule create vague distinctions between matters of "purely municipal concern" and matters of "statewide concern." For instance, the California constitution reads, "It shall be competent in any city charter to provide that the city governed thereunder may make and enforce all ordinances and regulations in respect to municipal affairs."[18] In *California Federal Savings and Loan Association v. City of Los Angeles* (1991), the California Supreme Court was faced with the question of whether a local tax on financial corporations was a matter of municipal concern or of statewide concern. The court in that case held that it was a matter of statewide concern. Like the California case, much of the litigation regarding home rule has centered on situations of conflict between state and municipal law, thereby calling on courts to determine what are local matters and what are state matters. When statewide affairs are involved, home rule municipalities may not act. When the matters in question involve shared statewide and local affairs, which comprise the majority of home rule powers, home rule municipalities may act, but they may also be preempted by the state. Where the affairs are exclusively of local concern, home rule municipalities may act and may not be preempted by the state. Of course, as Terrance Sandalow points out in "The Limits of Municipal Power Under Home Rule: A Role for the Courts," responsibility for the general welfare within a state cannot be neatly divided into areas of local and general concern (Frug 1994: 75–78).

The contemporary situation is that almost all states have constitutional home rule provisions, yet home rule powers are not exercised vigorously in every state (Mandelker et al. 1996: 129). Nonetheless, the doctrine of municipal home rule, like Dillon's rule, remains alive and well.

Requirement of Uniformity and Equality in State Taxation

Most state constitutions contain uniformity provisions that are closely linked to the equal protection concept requiring that similarly situated persons or objects be treated in a similar manner (Gelfand 2000: 10). The exact motives for the first uniformity clause have not been established (Stark 1993: 579). However, the period from 1838 to 1851 saw the first use of uniformity clauses phrased in "equal and uniform" language such as is used in existing uniformity clauses (Newhouse 1959: 616). This was the period when most state governments were incurring enormous debts to encourage commerce and economic development. Indeed, in Pennsylvania, the state uniformity clause was part of the 1874 amendments to the state constitution aimed at limiting the General Assembly's authority to enact economically preferential legislation (Hickman 1999: 1698–99). Therefore, the uniformity clause may have been a part of the people's reaction to the rising inequities in taxation and other economically preferential legislation in the early nineteenth century.

Newhouse (1959), in his compendious two-volume work on uniformity provisions in state constitutions details twelve variations of the basic constitutional provision requiring uniformity in state taxation. The basic form of the uniformity clause, as stated in Pennsylvania's constitutional provision, reads, "All taxes shall be uniform, upon the same class of subjects."[19] The state of Arizona's provision, which Newhouse lists as a different variation, reads, "All taxes shall be uniform upon the same class of property."[20] In general, state uniformity clauses require that taxation be "uniform and equal" to some degree.

However, state uniformity clauses have not been as clear as the preceding paragraph implies. They have produced, more than anything else, confusion and litigation (Newhouse 1959: 767). The cases on this subject generally involve the organization or classification of taxable subjects into groups that receive varying treatment (Gelfand et al. 2000: 10). Courts typically answer uniformity questions by analyzing the classification scheme that the challenged tax utilizes (Ibid.). Most celebrated of all uniformity cases is *Amidon v. Kane* (1971), in which the Supreme Court of Pennsylvania considered a challenge to Pennsylvania's adoption of the definition of "taxable income" from the U.S. Internal Revenue Code. The court held that the various tax preferences in the Internal Revenue Code, such as those for homeowners and for personal itemized deductions, violated the uniformity clause of the Pennsylvania Constitution, which required that "all taxes shall be uniform, upon the same class of subjects." In *Leonard v. Thonburgh* (1985: 320–21), the Supreme Court of Pennsylvania outlined the principles that govern the analysis of claims of nonuniform taxation. (1) The Legislature possesses wide discretion in matters of taxation. (2) The challengers of the constitutionality of state or local taxation bear a heavy burden to demonstrate that a classification, made for purposes of taxation, is unreasonable. (3) In cases where the validity of a classification for tax purposes is challenged, the test is whether the classification is based upon some legitimate distinction between the classes that provides a nonarbitrary and "reasonable and just" basis for the difference in treatment. (4) Tax legislation will not be declared unconstitutional unless it "clearly, palpably, and plainly violates the Constitution."

Most state courts, like the Supreme Court of Pennsylvania, review uniformity challenges to tax legislation under the rational basis test. Newhouse recommends that states formulate more definite policies to explain precisely what is necessary to achieve the policy goal that underlies the constitutional limitation of uniformity in taxation (Newhouse 1959: 767).

Prohibitions Against Enacting Local Laws or Special Laws

Provisions limiting local laws or special laws are, along with home rule provisions, the bulwark of a defense against meddling by the state legislature in local affairs. Most states were motivated to adopt these provisions during the latter half of the nineteenth century when the rapid growth of cities and towns produced lots of changes in social and economic conditions, and added greatly to the complex necessities of local communities (*Anderson v. Board of Commissioners* 1908). As a result, there was increased demand for legislation aimed at benefiting small localities, thereby leading to preferences and irregularities (Ibid.). Typically, members whose particular constituents were not affected by a proposed special law became indifferent to its passage and allowed the enactment of improvident, corrupt, and ill-considered legislation (Ibid.). In the alternative, members voted for local bills of others in return for comparable cooperation from them (Reynolds 1982: 86). For instance, over half the legislation passed by the Kansas legislature of 1905 constituted special acts with at least twenty-five special acts relating to bridges and thirty-five fixing the fees of officers in various counties and cities (*Anderson v. Board of Commissioners* 1908).

People in various states reacted to these inherent vices of special and local laws by changing their state constitutions to include specific provisions prohibiting the enactment of "local" or "special" legislation. The Supreme Court of Texas in *Maple Run at Austin Municipal Utility District v. Monaghan* (1996: 945) defined a local law as one limited to a specific geographic region of the state, while a special law is limited to a particular class of persons distinguished by some characteristic other than geography. Osborne Reynolds finds that provisions prohibiting local or special legislation take three main forms:

> One type of provision forbids special legislation as to certain listed subjects, and those subjects often include the incorporating of cities and towns, changing the chapters of municipalities. . . . A second type of provision commonly declares that all general laws shall have uniform application throughout the state and that no special law shall be passed where a general law could be made applicable. . . . A third type of provision merely requires that special legislation must undergo a specified procedure before it is considered, or at least before it is passed, by the state legislature. (Reynolds 1982: 86–87)

An example of the typical constitutional language is the Illinois Constitution, which states, "The General Assembly shall pass no special or local law when a general law is or can be made applicable."[21] Other state constitutions may take different forms, but like the Illinois constitutional provision, they all seem based on the belief that general legislation, rather than legislation aimed at specific cities, will curb state interference in city affairs (Frug 1994: 130).

States, however, have a legitimate interest in enacting legislation to solve problems found only in particular areas of the state because not every state law can appropriately be applied statewide (Ibid.). Much of the litigation in this area focuses on legislation that places cities in various categories or classes, classes that are most often defined by class with different legislative schemes for each class. The main issue that courts grapple with is whether the classification is reasonable and whether the law operates equally on all within the class. For instance, in *Maple Run at Austin Municipal Utility District v. Monaghan* (1996: 944), the Texas Supreme Court considered the constitutionality of a section of the Texas Local Government Code that singled out one specific municipal utility district for special treatment due to the code's specific requirements. The court held that the section of the code was an invalid local law because the state legislature singled out the district for special treatment without any reasonable basis for doing so (Ibid.: 947). In addition to singling out districts for special treatment using specific statutory requirements, some legislatures legislate for particular cities by name, as opposed to by population. Courts usually strike such individualized specification as an unconstitutional local law.[22]

Population is often a valid basis on which to distinguish categories (Reynolds 1982: 89). In *State v. Hoovler* (1996), for instance, the Supreme Court of Indiana held that a county economic development income tax statute that authorized counties having a population of more than 129,000 but less than 130,600 to increase the tax rate for certain purposes was not an unconstitutional local or special law. Courts also generally allow classification by size. For instance, a legislature may enact laws that pertain to cities of different sizes, although a particular size may contain only one member (Winters 1962; *Masters v. Pruce* 1973).

Over time, courts have become more liberal in allowing classifications (Sato and Van Alstyne 1977: 119). However, limits on special legislation remain of some importance because they are contained in the constitutions of a majority of the states (Reynolds 1982: 92).

Limitations Applied to School Finance

The majority of states delegate the task of providing public education to school districts (Gelfand et al. 2000: 143). School districts are a form of special districts that operate as limited-purpose units of local government (Mandelker et al. 1996: 89). School districts usually function independently of the general purpose county and city governments within whose territory they operate. Only a few cities have dependent school districts that operate as a part of a general-purpose government (Gelfand et al. 2000: 143).

Revenue for public school districts comes primarily from state and local revenues with minor assistance from the federal governments. Local revenues come from property taxes; state revenues, from general state revenue sources. The mix between state and local funding varies from state to state. For instance, in 1998, local property taxes accounted for 33 percent of the general fund revenues for school districts in Minnesota while 57 percent came from state aid (Office of the Legislative Auditor 2000: 11). In 1997, Michigan, the state with the highest allocation to education of state funds, allocated 28 pecent of its state spending to elementary and secondary education. That same year, New Hampshire, a state with no sales tax, allocated 6 percent (Schoettle 2001: ch. 1, sources cited).

Because of variations in property values within the boundaries of a school district there are "rich" school districts and "poor" school districts. These disparities are at the heart of the majority of the disputes concerning school finance (Schoettle 1971, 1972). Given equal tax rates and tax effort, rich school districts can generate revenues for higher per-pupil expenditures than can poor school districts (Schoettle 1971, 1972; Heise 1995: 1151). Variations in the tax base available to fund the public schools can lead to stunning differences in per-pupil spending. For instance, in Vermont, in fiscal year 1995, per-pupil expenditures varied from $2,979 per student to $7,726 per student (Verstegen and Knoeppel 1998: 562). In North Dakota, during 1990–91, disparities ranged from $11,743 per pupil in Twin Buttes elementary school district to $2,085 in Salund rural school district (Ibid.: 565).

Such disparities have evoked constitutional challenges to public school financing systems. Scholars currently divide such challenges into three waves:

1. The first wave of challenges relied upon the U.S. Constitution's Equal Protection Clause.
2. The second wave of challenges relied upon equal protection and education clauses in state constitutions and focused on inequality between school districts in the funds available for education.
3. The third, now current, wave of challenges relies upon the education clauses of state constitutions and focuses more on the adequacy of education than did the earlier challenges.

We turn now to look in more detail at these challenges to state public finance decisions and allocations of responsibility for funding the public schools.

The first wave focused primarily on the Equal Protection Clause of the United States Constitution (Heise 1995: 1153). This wave was ushered in by the U.S. Supreme Court's broad interpretation of the Fourteenth Amendment in the 1950s and 1960s and emphasis on the importance of education. Especially important was the landmark U.S. Supreme Court decision in *Brown v. Board of Education* (1954), holding segregation in the schools unconstitutional. The opinion of the Court proclaims the importance of education to our society. Proponents of education-financing reform during this era argued that education-financing disparities among school districts within a state violated the Equal Protection Clause of the U.S. Constitution, which stated that "nor shall any state . . . deny to any person within its jurisdiction the equal protection of the laws."[23] The first significant school finance case during this era was *Serrano v. Priest* (1971) in which the California Supreme Court concluded that the school finance system violated the federal Equal Protection Clause because it implicated a suspect class of individuals as well as a fundamental right and could not pass the strict scrutiny. The first wave was ended by the U.S. Supreme Court holding in *San Antonio Independent School District v. Rodriguez* (1973) that wealth was not a suspect class and education not a constitutionally guaranteed fundamental right. The *Rodriguez* holding effectively barred any arguments based on the Equal Protection Clause of the U.S. Constitution in challenging school finance systems.

The second wave was also committed to equity and focused on state constitutions' equal protection and education clauses. For instance, California's constitution states, "All laws shall have a uniform operation,"[24] which is identical to the federal Equal Protection Clause. A majority of state constitutional provisions have language similar to the New Jersey constitutional provision, which states, "The Legislature shall provide for the maintenance and support of a thorough and efficient system of free public schools for the instruction of all the children in the State between the ages of five and eighteen years."[25] Within days after the *Rodriguez* opinion, the New Jersey Supreme Court announced its decision in *Robinson v. Cahill* (1973), the first major school finance case in the second wave. The *Robinson* holding concluded that New Jersey's school finance system did not meet the state constitution's "thorough and efficient" requirement because of the interdistrict per-pupil spending disparities. However, second wave decisions had mixed results with almost as many state courts invalidating state school finance systems as upholding them between 1973 and 1989 (Heise 1995: 1159). Between 1984 and 1987, there were no decisions on the constitutionality of a state's plan for financing public schools, showing the loss of momentum in school finance litigation toward the end of the second wave (Strickland 1991: 1143).

In 1989, within months of each other, courts in Kentucky, Montana, and Texas declared their respective state school funding systems unconstitutional, thereby ushering in the now-current third wave. Reformers in the three states successfully argued that unequal school expenditures among the state's school districts were unconstitutional based on the education provisions in the states' constitutions. Decisions in this era reflect a general shift from the focus on equity, that is, per-pupil spending disparities, to a focus on adequacy, or the sufficiency of funds allocated to students and schools. Many proponents of school finance reform, using an adequacy theory, argue "that all children are entitled to an education of at least a certain quality and that more money is necessary to bring the worst school districts up to the minimum level mandated by the state education clause" (Heise 1998: 545). For instance, in *Abbott v. Burke* (1990), the New Jersey Supreme Court defined equal educational opportunity in terms of educational needs and held that certain poorer urban school districts did not provide a thorough and efficient education as required by the state constitution's education provision (Strickland 1991: 1149).

The new phase of the school finance reform movement that began in 1989 is bound to continue well into the early twenty-first century. Many states, for instance, Massachusetts, have yet to rule on the constitutionality of their school finance systems. However, opponents of the movement are likely to raise the traditional arguments against school finance reform that were raised in the early cases. The California Supreme Court in *Serrano v. Priest* (1971), for example, acknowledged that the state's school finance system furthered legitimate governmental interests, such as traditional notions about local control of schools (Heise 1995: 1155). The U.S. Supreme Court also recognized the sanctity of local control and that it is a legitimate governmental interest (*San Antonio Independent School District v. Rodriguez* 1973: 49–50). There is tension between local control and school finance reform efforts, which favor centralization. In addition, some politically powerful urban school districts are ambivalent about participating in equity litigation efforts because some urban school districts might lose financially in an effort to equalize per-pupil spending (Heise 1995: 1173). In general, however, American school districts continue to become more reliant upon state revenues, and not local property taxes, for funding (Heise 1998: 631). Whether successful adequacy lawsuits will increase centralization and improve education among poorer school districts will depend upon the outcomes of the current wave of school finance litigation.

Conclusion

This chapter has introduced the major legal strictures governing state and local government finance. Clearly, state and local governments do not have the power that they might otherwise have were there no debt limits, prohibitions against the lending of credit, public purpose doctrine, Dillon's rule, home rule, requirement of uniformity and equality in state taxation, and prohibitions against enacting local or special laws. Although the necessities that led to the enactment of most of these legal doctrines and rules have decreased over the years, many of the doctrines still remain alive and well. However, as detailed in discussion on the public purpose doctrine, courts are increasingly taking a deferential view to legislative decisions. This has not meant the death of these legal strictures, but merely a reluctance by courts to apply these doctrines as strictly as when they were first developed. As noted by the example of school finance, the debate between proponents of centralization and proponents of decentralization seems to be shifting more toward centralization.

Notes

Special recognition is gratefully extended to University of Minnesota law student, Fordam Otieno Wara, who very ably assisted in the preparation of this chapter.

1. *City of Chanute v. Polson,* 17 Kan App 2d 159, 161, 836 P 2d 6 (1992).

2. *Baker v. Carter,* 25 P. 2d 747, 755 (Okla 1933).

3. Wash Const, Art VIII, §7.

4. See, for example, La Const, Art VII, §14(A).

5. See, for example, Idaho Const, Art VIII, §14.

6. Wyo Const, Art XIII, § 3.

7. Ill Const, Art VIII, §1(a).

8. 164 Neb 223, 82 NW 2d 269; 378 Mich 273, 144 NW 2d 467; 39 Wis 2d 356, 376, 159 NW 2d 36, 46; 455 A 2d 1; 110 Wash 525, 531 188 P 538, 541.

9. 61 Ariz 238, 148 P 2d 353.

10. In applying the doctrine, most courts compare public and private benefits. Minnesota requires a showing of bad faith. Many state constitutions contain specific exemptions to the public-purpose requirement. For instance, government contributions to veterans, students, the needy, and the families of public safety employees are exempt from the public-purpose requirement in many state constitutions.

11. See *Brandes v. City of Deerfield Beach,* 186 So 2d 6 (Fla 1966) and *Opinions of the Justices,* 356 Mass 775, 250 NE 2d 547 (1969).

12. *State v. Lewis.*

13. T. Cooley, "A Treatise on the Constitutional Limitations Which Rest Upon the Legislative Power of the States of the American Union," (1927) quoted in (Frug 1994: 58).

14. Series of articles entitled "The Right to Local Self-Government," quoted in (Frug 1994: 58).

15. For Tennessee see *CARTA v. T.U. Parks Construction Co.* (1999); for Virginia see *W.M. Schlosser Co. v. School Board* (Va 1992) and *Norfolk Federation of Business Districts v. Department of Housing and Urban Development* (1996).

16. Wash Const, Art XI, § 11.

17. Art X, § 16, 1876; Swindler 1971.

18. Cal Const, Art XI, § 5(a).

19. Pa Const, Art IX, § 1.

20. Ariz Const, Art IX, § 1.

21. Ill Const, Art IV, § 13.
22. See *City of New Orleans v. Treen* (1983) and *Nichols v. South Carolina Research Authority* (1986).
23. US Const, Amend XIV, § 1.
24. Cal Const, Art IV, § 16.
25. NJ Const, Art VIII, § 4.

References

Cases

Abbott v. Burke, 575 A2d 359, 408 (NJ 1990).
Amidon v. Kane, 444 Pa 38, 279 A2d 53 (Pa 1971).
Anderson v. Board of Commissioners of Cloud County, 77 Kan 721, 95 P 583 (1908).
Asson v. City of Burley, 105 Id 432, 670 P2d 839 (1983), cert., denied *Chemical Bank v. Asson*, 469 US 870, 105 S. Ct. 219, 83 L. Ed. 2d 149.
Brown v. Board of Education, 347 U.S. 483 (1954).
California Federal Savings and Loan Association v. City of Los Angeles, 812 P2d 916, 283 Cal Rptr 569 (Cal 1991).
CARTA (Chattanooga Area Regional Transportation Authority) v. T.U. Parks Construction Company, 1999 WL 76074, 2 Tenn Ct App (1999).
Chemical Bank v. Washington Public Power Supply System, 666 P2d 329 (Wash 1983).
City of New York v. State of New York, 709 NYS2d 122 (NY 2000).
City of New Orleans v. Treen, 431 So 2d 390 (La 1983).
CLEAN v. State, 130 Wn 2d 782, 928 P2d 1054 (Wash 1996).
DeFazio v. Washington Public Power Supply System, 679 P2d 1316; 296 0.5550 (Ore 1984).
Hayes v. State Property and Buildings Commission, 731 SW2d 797 (Ky 1987).
Hunter v. Pittsburgh, 207 US 161, 52 LEd 151, 28 S. Ct. 40 (1907).
Leonard v. Thonburgh, 489 A2d 1349 (Pa 1985).
Maple Run at Austin Municipal Utility District v. Monaghan, 931 SW2d 941 (Tex 1996).
Masters v. Pruce, 274 So 2d 33 (Ala 1973).
Merriam v. Moody's Executors, 25 Iowa 163, 170 (1868).
Nichols v. South Carolina Research Authority, 290 SC 415, 351 SE2d 155 (SC 1986).
Norfolk Federation of Business Districts v. Department of Housing and Urban Development, 932 F Supp. 730 (1996).
Price Development Company v. Orem City, 995 P2d 1237 (2000).
Robinson v. Cahill, 303 A2d 273 (NJ), cert., denied, 414 US 976 (1973).
San Antonio Independent School District v. Rodriguez, 411 US 1 (1973).
Serrano v. Priest, 487 P2d 1241 (Cal 1971), cert., denied, 432 US 907 (1977).
Sharpless v. Mayor of Philadelphia, 21 Pa 147 (1853).
State ex rel. Tomino v. Brown, Ohio St 3d 119, 549 NE2d 505 (1989).
State v. Lewis, 86 Wash App 716, 717–18, 937 P2d 1325 (1997).
State v. Hoovler, 668 NE 2d 1229 (Ind 1996).
State v. Hutchinson, 624 P2d 1116 (Utah 1980).
W.M. Schlosser Co. v. School Board, 980 F2d 253 (4th Cir 1992).

Articles and Books

Alexander, Frank S. 2000. "Inherent Tensions Between Home Rule and Regional Planning." *Wake Forest Law Review* 35: 539–61.

Amdursky, Robert S., and Clayton P. Gillette. 1992. *Municipal Debt Finance Law, Theory and Practice.* New York: Little, Brown.

Dillon J.F. 1872. *Treatise on the Law of Municipal Corporations.* Boston: Lockcroft.

Frug, Gerald E. 1980. "The City as a Legal Concept." *Harvard Law Review* 93: 1057–1154.

———. 1994. *Local Government Law.* St. Paul, MN: West.

Gelfand, M.D.; Joel A. Mintz; and P.W. Salsich, Jr. 2000. *State and Local Taxation and Finance in a Nutshell.* 2d ed. St. Paul, MN: West.

Grad, F.P. 1970. "The State's Capacity to Respond to Urban Problems: The State Constitution." In *The States and Urban Crisis,* ed. A.K. Campbell, 27–58. Englewood Cliffs, NJ: Prentice Hall.

Heise, Michael. 1995. "State Constitutions, School Finance Litigation, and the 'Third Wave': From Equity to Adequacy." *Temple Law Review* 68: 1151–76.

———. 1998. "Equal Educational Opportunity Hollow Victories, and the Demise of School Finance Equity Theory: An Empirical Perspective and Alternative Explanation." *Georgia Law Review* 32: 545–631.

Hickman, Kristin E. 1999. "The More Things Change, the More They Stay the Same: Interpreting the Pennsylvania Uniformity Clause." *Albany Law Review* 62: 1695.

Hirshman, L.R. 1985. "The Second Arbitration Trilogy: The Federalization of Arbitration Law." *Virginia Law Review* 71: 1305–78.

Hurst, J.W. 1950. *The Growth of American Law: The Law Makers.* Boston: Little, Brown.

Mandelker, Daniel R.; Dawn C. Netsch; P. W. Salsich, Jr.; and Judith W. Wegner. 1996. *State and Local Government in a Federal System.* Miamisburg, OH: Michie, Division of Reed Elsevier.

McBain, H.L. 1916. "The Doctrine of an Inherent Right of Local Self-Government." *Columbia Law Review* 16: 190–219, 299–322.

McQuillin, E. 1911. *A Treatise on the Law of Municipal Corporations.* Chicago: Callaghan and Company.

Missouri Law Review. 1976. "The Dillon Rule—A Limit on Local Government Powers." 41: 546–69.

Newhouse, Wade J. 1959. *Constitutional Uniformity and Equality in State Taxation.* University of Michigan Law School.

———. 1984. *Constitutional Uniformity and Equality in State Taxation.* Buffalo: W.S. Hein.

Office of the Legislative Auditor, State of Minnesota, Program Evaluation Report (February 2000). School District Finances, www.auditor.leg.state.mn.us (August 5, 2001).

Oldman, Oliver, and Ferdinand P. Schoettle. 1974. *State and Local Taxes and Finance.* New York: Foundation Press.

Owens, David W. 2000. "Local Government Authority to Implement Smart Growth Programs: Dillon's Rule, Legislative Reform, and the Current State of Affairs in North Carolina." *Wake Forest Law Review* 35: 671–706.

Pinsky, D.E. 1963. "State Constitutional Limitations on Public Industrial Development Financing: An Historical and Economic Approach." *University of Pennsylvania Law Review* 111: 265–326.

Reynolds, Osborne M., Jr. 1982. *Local Government Law*. St. Paul, MN: West.

Rubin, Dale F. 1993. "Constitutional Aid Limitation Provisions and the Public Purpose Doctrine." *Saint Louis University Public Law Review* 12: 143–67.

———. 1999. "Public Aid to Professional Sports Teams—A Constitutional Disgrace: The Battle to Revive Judicial Rulings and State Constitutional Enactments Prohibiting Public Subsidies to Private Corporations." *University of Toledo Law Review* 30: 393–418.

Rutgers Law Journal. 1999. "Local Government—Home Rule Doctrine and State Preemption—The Iowa Supreme Court Resurrects Dillon's Rule and Blurs the Line Between Implied Preemption and Inconsistency. Goodell v. Humboldt County, 575 N.W.2d 486 (Iowa 1998)." 30: 1555–58.

Sato, Sho, and Arvo Van Alstyne. 1977. *State and Local Government Law*. 2d ed. New York: Little, Brown.

Schoettle, Ferdinand P. 1971. "The Equal Protection Clause in Public Education." *Columbia Law Review* 71: 1355–419.

———. 1972. "Judicial Requirements for School Finance and Property Tax Redesign: The Rapidly Evolving Case Law." *National Tax Journal* 25: 455–72.

———. 2001. "State and Local Taxes and Finance." (Draft).

———. 2002. *State and Local Taxes and Finance*. Miamisburg, OH: Lexis.

Sebree, Michael M.K. 1989. "One Century of Constitutional Home Rule: A Progress Report." *Washington Law Review* 64: 155–78.

Shattuck, R. 1984. "A Cry for Reform in Construing Washington Municipal Corporation Statutes." *Washington Law Review* 59: 653–73.

Stark, Jack. 1993. "The Uniformity Clause of the Wisconsin Constitution." *Marquette Law Review* 76: 577–623.

Strickland, Kate. 1991. "The School Finance Reform Movement, a History and Prognosis: Will Massachusetts Join the Third Wave of Reform?" *Boston College Law Review* 32: 1105–77.

Swindler, W.F. 1971. "State Constitution for the 20th Century." *Nebraska Law Review* 50: 577–99.

University of Missouri at Kansas City Law Review. 1985. "Tax Increment Financing for Redevelopment in Missouri: Beauty and the Beast." 54: 77–108.

Verstegen, Deborah A., and Robert C. Knoeppel. 1998. "Equal Education Under the Law: School Finance Reform and the Courts." *Journal of Law and Politics*, University of Virginia Law School 14: 555–89.

Virginia Law Review Association, A.E.S. 1982. "Dillon's Rule: The Case for Reform." *Virginia Law Review* 68: 693, 693–712.

Williams, Joan C. 1986. "The Constitutional Vulnerability of American Local Government: The Politics of City Status in American Law." *Wisconsin Law Review* 986: 83–94.

Winters, J.M. 1962. "Classification of Municipalities." *Northwestern University Law Review* 57: 279–304.

Wohabe, D.P. 1984. "Chemical Bank v. Washington Public Power Supply System: The Questionable Use of the *Ultra Vires* Doctrine to Invalidate Governmental Take-or-Pay Obligations." *Cornell Law Review* 69: 1094–118.

Part 2

The Developer Pays

3

Tax Incremental Financing in Theory and Practice

Rachel Weber

Introduction

If the past quarter of a century is any indication, tax incremental financing (TIF) is likely to remain one of the most popular forms of finance for local economic development in the United States. TIF is neither a new tax nor a tax abatement in the conventional sense. Rather it is a reallocation of property tax revenues from the municipality's general fund to a smaller enclave of contiguous properties: a TIF district. TIF allows a municipality or redevelopment authority to designate an area for improvement and then earmark any future growth in *ad valorem* property tax revenues from the district to pay for the initial and ongoing economic development expenditures there.

The popularity of TIF can be explained in part by the rapidly changing fiscal and political context in which municipalities operate. The flow of federal funds for redevelopment activities has been stemmed by a series of deep cuts, restrictions on tax-exempt bonds, and the administrative devolution of urban policy to lower levels of government (Clarke and Gaile 1998; Eisinger 1988; Briffault 1997). States, responding to threats of taxpayer revolt, have imposed caps on municipal property tax collections and limits on the amount and nature of municipal expenditures. At the same time, a heightened awareness of "corporate welfare," due in no small part to a nationwide movement for subsidy accountability, has made it harder for local governments to indiscriminately provide tax breaks to select private firms.

In response, local officials have adopted redevelopment strategies that do not rely heavily on federal funds, circumvent the state-imposed revenue and expenditure limits, and, at least on the surface, do not resemble the giveaways of yore. TIF addresses each of these concerns. Its funding is derived from a local source: the municipality's property tax revenues.When changes were made to the federal tax code in the 1980s prohibiting the use of tax-exempt status for bonds that funded certain kinds of private development, municipalities turned to TIF as a means of circumventing these restrictions. TIF funds have also evaded state debt limits, which typically restrict borrowing to a percentage of the municipality's assessed property base. Because the subsidized firm's future property taxes are used as leverage to pay for the initial costs of the development, TIF is often perceived as a "self-financing" form of subsidy, and, therefore, less of a drain on public resources.

But just as TIF's popularity has grown, so too has scrutiny of its operations and impact. Substantial abuses, public costs, and inequities have been unearthed in localities around the country. This scrutiny makes it imperative that policymakers fully understand how the mechanism operates in practice as well as what TIF's larger implications are for the fiscal health of municipalities. In this chapter, I describe the mechanics of using TIF to finance redevelopment projects. I then discuss the situations in which its use is appropriate and those in which benefits of using TIF, as opposed to other combinations of public and private capital, are not as evident. The chapter ends with a summary of the criticisms that have been leveled at TIF and suggestions for policy reform.

The Mechanics of Tax Incremental Financing

State-enabling legislation defines two key legal parameters for TIF designation. First, in most states, TIF can be used only to redevelop areas where a sufficient number of the properties are considered "blighted." In Indiana, for example, the authorizing statute defines a "blighted area" as one in which "normal development and occupancy are undesirable or impossible" due to "lack of development, cessation of growth, deterioration of improvements, age or obsolescence of the area, character of occupancy, substandard buildings," or presence of "other factors that impair values or prevent a normal use or development of property" (Indiana Code § 36-7-1-3). The municipality, in concert with developers and consultants, will write up an eligibility study to demonstrate that the area in question meets the state's definition of blight, documenting the deterioration, the age of the building stock, zoning and land use designations, vacancies, and changing property values. In some states, nonblighted areas may be designated as TIF districts so long as they serve other legislated goals, such as industrial job creation or military base conversion. In Michigan, for example, the original TIF legislation limited funds to roads, sewers, and other "pure public good" infrastructure expenses until the statute was amended in 2000 to include land acquisition and improvements for private businesses and incubators (Wisniewski 2000).

Second, states require the municipality to demonstrate that the area in question could not be redeveloped "but for" the use of TIF. Herein lies the counterfactual that most economic development incentives must address. This provision requires municipal officials to attest to the fact that (a) the redevelopment would not occur without incentives; and (b) other available sources of incentive, such as a combination of bonds, abatements, and tax revenues, would not be sufficient to attract private investment. There is no definitive case law or statutory authority on the "but for" condition (Redfield 1995; Peddle 1997), an absence that is somewhat understandable given the methodological hurdles one would need to traverse in order to prove the counterfactual *ex ante* (Persky, Felsenstein, and Wiewel 1997; Bartik 1991). If these conditions are met, however, a TIF district may be formed by municipal ordinance after notice is given and a public hearing is held to discuss the redevelopment plan.

Once an area becomes designated as a TIF district, the initial assessed property valuation for the district is held constant for a designated period. In most states, the lifetime of a TIF is around twenty years, while in some others, there is no limit on how long a TIF district can be in existence. The sum of the initial assessed values of the properties in the district forms "the base" against which growth will be measured. The municipality or authority then uses its powers of eminent domain, land assembly and sale, site clearance, relocation, utility installation, and street repair to improve the district and make it more attractive to potential businesses and developers. As private investment is attracted to the area, the assessed value of property and its taxes are expected to rise. The difference between the base value and new assessed value is the "tax increment" (see Figure 3.1).

Instead of channeling the increments to the municipality's general fund and to other taxing bodies with jurisdiction over the area (such as school and park districts), they are diverted to the TIF authority and used to finance any debt the authority accumulated when making improvements. In other words, any increase in the assessed property values of the district over the next twenty-plus years will pay for TIF activities, while taxes on the base value of the properties will remain the same and will continue to be paid to the local taxing bodies. Without TIF, each overlapping jurisdiction would levy its individual tax rate on the assessed value available in its district, and the municipality would be but one of several that receives revenues.

In order to realize an increase in property values and produce the coveted TIF increment, the municipality must find ways of paying for the up-front costs of those improvements that will make the TIF district attractive to new development. Some of these expenditures are for infrastructure, while others are for developer incentives. TIF districts do not generate funds for incentives or infrastructure immediately; instead, increments trickle in over the lifespan of the district. TIF increments, therefore, are committed *before* they are gener-

Figure 3.1 **The Allocation of Assessed Value (AV) in a Tax Incremental Finance District**

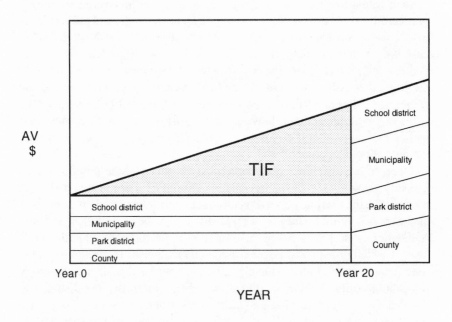

ated. Tax revenues and expenses flow in and out at different times, even though the municipality must meet all obligations as they come due.

Thus, TIF is, in essence, a means of smoothing cash flows in a development project because most expenses come up front while tax revenues and corporate profits come in further down the road. This mechanism provides the municipality with the legal means and security to borrow against the future property tax revenues for current spending. Municipalities prefer TIF because it provides the public redevelopment agency with its own budget funded with earmarked funds for economic development; it does not have to compete with other city departments at budget time. Proponents also argue that TIF also enables municipalities to keep tax rates low because the development increases the taxable base.

Municipalities rely on two primary methods of "front funding" expenditures from the expected increments. Under the first method, the municipality floats revenue bonds for the total amount of the redevelopment, dedicating the expected tax increments to pay the debt service. Revenue bonds allow municipalities to circumvent constitutional and statutory debt limitations as well as voter referenda. Some TIF bonds, however, do carry a general obligation or general fund pledge and are tax-exempt, allowing investors to earn a slightly higher than normal return. In Colorado, TIF bonds can also be secured by a captured sales tax pledge or a blended structure of property and sales tax increment. For many years TIF debt comprised a small, not rated, and obscure segment of the bond market, but as the mechanism's popularity has grown, so too has the amount of bonded debt (Johnson 1999). Once a municipality develops a track record of development that generates incremental tax revenues, it can secure insurance, higher ratings, and, therefore, cheaper debt.

The second method of front funding—commonly known as "pay-as-you-go"—requires the private developer to pay initially for the costs of the project. The municipality then reimburses the developer annually as it receives the incremental property taxes. Because developers require initial sums of money larger in amount than the increments trickling in, they often turn to banks to fill their financing gaps and pay for TIF-eligible costs such as land acquisition. Lenders require some assurance that the municipality will assist the borrower to pay its debt service.

The beauty of TIF lies in its promise that subsidized development will eventually pay for itself through increased property values. Unlike redistributive programs, which involve a transfer of resources from those who contribute them to those who need them, TIF is a mechanism that explicitly ties the level of contribution to the level of compensation (Peterson 1981).

When Is Tax Incremental Financing Used?

The short answer is all the time. Each municipality, however, has its own political process for designating TIF districts and distributing the increment generated within the district. Even before the TIF designation, the local redevelopment authority or planning department must draft a "redevelopment plan," a wish list of the future redevelopment projects in the district. After the development plan has been approved and the boundaries designated, individual developers must apply and be approved for an allocation of increment by the local administration and city council. In most municipalities, the applicant must describe the particular project in detail, providing specific figures for total development costs, sources and uses of funds, and expected job creation impact. If the authority or city council decides that the project will further TIF objectives and has sufficient front funding from other sources, it will enter into a redevelopment agreement with the individual developer or business tenant that spells out the details of the subsidy for a specific project.

Unlike the federally funded categorical programs that preceded it, TIF can be used for most kinds of projects that demonstrate financial feasibility and promise increases in property value. In general, the only significant restrictions imposed by state statutes are those directing TIF to certain redevelopment areas, defining "blight," and limiting the project term (Paetsch and Dahlstrom 1990). Because of its flexibility, this tool has enabled municipalities to channel funds to infrastructure improvement, industrial expansion, downtown redevelopment, historic preservation, firm-specific subsidies, and military base conversion.

States can also delimit the eligible costs that the TIF increment can subsidize. These typically include the cost of demolition, parcel assembly, land preparation, historic rehabilitation and other façade improvements, planning studies, and, occasionally, workforce development and training. Most TIF legislation also allows municipalities to offer subsidized, below-market rate financing from the increment. By providing financing for the total development costs, TIF reduces the amount of equity investment required of the developer for the project. Lower mortgage payments decrease the project's total leverage and financial risk, therefore making it appear more viable. Indeed, reducing the up-front costs of development (primarily those costs related to land development) can make an immediate and substantial impact on a developer's bottom line. In this sense, TIF can be more attractive to the developer (and also more costly to the local government) than conventional abatements that reduce a developer's tax burden over time.

The Public Investment Decision

The decision point for the municipality in allocating the increment is that the subsidized project must create substantial increases in the value of the property. After all, it is the difference between the value of the property in its undeveloped state and the value of the same property after it has been redeveloped (i.e., the increment or "rent gap") that is the basis for the operation of this mechanism.

In practice, property owners and developers seeking increments must demonstrate that their investments will equal or exceed the sum of discounted future increases in property tax revenues. For example, if the owner of a manufacturing plant were to consider building a new 100,000-square foot warehouse in a TIF district in Chicago, the city would embark on the following analysis. The city would identify the current ownership and use of the parcels within the TIF district being slated for redevelopment. Let us assume that they currently are being used as a parking lot and generate $40,000 in annual property taxes in the base year (i.e., the year the TIF is designated). The city then would estimate how much property tax the manufacturer would pay if the proposed warehouse were constructed and became fully operational (see Table 3.1). In this case, the *difference* between the taxes generated as a parking lot

Table 3.1

Tax Increment for Proposed Warehouse Construction in Year One

Cost per square foot	$50.00
Proposed size (sq. ft.)	100,000
Total cost	$5,000,000
Cost discount factor[a]	80%
Fair market value	$4,000,000
Assessment ratio[b]	36%
Assessed value	$1,440,000
Equalizing multiplier	2.149
Equalized assessed value (EAV)	$3,094,560
Occupancy rate	100%
Total EAV	$3,094,560
Tax millage rate	9.00%
Estimate property tax revenue	$278,510
Property tax revenue as warehouse	$278,510
Property tax revenue as parking lot	($40,000)
Tax increment in year one	$238,510

[a]The county applies this factor to new construction to bring the assessments more in line with comparable buildings.

[b]Cook County uses a bifurcated classification system that assesses industrial and commercial properties at a higher rate than residential.

and those potentially generated as a warehouse would amount to $238,510 in the first year. In theory, this increment would be available to use for economic development expenditures in the TIF district.

Although it provides a good snapshot, this calculation does not take into account the estimated lifetime of the TIF or the time value of money. In Illinois, TIF districts are designated for a period of twenty-three years. The city would make assumptions about the rate at which one could reasonably expect property tax revenues to increase if the facility were built. Looking at comparable warehouses, it might assume a 12 percent increase every three years (in Cook County, property taxes are reassessed every three years).

Moreover, the city will want to take into account the various risks, opportunity costs, and contingencies that arise when relying on any kind of payment or income that is generated in the future. Because the city wants to figure out what the value of receiving income in the future is worth today and because it does not know what kind of front funding mechanisms will be used at the onset, it cautiously discounts the future increments by an amount roughly equivalent to the cost of capital, inflation rate, and the perception of future risks. If the city relied on an 8 percent discount rate, the present value

Table 3.2

Net Present Value of Future Property Tax Increments

Year	Increment ($)
1	238,510
2	238,510
3	238,510
4	267,131
5	267,131
6	267,131
7	299,187
8	299,187
9	299,187
10	335,089
11	335,089
12	335,089
13	375,300
14	375,300
15	375,300
16	420,336
17	420,336
18	420,336
19	470,777
20	470,777
21	470,777
22	527,270
23	527,270
Total proceeds	8,273,530
Net present value @ 8.00%	3,294,998

of the increment would total approximately $3.2 million over twenty-three years (see Table 3.2). For the savvy local official, this figure would represent the upper limit of assistance available to the manufacturer to build the warehouse.[1] The city may pay for the site assembly, demolition, or environmental remediation with leveraged TIF funds. If the city planned to go to the bond market for the front funding (an unlikely event given the small size of the issuance), it would subtract the cost of debt service and other fees from the stream of increments to get a better estimate of the upper limit of assistance.

This example makes several assumptions. The first is that there is only one proposed redevelopment project in the TIF district that needs all the incentives and generates all the increment. In reality, and especially after the initial designation occurs, a queue of projects seeking assistance forms. Some of these projects may be part of the original redevelopment plan, and they are typically given priority. Second, increments are generated by all properties in the district that appreciate in value over time. Any property appreciation within the TIF district can be used to fund other, unrelated projects as long as they fall within the designated boundaries. In our case, the City of Chicago could use a portion of the increment generated by the warehouse to pay the demolition costs for a strip mall sited down the street. In Chicago, the increments are not infinitely portable across the city; they must be used in the district in which they were generated or in an adjacent TIF district. In Milwaukee and other cities, the increment can be used to pay down costs incurred in any TIF district in the city.

Third, and perhaps most important, it is likely that the future tax revenues in the TIF district (the $3.2 million from our example) will include, in no small part, property appreciation that was not in any way induced by the initial TIF-subsidized investments. Therefore, TIF, as many critics have argued, has the potential to "capture" increment to which the municipality has no singular claim (Dye 1997; Hissong 2001; Jolin, Legenza, and McDermott 1998). This perspective challenges that which fully attributes all of TIF increment to the subsidized redevelopment projects. The "but for" provision in the enabling legislation, proponents would argue, ensures that TIF was responsible for the increment in the first place.

TIF-funded Redevelopment

TIF has been used for a wide range of redevelopment projects around the country. Chicago has spent approximately $60 million of TIF funds to rehabilitate and restore the historic buildings in its downtown theatre district, and, on a very different kind of project, used $11 million to help the Ford Motor Company build a supplier park on a brownfield site on the city's southwest side (Neighborhood Capital Budget Group 1999). Philadelphia is planning to use TIF for a $174 million mixed-use family entertainment center at Penn's Landing, one mile east of downtown (Higginbotham 2000). Kansas City wooed big-box retailers like Home Depot with land preparation and developer incentives, while San Diego built mixed retail-residential developments. Smaller cities and towns are using TIF to revitalize the sagging main streets and downtown shopping areas depopulated by malls in the 1980s. New Ulm, Minnesota, helped Kraft Foods to expand its Velveeta facility in town (State of Minnesota 1996). Following Hurricane Andrew in 1993, the city of Homestead, Florida, was rebuilt using $54 million in TIF for everything from signage to a new community center (McEntee 1998).

Compared to most state and federal programs, TIF is considered a very flexible tool. The TIF process can be initiated any time a development opportunity presents itself, and TIF can be used for a variety of reimbursable costs (Paetsch and Dahlstrom 1990). In Chicago, for example, community-based economic development organizations have received TIF funding for workforce development to complement the city's focus on industrial retention and expansion.[2] One such organization, the Local Economic and Employment Development (LEED) Council, recently assisted Federal Express in securing $1.4 million of TIF funds to reconstruct a seawall on its property, after which the company signed an agreement that committed Federal Express to hiring its new employees through LEED's placement services (Barancik 1998). Federal Express front-funded the money for job training, and the city agreed to reimburse the company when tax increments were generated. LEED was able to provide follow-up support and encouragement to program graduates to help ensure that they not only remained on the job but advanced up the ladder to higher-paying jobs. TIF works especially well with these kinds of one-time allocations, especially when the employer is willing to commit its own funds up front and be paid back after time.

The design of TIF also works well with large, expensive projects that promise quick and substantial spikes in tax increment. Most municipalities are reluctant to use their bonding authority to sell revenue bonds for smaller (under $1 million) projects. This is because the amount of deficit financing needed for small projects—for a new roof or small parking lot for an existing business—is not likely to clear the minimum threshold for new issues or justify the high transaction costs (e.g., $50,000 for bond counsel). TIF is also a useful tool in instances where land uses are up-zoned, that is, when property moves from less-intensive usage to more-intensive usage. Such a move is likely to produce an immediate increase in taxable area. If increments generated are sufficient to pay for the wish list of redevelopment projects in the district, the TIF designation may be retired early and new property taxes can revert back to the overlapping jurisdictions.

From the example of the new warehouse, it should be clear why TIF operates well in areas where property values are initially low relative to other parts of the municipality or are growing at a slower pace. Government-owned (i.e., tax exempt) property, abandoned buildings, or derelict sites in appreciating neighborhoods are especially ripe for TIF-financed in-fill development. In these cases, the base value of the property (the value in the year of the TIF designation) is low enough so that when the property values start to grow in subsequent years, a substantial amount of increment can be generated. However, TIF designation is also a signaling mechanism to developers and speculators that the municipality expects property values to increase in the designated district. If the municipality is unable to act quickly, developers may flock to the proposed district, purchasing property and driving the prices up. The municipality's ability to quickly designate the TIF district is critical to locking in the lowest base value.

Evaluating Tax Incremental Financing

Judging the success of TIF is difficult, given the measurement problems involved. Municipal officials are quick to attribute new developments and increases in property values to their own economic development policies. Studies commissioned by municipalities simply add up the increases in property value since their program was initiated and either state or imply that the program caused the increases—an example of the kind of "credit-claiming" so prevalent in public policy (Bartik 1991; Rubin 1988). Local officials point to TIF-funded parking garages and office buildings, public improvements, and demolitions as evidence of the tool's success. The City of Chicago, for example, attributes the creation of 9,500 jobs and retention of another 25,000 jobs to its aggressive use of TIF in industrial areas (City of Chicago Department of Planning and Development 1998).

In contrast, most academics agree that determining the causal effect of tax abatements, low-interest loans, enterprise zones, or TIF is difficult because of the need to "control" by reasonable assumption or appropriate statistical technique for what would happen *without* the program (see, e.g., Bartik 1991; Persky et al. 1997). Those studies that use appropriate statistical methodology for dealing with causation have found mixed results. Man and Rosentraub (1998) found TIF had a positive effect on median housing values in Indiana. In Dardia's study of California (1998), he found that TIF had a substantial and positive impact on development.

However, Dye's and Merriman's (2000) comparison of TIF-adopting and nonadopting municipalities in 247 municipalities around metropolitan Chicago found a negative impact of TIF adoption on the growth in municipal-wide property values. They found that where there was a positive effect on growth in property values within the TIF district, it was more than offset by a negative impact on the non-TIF portion of the same city. Anecdotal evidence supports the view that TIF is frequently used to move existing retail to different parts of the same region (Redfield 1995). In such cases, the municipality's real revenues will increase only by the net change in property taxes and wages (i.e., minus the substitution effect).

The debate about the independent influence of TIF on development and property values is at the heart of the controversies around the impact and benefit distribution of this financing mechanism. For example, if TIF has no independent effect on property values, then school districts and other overlapping tax jurisdictions are justified in arguing that TIF "captures" revenues that would otherwise be going to them. Property taxes support the operations of many taxing jurisdictions in addition to those of the municipality, including school, park, and library districts. Because TIF redirects property tax revenues away from overlapping jurisdictions for over twenty years, these affected taxing bodies lose all the taxes derived from normal inflationary pressures and reinvestment. On the other hand, without the use of TIF as a development incentive, there may not be any or much new revenue to distribute in the first place. Everything hinges on the "but for" question.

Even if TIF can be said to independently increase property values, it is possible that existing residents may not be prepared for the higher tax burden that comes with it. For example, small business tenants may be unable to pay inflated rents, and larger industrial users and "big box" retailers may be the only ones that can afford the higher prices. Because there is no mechanism through which these owners or renters may give or withhold their consent to the TIF designation, businesses gentrified out by spiraling property values and taxes may be forced to submit to a potentially coercive arrangement.

Fear of rapid development, aggravated by the municipality's desire to move ahead on TIF designation quickly in order to lock in the lowest base, has prompted popular protest against the use of TIF. Residents in Richmond Heights, a middle-class suburb of St. Louis, attempted to stall a TIF-funded shopping mall project through voter referenda. Mexican immigrants waged protests against a proposed industrial TIF district in their Chicago neighborhood, fearing they would be displaced by rising property values. Because of the premium placed on speed and the cooption of political opposition, TIF is especially popular in municipalities with strong pro-growth mayors and city councils or those without strong opposition to development.

TIF encourages municipalities to spend now for projects that will be paid off with future increments. In doing so, municipalities take on the risk that those increments may never materialize. The fiscal exuberance of the 1990s was fueled by rapidly appreciating urban property values, and many municipalities found themselves sitting on small goldmines of tax revenues with the discretion to use them for pet development projects. As the economy slows and the sheer number of TIF districts tests the financial management skills of local bureaucrats, the speculative roots of TIF are being exposed. When the Kellogg Corporation announced plans to close its Battle Creek, Michigan, plant, for example, the city's Downtown Development Authority had to scramble to cover more than $60 million in TIF bonds it had issued (Ward 1999). In California and Colorado, several TIF bonds have defaulted (Johnson 1999). Even those TIF bonds secured with strong back-up pledges may falter when the local economy starts to decline.

Moreover, the flip side of the flexibility that this local funding source offers is a concomitant lack of accountability. TIF has been subject to misuse in certain instances, where expenditures have been made for golf courses, luxury car dealerships, fireworks displays, parades, marketing efforts, and the normal operating expenses of local governments. These kinds of project expenditures go beyond the intent of state legislation, but municipal agencies lack uniform guidelines for choosing which projects receive funding, resorting to a reactive deal-making mode with prospective developers. The competition for scarce economic development funds has increased the pressure to create additional TIF districts, rather than improve existing ones. Like the tax abatements and industrial revenue bonds before them, TIF has become a general purpose economic development tool that is playing a key role in perpetuating the border wars for private investment (Peddle 1997; Anderson and Wassmer 1995).

Suggestions for Reform

Although the early TIF legislation contained some very laudable goals, the actual administration of this financing tool has not always lived up to them. Several states have audited municipal use of TIF, and most have amended their enabling legislation to try to curb abuses. Some have tightened their definitions of blight and have tried to restrict reimbursement for parking garages, "ordinary" municipal services, and poaching retail from adjacent localities (Redfield 1995). However, even in such cases, the ambiguity of most legislated criteria will afford municipal officials a substantial amount of discretion in making the final allocation decision.

Although it would slow the process down, there is clearly a need for formal participation by the overlapping taxing jurisdictions in the TIF adoption and allocation decisions of municipalities. TIF enables municipalities to shift part of the cost of financing development to these other overlapping jurisdictions. Without state-granted rights, municipalities are under no obligation to recognize when TIF would seriously harm a school or park district's financial condition, and these districts lack legal authority to demand that their interests be taken into account. Some states require Joint Review Boards on which representatives of all districts sit, but in all but nine states, these boards have no official veto authority (Redfield 1995).[3] Schools, in particular, need to be compensated by the TIF when new residential development leads to a net increase in their student population.[4] To the extent that there is pro rata sharing of the tax increment, the negative fiscal consequences for these jurisdictions can be reduced. Moreover, the twenty-plus-year lifetime of a TIF is an arbitrary and lengthy period for jurisdictions to go without increases in tax revenues. A shorter time frame would return increment to the general fund.

States may want to consider an "inflation factor" in the frozen base to allow overlapping districts to recapture some of the increment that is not attributable to the new development. The state of Minnesota, for example, requires that the original tax capacity (base assessed value) be adjusted by the inflation rate on property values in the district so that only increases above and beyond inflation will be captured (State of Minnesota 1996). Minnesota also attempts to distinguish between the increment "caused" by TIF and increases in value due to other unrelated factors (e.g., low interest rates). If building permits were not issued in the eighteen months before the assessment, if parcels were not redeveloped within four years of the district designation, or if the municipality never issued bonds or acquired property, then it cannot claim the full amount of the increment. In this way, the legislation requires municipalities to demonstrate responsibility for creating the value that is appropriated for economic development.

Municipalities also need to migrate more of the fiscal risks back to the developers and big-box tenants receiving generous TIF subsidies. Imperiling the public purse with speculative TIF bonds makes less sense than asking developers to pay for the initial costs and paying them back as the increments are generated (Weber 2002). Some municipalities, like the city of Chicago, have taken a more cautious approach to bonding for TIF expenditures. In all but the largest and least risky projects, the city has opted for a pay-as-you-go arrangement while suburban development agencies have compromised their bond ratings with excessive TIF debt. As long as the municipality controls the financing, it can also control the reciprocal obligations of subsidized firms that partake. Developers receiving TIF assistance could agree to certain standards of employment (i.e., adherence to living wage ordinances) and environmental conduct.

Other suggestions for reform involve looking to other kinds of incentives and public spending to further economic development goals. Despite evidence of a broad national trend toward TIF, the use of this device is by no means ubiquitous across the landscape of municipal governments. TIF districts are concentrated in certain cities and regions. While municipalities in the Midwest and West Coast rely heavily on TIF revenues to fund economic development activities, New York City, Seattle, and Durham, North Carolina, rely more on conventional property tax abatements, tax increases, and voluntary tax levies like business improvement districts. The decline of federal funding and the intensified competition for private investment need not translate the requirement to "do something" into a mandate to "do anything." For municipalities, TIF has serious fiscal implications that need to be considered before increasing dependence on this fragile and controversial mechanism.

Notes

1. In theory, the municipal agency or redevelopment authority responsible for TIF allocations would go through this kind of rational decision-making process to determine the amount of subsidy available. However, political considerations of reputation, party politics, and threats of relocation enter into the decision to subsidize private firms, as cases of TIF abuse and other studies of economic development deal making have demonstrated (Molotch 1990; Reese 1991; Rubin 1988; Wolkoff 1992; Wolman 1988).

2. Job training is considered a "TIF-eligible" activity in Illinois. State-enabling legislation allows funds to be allocated toward "job training, advanced vocational education and career education including but not limited to courses in occupational, semi-technical or technical fields leading directly to employment in the TIF district."

3. In Wisconsin and New Mexico, for example, state law requires that a majority of representatives of overlying districts approve the TIF district (Lemov 1994). In Kansas, a county or school board can veto the designation.

4. A recent amendment of the Illinois TIF statute allows school districts to demand reimbursement for new expenses because of TIF-induced residential growth but does not mandate this reimbursement. Overlapping jurisdictions in Illinois can also sign intergovernmental agreements with municipalities to cover all or a portion of additional, TIF-induced expenses.

References

Anderson, John, and Robert Wassmer. 1995. "The Decision to 'Bid for Business'." *Regional Science and Urban Economics* 25, no. 5: 739–57.

Barancik, Marsha. 1998. "TIF Advocates Link Local Labor with Incoming Businesses." *Illinois Real Estate Journal* (May 11): 9–10.

Bartik, Tim. 1991. *Who Benefits from State and Local Economic Development Policies?* Kalamazoo, MI: Upjohn Institute.

Briffault, Richard. 1997. "The Law and Economics of Federalism: The Rise of Sublocal Structures in Urban Governance." *Minnesota Law Review* 82: 503–34.

City of Chicago Department of Planning and Development. 1998. "Review of Tax Increment Financing in the City of Chicago." Chicago: Department of Planning and Development.

Clarke, Susan, and Gary Gaile. 1998. *The Work of Cities*. Minneapolis: University of Minnesota Press.

Dardia, Michael. 1998. *Subsidizing Redevelopment in California*. San Francisco: Public Policy Institute of California.

Dye, Richard. 1997. "A Comparative Analysis of Tax Increment Financing in Northeastern Illinois." In *Assessing the Impact of Tax Increment Financing in Northeastern Illinois*, ed. Roland Calia, 9–28. Chicago: Civic Federation.

Dye, Richard, and David Merriman. 1999. "Does Tax Increment Financing Discourage Economic Development?" *Journal of Urban Economics* 47: 306–28.

Eisinger, Peter. 1988. *The Rise of the Entrepreneurial State.* Madison: University of Wisconsin Press.

Higginbotham, Stacey. 2000. "Philadelphia to Borrow $62 Million in Largest-Ever TIF Deal." *Bond Buyer* (September 7): 5.

Hissong, Rodney. 2001. "Guest Editor's Symposium Introduction." *Municipal Finance Journal* 22, no.1: iv–v.

Johnson, Craig. 1999. "TIF Debt Finance: An Analysis of the Mainstreaming of a Fringe Sector." *Public Budgeting and Finance* (Spring): 47–67.

Jolin, Marc; Sharon Legenza; and Matt McDermott. 1998. "Tax Increment Financing: Urban Renewal of the 1990s." *Clearinghouse Review* (July–August): 81–99.

Lemov, Penelope. 1994. "Tough Times for TIF." *Governing* 7: 18–19.

Man, Joyce. 1999. "Fiscal Pressure, Tax Competition and the Adoption of Tax Increment Financing." *Urban Studies* 36, no. 7: 1151–67.

Man, Joyce, and Mark Rosentraub. 1998. "Tax Increment Financing: Municipal Adoption and Effects on Property Value Growth." *Public Finance Review* 26, no. 6: 523–47.

McEntee, Christopher. 1998. "Tips on TIFs: Panelists Explain How to Gain Maximum Benefits, Quickly." *Bond Buyer* (February 17): 34.

Molotch, Harvey. 1990. "Urban Deals in Comparative Perspective." In *Beyond the City Limits*, ed. John Logan and Todd Swanstrom, 175–98. Philadelphia: Temple University Press.

Neighborhood Capital Budget Group. 1999. *Chicago TIF Encyclopedia.* Chicago: NCBG.

Paetsch, James, and Michael Dahlstrom. 1990. "Tax Increment Financing: What It Is and How It Works." In *Financing Economic Development*, ed. Richard Bingham et al., 82–98. Newbury Park, CA: Sage.

Peddle, Michael. 1997. "TIF in Illinois: The Good, the Bad, and the Ugly." *Northern Illinois University Law Review* 17: 441–58.

Persky, Joe; Dan Felsenstein; and Wim Wiewel. 1997. "How Do We Know That 'But for the Incentives' the Development Would Not Have Occurred?" In *Dilemmas of Urban Economic Development*, ed. Richard Bingham and Rob Mier, 28–45. Thousand Oaks, CA: Sage.

Peterson, Paul. 1981. *City Limits.* Chicago: University of Chicago Press.

Redfield, Kent. 1995. *Tax Increment Financing in Illinois: A Legislative Issue.* Springfield: Taxpayers Federation of Illinois.

Reese, Laura. 1991. "Municipal Fiscal Health and Tax Abatement Policy." *Economic Development Quarterly* 5: 24–32.

Rubin, Herbert. 1988. "Shoot Anything That Flies; Claim Anything That Falls." *Economic Development Quarterly* 2: 236–51.

State of Minnesota. 1996. *Tax Increment Financing.* Saint Paul, MN: Program Evaluation Division of the Office of the Legislative Auditor.

Ward, Andrew. 1999. "Possible Kellogg Plant Closure Imperils Michigan TIF Bonds." *Bond Buyer* (June 29): 1.

Weber, Rachel. 2002. "Do Better Contracts Make Better Economic Development Incentives?" *Journal of the American Planning Association* 68, no. 1: 43–56.

Wisniewski, Mary. 2000. "Smart Zones: Michigan's Plan to Keep Its Geniuses at Home." *Bond Buyer* (August 16): 26.

Wolkoff, Michael. 1992. "Is Economic Decision Making Rational?" *Urban Affairs Quarterly* 27: 340–55.

Wolman, Hal. 1988. "Local Economic Development Policy: What Explains the Divergence between Policy Analysis and Political Behavior?" *Journal of Urban Affairs* 10: 12–28.

4

Adding a Stick to the Carrot

Location Incentives with Clawbacks, Recisions, and Recalibrations

Larry Ledebur and Douglas P. Woodward

As economic development has moved to the forefront of state and local policy in the United States, mayors and governors now measure their performance, however crudely, by plant announcements and job creation. The Reagan era's New Federalism thrust industrial recruitment to the top of the state and local policy agenda. With many federal development programs eliminated or reduced sharply, the amount of state and local money to "buy payroll" during the 1980s has spiraled upward.[1] Public officials battle fervently against one another for new plants, expansions, and relocations, armed with increasingly expensive incentive packages.

These packages tie together everything from land acquisition and job training to new roads and sewers, subsidized loans, and tax credits. Deals to entice automotive assembly plants to the Midwest and Southeast are among the best known (see Table 4.1). The interstate bidding war to subsidize the paving of the Japanese-American "auto alley" perhaps peaked in 1985 when Kentucky won a new Toyota plant with a package valued at more than $300 million.[2]

Besides these and other efforts to attract large manufacturing plants, multimillion dollar deals have been offered to retain or relocate major office facilities. In 1988, New York City bestowed upon Chase Manhattan a $235 million incentive bundle to keep the bank's 5,000 jobs from moving to New Jersey. The next year, Hoffman Estates, Illinois, won the bid for the relocation of 6,000 employees of the Sears Merchandising Group with a $240 million package, providing free land, worker retraining, infrastructure improvements, and tax abatements.

From *Economic Development Quarterly* 4, no. 3: 221–37. Copyright © 1990 by Sage Publications. Reprinted by permission of Sage Publications, Inc.

A growing chorus of academics, practitioners, and politicians charges that incentives are getting out of control (Fiordalishi 1989: 11–12). They contend that the economic development climate is fraught with everything from "fend-for-yourself federalism" to "fiscal fratricide" (Tolchin and Tolchin 1988). A major objection is that the bargaining process often lacks any form of accountability, Even a successful effort may turnout to be a Pyrrhic victory when a prized plant is closed or scaled back, as Pennsylvania found when Volkswagen shut down in 1988.[3] Although the expected benefits of a new plant may never reach employment, tax, and other targets that justify the costs of public subsidies, public officials rarely monitor shifting costs and benefits.

This article addresses a neglected facet of bargaining between government and business for industrial recruitment—generically called clawbacks. In addition to analyzing incentive clawbacks, we identify three related areas for policy intervention: penalties, recisions, and recalibrations. These provisions entail financial recourse to reclaim all or some of an incentive package whenever a firm fails to meet negotiated performance requirements.

The intent of this article is to show that policymakers can avoid expensive mistakes if they tie incentives to written guarantees of job creation and other benefits. All private business transactions work within a framework of legally binding contracts. The time has come for public-private bargaining with some form of reasonable, guaranteed quid pro quo. European regional policymakers have used a carrot-and-stick approach to industrial recruitment, binding clawback provisions to incentive awards. However, to date there has been little discussion and only limited use of clawbacks in the United States.

The following is organized into four sections. First, we review the political economy of state incentive programs, focusing on their growing role in industrial recruitment. Next, we explain the economic justification for clawback provisions and other forms of policy action when governments use public money to entice new facilities. The third section presents various incentive control options in a simple cost-benefit framework. Finally, we offer guidelines for economic development policy and industrial recruitment, suggesting directions for further discussion and research.

The Proliferation of Incentive Programs

Figure 4.1 shows how state development programs have grown before and after the advent of the New Federalism in the early 1980s. Although some states already had financial assistance and tax incentive programs in place during the 1970s, they were in the minority. The slowdown in national economic activity and greater mobility of capital during the stagflation period

Table 4.1

Automotive Plant Incentive Packages

Company/Location	Completion date	Company's investment ($ millions)	Estimated amount production	Estimated employment	Incentives	Total incentives ($ millions)
General Motors (Saturn) Springhill, TN	1990	3,500	200,000–250,000	3,000	Job training, road improvements, forty-year local tax abatement (GM makes payments in lieu of taxes)	70.0+
Toyota Motor Company Scott County, KY	1988	800	200,000	3,000	Land purchase assistance, Site preparation, skills center, job training, highway improvements, educational programs for Japanese employees and families	325.0+
Diamond-Star (Mitsubishi/Chrysler), Bloomington/Normal, IL	1988	650	180,000	2,900	Road, water, sewer installation; site improvements; land purchase assistance; job training; property tax abatement; tax credits on investment state sales tax; local utility tax pollution control bonds; water and sewer fee savings	118.3+

Isuzu/Fuji Motors, Lafayette, IN	1988	500	120,000	1,700	Road, highway, sewer improvements; land acquisition assistance; job training; $1 million cultural transition fund to aid Japanese workers and families	86.0+
Mazda/Ford Motor, Flat Rock, MI	1987	550	240,000	3,500	Road, rail, sewer, site special improvements; job training; $500,000 loan; tax abatements; Mazda makes payments in lieu of taxes	52.0+
Nissan Motor Co., Smyrna, TN	1983	850	240,000	3,300	Job training; road, sewer, water, rail improvements; local property tax abatements: company makes special payments in lieu of taxes	66.0+
Honda of America, Marysville, OH	1982	870	330,000	4,200	Property tax abatement on buildings; previous $16.4 million grant to Honda for adjacent motorcycle factory	16.4+
Volkswagen AG, East Huntington, PA	1978	236	90,000	2,500	Low interest loans; rail and highway improvements; job training; local tax abatements; company makes payments in lieu of taxes	86.0+

Source: Glickman and Woodward 1989, pp. 230–31.

Figure 4.1 **State Incentives for Industrial Development, 1974–1988**

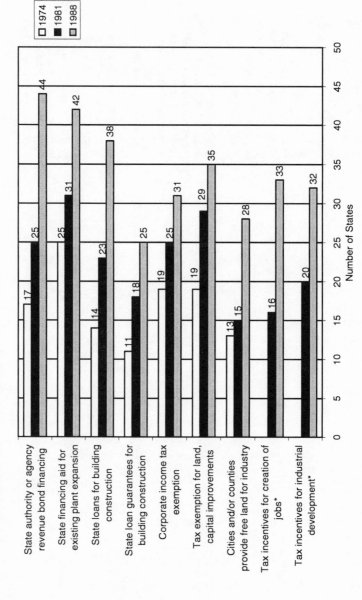

Source: "Annual Survey: 50 Legislative Climates," *Industrial Development and Site Selection 1974, 1981, 1988.*
*Figures not available before 1980.

of the 1970s intensified the interstate rivalry over economic development. Boosterism turned more aggressive, resulting in the "new war between the states" and the notorious Sunbelt-Frostbelt contest.

The New Federalism ushered in a more intense phase in this interregional competition.[4] By the late 1980s, a majority of states had programs for a broad range of incentives available to firms (see Figure 4.1). The number of states with tax incentive schemes for job creation and industrial development, including attempts to develop distressed areas, expanded significantly between 1981 and 1988.[5]

Such inventories fail to account for the size of state and local financial commitments and the way they are practically deployed. No doubt, an increase in the dollar volume of public resources invested has accompanied the proliferation of incentive programs.[6] Unfortunately, an accurate tally is not available, in part because some programs are carefully hidden or disguised by economic development agencies.

At any rate, what stands out during the Reagan era is the rise of ad hoc industrial targeting at the state and local level. Today's economic development practitioners do more than just attempt to "pick winners." Interviews disclose that they tend to "shoot anything that flies and claim anything that falls" (Rubin 1988).

In principle, subsidies for site location result from bargaining between government and private industry. In practice, however, private firms have been permitted to dictate many of the terms of the final location agreement. Companies always have the advantage of choosing another location. Although there are only a few winners and many losers, states and localities enter an often counterproductive gambit to attract new capital.

The strongest argument in favor of using public money to attract new plants and expansions is straightforward: A jurisdiction would receive no new tax revenue, jobs, or other benefits if a firm chose an alternative location. The critical question then becomes whether incentives have any discernible influence on private location choices. Unfortunately, the efficacy of economic development programs is hard to evaluate systematically because they vary widely and are tailored to individual cases. Still, most studies show that incentives have little influence on location decisions. A recent report to the National Governors Association noted that "many manufacturers make the decision to locate a new facility without the benefit of state-supported incentives" (Liner and Ledebur 1987: 5). Empirical work dating back to the 1960s suggests that most promotional activities are insignificant determinants of site selection decisions, especially when statistical tests include access to markets, resources, labor force characteristics (quality, availability, and cost), and other important determinants as control variables.[7] Firm surveys find that most businesses consider financial incentives a minor influence on plant openings and relocations.[8]

It is not surprising that incentives carry so little weight in these studies. If a firm follows profit maximization, the location offering the greatest margin between revenues and costs will dictate the decision. Governments have little or no control over the fundamental determinants of a firm's demand and costs. Policymakers can only alter location factors like markets (on the demand side) and energy and wage costs (on the cost side) over a very long time period, if at all.

Why, then, are incentive programs proliferating? Their popularity arises in part because they provide policymakers with one of the few discretionary tools available that could sway private decisions in the short run. In other words, development officials focus their efforts on the factors they can immediately control (Rubin and Zorn 1985). Indeed, incentives could be effective at the margin—acting as tiebreakers when all else is the same among the communities under consideration. Empirical studies downplay the role of incentives in plant location, but this does not invalidate the argument that government policy can be influential in the final stage of a site location decision.[9]

Incentives work best after a firm has chosen a region (the Southeast or Midwest, for example) and has drawn up a final checklist of local sites. The list is often highly visible and encourages intense competition among states and localities. Some companies, Japanese multinational corporations in particular, take as long as five years to narrow their selection. Yet development agencies often have no more than a month to assemble an incentive package. There is little time for sound economic and fiscal impact analysis.

Nevertheless, states and cities believe they must act. If they seriously banned or limited the use of differential subsidies for industrial recruitment, they could miss an opportunity to add hundreds or even thousands of jobs to state payrolls. Given the emphasis on job creation, action at this point appears to be politically expedient. North Carolina, for example, ostensibly refrains from using costly "giveaways."[10] Even so, both Charlotte and Raleigh, North Carolina, managed to assemble heavy subsidies in their unsuccessful attempt to relocate the Sears Merchandising Group in 1989.

In fact, incentive programs naturally tend to propagate. Often, localities feel they must offer incentives to remain competitive with neighboring jurisdictions (Morgan and Hackbart 1974; Harrison and Kantor 1978). A recent study of four categories of incentives—industrial revenue bonds, loans, property tax exemptions, and income tax reductions—found empirical support for the "competitive adoption" hypothesis (McHone 1987). Changes in state incentive programs prompt neighboring states to adopt similar programs. Accordingly, one state program may quickly spread throughout a whole region.

The Justification for Incentive Controls

Recent evidence, then, suggests that incentive bidding tends to feed on itself, with more expensive items often added at the last minute in an attempt to keep ahead of the competition. These hastily assembled packages act like economic steroids—in the short run, they strengthen communities in the race for new plants and expanded payroll. Of course, that does not justify their use. Even when they are effective, incentives are open to serious objections. Not surprisingly, the opposition to incentive "giveaways" began to gather steam during the mid-1980s.

A major objection is that most locational incentive programs are highly selective and firm specific. This distinguishes incentives from economic development programs that seek to enhance the "business climate" through educational reform, research and development, support for small business, and general tax relief. State money is allocated neither uniformly nor necessarily efficiently, but on an ad hoc, case-by-case basis. It often favors large, visible projects over smaller, lower profile investments. More than anything else, this raises the question of their legitimacy. There is some evidence, largely anecdotal, that shows that tax breaks favoring individual plants can crowd out existing businesses.[11] Moreover, tax breaks and other subsidies represent lost revenue—money that cannot be spent on education, better infrastructure, and other things that most firms, and, indeed, most citizens, want.

Critics, crossing the spectrum of political opinion, now recognize that governments must carefully assess the possible benefits of an incentive package against competing uses of public money. The justification for controlling incentives stems from possible unfair state-supported advantages given to certain firms. Laissez-faire advocates argue that state-imposed controls, especially performance requirements, distort business decisions. They must agree, though, that it is industrial incentives, not these requirements, that upset private capital accumulation and allocation. With industrial subsidies, as with any other payment for product or services, failure to perform to contract specifications should result in partial or full recovery of past payments and forfeiture of future payments. Unfortunately, firms subsidized by state or local governments in the United States are rarely obliged to pay penalties for nonperformance to subsidizing governments, usually because no contract exists.

The mood is clearly changing. Some states and cities have brought lawsuits against corporations that received incentives and then closed facilities. The most significant case to date involved Duluth, Minnesota, and Triangle Corporation. The city signed a contract with the company in 1982 stipulating that Triangle could not move equipment financed by tax-exempt industrial bonds. Yet seven years later, Triangle cut the Minnesota workforce by one-half and moved some of its operations to Orangeburg, South Carolina. Duluth sued the company and won in February 1988, with the court ordering Triangle to return the relocated equipment. The verdict was overturned a year later, when the Minnesota Court of Appeals barred Triangle from moving any more equipment, but allowed Triangle to keep the existing equipment in South Carolina.

Another significant court challenge came in 1980, after the city of Chicago gave Playskool, Inc. a $1 million industrial revenue bond with the understanding that the company would create 400 jobs. When the plant closed after four years, city officials threatened to sue and eventually settled out of court. Playskool agreed to keep the plant open ten more months, to set up a job placement program, and to create a $50,000 fund for displaced workers.

The lesson of both the Chicago and Minnesota cases is that communities fare better if they carefully specify a financial recovery procedure *before* a plant shuts down or scales back. Apart from these isolated legal disputes, little has been done to control the bidding war for business. Occasionally, states have proposed forming compacts to control interregional competition. In 1987, Michigan spearheaded a drive in the Midwest to limit incentives, agreeing to end tax abatements if other states reciprocated. But the initiative never took hold. Likewise, the Massachusetts legislature proposed an interstate moratorium on incentives. However, most states have shown that they are unlikely to sign such pacts and will continue to do everything they can, within their budget constraints, to entice more investment.

In lieu of an interstate compact on controlling the costs of attracting new plants and expansions, enforceable penalties imposed by individual states remain the only viable, if second-best, solution to the incentive game. Overseas such penalties are often called *clawbacks*, a comprehensive term for cancellation, reduction, and recovery of subsidies.[12] West European countries, all with very generous incentive programs by U.S. standards, establish contractual relationships with firms they subsidize. They specify investment, employment, or output standards and penalties for failure to perform at these contractual levels. As the following examples illustrate, clawbacks are used with almost every form of industrial subsidy in these European nations.

Tax Concessions

The Netherlands subsidizes almost all types of business investment through reduced tax payments if the operation is profitable or through negative tax payments if it incurs losses. If the subsidized asset is sold within a given period, all or a portion of the subsidy must be repaid. France provides local business tax concessions to firms for qualified projects. If a firm fails to meet job targets, the concession is revoked and firms must repay the conceded tax plus interest penalties.

Employment Creation Subsidies

Italy has provided concessions on social security contributions paid by employers for new employment. Where contributions have been withheld for jobs not created, this amount can be clawed back with penalties of five times this amount. Other nations limit grant payments to employment levels as well. Great Britain and Northern Ireland both dispense grants for job creation. Yet the government pays the grants in installments, which can be reduced if job targets are not met.

Capital Grants

In addition to job-creation incentives, direct grants to stimulate investment are common in Europe. Almost all of these grants include clawback features of varying degrees of severity. In Germany and Northern Ireland, grants can be revoked and full repayment required. Belgium and France make grant payments in installments. If investment or job targets are not met, future installments can be revoked. France also allows for pro rata reductions. Italy can suspend further payments, but must sue to recover past payments.

Loans and Interest Subsidies

Several European countries administer industry subsidy programs that reduce commercial interest rates on loans for eligible projects. In Belgium, Germany, and Luxembourg, these subsidies can be reduced or withdrawn if the firm fails to meet the conditions for the incentive award. These nations also enforce penalties in soft loan programs. In Denmark and Great Britain, for example, loans can be called in. The state may require special payments if conditions are not fulfilled.

These examples of relatively simple clawback schemes reveal that a menu of options is available. Despite the growing interest among state and local development analysts and the increasing number of initiatives discussed earlier, so far the U.S. literature has been silent on the issue. What is needed to open the dialogue is a conceptual framework that clarifies how state and local governments can design contractual performance agreements with subsidized firms. In the next section we present the rudiments of how various options would work.

Recisions, Clawbacks, Penalties, and Recalibrations

Just as incentive packages come in many forms, incentive controls can be tailored to individual cases. In general, however, modifications for performance deficits will fall into four basic categories:

- recisions: canceling a subsidy agreement;
- clawbacks: recovery of all or part of the subsidy costs;
- penalties: special charges for nonperformance or relocation;
- recalibrations: subsidy adjustments to reflect changing business conditions.

To see how each of these options would work, consider the following hypothetical case. Footloose, Inc., a successful athletic shoe company, announces it will open a major production facility and promises it will move its corporate headquarters and marketing research operations to the new location. The production facility alone will hire 2,000 workers. Having made the final site selection cut for the new plant, the city of New Prosperity wants to explore the possibility of bidding for the plant with an incentive package, which may include a tax abatement.

The city then asks the Department of Economic Development to evaluate the incentive package within a cost-benefit framework. Their first step is to define the time stream of costs and benefits.

Benefits. In practice, the government may define benefits in a variety of ways, including jobs created, private investment, and tax revenues generated. For purposes of this analysis, benefits are defined by New Prosperity as the sum of the tax revenues resulting from the direct and indirect impact of new investment, output, and payroll.

Costs. All state and local development agencies must allocate limited financial resources among many competing, worthwhile projects. The city acknowledges that public resources used for subsidies, including tax expenditures, will have opportunity costs. Thus, the city decides to strive to get the greatest possible return from its budget—taking all relevant direct and indirect costs into account. The full costs of a subsidy encompass the

Table 4.2

Hypothetical Schedule of Benefits and Costs of Subsidies
(in thousands of dollars)

Year	1 Annual benefit	2 Annual cost	3 Annual benefit minus annual cost	4 Realized benefits	5 Realized benefits minus annual costs
1	5	52.5	−47.5	3.34	−49.16
2	10	52.5	−42.5	6.68	−45.82
3	15	52.5	−37.5	10.02	−42.48
4	20	52.5	−32.5	13.36	−39.14
5	25	52.5	−27.5	16.70	−35.80
6	30	52.5	−22.5	20.04	−32.46
7	35	52.5	−17.5	23.38	−29.12
8	40	52.5	−12.5	26.72	−25.78
9	45	52.5	−7.5	30.06	−22.44
10	50	52.5	−2.5	33.4	−19.10
11	55	52.5	2.5	36.74	−15.76
12	60	52.5	7.5	40.08	−12.42
13	65	52.5	12.5	43.42	−9.08
14	70	52.5	17.5	46.76	−5.74
15	75	52.5	22.5	50.10	−2.40
16	80	52.5	27.5	53.44	0.94
17	85	52.5	32.5	56.78	4.28
18	90	52.5	37.5	60.12	7.62
19	95	52.5	42.5	63.46	10.96
20	100	52.5	47.5	66.80	14.30
Total	1,050	1,050.0	0.0	701.40	−348.60

dollar value of the subsidy, including tax revenues forgone, and any public infrastructure and service costs imposed by the anticipated activity of the firm.

Next the city identifies the upper bound of the subsidy—the cost ceiling that would not be exceeded if economic rationality guided the public decision. This maximum subsidy is determined by comparing the stream of anticipated benefits and alternative subsidy levels. The subsidy limit can be readily identified. Consider Column 1 of Table 4.2, a hypothetical stream of anticipated benefits from an annual tax abatement given to Footloose, Inc. All figures in Table 4.2 are discounted present values (DPV). Over a twenty-year period, the cumulative anticipated benefits are $1,050 thousand. This is the ceiling that should not be exceeded by the discounted cost of the public subsidy over this same period. An annual tax abatement with a DPV of $52.5 thousand per year (Column 2) will result in a total subsidy cost over the twenty years equal to cumulative anticipated benefits. Note that annual subsidy costs will exceed anticipated annual benefits in years 1–10, and annual net benefits will be anticipated over the remaining ten years of the subsidy program (Column 3).

The case where the DPV of benefits equals the DPV of subsidy costs is the breakeven, or zero rate of return, level of subsidization. Enterprising state and local governments will want to achieve some positive rate of return on these public expenditures, one that exceeds the opportunity cost of the public resources. The depth of the subsidy should be established to achieve this desired rate of return on public expenditures (i.e., the ratio of DPV of benefits to DPV of costs = 1 + target rate of return).

After completing the preliminary analysis, New Prosperity presents the package to Footloose, Inc. The company accepts the offer as specified in a contract, which is to be administered by the city's Department of Economic Development. The agreement with the recipient firm is contingent upon target levels of activity (investment, employment, and output). The city also retains the ability to modify the depth of the subsidy if Footloose fails to perform at these contractual levels (i.e., when the stream of realized benefits is less than that of anticipated benefits).

The need for any adjustment would follow from monitoring and further cost-benefit analysis. Say Footloose's activity is evaluated in year 5, when it appears that the company's promises about headquarters and marketing research expansion plans will not come to pass. The new situation is presented in Table 4.2, Column 4. Here the stream of annual benefits falls below the anticipated stream used to establish the threshold subsidy level. The development office of New Prosperity recognizes that the stream of realized benefits is not meeting the originally anticipated targets. Under the new stream of expected benefits, the annual benefits will not exceed annual costs until after year 15 (Column 4), and, over the twenty-year period, public costs will exceed benefits by $348.6 thousand. At this point, New Prosperity development officials have several alternatives to consider.

Recisions

As one option, the development office can simply cancel the subsidy agreement with the firm for nonperformance. In Table 4.2, cancellation to the subsidy after year 5 will result in a net loss of $212.4 thousand, the difference between cumulative costs and realized benefits over the five-year period. This may not be a net loss to the government in the long run, however, if the now unsubsidized firm continues to operate and generates future benefits.

Clawbacks

Next consider the clawback, which specifically refers to recovery of all or part of past subsidy costs. Here the government faces three choices. First, it can attempt to clawback a part of the subsidy equal to the stream of unrealized benefits over the five-year period. In Table 4.2, the amount to be clawed back is $24.9 thousand: the sum of the difference between anticipated benefits in years 1–5 (Column 1) and realized benefits (Column 4).

Second, the government can attempt to recover the subsidy costs for years 1–5 in excess of realized benefits. In Table 4.2, this amount is equal to $212.4 thousand: the sum of the difference between subsidy costs for years 1–5 (Column 2) and anticipated benefits (Column 1).

Third, if New Prosperity wished to penalize the firm for nonperformance more stringently, it could attempt to clawback the entire subsidy for the first five years, or $262.5 thousand in the example in Table 4.2. This more severe clawback option might be used, for example, if Footloose, Inc. made the decision to relocate to another jurisdiction after the initial five years.

Penalties

Disincentives for nonperformance can be increased by adding penalties to clawback provisions. For example, if the incentive is a tax abatement or tax credit, the government could clawback the taxes forgone, plus charge interest on these unpaid taxes as a penalty for nonperformance. Similar interest penalties can be applied to all forms of interest subsidies on loans (direct interest subsidies, soft loans, and loan guarantees). A variety of penalties can be devised, including foreclosure of subsidized assets (land, building, and equipment). This would be a likely option only if a plant relocated rather than scaled back its operations.

Recalibrations

An alternative to canceling the subsidy or attempting to clawback past subsidy costs is to adjust or calibrate the level of subsidy to reflect the new projected benefit stream. Three primary calibration options are available.

Option 1: De Novo Recalibration

The recalibration can be made in view of historical and future benefits without reference to past subsidy costs. In this case, the recalibrated annual subsidy had been paid over the entirety of the twenty-year period; the DPV of

Table 4.3

Recalibration Options (in thousands of dollars)

	(1)	(2)	(3)	(4)	(5)	(6)	(7)
						Recalibrations	
						Option 2	
	Annual	Annual	Realized			with	Option 3
Year	benefit	cost	benefits	Option 1		clawbacks	racheted
1	5	52.5	3.34	35.07	—	52.50	52.5
2	10	52.5	6.68	35.07	—	52.50	52.5
3	15	52.5	10.02	35.07	—	52.50	52.5
4	20	52.5	13.36	35.07	—	52.50	52.5
5	25	52.5	16.70	35.07	—	52.50	52.5
6	30	52.5	20.04	35.07	43.4	29.28	49.6
7	35	52.5	23.38	35.07	43.4	29.28	46.7
8	40	52.5	26.72	35.07	43.4	29.28	43.8
9	45	52.5	30.06	35.07	43.4	29.28	40.9
10	50	52.5	33.40	35.07	43.4	29.28	38.0
11	55	52.5	36.74	35.07	43.4	29.28	35.1
12	60	52.5	40.08	35.07	43.4	29.28	32.2
13	65	52.5	43.42	35.07	43.4	29.28	29.3
14	70	52.5	46.76	35.07	43.4	29.28	26.4
15	75	52.5	50.10	35.07	43.4	29.28	23.5
16	80	52.5	53.44	35.07	43.4	29.28	20.6
17	85	52.5	56.78	35.07	43.4	29.28	17.7
18	90	52.5	60.12	35.07	43.4	29.28	14.8
19	95	52.5	63.46	35.07	43.4	29.28	11.9
20	100	52.5	66.80	35.07	43.4	29.28	9.0
Total	1,050	1,050.0	701.40	701.40	651.0	701.70	702.0

the twenty-year stream of public costs would have been equal to that of the corresponding benefit stream (Column 3). However, the rate of return to the expenditure of public monies falls below the target rate of return because the subsidy level in years 1–5 exceeded the new threshold subsidy.

Alternatively, the recalibration can be made without reference to historical costs or benefits. The new subsidy level would be set to achieve the targeted rate of return on the public expenditure over the remaining fifteen years. In the example of Table 4.3 (Column 5), this annual subsidy level would be approximately $43.4 thousand.

Option 2: Recalibration with Clawbacks

The recalibration can also include clawback features. New Prosperity could reduce the level of the annual subsidy for years 6–20 to recover the overpayment in years 1–5. The new subsidy level would be calibrated so that the ratio of the DPV of realized benefits in years 1–5 plus that of anticipated benefits in years 6–20 over the DPV of the previously paid subsidy in years 1–5 plus the DPV of the cost stream of the subsidy for years 6–20 equaled the target rate of return. This recalibration is presented in Column 6 of Table 4.3. The annual subsidy for years 6–20 would be equal to $29.28 thousand.

Option 3: Racheted Recalibration

An abrupt reduction of the annual level of the subsidy might, in itself, adversely affect a troubled company like Footloose, Inc. To provide time for the firm to adjust to the lower subsidy level, the recalibration can be accomplished by a downward rachet in the annual subsidy over the years 6–20.

The downward rachet would be calibrated to achieve the targeted rate of return by the end of the subsidy period. Thus the subsidy would be reduced in each succeeding year starting in year 6 with the extent of the annual reductions scaled to achieve the targeted rate of return, as illustrated in Column 7 of Table 4.3.

Policy Guidelines: Preparing for the Decade Ahead

By considering any one of the options described in the previous section, public officials would be forced to look at how the consequences of their recruitment efforts go beyond initial job tallies advertised in the media. For example, they would be compelled to examine whether, by exempting from property taxes a plant that employs 2,000 people, they still guarantee that the community will have safe roads and drinking water, fire and police protection, parks, and a first-rate educational system.

Still, ribbon-cutting photo opportunities for major new plants often appear more politically expedient than a careful economic development plan for the future.[13] Hence the push for greater accountability is less likely to come from gubernatorial and mayoral offices than from financial officers, who are more familiar with the opportunity costs associated with development programs. Edward V. Regan, comptroller of New York State, for example, issued a stinging indictment of undisciplined development programs and of the failure of public officials to make them accountable to analytical inspection. He noted, "The major players—the business community and, especially elected officials—either do not want to or do not know the costs versus benefits of playing the development game or how to change the game. Such an evaluation, by default, is now left to finance officials" (Regan 1988).

Is there reason to believe that states and communities offering public incentives to the private sector will make development programs more accountable to analysis and inspection? Already more rigorous cost-benefit analysis is being given consideration in state governments. In 1988, legislation in the state of New York proposed that every tax abatement and exemption include a statement of benefits and the costs to the taxpayers of all subsidies. The state of Illinois passed a law in 1987 requiring an economic impact study before the authorization of incentives to attract foreign investment.

The first signs that governments are moving toward clawback provisions come from Wisconsin and Vermont. Wisconsin's constitution prohibits using differential tax abatements, but to attract industry the state established assistance programs for labor training and technology development during the 1980s. The Department of Development operates under an administrative rule that requires a contract with the recipient firm. Wisconsin may void state funding when the company relocates, downgrades skill levels, or otherwise does not perform according to contract. Similarly, Vermont stipulates under contract that a company must meet employment targets and wage levels when labor training assistance is offered.

It remains to be seen whether other states and cities will follow the lead of Wisconsin and Vermont. Even so, as public officials continue to engage in subsidized industrial recruitment during the 1990s, they should at least become more skilled than they have over the past decade. Toward that end, this article has focused on one important new area for state and local policy. But the suggestions we make for improving and protecting the integrity of public funds used for industrial recruitment should be embedded in a set of state and local economic development guidelines. Seven important steps are summarized next.

Policy Framework

State and local governments should establish clear and consistent policies on industrial subsidies and avoid operating on an ad hoc, case-by-case basis. Governments engaged in subsidizing private enterprise need to operate from a consistent framework of policies that can be effectively communicated, understood, and defended in working with potential industrial opportunities. One component of these guidelines should be a clear rationale for assisting target firms.

Subsidy Budgets

State and local governments should establish budgets for industrial subsidies, including tax concessions, that identify the amount that the unit of government is willing to invest in each fiscal year. Often, subsidy programs are administered but there is no clear understanding of accounting or their costs, especially those resulting from off-budget programs and tax expenditures. Administering officials should be required to conform to these budget limitations. Creation of subsidy budgets, besides controlling public costs, also encourages development authorities to establish priorities among projects based on their rate of return to the administering government.

Target Rate of Return

State and local governments should identify a target rate of return on the investment of public funds in industrial subsidies. This target rate of return should be no less than the opportunity cost of these public resources (i.e., the rate of return in the highest alternative uses). Projects that do not meet or exceed this target rate of return should not receive public subsidies.

Evaluation

State and local governments should develop the analytical capacity to evaluate the public benefits and costs of industrial subsidies. Analysis of every project considered for public subsidies should be undertaken to identify the benefits derived by the administering jurisdiction, the costs to the administering government, and the rate of return to the investment of public funds.

Cost-Effectiveness

Jurisdictions should use the most cost-effective instruments in administering industrial subsidies.[14] Tax abatements, although one of the most common subsidies, are seldom cost-effective. The more cost-effective instruments are those that leverage investment from commercial lending and investment institutions. Among these are loan guarantees, direct interest subsidies, and incentives targeted to nondepreciable assets.

Negotiating Skills

State and local governments should develop the capacity to sit with business at the negotiating table as equal partners. Business executives will respect government officials who are "businesslike," have a clear understanding of the public "bottom-line," and are skillful negotiators.

Subsidy Contracts

Governments should require legally enforceable contracts with firms as a condition of award of subsidies. These contracts should carefully specify performance criteria such as investment, employment within their juris-diction, and public recourse for nonperformance. Subsidy contracts should include clauses that specify recisions, clawbacks, penalties, and recalibrations that will be enforced if the subsidized firm fails to meet its promises.

These seven guidelines would help deter the often haphazard and coun-terproductive bargaining over incentives that has arisen inexorably over the past decade. With a comprehensive economic development program in place, states and cities could act more prudently when they make the site selection cut for a major facility. By presenting these objectives for economic development policy in this article, including specific clawback and other incentive controls, we hope to stimulate further discussion and research.

Notes

1. A review of the literature on the use of industrial development incentives in the United States can be found in Luker (1998).

2. For details, see Glickman and Woodward (1989, esp. ch. 8). See also Tolchin and Tolchin (1988, ch. 4).

3. A decade earlier, the state offered Volkswagen a multimillion dollar incen-tive package following a fierce bidding war with neighboring Ohio. The pack-age included $30 miilion for rail and highway connections to the plant and a $40 million loan not due until ten years after the plant closed.

4. During the 1980s, major cutbacks affected most federal programs de-signed to stimulate local economies. Under the Reagan administration, real spending on Urban Development Action Grants and Economic Development Administration programs fell about 53 percent. Even the popular Community Development Block Grant program was cut 20 percent (after adjusting for infla-tion) from 1980 through 1986. See Fainstein and Fainstein (1989).

5. The best-known examples are enterprise zones used to stimulate eco-nomic development in depressed urban areas. This centerpiece of Reagan's ur-ban policy was never implemented nationally, but became popular with states and communities.

6. It is difficult to assess how the size of incentives has grown over time. For 1985, the dollar volume of state incentive programs is presented in National Association of State Development Agencies (1986).

7. A good summary of the literature may be found in Blair and Premus (1987). For a review of early research, see Benjamin Bridges, Jr. (1965). A recent empirical study of industrial development effectiveness tested a broad range of general state programs, including some of the plant location inducements con-sidered in this article. It found that land and building subsidies, tax programs, post-secondary education assistance, advertising and other outreach programs, and research and development support are either too small to have an impact on state economic performance or are inherently ineffective. The author concludes that they tend to waste resources. See Luger (1987).

8. Schmenner's 1980 survey of Fortune 500 plant openings and relocations demonstrated "fairly convincingly that tax and financial incentives have little influence on almost all plant location decisions" (Schmenner 1982) More recently, the 1989 Grant Thornton survey found that manufacturers ranked state incentives seventeenth out of twenty-one factors that companies consider when deciding on locating new sites. See Thornton (1989).

9. As for the impact of taxes on intrametropolitan and interstate location, one exhaustive review of pertinent empirical research concluded that the issue is an "open rather than a settled question" (Newman and Sullivan 1988) At the urban level, studies have shown that once available land, properly zoned, is accounted for, general tax levies may influence final manufacturing location decisions (Wasylenko 1980).

10. North Carolina claims to have only four types of tax breaks, with strict limitations, and one type of financial assistance. South Carolina, by comparison, offers ten categories of tax breaks and eleven varieties of financial assistance (Myers 1987).

11. In one case during the late 1970s, a maker of hydraulic equipment announced that it would close its Columbus, Ohio, facility after the city government subsidized a West German competitor with a large tax break (Testa and Allardice 1988). More recently, auto parts suppliers have complained that subsidies to foreign companies are driving them out of business.

12. See Yuill and Allen (1980) and subsequent volumes of this catalog for a discussion of clawbacks in European incentive programs. The clawback schemes discussed in this article are drawn from this catalog.

13. The economic myopia of some mayors and governors may ultimately prove to be politically short-sighted. The mayor of Flat Rock, Michigan, was voted out largely because of anger about the fourteen-year tax holiday given to Mazda Motor Corporation.

14. For information on the cost-effectiveness of alternative forms of industrial incentives, see Hamilton, Ledebur, and Matz (1985); Bendick, Rasmussen and Ledebur (1982); and Rasmussen, Bendick, and Ledebur (1984).

References

Bendick, Marc; David Rasmussen; and Larry Ledebur. 1982. "Evaluating State Economic Development Incentives from the Firm's Perspective." *Journal of Business Economics* 17, no. 3 (May): 23–29.

Blair, John P., and Robert Premus. 1987. "Major Factors in Industrial Location: A Review." *Economic Development Quarterly* 1: 72–85.

Bridges, Benjamin Jr. 1965. "State and Local Inducements for Industry, Parts I and II." *National Tax Journal* 18, no. 1 (March): 1–14 (Part I); and 18, no. 2 (June): 175–92.

Fainstein, Susan S., and Norman Fainstein. 1989. "The Ambivalent State Economic Development Policy in the U.S. Federal System Under the Reagan Administration." *Urban Affairs Quarterly* 25, no. 1: 41–62.

Fiordalishi, Georgina. 1989. "How to Avoid a Bum Deal When Using Incentives to Win Business Jobs." *City and State* (June 19–July 2): 11–12.

Grant Thornton. 1989. *The 10th Annual Manufacturing Climates Study.* Chicago: Grant Thornton, June.

Glickman, Norman J., and Douglas P. Woodward. 1989. *The New Competitors: How Foreign Investors Are Changing the U.S. Economy.* New York: Basic Books.

Hamilton, William; Larry Ledebur; and Deborah Matz. 1985. *Industrial Incentives: Public Promotion of Private Enterprise.* Washington, DC: Aslan Press.

Harrison, Bennett, and Sandra Kantor. 1978. "The Political Economy of States' Job-Creation Business Incentives." *Journal of the American Institute of Planners* 44: 424–35.

Liner, Blaine, and Larry Ledebur. 1987. *Foreign Direct Investment in the United States: A Governor's Guide.* Paper prepared for the seventy-ninth meeting of the National Governors Association, Washington, DC: Urban Institute, July, 5.

Luger, Michael I. 1987. "The States and Industrial Development: Program Mix and Policy Effectiveness." In *Perspectives on Local Public Finance and Public Policy,* Vol. 4, ed. John Quigley, 29–63. Greenwich, CT: JAI Press.

Luker, William Jr. 1998. "'Buying Payroll': Industrial Development Incentives and the Privatization of Economic Development." Paper presented at the annual meeting of the Western Social Science Association, Lyndon B. Johnson School of Public Affairs, University of Texas at Austin, April, mimeographed.

McHone, W. Warren. 1987. "Factors in the Adoption of Industrial Development Incentives by States." *Applied Economics* 19, no. 1: 17–29.

Myers, Greg. 1987. "Bidding Wars." *Business and Economic Review* (January–March): 8–12.

Morgan, W.E., and M.M. Hackbart. 1974. "An Analysis of State and Local Industrial Tax. Exemption Programs." *Southern Economic Journal* 41: 200–205.

National Association of State Development Agencies. 1986. *Directory of Incentives for Business Investment and Development in the United States: A State-by-State Guide.* Washington, DC: Urban Institute Press.

Newman, Robert J., and Dennis H. Sullivan. 1988. "Econometric: Analysis of Business Tax Impacts on Industrial Location: What Do We Know, and How Do We Know It?" *Journal of Urban Economics* 23: 215–34.

Rasmussen, David; Marc Bendick; and Larry Ledebur. 1984. "A Methodology for Selecting Economic Development Incentives." *Growth and Change* 15, no. 2 (January): 18–25.

Regan, Edward V. 1988. "Government Inc.: Creating Accountability for Economic Development Programs." Washington, DC: Government Finance Research Center of the Government Finance Officers Association, April, mimeographed.

Rubin, Barry M., and C. Kurt Zorn. 1985. "Sensible State and Local Economic Development." *Public Administration Review* (March/April): 333–39.

Rubin, Herbert J. 1988. "Shoot Anything That Flies; Claim Anything That Falls: Conversations with Economic Development Practitioners." *Economic Development Quarterly* 2, no. 3: 236–51.

Schmenner, Roger W. 1982. *Making Location Decisions.* Englewood Cliffs, NJ: Prentice-Hall, 1982.

Testa, William A., and David R. Allardice. 1988. "Bidding for Business." *Chicago Fed Letter* 16 (December).

Thornton, Grant. 1989. *The 10th Annual Manufacturing Climates Study.* Chicago: Grant Thornton.

Tolchin, Martin, and Susan Tolchin. 1988. *Buying Into America: How Foreign Money Is Changing the Face of Our Nation.* New York: Times Books.

Wasylenko, Michael J. 1980. "Evidence of Fiscal Differentials and Intra-metropolitan Firm Relocation." *Land Economics* 56, no. 3: 341–49.

Yuill, Douglas, and Kevin Allen. 1980. *European Regional Incentives.* Glasgow: Centre for the Study of Public Policy, University of Strathclyde.

5

Development Exactions

Michael T. Peddle and Roger K. Dahlstrom

A few years ago, a small community in Illinois was approached by a residential developer who sought to build a subdivision that was proposed to include more housing units than the number of existing residents in the community. That is, at build out, this subdivision was expected to triple or quadruple the community's population and to produce more than 500 new students who would need to be educated by the local school districts. With no growth management plan in place, no comprehensive capital facilities plans for schools or other public infrastructure, no policies in place for development exactions, and no level of sophistication in development negotiations, the long-term ramifications of the development decisions faced by the community were hard to overstate.

The amount of new public infrastructure required to support the new development, including the possible need for new school buildings, was overwhelming. Yet, new school buildings and large-scale infrastructure improvements were likely to require voter referenda for bond issues and corresponding real estate tax hikes. Under normal conditions, such a bond issue would be difficult to pass. Under conditions where much, if not all, of the need for the new infrastructure, and the vast majority of the benefits of the new infrastructure, flows from new development, a tax increase on existing residents may be even harder to swallow. The local school district sought outside counsel and a short delay in the municipality's decision on the project so as to better inform the village board of the potential ramifications of their decision on the fiscal health of the schools. Unfortunately, the district's pleas fell on deaf ears, and the development was approved with the stipulation that any future impact fees or development exactions that might otherwise apply to the project would be waived via the development/annexation agreement.

The concept of giving up or sacrificing some of one's property or wealth for the purpose of promoting the greater good is at the heart of much charitable behavior. The adage "you've got to spend money to make money" is also a familiar mantra of those offering advice to fledgling businesses. Intellectually, development exaction systems are designed with a hope to capitalize on both of these sentiments on the part of the development community as a means to provide greater amounts of high-quality public infrastructure and services at a more affordable price for taxpayers. Politically, development exaction systems are designed to shift the burden of financing infrastructure away from the voters who have elected the community's leaders (and will be asked to vote for their reelection) to groups not yet present (and, therefore, not yet voters) in the local community. What politician would not drool at the chance to provide improved public services and infrastructure and not have to burden his or her constituents with a tax increase to do it? Development exactions are often viewed by politicians and local residents as such a silver bullet.

A development exaction is a provision in the development approval process that requires a developer to give or provide something to, or on behalf of, a local government unit or service district. Development exactions include things such as dedicating and donating to the community a parcel of land in a subdivision to be used as a park, building, or fire station, or making cash donations/payments to a fund established for the purpose of making open-space land acquisitions. Development exactions are different from altruistic donations to local governments and service districts in that the donation or payments made as part of a development exaction are required (legally, politically, or through moral suasion) in order for some form of development approval to take place. There is generally a clear quid pro quo relationship that underlies development exactions.

Impact fees represent one common means by which development exactions are implemented. Impact fees are development exactions that compel a cash payment as opposed to many other types of development exactions that provide an opportunity for the developer to make a land, building, or other in-kind donation in lieu of paying the exaction in cash. Impact fees are based upon a fixed fee schedule that is published, available, and enforced through ordinance or resolution. An example of an impact fee would be the cash payments required of builders or developers by many Chicago suburbs. These are based upon a schedule of fixed fees that vary by the number of bedrooms in a new home. These fees must be paid in order to obtain a building permit for a new home. The proceeds are earmarked and escrowed by the municipality for disbursement to their local school district to help finance new school buildings that will service the residents of the home whose permit is being obtained. Impact fees are also charged for things such as building a new branch library, building a new fire station, expanding a wastewater treatment plant, and buying a new piece of fire equipment. Understanding development exactions and their use can be very important for economic developers, students of economic development, public policymakers, and resident taxpayers.

Development exactions are an increasingly popular means of financing the public costs associated with economic development projects and economic development activity (Peddle and Lewis 1996). They are also unique and richly diverse financing tools. Exactions provide a means by which public infrastructure and other capital projects can be built or provided without resorting to unpopular tax increases or cuts in alternative projects, or at least a means by which to reduce the necessary magnitude of those actions. Furthermore, negotiated exactions provide one of the few means by which infrastructure and government services can be paid for using revenue sources other than tools of compulsory finance such as taxes and charges. Like fees and charges, development exactions are generally linked to some form of benefits received by the person paying the exactions. However, unlike most other government and economic development finance tools, development exactions commonly are paid fully or in part through in-kind contributions or fee offsets. Furthermore, depending on their form, development exactions often require a rational nexus to some form of development activity, a higher standard than is applied to almost any other form of government finance mechanism.

The Growing Use of Exactions

There are a number of reasons why the use of development exactions has exploded over the past thirty years or so (Altshuler and Gómez-Ibáñez 1993). First, the late 1960s brought a significant increase in concern about the environment and quality of life. This concern has continued into the twenty-first century, and has meant a more ambivalent attitude toward growth. Development exactions are often adopted as part of comprehensive growth management plans that are often motivated by a desire to slow growth to a more manageable level. Perceptions are that development exactions can increase the costs of development, thereby slowing the rate at which development would be expected to occur (other things equal).

Second, development exactions provide a logical and focused means for newly empowered neighborhood groups to counteract the harsh effects of many types of local development projects. An example of this is the building of a large new subdivision in DeKalb, Illinois, that will take forest lands, open space, and children's play areas away from existing, adjacent residents while adding more traffic, congestion, and drainage problems to the existing neighborhood. At minimum, development exactions help to pay for some of the negative externalities (spillover effects) associated with some types of development activities (e.g., in the DeKalb case impact fees could be used to make road improvements, provide drainage enhancements, and build buffers to mitigate negative effects on the existing neighborhood).

Third, over time, stagnating incomes and the tax revolt movement have made it more difficult to rely on traditional revenue sources like property taxes and sales taxes. In addition, changes in the municipal bond market have made some types of debt issues for infrastructure more difficult (e.g., changes in rules that resulted in limiting the use of industrial revenue and industrial development bonds). Development exactions have helped to fill the gap.

Fourth, deferred maintenance and a backlog of capital improvement projects have created a financing bottleneck. That has made it impossible to finance all critical projects out of traditional tax sources on a timely basis, despite the common occurrence and increased probability of infrastructure failures. Development exactions provide another means to overcome the financing bottleneck.

Finally, more sophisticated fiscal impact analysis has provided greater and more precise evidence that most forms of new development, particularly residential, do not pay for themselves, especially when one looks at both the capital and operating costs of government (e.g., see the work of Robert Burchell and David Listokin [1978, 1994]). This is a controversial notion in the home building community, as they maintain that this work does not reflect the property taxes that a home will pay over its useful life. However, few challenges to Burchell's and Listokin's work appear to accurately reflect capital costs, operating costs, and the time value of money in the alternative calculation of the net fiscal effect of a new home or other development unit. The common popular acceptance by local officials of the general conclusions of analysts like Burchell and Listokin has created an even greater demand and incentive for local communities to shift some of the burden of infrastructure finance to new developments through exactions. Yet, while all of these developments have contributed to growth in the use of exactions as a means of financing economic development, there are other reasons for the growing use of exactions that are grounded in economic, political, and social theory and practice.

Why Do Communities Adopt Exactions?

Communities adopt development exactions for a wide variety of reasons and in a wide variety of situations. However, there seem to be a few particularly common reasons why communities choose to add development exactions to their economic development finance portfolio.

Perhaps the most important reason why development exactions are widely used by communities is that they help to hold property taxes down by providing an alternative revenue source for expenditures that would otherwise be financed through such taxes. This is particularly notable because property taxes have almost universally been found in citizen surveys over the past thirty years to be the least popular form of taxation at the state and local level. Lower property taxes will generally be perceived to make an area more attractive as a place of residence and a place to do business. Any offsetting effect of development exactions is generally more hidden from view, especially for existing properties. Furthermore, exactions typically are of a "one-payment" nature. Unlike property taxes or other "pay-as-you-use" financing tools, the magnitude of the exaction is known and fixed up front, and the responsibility for further payments generally does not exist. Thus, past development exactions are invisible to future buyers of a given piece of property. This removes a great deal of uncertainty for the taxpayer, as compared with a property-tax-based system that passes on a future stream of property tax payments and the prospect of additions to that future stream as more infrastructure is brought on line. These effects make exactions that much more politically attractive to elected officials.

Another related reason why development exactions are an increasingly popular local finance tool is that they add diversity to the revenue structure used to finance economic development. Over the years there has been heavy reliance on the property tax to finance the local infrastructure and public services that support economic development activity and daily life in communities. Development exactions can help reduce reliance on the property tax, in the process providing a revenue structure that is more evenly divided among a diverse set of revenue tools.

Remember from the previous point that while the property tax remains a widely used form of local government finance, it also remains a flash point for tax revolt efforts and widespread resident dissatisfaction. As a result, tax and spending limitations have placed significant constraints on continued use of the property tax as the major source of funds for financing local infrastructure and services. This has contributed to fiscal stress at all levels of government, as cuts in the revenue available from property taxes have come at the same time as increased devolution of responsibility down the fiscal federalism chain. This combination has made local program cuts seem inevitable. It has also meant that the cries from communities for assistance from higher levels of government are more frequent, more urgent, and more fervent.

Development exactions often provide a way to help stem the downward slide for many growing communities. Relief comes both in terms of the revenue stream they provide and in the way they improve the fiscal health of general funds (as well as other government funds) in these communities through their revenue diversification effects. For example, funds that would have otherwise been used to pay for the infrastructure and services supporting economic development can be freed up through development exactions and put to alternative uses. As a rule, revenue diversification aids in the stability and health of a government's finances. The effects are often seen in improved municipal bond ratings and the reduction in borrowing costs that comes with such improved ratings. Development exactions help to provide this valuable diversification.

Another reason why development exactions are popular with local governments is their perceived effectiveness as a tool of growth management. Development exactions have the reputation as a tool for helping "make growth pay for itself." In addition, development exactions raise the cost of developing a given piece of property (though some or all of these costs may be passed through to buyers or other participants in the development process) (Skidmore and Peddle 1998). Thus, development exactions are commonly expected to slow the growth that a community might expect to take place, and, therefore, can be an attractive tool for growth management. Empirical evidence of this was provided by Skidmore and Peddle (1998), who estimated that impact fees in DuPage County, Illinois, had been responsible for a 25 percent reduction in the residential growth rate in the county below what it would have been without the fees. It is notable that the county still experienced significant growth during the time period they studied, but that the fees imposed by municipalities in the county appeared to be an effective tool in dampening both the explosive growth of the county and the fiscal effects of that growth.

John Shannon, former executive director of the Advisory Commission on Intergovernmental Relations (a now defunct, national level, independent federal agency), coined the term "fend for yourself federalism" to describe the massive devolution of responsibilities from the federal and state governments down to the local level. Development exactions provide an attractive means of financing activities in such a setting because of their basis in the benefit principle of public finance. The benefit principle says that individuals should pay for government goods and services based on their degree of consumption of those goods and services. "Application of the benefit principle to growth management means that the costs of providing infrastructure should be borne by those economic units that create the need for that infrastructure" (Peddle and Lewis 1998: 22).

While the operating costs of government are generally difficult to attribute to individual households or businesses, infrastructure and capital costs are more discrete and attributable to individual economic units. In addition, "by tying the costs of infrastructure more directly to the beneficiaries of the services provided by that infrastructure, economic efficiency in the allocation of public infrastructure investment dollars should be enhanced" (Peddle and

Lewis 1998: 23). Development exactions, and impact fees in particular, provide governmental units an opportunity to attribute and allocate certain capital costs to individual economic units. This provides a tangible justification for impact fees based on economic theory. Besides being economically efficient, it is also intuitively appealing to have the costs of government services paid for by the people who use the services or for whom particular infrastructure is built. Yet, efficiency is not the only possible criterion by which the economic benefits of development exactions might be appropriately judged.

Equity Issues and Development Exactions

Because development exactions can be expected to alter the prevailing distribution of the costs of financing government services and infrastructure, one would expect that they might also have some effects on the income distribution and relative economic well-being in the community. While the potential efficiency gains from the use of development exactions are identifiable and attractive, the equity or fairness effects of development exactions, attributable generally to changes in the income distribution or living standards of different citizen groups in the community, are much more difficult to discern and generalize. Yet, these equity effects are not only important but also provide an insight into another popular argument often made by existing community residents in favor of the adoption or enhancement of a development exaction system.

If they do nothing else, development exactions generally alter the distribution among economic actors of the costs of financing public infrastructure. In particular, development exactions are designed to increase the share of the cost of new infrastructure that is paid by new growth. Getting growth to "pay its own way" is one of the most common justifications offered for adopting a development exaction or impact fee system. In the absence of development exactions, the costs of the infrastructure required to service new growth would typically be borne by the community's taxpayers as a whole, often through compulsory finance tools like the real property tax.

Development exactions are generally levied against the developer of projects that require building new infrastructure or that make use of excess infrastructure capacity built to accommodate or service new development projects. It is an empirical question as to which economic actors (e.g., developers, builders, home buyers, existing residents) bear the effective burden of any set of development exactions, and the allocation of this burden among those actors who share the real costs of the exactions.

The precise allocation of the burden of exactions will be dependent, among other things, on the price elasticity of demand and the price elasticity of supply for a particular type of development (e.g., new, upscale, four-bedroom and larger homes) in a particular geographic market. In general, a particular set of economic actors will bear less of the burden when they have the ability to avoid the exactions by choosing to move their economic activity away from the jurisdiction that imposes the exactions. For example, if home buyers can easily choose to go to an adjacent, nonexaction community to buy a comparable house, then it is likely that the market reaction, other things equal, will be to have those buyers pay less of the impact fee or development exaction than in a situation where they would not have the ability to flee the fee by locating in another nearby community.

However, a scenario in which development exactions do not shift at least some of the burden of infrastructure finance to developers and builders is very unlikely (as is a scenario where home buyers bear none of the burden of the exactions). These scenarios would presume absolute and total inability on the part of at least one type of economic actor to alter their economic behavior to avoid the development exaction (a situation of perfectly inelastic demand or supply in the housing or land market). Such a scenario borders on impossibility. Furthermore, whether justified by reliable empirical evidence or not, perception among the general public is that development exactions help make sure that development pays for itself. Yet, in almost every community, much of the capital infrastructure was built at a time when development exactions were not used, or at least were not used extensively.

Thus, adopting a development exaction program typically begs the question of whether new residents and new businesses are being singled out for inequitable treatment. To the extent that the infrastructure to support the existing homes and businesses in a community was financed by the community as a whole, without special exactions or assessments paid by the new development, one might perceive that such new development is asked to bear an unfairly disproportionate share of financing the public infrastructure needed to support the new homes and businesses.

In addition, one can expect that the market price for housing, both existing and new units, will increase in the presence of a development exaction system, though the extent of that increase is again subject to the empirical conditions outlined above. Thus, one further equity issue raised by development exactions is the degree to which they decrease the affordability of housing in a community, thereby threatening the ability of lower and moderate-income households to afford to buy or rent housing in the community. In some of the most sophisticated exaction systems, the provision of affordable housing is a required element of the donations made by developers of projects in the community (Altshuler and Gómez-Ibáñez 1993). Thus, one key issue for a community evaluating a development exaction system for adoption or continuation is the extent to which those development exactions are consistent with the community's values regarding the appropriate distribution of the costs of financing public infrastructure and public services. A concurrent concern is the preservation of an affordable housing base in the community.

Yet, even after a community has decided to implement a development exactions system, much work must be done to establish clear policies to guide the imposition and administration of the system. One key issue is how to appropriately calculate the costs of growth and allocate those costs among economic units.

General Approaches to Calculation

Development exactions are grounded in the notion that successful development in a community typically increases the need/demand for public infrastructure and services. Furthermore, the quantity or quality adjustments in public services or infrastructure are such that they can often be attributed in whole or in part to particular development projects. Finally, it is typically recognized that economic or community development projects typically also result in some form of additional revenue stream for the community hosting those projects (e.g., real property taxes, sales taxes). Calculating an exaction requires that one investigate three components. The first is demand (i.e., the increased need for infrastructure/services). The second is cost (i.e., the outlay necessary to provide the newly demanded infrastructure/services). And the third is revenue (i.e., the enhancement to the resources of the government provided through the new development). The combination is needed in order to produce an exaction amount that accurately reflects the appropriate net effects of a given development project on a community's infrastructure and public services.

In order to address the subject of exaction calculation, it is necessary to adopt definitions of various relevant terms. A demand unit is the discrete, identifiable entity whose addition will require improvements to capital facilities. For example, an additional student requires additional school facilities, and an additional family requires additional parks and active recreation facilities. A service standard is the quantity of capital facilities that will be required by new development (Nicholas, Nelson, and Juergensmeyer 1991). Furthermore, for purposes of clarity, we will make a distinction between an exaction and an impact fee. An exaction is a condition of development approval that requires a builder or developer to give or provide something to (or on behalf of) a local government or service district. This could include dedication of sites for common or public facilities; construction of common or public facilities; provision of vehicles and equipment for common or public use; payments to defray the costs of land, facilities, vehicles, and equipment; or some combination of these items (Frank and Rhodes 1987). In contrast, we define an impact fee as a form of cash-based development exaction according to a fixed fee schedule that is typically published in an adopted ordinance or policy statement. In addition to a fixed fee schedule, development impact fee programs are usually based on a specific calculation methodology that considers and then allocates the proportionate share of the impact that is generated on a facility by new development.

Although the actual calculation of appropriate exactions can take many forms and require rigorous investigation, the essential elements of analysis and calculation generally remain demand, cost, and revenue (Dahlstrom 1995). Therefore, if one accepts the definitions and distinctions provided above regarding exactions and development impact fees, then the determination of an appropriate *negotiated* exaction (i.e., one not based on a fixed fee schedule) *may*, like a development impact fee, be influenced by the measurement of and balance among demand, cost, and revenue. In contrast, determination of an appropriate *impact fee* will be narrowly limited by the measurement and balance among demand, cost, and revenue reflected in some form of fixed fee schedule.

Full consideration of demand, cost, and revenue is often overlooked in the rush to implement a development impact fee requirement to relieve capital cost burdens in rapidly growing communities. In general, demand and cost factors are easily determined, and while the revenue side of the equation can be more challenging, its importance should be apparent. We discuss each of the calculation components separately, and then develop a particular example of an impact fee methodology to illustrate how the calculation process might proceed in practice.

Demand

In order to sustain an active and vital community, some level of public infrastructure is required to support businesses, workers, and residents. This public infrastructure typically includes things like roads, water and sewer systems, police and fire protection, a judicial system, and schools. It may also include things like parks, recreation centers, community centers, hospitals, public libraries, convention centers, and a myriad of other local amenities. Despite the variety of forms that it can take, public infrastructure is typically characterized by two features: (1) investment must be in discrete large units that are "lumpy"; and (2) each unit has some finite capacity. These features have implications for the developing community.

First, public infrastructure, when initially built, will have excess capacity that can be used to accommodate future development. The prudent community actively plans for the development and use of this excess infrastructure capacity. The best and most common way of planning is through a comprehensive capital improvement plan and program.

Second, a small change in the cumulative level of development activity can trigger the need for a significant new investment in public infrastructure. The need for new infrastructure, or the recapture of the costs of the excess capacity built into old infrastructure, provides an important motivation for development exactions. At the most basic level, development increases the amount of demand for various types of public infrastructure, and, therefore, increases the need for ways to pay for this infrastructure. The demand component of development exaction calculation allocates the capacity of infrastructure to a particular type of unit that is associated with the increased need for the particular type of public infrastructure. This unit is called a "demand unit," as it is a single, discrete, identifiable entity that creates the need for and uses public infrastructure.

Cost

Without costs, there would be no development exactions. In particular, development exactions exist as a result of the need to finance the cost of the public infrastructure required to service new developments. Typically, this infrastructure is financed up front through some form of debt finance (e.g., general obligation bonds, revenue bonds, tax increment financing bonds, installment contracts) or a leaseback arrangement.

In many ways, costs are the easiest of the key variables to estimate. This is especially true if the infrastructure is built prior to the first demand units coming on line. The total capital cost of the infrastructure can then be reliably and objectively fixed (no contingencies should be necessary because the project has been completed). Even in the case of infrastructure not yet built, but proposed in a comprehensive capital-facilities plan, costs are typically estimable. Within an acceptable level of confidence, building costs are predictable from tables and experience, land costs can be hedged through banking and/or developer donations, and the capacity of the infrastructure can generally be determined.

Of course, these costs must then be allocated to demand units, as well as revenue sources (because it may be desired to have exactions only as one of the financing sources for the infrastructure—more on this later). However, these issues are not issues of cost, but rather issues of demand and revenue structure.

Revenue

While proponents of development exactions often extol the virtues of having new growth pay for itself, most also recognize the need not to "double charge" the new growth for community infrastructure. Furthermore, it should be recognized that particular development units may differ in their expected capacity to produce revenue for the local governments, even though, as demand units, their impact on the infrastructure can be expected to be the same. For example, a starter three-bedroom home and an upscale three-bedroom home would be expected to generate roughly the same number of students for a school district over time. But the upscale home is likely to have a higher market value, and, therefore, will pay more in property taxes that can be used to help pay for the services that its occupants require. Put another way, the upscale home is more likely to produce an excess of tax dollars above and beyond the services that it and its occupants consume (the higher the value of the home, the more likely this is to occur). This fiscal surplus could then be used to offset fiscal deficits created by other demand units. However, given that development exactions are designed solely to offset the capital, rather than the operating, costs attributable to new growth, calculations of a revenue offset must be done carefully and conservatively.

In effect, the revenue calculation attempts to credit new growth for two separate contributions it makes to the fiscal health of the community. First, new growth should not be asked to simultaneously pay a disproportionate share of financing infrastructure to service its needs while also being asked to pay for the bond issues used to finance previous iterations of infrastructure built (solely) to service other areas of the community. Second, if the new growth will produce a fiscal surplus, this should be taken into account as a contribution to the community's finances and be credited against the exaction. One can quickly see the link between this analysis and fiscal impact analysis.

There are obvious similarities between the methodologies employed in fiscal impact analysis and the calculation of development impact fees. Both should be based on a comprehensive analysis of an extensive array of relevant data. However, development impact fee analysis should be carried to higher levels of detail, because the objective is to determine an individualized assessment of impact. While fiscal impact analysis focuses on the effects of an entire development on an entire community, development impact fee analysis should focus on the effects of the development of an individual parcel of land on specific capital components of applicable community facilities. We present an example of an impact fee calculation later in this chapter.

Types of Exactions

As mentioned above, communities adopt exactions in a wide variety of situations, and, as a result, it would be impossible to provide an exhaustive list. However, some forms of exactions are relatively common in high-growth situations, and some generalizations are achievable (Nicholas, Nelson, and Juergensmeyer 1991). Exactions may be applicable to residential development or nonresidential development, or both. Furthermore, the majority of exactions falls into three categories that may be distinguished generally by the means used to measure demand units. The first category uses residential population as the demand unit. This form of analysis is commonly applied to exactions for the following:

- Schools
- Parks
- Libraries
- Water Systems
- Sanitary Sewer Systems
- Police Protection
- Emergency Medical Facilities
- General Governmental Facilities

In general, exactions based on residential population require an exact enumeration of dwelling units and conversion of those counts to an estimated population figure derived from a reliable source. This procedure considers the probable population load of the dwelling unit and allows the exaction to be sensitive to the demand unit that actually generates the need for the facility (population).

While sensitivity to population is desirable in the calculation of residential exactions, it is not always possible to accomplish, due to a lack of acceptable data. For example, data available from the Institute of Transportation Engineers (ITE) are a widely cited source for vehicle trip generation factors applied in the design of roadway exactions. ITE data for residential land uses are gathered and made available by basic dwelling-unit type. Consequently, a second category of residential exactions uses dwelling units for demand measurement rather than population. This form of analysis is commonly applied to exactions for the following types of facilities:

- Fire Protection
- Roads
- Storm Water Control Systems

It should be noted that residential exactions commonly based on population may be based on dwelling units in situations where reliable demographic data are not available.

Exactions for nonresidential land uses may be based on a broad range of demand unit measurements, depending upon the manner in which primary or secondary data are available. Most methodologies attempt to convert nonresidential demand to some population equivalent or use locally generated information regarding consumption by land area or floor area. This form of analysis is commonly applied for the following:

- Sanitary Sewer Systems
- Water Systems
- Storm Water Control Systems
- Public Safety (police, fire, emergency medical facilities)
- Roads
- General Governmental Facilities

We now turn our attention to an example of impact fee calculation.

Calculating an Impact Fee: An Example

Due to the numerous variations in exactions and development impact fees, a discussion of methods for calculation may be best advanced by providing a specific example. The example that follows is an explanation of the data sources and basic calculations for the Applied Planning Techniques (APT) school district capital improvement development impact fee program. The APT program has been adopted in a number of annexation agreements in the state of Illinois and was developed in consideration of that state's "specifically and uniquely attributable" standard for evaluation of such programs. Although it is not always entirely clear what is intended or required under the specifically and uniquely attributable standard, it is acknowledged to be the most stringent standard for evaluating and judging exactions in that it implies a direct and material benefit in exchange for the exaction (Cope 2000).

The APT program is demand, cost, and revenue sensitive. Revenue sensitivity is achievable to extremely high levels of detail. The program requires a substantial amount of system-specific input data and can generate a substantial volume of unit-specific output data that are often presented in tabular form. The required data for the APT school district capital improvement development impact program includes details regarding the following:

1. District enrollment.
2. Square footage of school facilities.
3. School district operational and capital budgets.
4. School district equalized assessed valuation and real estate tax factors.
5. Capital facility projects completed by the district.
6. Existing and projected debt for capital facilities.

With respect to cost, the APT model is designed to recognize many of the unique qualities of individual school districts. For example, data input for the model is based generally on the prevailing service standard in the subject school district rather than on a regional, state, or national standard. In most instances, the service standard is measured in square footage of facilities per student, and the cost of delivering that service standard to a new student population is estimated based on a database of school facilities built in Illinois over the past nineteen years. Construction cost figures from the subject school district are introduced into the database and are doubled-weighted to reflect any unique circumstances that may affect that district. The intent is to produce locally sensitive yet broadly based construction cost factors. Historic cost information is updated to current levels through the application of a building construction cost index like the ones published regularly in *Engineering News Record*. The derived construction cost is compared to a national source of school construction data, *School Planning and Management*, from time to time as a monitoring measure.

The generation of demand factors for school district capital improvement impact fees is based on the specifics of dwelling unit type and number of bedrooms. Commonly, student generation data are obtained through the application of demographic factors from generally accepted, objective sources for single-family detached, single-family attached, and multi-family dwelling units. An example of a widely used source of demographic data and population tables in Illinois is the "Table of Ultimate Population per Dwelling Unit" published every five years or so by the Illinois School Consulting Service/Associated Municipal Consultants.

Because development generates value, and, therefore, revenue in addition to demand, credits are applied in the overall impact analysis. Failure to consider credits may result in double-charging new residents for required capital facilities. The consideration of credits focuses on the extent to which a school district can direct revenue from new development to capital facilities. Generally, this revenue credit is based on projected participation in the retirement of capital debt. There are a variety of ways to determine credits for school capital facilities. The APT model applies credits on a dollar-value basis. Although complex, that form of credit calculation produces a high degree of sensitivity (Nicholas, Nelson, and Juergensmeyer 1991).

A dollar-value credit calculation is based on the "spreading" of the debt service cost over the valuation of the taxing district's equalized assessed valuation, as modified by the proposed development. That is, the existing debt service of the taxing district is allocated to the expected total assessed valuation of the district after the development project is undertaken. For example, if the district has $4.5 million in debt service per year, a current assessed valuation of $400 million, and an expected increment to the assessed valuation of $50 million from a new subdivision (for a new, total equalized assessed valuation of $450 million), the allocation would be $.01 per $1.00 of assessed valuation. A present value is calculated for the cumulative annual charge per dollar of valuation for the life of the debt service. For example, if in the previous example the debt service were to continue for thirty years, the present value of a thirty-year stream of allocated debt service payments would be taken. Due to variations in initial and effective bond terms, and other individual qualities of the overall debt structure, a series of independent calculations must be made for each outstanding capital bond issue and for each property value. Depending upon volume of output, the methodology can require several thousand individual calculations.

However, a straightforward numerical example for a given home can provide a basic understanding of the concept of credits. A $300,000 home located in a school district in Cook County, Illinois, and subject to a real estate tax rate including a .5303 factor for bond debt would pay $548.99 annually for debt service, after adjusting for the assessment percentage, the equalization rate, and a homeowner's exemption. This is the amount that the homeowner is contributing to pay for past capital projects in the district through the real property tax. In simple terms, because the homeowner is paying the impact fee for essentially the same or substitute capital facilities, asking them also to pay a property tax bill for the facilities unfairly burdens them with paying twice for essentially the same facilities.

Over time, these property taxes for capital facilities can add up. The present value of the amount in this example (over thirty years at a 5 percent rate of discount) is $8,439.29. In fact, some development impact fee programs employ a calculation methodology that credits this full present value against the calculated impact fee. Most impact fee calculations credit a portion of this present value, recognizing the collective benefits of the infrastructure and services that should be shared by all, including those who also pay an impact fee. It should be noted that a real-estate-tax-based form of credit calculation is applicable only in those situations in which debt for capital facilities is funded through the property tax. However, regardless of credit calculation methodology, the intent is to produce a "net impact" measurement that considers the revenue generation attributable to the demand unit and is sensitive to not having the demand unit pay twice for the same infrastructure or services.

The limitations of the APT program, and similar programs, are generally those associated with a lack of available local data. All development impact fee programs should be based on a careful evaluation of relevant service standards and identification of appropriate demand units. However, many local governments and service districts do not collect data in a form that facilitates analysis of service standards and demand units. For example, most communities can provide information regarding the daily pumping volumes of municipal water as well as an estimate of the current population. As a result, these communities often believe that they have the necessary information (per capita water consumption) to implement a water system, capital-improvement development impact fee program. The problem is that nonresidential development also consumes water, and many water system engineering studies do not identify water consumption factors for nonresidential development to the level of detail required for accurate impact measurement.

Further, supporting architectural and engineering studies should provide discrete cost data for the various components of the capital facility systems. Again using a water system example, the system is usually comprised of elements for extraction, treatment, storage, and transmission; and the distribution of cost for these elements may not be uniform throughout the system. This would seem to be of particular importance in large, complex water systems that may include multiple pressure zones due to elevation changes in the service area. In order to avoid the necessity of revising otherwise valid studies, future consideration of a development impact fee program should be an integral part of the capital improvement planning process rather than an afterthought.

In addition to the need for suitably detailed architectural and engineering studies for capital projects, comprehensive development impact fee programs should be supported by up-to-date comprehensive plans and capital-improvement programs. These documents usually provide the projections that are essential to development impact fee program design and can be useful tools for explaining why such fees often are necessary components of a growth management program.

Conclusion

Development exactions are an increasingly popular means of financing the infrastructure costs associated with economic and community development.

Exactions can be powerful growth management tools that can be used to improve the fiscal capacity and health of developing communities. However, exactions must be based on careful and predictable calculations of the costs imposed by growth and of the allocation of those costs to demand units in the community. When combined with a careful and comprehensive capital improvements program, development exactions provide a means for assuring infrastructure concurrency and fiscal solvency for communities.

References

Altshuler, Alan A., and José A. Gómez-Ibáñez. 1993. *Regulation for Revenue.* Cambridge, MA: Lincoln Institute of Land Policy.

Burchell, Robert W., and David Listokin. 1978. *The Fiscal Impact Handbook: Estimating Local Costs and Revenues of Land Development.* New Brunswick, NJ: Center for Urban Policy Research, Rutgers University.

Burchell, Robert W.; David Listokin; and William R. Dolphin. 1994. *Development Impact Assessment Handbook.* Washington, DC: Urban Land Institute.

Cope, Ronald S. 2000. "Impact Fees: Constitutional Calculations for Future Growth." De Kalb: Illinois Association of School Business Officials.

Dahlstrom, Roger K. Summer 1995. "Development Impact Fees: A Review of Contemporary Techniques for Calculation, Data Collection, and Documentation." *Northern Illinois University Law Review* 15: 557–69.

Frank, James E., and Robert M. Rhodes. 1987. *Development Exactions.* Chicago: American Planning Association.

Illinois School Consulting Service. 1996. "Table of Estimated Ultimate Population per Dwelling Unit." Naperville: Associated Municipal Consultants.

Nicholas, James C.; Arthur C. Nelson; and Julian C. Juergensmeyer. 1991. *A Practitioners Guide to Development Impact Fees.* Chicago: American Planning Association.

Peddle, Michael T., and John L. Lewis. March 1998. "Would Illinois Benefit from Impact Fee Legislation?" *Illinois Developer* 1: 21–26.

———. 1996. "Development Exactions as Growth Management and Infrastructure Finance Tools." *Public Works Management and Policy* (October): 129–44.

Skidmore, Mark, and Michael T. Peddle. 1998. "Do Development Impact Fees Reduce the Rate of Residential Development?" *Growth and Change* 29: 383–400.

Part 3

Public Financing

6

Enterprise Zone Incentives

How Effective Are They?

Alan Peters and Peter Fisher

Over the past two decades, enterprise zones have become central to many states' economic development policies. While in a few states enterprise zones are little more than the institutional means of delivering traditional economic development funds to business, in most states enterprise zones have been used to focus economic development policy—and sometimes community development and housing policy—on poorer areas and thus poorer people. The intuitive justification for this geographical focus is straightforward. If economic development policy is essentially about the creation of jobs, then those areas of a state with the highest unemployment rates—or lowest labor force participation rates, or lowest wages—should be the first beneficiaries of policy. This justification seemed to gain greater credence during the boom years of the latter 1990s when overall unemployment plummeted downward in all but the most disadvantaged American communities.

Tax incentives are the primary tool for promoting development and reducing unemployment in most enterprise zone programs. In this chapter we look at four important questions that together speak to the likely effectiveness of enterprise zone incentives:

- What incentives are offered in enterprise zones? How big are these incentives and how much of an incentive advantage do states and localities provide to firms that locate in zones?
- Do zone incentives induce new job growth?
- If they do create jobs, who gets the jobs?
- How costly are zone incentives to government?

This leads us to a broader evaluation of the effectiveness of enterprise zones. Given their relative costliness and effectiveness, are other policy instruments likely to better attain the avowed goals of enterprise zones—in other words, do enterprise zones make policy sense?

The Justification for Enterprise Zones

The scholarly justification for pursuing a geographically targeted enterprise zone policy is centered on two issues. The first is the spatial-mismatch hypothesis. This is the claim that a major part of the reason for the underemployment so endemic to poorer, particularly minority, urban neighborhoods, is that jobs have suburbanized since the early 1950s but poorer urban minorities have not. Given the difficulties in commuting from downtown to suburban work sites, urban minorities have become trapped in dying labor markets and as a result are much more likely to be unemployed or out of the labor force. The second is an argument first made by Timothy Bartik (1991) in his influential book *Who Benefits from State and Local Economic Development Policies?* Bartik's argument is that economic development policy is likely to be more cost-effective if pursued by (or in) poorer, high-unemployment communities rather than wealthier, low-unemployment communities. The major reason for this claim is that there is evidence that a job paying the same wage will generate greater benefits when placed in a poorer community than when placed in a wealthier community.

Even though enterprise zones appear to make a lot of policy sense,[1] there is still a need to answer some basic questions about their actual effectiveness. One would hope that a policy instrument would create new jobs; thus, a crucial test of economic development instruments is whether they are capable of "inducing" new jobs. And by "inducing" we usually mean creating jobs that would not exist "but for" the policy instrument. Unfortunately, determining whether incentives induce jobs is a daunting task. Because true policy experiments are out of the question, econometric analysis has typically been used to answer the induction question, although other methods—such as surveys and case studies—are viable. The problem here is that although this literature is very well developed, the results are highly variable. Consequently, we do not know for certain whether enterprise zone incentives do or do not induce jobs. This difficulty has led some researchers to take a different tack—measuring the actual impact of enterprise zone incentives on a firm's income, and deducing whether that impact is likely big enough to get a firm to change its behavior. This technique has one other benefit: It requires the researcher to measure, as accurately as possible, both the relative size of incentives and their interaction effects.

Showing that enterprise zone incentives are effective in inducing jobs is not enough. We also need to know if the jobs we induce are being filled by the "right sort" of job seekers—in other words, we want to know if the policy is helping those who have trouble in the labor market rather than those who do not. We would also want to know whether enterprise zone incentives are effective relative to other possible policy instruments—that they are efficient. These two questions are even more difficult to answer than the induction question. National data on who works in enterprise zones are sketchy to say the least. And as yet no researchers have felt competent to assess the relative efficiency of enterprise zones compared to alternative policy instruments. In this chapter, we do give estimates of the likely workers in enterprise zones but acknowledge that many more data are necessary before any firm conclusions can be drawn. And instead of comparing the effectiveness of zones to all other instruments, we focus instead on their costliness. This allows us to deduce some important conclusions about the relative efficiency of enterprise zones.

What Incentives Are Offered and How Much Are They Worth?

Any attempt to estimate the influence of economic development incentives on firms' behavior must begin with an assessment of the value of those incentives to the firms. In this study we employ a computer microsimulation model, TAIM^{ez}, to measure how the actual incentives in place in each of the enterprise zones in our study would improve a firm's rate of return on an investment in a new manufacturing facility in that zone. TAIM^{ez} is a hypothetical firm model that includes computer algorithms for the calculation of corporate taxes and incentives as they existed in twenty states from 1990 to 1998, and in a sample of about seventy-five enterprise zones within thirteen of those states. The "firms" in the model are actually a set of financial statements constructed to be representative of actual firms in each of sixteen manufacturing sectors. (The workings of the model are described in Peters and Fisher, forthcoming, and in Fisher and Peters 1998.)

The TAIM^{ez} model calculates, for each representative firm and each locality, the gross property taxes that the firm would pay each year for the first twenty years after a new plant is built, based on the value of its taxable property each year and a constant local property tax rate. It then calculates the size of the abatement it would receive from the local government being modeled. The model also measures the state and local sales taxes paid on purchases of machinery and equipment and on purchases of fuel and electricity for the new plant, and the increase in state and local income taxes paid, and then deducts all state credits resulting from the new plant investment. The result is an estimate, year by year for twenty years, of the increase in after-tax cash flow attributable to the firm's investment in a particular city and enterprise zone, with and without generally available tax incentives, and with and without incentives available only in the zone.

Most states provide incentives for new investment that are not tied to location; we call these "general incentives." Some states also permit localities to offer such incentives, generally in the form of local property tax abatements. The states in our study also, for the most part, provide state tax incentives that are spatially targeted—available only to firms locating in an enterprise zone or the equivalent. In only a few states are local incentives restricted (by state law) to enterprise zone firms.

The kinds of incentives offered in each of the thirteen enterprise zone states in our study as of 1998 are shown in Table 6.1. Eight of the states had investment tax credits (ITCs) available statewide by 1998, and three of these offered more generous versions within enterprise zones. Another three states offered ITCs only within enterprise zones. Investment tax credits typically allow a firm to deduct from their state corporate income tax liability a credit equal to some percentage of the cost of new manufacturing facilities and machinery. Five states offered a jobs credit statewide (and four of these provided larger credits in zones); another five offered jobs credits only in enterprise zones. The jobs credits also allow a credit against income taxes, but with the credit equal to a dollar amount per new job created. Four states offered a credit for job training expenses (two statewide, two only in zones), and four allowed a credit for a percentage of wages paid, or payroll or income taxes withheld, for new jobs (three statewide, one in zones only). Credits for sales taxes paid on goods purchased for the new plant, or for local property taxes paid on the new plant, were available in five states, in all cases for zone establishments only. Three states excluded all or a portion of income generated within a zone from corporate taxable income.

How significant are these incentives? In the average zone among our seventy-five cities, the total tax incentive package available in the zone lowered the effective tax rate on a new plant by about a third. In thirteen of the seventy-five zones, the incentive package cut the tax rate by more than half. (The effective tax rate is the state and local tax bite as a percent of the pre-tax cash flow from the new plant.) As Table 6.2 shows, the average tax rate before incentives among the cities ranged from 5.2 percent to 22.8 percent, while the average rate after incentives ranged from 1.4 percent to 11.7 percent.

Another way to judge the size of incentives is to measure the dollar value to the firm per new plant job. Such measures are common in newspaper stories about the incentive packages awarded to automobile manufacturers and others, though the common practice is to present these figures as the gross cost to the state and local government summed over all the years for which incentives are granted. Our measure is the value of the incentives to the firm

Table 6.1

Tax Incentives Available in Thirteen States, 1998

	State incentives	Local incentives
California	ITC; EZ jobs credit; EZ sales tax credit.	Abatements not allowed.
Connecticut	ITC; training credit; EZ income exemption.	Abatements allowed.
Florida	ITC; EZ jobs and property tax credits.	Abatements little used.
Illinois	Two ITCs; EZ ITC; EZ jobs credit.	Abatements allowed but little used outside of EZs.
Indiana	Credit for up to 3.1 percent of new employee payroll; EZ jobs credit.	Abatements allowed in Economic Revitalization Areas.
Kentucky	ITC; jobs credit; payroll credit; training credit; EZ jobs credit; EZ sales tax exemption for M and E.	Property tax rate reduction allowed.
Missouri	ITC and jobs credit; EZ income exemption; EZ ITC, training and jobs credits.	Abatements allowed.
New York	ITC; EZ ITC and wage tax credit.	Abatements allowed.
Ohio	ITC; jobs credit; EZ income exemption, training credit, and jobs credit.	Abatements allowed in EZs.
Pennsylvania	Jobs credit; wages credit; EZ ITC.	Abatements allowed.
Texas	EZ property tax refund; EZ sales tax refund; EZ property deduction.	Abatements allowed.
Virginia	Jobs credit; EZ income exemption; two EZ ITCs; EZ jobs credit	Very limited abatements allowed.
Wisconsin	EZ ITC, jobs credit, and sales tax credit.	Abatements not allowed.

Note: ITC = investment tax credit; EZ = enterprise zone or equivalent; M and E = machinery and equipment.

Table 6.2

State and Local Tax Rates and Incentives in Seventy-five Enterprise Zone Cities, 1994 (weighted average across sixteen manufacturing sectors)

	State-local tax rate			Value of state and local incentives per new plant job		
	Without incentives	With all incentives	Percent reduction	General ($)	Zone ($)	Total ($)
Average by state						
California	8.9	6.8	23.6	2,682	952	3,634
Connecticut	8.9	5.7	36.1	3,547	1,822	5,370
Florida	8.3	6.7	19.4	0	2,301	2,301
Illinois	6.2	4.7	22.8	661	1,686	2,347
Indiana	15.2	7.4	50.9	3,485	9,284	12,769
Kentucky	8.1	4.0	50.3	5,462	1,681	7,143
Missouri	10.4	6.1	42.8	4,635	2,710	7,346
New York	6.9	2.8	60.2	5,597	1,017	6,615
Ohio	9.8	5.6	42.4	1,268	5,533	6,800
Pennsylvania	10.6	8.2	24.1	782	3,238	4,019
Texas	11.1	9.0	18.8	1,055	2,377	3,432
Virginia	7.0	6.1	12.5	0	1,045	1,045
Wisconsin	7.3	5.3	27.9	0	3,237	3,237
Among the 75 cities						
Highest	22.8	11.7	75.6	7,359	19,193	22,678
Mean	9.1	6.1	32.9	2,199	2,849	5,048
Lowest	5.2	1.4	10.1	0	720	1,045

(which is about 60 percent of the cost to government, on average, because incentives lower the firm's deduction for state and local taxes and hence increase the firm's federal taxes), discounted over twenty years at 10 percent. In other words, it is the lump-sum, tax-free grant that would be equivalent in value to the incentives, for a firm with a twenty-year planning horizon. In the average zone, the total incentive package was worth about $5,000 per job, but reached a value of $10,000 per job or more in five zones and was less than $2,000 per job in eight zones (see Table 6.2).

What is the comparative advantage provided to enterprise zones by the kinds of incentives offered in these states? Presumably, the goal of establishing enterprise zones is to entice firms to establish plants there by making the tax burden lighter than elsewhere. But states have also been engaged in tax competition among themselves for many years, and the result in most states has been the enactment of incentive programs available statewide. Is the additional incentive provided in zones significant enough to attract investment

| General incentives | | Zone incentives | | |
State (%)	Local (%)	State (%)	Local (%)	Combined (%)
73.8 0.0	26.2	0.0	26.2	
32.4	33.7	33.9	0.0	33.9
0.0	0.0	100.0	0.0	100.0
28.1	0.0	20.9	51.0	71.8
'	0.0	7.6	65.1	72.7
71.6	4.8	19.7	3.9	23.5
31.3	31.8	36.9	0.0	36.9
56.3	28.3	15.4	0.0	15.4
18.6	0.0	0.0	81.4	81.4
5.4	14.1	80.6	0.0	80.6
0.0	30.7	69.3	0.0	69.3
0.0	0.0	100.0	0.0	100.0
0.0	0.0	100.0	0.0	100.0
78.6	48.6	100.0	86.9	100.0
27.0	10.1	47.6	15.3	62.9
0.0	0.0	0.0	0.0	12.2

Percent of total incentive package

to such places? In three of the thirteen states (Florida, Virginia, and Wisconsin), there are no general incentives, and in all three of these states, the zone incentives are entirely in the form of state credits. At the other extreme are five states (California, Connecticut, Kentucky, Missouri, and New York) that provide the least relative advantage to zones; here the zone incentives make up less than 40 percent of the total incentive package. In the remaining five states, there are both general and zone incentives, but the zone incentives make up 69 percent to 81 percent of the package. The average across all seventy-five zones was a 63 percent share for zone incentives. In most zones, the state zone incentives were worth more than the local zone incentives. Only three states (Illinois, Indiana, and Ohio) put most of the burden on the locality to provide the tax advantage for zone firms.

Another way of getting at the question of incentive size and importance is to consider the size of the wage premium that a given incentive package would just offset. Wages are a much larger component of costs than are taxes (about fourteen times as large, on average), and wage rates can vary substantially from one place to another. Wages might be only slightly higher in a particular locale, but a large percentage reduction in taxes would be required to offset the wage disadvantage. To put it another way, if wage differentials of $1.00 per hour or more are common when manufacturers compare sites, then an incentive package that provides the equivalent of a $.10 wage reduction is unlikely to exert a significant influence on location decisions; tax differences will be swamped by wage differences.

Again using TAIM^{ez}, we calculated the hourly wage differential at a new plant location that would provide the firm with the same present value of cost savings over twenty years as the incentives available at that location. These equivalent wage reductions were, for the most part, in the range of $.10 to $1.00 per hour, with considerable variation both by state and by sector, as can be seen in Table 6.3. If we look at the average across the sixteen sectors for each of the states, we find that the incentive packages were equivalent to a 0.8 percent to 9.4 percent cut in wages. The median among the states was 3.1 percent and in only one state did it exceed 5.3 percent. A relatively small wage premium (5 percent or less) would be sufficient, in most locations, to wipe out the advantages created by the incentive packages there. (Considering each of the sixteen sectors in each of the thirteen states separately, in 74 percent of cases the wage premium was 5 percent or less.)

Given the small size of the typical incentive package offered in an enterprise zone, when put in terms of the wage reduction that would provide an equivalent cost savings to the firm, we would not expect incentives to have much impact on the location of new business investment. This is particularly the case if we compare the wage equivalent of the zone incentives alone. After all, tax incentives are usually thought to have their largest effects on the intrametropolitan location decision, where other spatially variable factors, such as labor and transportation costs, are about equal. Within a metro area, at least within a given state, the nonzone incentives will be equal. Only the additional differential provided by a zone location will affect the intrametropolitan location decision, and then only if it is sufficient to overcome the lower property tax rates that are probably available in suburban locations and the inherent disadvantages of zones in distressed areas. As can be seen in Table 6.3, Indiana provided the most valuable zone differential at 6.8 percent of wages. But the zone incentives were equivalent (on average across sectors and cities) to a wage reduction of just 0.7 percent to 2.5 percent in eleven of the thirteen states; it is difficult to believe that inducements of this magnitude will be very effective.

Table 6.3

Wage Equivalent of General and Zone Tax Incentives, 1994
(averaged by state for seventy-five cities)

State	Average hourly wage equivalent[a] across 16 sectors			Range of wage equivalents for all incentives		Percent reduction in wage	
	General incentives ($)	Zone incentives ($)	All incentives ($)	Lowest sector ($)	Highest sector ($)	Zone incentives (%)	All incentives (%)
California	0.25	0.09	0.34	0.08	0.61	0.7	2.7
Connecticut	0.34	0.18	0.52	0.19	0.91	1.4	4.1
Florida	0.00	0.21	0.21	0.08	0.32	1.7	1.7
Illinois	0.06	0.15	0.21	0.07	0.36	1.2	1.7
Indiana	0.32	0.86	1.18	0.47	2.25	6.8	9.4
Kentucky	0.52	0.16	0.68	0.22	1.35	1.2	5.3
Missouri	0.42	0.25	0.67	0.23	1.22	2.0	5.3
New York	0.53	0.10	0.63	0.25	1.57	0.8	5.0
Ohio	0.12	0.53	0.65	0.24	1.11	4.2	5.2
Pennsylvania	0.08	0.32	0.39	0.13	0.69	2.5	3.1
Texas	0.09	0.21	0.31	0.09	0.52	1.7	2.4
Virginia	0.00	0.10	0.10	0.05	0.10	0.8	0.8
Wisconsin	0.00	0.30	0.30	0.12	0.48	2.4	2.4

[a]Wage equivalent is the hourly wage reduction that is equivalent in value to the total state-local incentive package over twenty years.

Do Zone Incentives Induce New Job Growth?

The conclusion of the previous section suggests that most enterprise zone incentives are too small to materially affect the investment and location behavior of firms. It follows that they will not induce new jobs locally. Do empirical studies of the impact of enterprise zones on local growth provide any reason to doubt this deduction?

There is fairly widespread agreement that the connection between incentives and growth is best analyzed using econometric techniques. The central benefit of such techniques is that they allow the various potential causes of growth to be controlled statistically, thus allowing the specific effect of incentives on growth to be identified. In this section we focus on the findings of the scholarly literature, because it would be a mistake to draw definitive conclusions from a single econometric study.

Studies of enterprise zones fall into a much broader literature looking at the effect of taxes on growth and the effect of nontax fiscal incentives—such as grants and loans—on growth. This literature has been surveyed a number of times over the past decade, and we will not repeat that work here. (With regard to reviews on taxes and growth, see Newman and Sullivan 1988, Bartik 1991, and Wasylenko 1997; for a review of incentives and growth see Fisher and Peters 1997). Suffice it to say that on the issue of taxes and growth there is a growing consensus that state and local taxes can and do have an impact on local growth. It is now fairly widely assumed that the elasticity of growth with respect to taxes is somewhere around -1.0 at the local level and in the range of -0.1 to -0.6 at the regional level. In other words, at the regional level, lowering taxes by 10 percent would increase long-run growth by about 1 percent to 6 percent. Most of the studies looking at the effect of nontax fiscal incentives also find that larger incentives induce new growth. But there is reason to use these results with caution. As Fisher and Peters (1997) in their review of the incentive literature point out, most of the studies are seriously flawed and all make use of very poor data on incentives. Others have pointed to the difficulties of replicating the tax results for other years and in other settings, and so on (McGuire 1992, 1997; Netzer 1997). Certainly, a significant minority of researchers in this area believe the matter is anything but settled, and many still believe that taxes and other incentives have little, if any, impact on local economic growth.

What of enterprise zones and growth? Intuitively, one would expect enterprise zone incentives to have a greater effect on growth than do more widely available incentives, precisely because zone incentives are spatially targeted, relatively more generous, and, presumably, more focused on generating local growth. In fact, the econometric literature on the effects of enterprise zones on growth is small at best, and most of this evidence suggests that zones have almost no influence on local growth. Nevertheless, a few early studies have found enterprise zones to be effective. Erickson and Friedman (1990) looked at the jobs created or saved by firms in zones after zone designation and at the number of firms investing in zones after designation. They found that their proxy for zone incentives had a strong positive effect on both jobs and establishments. Papke's (1994) considerably more sophisticated analysis of Indiana enterprise zones found that designation leads both to an increase in inventories and a decrease in local unemployment claims. This suggests that, at least in Indiana, enterprise zones do result in new growth.

However, Boarnet and Bogart (1996), using methods similar to Papke's, found no evidence that the New Jersey enterprise zone program had resulted in increased economic activity. Likewise Greenbaum (1989), Greenbaum and Engberg (2000), and Bondonio and Engberg (2000), in various studies that covered multiple states, found that enterprise zones have little impact on business, income or employment outcomes. Our own recent study covered, on the one hand, a sample of sixty-five zones in thirteen of the biggest states in the nation with enterprise zones programs, and, on the other, a sample of 104 zones in Ohio. The study found no evidence to suggest that zone incentives result either in more businesses moving into the zones or more firms being born in the zones (Peters and Fisher forthcoming). All this strongly suggests that, on average, zones do not induce new job growth.

As we indicated earlier, there are various alternative ways of analyzing the effectiveness of enterprise zones. Rubin and Richards (1992), Wilder and Rubin (1996) and Fisher and Peters (1997) have reviewed this literature. We will not examine this literature here, since it will take us too far from our central concern with induction. Nevertheless, it appears that most of the noneconometric evidence suggests that enterprise zones have not been effective.

Why do enterprise zones perform so poorly? We believe there are two main answers here. First, although enterprise zone incentives are very costly for government (as we will show later), they have too small an effect on the bottom line of firms to have a large impact on the locational and investment choices of most businesses. Second, many enterprise zones are in economically impoverished areas—areas with poor infrastructure, poor connections to the transportation system, high crime, and so on. As Dabney (1991) has argued, enterprise zone incentives would have to be very large indeed to make up for these obstacles to investment.

Who Works in Zones?

Let us suppose for the moment that enterprise zones, in spite of the evidence just cited, do induce at least some new jobs. Still, for zones to be judged successful, as we argued earlier, a substantial share of these jobs must be filled by inhabitants of enterprise zones and surrounding poor neighborhoods. How likely is this to happen?

The first point to emphasize is that in some states enterprise zones are not targeted in any meaningful sense. Louisiana has thousands of zones; a full one-third of Ohio is covered by enterprise zone legislation. In such places zones are little more than delivery mechanisms for traditional state economic development policy. Our research on enterprise zones has focused only on those states where there is targeting—state code or administrative rules requiring the zones to be established only in distressed areas—or, as in the case of Ohio, where there is targeting within a subset of zones. The results presented in this section thus ignore those states that do not target.

Even where enterprise zones are geographically targeted, the jobs may be taken by individuals living far from the targeted areas. For example, if the skills demanded by, say, a high-technology firm locating in a zone are much higher than can be supplied locally one would naturally expect those jobs to go to commuters. Many states attempt to counter this problem by restricting incentives to jobs filled by certain kinds of persons. Of the thirteen states we looked at, eleven offered some sort of job-credit program, and all eleven targeted those credits, either to zone residents or to population groups that were, in some way, economically disadvantaged. During the mid-1990s, Indiana was the only state that restricted credits to new hires who were residents of the enterprise zone, though two states (Virginia and Wisconsin) provided larger credits for zone residents than for other new hires. Four states (Illinois, Kentucky, Ohio, and Wisconsin) restricted credits to employees who fell into one or more categories of economic disadvantage, such as welfare recipients, the unemployed, or those eligible for Job Training Partnership Act services. New York provided credits for all new hires, but allowed larger credits for those who were economically disadvantaged. Four states (California, Connecticut, Florida, and Missouri) provided credits for new hires who were *either* zone residents *or* fell into one or more categories of economic disadvantage. Missouri had a second credit program requiring that at least 30 percent of new hires be either zone residents or economically disadvantaged, but if this threshold is exceeded, the firm receives credits for all new hires. All this suggests significant targeting of enterprise zone incentives at economically disadvantaged individuals.

However, it is important not to overemphasize the extent of targeting at economically distressed individuals. In the states we examined, nontargeted capital (and other) incentives tend to dominate labor incentives. Firms are presumably attracted by the total incentive package, but if the jobs credit component is only a small part of the package, the jobs credit may be viewed as irrelevant. Also, the targeting of jobs credits is effective only if firms are able and willing to use them. The Ohio jobs credit, for example, is fairly generous ($3,000 per job), but fewer than 10 percent of firms locating in enterprise zones take advantage of the credits (Ohio Enterprise Zone Annual Report). One reason may be the onerous task of certifying eligibility under one of five criteria, employee by employee. The other reason may be that at least 25 percent of new hires must meet the eligibility criteria for the firm to receive any credits at all. This threshold may be too difficult for most firms to attain readily, and they may judge that the credits are not worth the cost of restricting their hiring criteria.

Furthermore, jobs credits may be too small to materially alter a firm's hiring behavior. For instance, take a fairly average jobs credit of $2,000 per job, and an average manufacturing wage of about $25,000 annually or $12.00 per hour. Let us assume the credit is fully utilized in the first two years; then it effectively reduces wage costs for the first two years by 4 percent, which is equivalent to a cut in the hourly wage rate of about $.48. The question is: How many targeted individuals become attractive hires at a wage of $11.50 for the first two years (which could be viewed as a sort of training wage), who would not have been hired at the standard wage of $12.00? To make a difference in hiring decisions, the $.50 wage differential must be enough to overcome employers' assessments of productivity differences. If zone employers are indifferent between hiring members of the targeted group and hiring others, then, of course, a small wage differential could have a large effect. On the other hand, it is easy to imagine that there are real or perceived productivity differences that would be valued at far more than $.50 to most zone employers.

The question naturally arises, who actually works in zones? Because of both data and modeling difficulties, we analyzed commuting patterns in only a subset of zones—fourteen zones in nine states. The data here come from the *Census Transportation Planning Package,* which allows commuting destinations (work sites) to be connected to commuting origins (homes). We found that, on average, only 10 percent of working zone residents actually worked in the enterprise zone. Moreover, of the jobs on offer in zones, only about a fifth were taken by zones' residents. While these numbers varied widely across zones, they strongly suggest that zones are not creating localized employment opportunities for enterprise zone residents.

Of course, it is possible that zones are pulling in workers from surrounding distressed neighborhoods. If this is true, then one would expect the commuting distance of those working in zones to be well under that for the transportation region as a whole. In order to test this, we built regression equations for each sample zone with time-dependent controls and controls for income (wealthier people tend to work further away from home) and mode (users of public transit will, all else being equal, tend to take longer to get to work). We found that in almost all cases, zone workers had a longer commute time than nonzone workers. Thus, zones are pulling in workers from far and wide.

In summary, although the enterprise zones we looked at were geographically targeted and although almost all also included some targeting of incentives at poorer workers, there is little to no evidence that enterprise zones actually create localized employment opportunities for residents of zones and surrounding neighborhoods.

How Costly Are Enterprise Zone Incentives?

While job creation is the primary objective of economic development incentives, expansion of the tax base is an important secondary rationale. It is true, of course, that as long as an incentive makes a difference for just one firm's location choice, it will increase the tax base. But the proper question is: Do incentives produce a gain in *revenue*? The incentives will be provided to many firms that would have expanded in that state or enterprise zone anyway, and these incentives drain revenues. The question we address here is: Will the revenues gained from the establishments induced to expand or locate in an enterprise zone exceed the revenues lost by providing incentives unnecessarily to other firms?

Enterprise zones are a state policy. States determine the criteria for establishing zones, limit the number of zones, and usually provide a majority of the incentives within the zones (though in some states the bulk of incentives are locally financed). Arguably, then, the appropriate question is whether state and local governments, in the aggregate, gain or lose revenues as a result of enterprise zones. In our study of seventy-five enterprise zones in thirteen states, we found that, on average, state and local governments would gain about $18,000 in revenue over a twenty-year period for each job that was induced to locate in the state because of the incentive package available in an enterprise zone in that state.[2] On the other hand, governments would lose about $6,600 for every job that received incentives unnecessarily (the plant would have been built in the state anyway).

So how do we know which jobs were induced by the incentives? As we indicated earlier, there has been extensive research on the interstate elasticity of economic activity with respect to taxes. And there is some agreement (not without dissension) that this elasticity is probably in the range of –0.1 to –0.6; in other words, incentives (reductions in taxes) have a positive but weak effect on investment and job creation. If we take –0.3 as the elasticity, this implies that the typical incentive package (which represents about a 26 percent reduction in taxes for the firm) in our sample cities would produce less than a 10 percent increase in the flow of new jobs into the state. This, in turn, means that there are far more jobs draining revenues from the state and locality at the rate of $6,600 per job than there are jobs providing the net gain in taxes of $18,000 per job. The net effect in our seventy-five-zone sample was a total state-local revenue loss of about $59,000 for every new job induced by incentives. In other words, if –0.3 is the correct elasticity, enterprise zones represent a sizable drain on revenues and are a costly means of creating jobs. Given the average size of a zone and the average level of economic activity (gross job creation) in these zones in our sample, the total cost per zone would eventually reach about $1.5 million per year, if all new establishments were eligible for and received the full incentive package. Furthermore, the picture worsens if we consider that our research indicates that even the elasticity of –0.3 is much too optimistic for enterprise zone incentives.

These net state-local fiscal effects mask some redistribution of local revenues. The calculations presented above address the question of whether state and local governments collectively gained revenue by attracting out-of-state investment into zones. But spatially targeted incentives may be most effective in redirecting economic activity within a metropolitan area. When economic activity is redirected *within* the state, from a nonzone locality to a zone, rather than from out of state, the fiscal effects consist of: (1) state revenue losses for every zone job (redirected or not) receiving state incentives, plus (2) revenue losses to the nonzone localities for every job redirected to the zone, plus (3) revenue losses to the zone city because of local incentives provided to businesses that would have expanded in that city anyway (including some firms redirected from nonzone to zone locations within the city), offset by (4) revenue gains to the zone city for each job redirected to the zone from a different locality.

The zone locality could experience a net gain in local revenue in such an instance. This could occur in two ways. First, even if there are no state incentives for zone firms, if the intrametropolitan elasticity of economic activity with respect to local tax rates is greater than one, the zone locality will gain revenue.[3] Unfortunately, the research in this area, particularly with respect to enterprise zones, is very sparse and the results widely scattered (see Peters and Fisher forthcoming). Second, local revenue gains can occur when state incentives are substantial while local incentives are small. The sizable state incentives jack up the redirection effects, while the small local incentives keep local revenue losses for noninduced jobs to a minimum and increase the net local revenue gains for induced jobs. In these circumstances, the zone-city could be a fiscal winner even with a weak relocation effect (i.e., an intrametropolitan elasticity of much less than one). But the zone-city revenue gains will come at the expense of substantial revenue losses for the state and for nonzone localities.

Conclusion: Do Zones Make Sense?

Enterprise zone incentive programs do not seem to provide enough benefit to firms to materially alter their investment and locational habits; as a result, they do not induce much, if any, new growth. Moreover, although enterprise zones are justified by politicians and academics alike as helping economically disadvantaged areas, zones do not appear to provide much in the way of employment opportunities to zone inhabitants. Furthermore, they tend to be very costly for government.

Can the enterprise zone strategy be redesigned to work more effectively? One temptation is to increase massively the size of enterprise zone incentives so that new investment would indeed be induced. This would be a mistake. Increasing the size of incentives would increase the cost to government of supplying those incentives. The fundamental problem from the state perspective is the low sensitivity of investment to tax incentives; as long as this is the case, increasing the size of incentives will actually increase the cost per induced job, even though more jobs may be induced. One could at least eliminate the fiscal drain on zone cities by prohibiting localities from competing with one another through local incentives, and providing state incentives only within enterprise zones. And one could eliminate capital incentives in favor of labor incentives. But these reforms do not solve the basic problem; states would still have to spend a lot of money to create a few zone jobs, only some of which go to the intended beneficiaries.

Can we find more efficient ways of spending the resources that government devotes to enterprise zones? Almost certainly. As a first step, one should simply abandon the idea of basing an income strategy for poor urban neighborhoods on a very localized "jobs-to-people" approach. While neighborhood-based community development efforts may be effective in improving housing, social services, school dropout rates, or the quality of life in general for neighborhood residents, place-based strategies have their limits. A strategy for raising the labor-market incomes of zone residents should not be place-based but should be directed at the people themselves. Instead of attempting to bring export industries to the neighborhood, states and cities should use the funds now spent on zone incentives to expand the access of zone residents to opportunities in the broad metropolitan labor market. This becomes clear once you recognize that most zone residents work outside the zone, and most zone jobs go to nonzone residents.

What kinds of labor market programs could be funded with the money now spent on enterprise zone incentives? We cannot evaluate here the effectiveness of all of the alternatives, but the possibilities include such things as reverse commuting programs, job screening and readiness programs combined with vanpools delivering workers to suburban employment centers, or the purchase of cars for residents. If state legislatures and governors are wedded to the tax incentive approach, such incentives should be tied to hiring the difficult-to-employ, regardless of where the person lives or where the job is located. In other words, incentives should be focused on changing the hiring decisions of firms, not their location decisions. Our overall assessment is that spending is bound to be more cost effective if it is focused directly on the problem—the lack of access to jobs and the lack of "employability" (or the perception of such) on the part of residents of certain areas of cities. Trying to solve these problems in a roundabout way by altering the location choices of firms is a costly and largely futile exercise.

Notes

1. The spatial-mismatch hypothesis and Bartik's argument are not free from controversy. There is considerable evidence that the spatial-mismatch hypothesis explains only a small portion (if any) of inner-city unemployment. Bartik's argument rests on the belief that the reservation wage of workers in high-unemployment areas will be lower than in low-unemployment areas. Unfortunately this is a claim that has been little studied in the United States.

2. This is the present value of increased state and local income, sales, and property taxes directly attributable to a new manufacturing plant, discounted at 10 percent over the first twenty years after the plant is built.

3. See Bartik (1994) for a proof of the elasticity required for fiscal break-even and Peters and Fisher (forthcoming) for a discussion of what we know about actual intrametropolitan elasticities.

References

Bartik, Timothy J. 1991. *Who Benefits from State and Local Economic Development Policies?* Kalamazoo, MI: W.E. Upjohn Institute for Employment Research.
———. 1994. "Jobs, Productivity and Local Economic Development: What Implications Does Economic Research Have for the Role of Government?" *National Tax Journal* 57, no. 4 (December): 847–61.
Boarnet, Marlon, and William Bogart. 1996. "Enterprise Zones and Employment: Evidence from New Jersey." *Journal of Urban Economics* 40: 198–215.
Bondonio, Daniele, and John Engberg. 2000. "Enterprise Zones and Local Employ-

ment: Evidence from States' Programs." *Regional Science and Urban Economics* 30: 519–49.

Dabney, Dan. 1991. "Do Enterprise Zone Incentives Affect Business Location Decisions?" *Economic Development Quarterly* 5, no. 4: 325–34.

Erickson, Rodney, and Susan Friedman. 1990. "Enterprise Zones 1: Investment and Job Creation of State Government Programs in the USA." *Environment and Planning C: Government and Policy* 8, no. 3: 251–67.

Fisher, Peter S., and Alan H. Peters. 1997. "Tax and Spending Incentives and Enterprise Zones." *New England Economic Review* (March/April): 109–30.

———. 1998. *Industrial Incentives: Competition Among American States and Cities.* Kalamazoo, MI: W.E. Upjohn Institute for Employment Research.

Greenbaum, Robert. 1998. "An Evaluation of State Enterprise Zone Policies: Measuring the Impact on Business Decisions and Housing Market Outcomes." Ph.D. dissertation, H. John Heinz III School of Public Policy and Management, Carnegie Mellon University, Pittsburgh.

Greenbaum, Robert, and John Engberg. 2000. "An Evaluation of State Enterprise Zone Policies." *Policy Studies Review* 17: 29–46.

McGuire, Therese. 1992. "Review of Who Benefits from State and Local Economic Development Policies?" *National Tax Journal* 45, no. 4: 457–59.

———. 1997. "Discussion of 'Taxation and Economic Development' and 'The Effects of State and Local Public Services on Economic Development.' " *New England Economic Review* (March/April): 76–77.

Newman, Robert, and Dennis Sullivan. 1988. "Econometric Analysis of Business Tax Impacts on Industrial Location: What Do We Know, and How Do We Know It?" *Journal of Urban Economics* 23 (March): 215–23.

Netzer, Dick. 1997. "Discussion of 'Tax and Spending Incentives and Enterprise Zones.' " *New England Economic Review* (March/April): 131–35.

Papke, Leslie. 1994. "Tax Policy and Urban Development: Evidence from the Indiana Enterprise Zone Program." *Journal of Public Economics* 54, no. 1: 37–49.

Peters, Alan H., and Peter S. Fisher. 2002 (forthcoming). *Enterprise Zones: Do They Work?* Kalamazoo, MI: W.E. Upjohn Institute for Employment Research.

Rubin, Barry, and Craig Richards. 1992. "A Transatlantic View of Enterprise Zone Impacts: The British and American Experience." *Economic Development Quarterly* 6, no. 4: 431–43.

Wasylenko, Michael. 1997. "Taxation and Economic Development: The State of the Economic Literature." *New England Economic Review* (March/April): 37–52.

Wilder, Margaret, and Barry Rubin. 1996. "Rhetoric Versus Reality: A Review of Studies on State Enterprise Zone Programs." *Journal of the American Planning Association* 62, no. 4: 473–91.

7

The Efficacy of Local Economic Development Incentives

Rod Hissong

This chapter reviews the current state of the debate centering on the efficacy of local economic development incentives. It discusses the inherent problems of conducting evaluations of the incentive policies and what researchers do to overcome the difficulties. Addressing the criticisms should ideally produce reliable and consistent results and lead to a definitive recommendation for policymakers regarding the efficacy of local economic development incentives.

The local economic development incentive evaluation literature is expansive both in quantity and quality. It contains qualitative studies (Wallace 1999), action research studies (Jenkins and Bennett 1999), and a plethora of quantitative studies. The quantitative studies include descriptive reports, case studies, and causal analysis. The quality has improved over time, but some local governments continue to pay for studies by consultants who know the answers before they begin the evaluation. Some critics contend the quality will improve when evaluators broaden their scope of the expected impact (Fasenfest 1997). The bottom line is that the vastness of the research has not produced a consensus on what does and does not work.

The first section of the chapter addresses the problems of conducting evaluation studies in general and evaluation studies of fiscal incentives in particular. These difficulties contribute in no small way to the variety of research results. Researchers have not reached consensus on a generally accepted definition of economic development or ways to measure it. The studies normally are conducted without the benefit of random assignment in a controlled environment. Economic development occurs, or does not occur, as the result of the confluence of numerous factors of which policymakers control relatively few.

The second section of the chapter discusses an econometric approach to evaluation that is an improvement over previous work. Panel data procedures have been in use in this arena since the early 1990s and are now commonly used (Sjoquist 2001) when evaluating local economic development incentives.

The chapter then turns to simultaneous equations modeling. The strength of this model is in its recognizing the endogeneity of local economic development incentives. The model estimates the effect of adopting an incentive on the poverty rate of the community as well as the employment rate. This methodology is used to avoid biased and inconsistent estimates.

The fourth section presents an approach that goes in a different direction but has much promise for accurately estimating the effects of the local fiscal incentives. The "hypothetical firm" approach avoids many of the pitfalls of traditional evaluations by asking what value the firm places on the incentive. Incentives of greatest value may make the move worthwhile.

Each section closes with a discussion of how each has expanded what we know about the efficacy of economic development incentives. The chapter ends with a summary of what we know and recommendations for the direction of research in this area.

Challenges in Evaluating Efficacy

One problem of evaluating local economic development incentives will likely never be resolved. Local officials do not implement the incentive policies in a controlled laboratory environment. Most of the local incentives are site specific. Enterprise zones, tax increment finance districts, downtown redevelopment districts, and free-port exemption zones are examples of policies that are designed to stimulate the economy in a particular area of the city. A multitude of economic, social, and political forces has brought the area to its current state. The composition and influence of forces change from one area to another. We should expect the same incentive to have different effects across areas. This geographical heterogeneity is extremely difficult to correct for statistically (Courant 1994). It also makes generalizing results precarious. The effects will, in fact, vary by place, the controls for such variation will be imperfect, and, willy-nilly, studies that look at different places and times will obtain different estimates of the effects of independent variables as measured (Courant 1994). Evaluations that use the county level or higher as the unit of analysis average out this geographical heterogeneity. The influence of the heterogeneity will bias the estimates and lead to inaccurate policy recommendations.

Netzer (1997) contends researchers too often insufficiently understand the theoretical model on which they base their analysis. For example, they naively overlook the link between relative input prices and input substitution. Most incentives involve the reduction of the price of capital. A sales tax abatement on the purchase of capital goods or a property tax abatement on the value of machinery is such an incentive. Any effective incentive that decreases the price of capital will cause the firm to increase its demand for capital relative to labor. This leads to a decrease in the demand for labor as the firm becomes relatively more automated. Only if the production effect offsets the substitution effect of capital for labor will the incentive create more jobs. Ironically, a common outcome measure is job growth. The incentive may have a significant impact, but it will not manifest in increased jobs. Some researchers, or what Netzer refers to as "pop economists and economic journalists"(Netzer 1997) have little understanding of factor substitution. So, it is important to distinguish between capital and labor subsidies, especially in enterprise zones, where job creation is usually by far the overriding objective (Netzer 1997). The flawed theories in the literature contribute to the wide variation in results.

Different studies, all well based in valid theory, can come to different findings and conclusions because of how they measure economic development. Courant compiles a list of over fifteen outcome measures reported in the 1991 Bartik survey. The list includes average growth rate of state product, employment growth, value added in manufacturing, value of building permits, and amount of industrial land (Courant 1994). Economic development is defined variously in terms of value, physical units, or rates of change. The geographical perspective also influences results. Local tax abatement incentives have less influence over firms in neighboring states than over firms in neighborhoods adjacent to the enterprise zone. It is not surprising the literature has failed to come to a consensus. A single incentive can influence dissimilar outcome measures with distinct geographical perspectives differently, even though the measures are defined as "economic development."

Researchers less interested in purely economic impacts argue the list of outcome measures is too narrow. The social and political forces mentioned above need to be included as outcome measures. The economy is a component of society, and some effects of economic development incentives are not captured by changes in employment or the number of new plants in the area. Social trends and past political decisions contribute to the depressed or blighted conditions. An incentive program that increases property values may add stress to renters who live in the neighborhoods. The higher property values are reflected in higher rents. Renters with very low incomes may be forced to find housing elsewhere. We need to begin to understand the community as something in which the economy is embedded as part of the overall social relations; markets do not emerge out of a vacuum but out of the social circumstances that surround them (Fasenfest 1997, paraphrasing Polanyi).

Most studies base their conclusions on the interpretation of statistical estimates of elasticities. Authors often declare the incentive as effective when statistical results indicate the incentive has a significant and positive impact on the outcome measure. The wide range of elasticities of growth with respect to incentives, -0.1 to -0.6 (Papke 1997), requires close scrutiny of the economic as well as the statistical impact. Papke points out the difference between statistical significance and economic significance. Statistical significance is a necessary but not sufficient condition for efficacy.

Economists require the benefits to outweigh the costs of the incentive. For example, in the case of tax abatements, the cost of the program would include the value of the taxes abated. Benefits would include taxes generated for the locality by the salaries of the new employees, multiplier effect of salaries paid to employees living in the jurisdiction, and so forth (Bartik and Bingham 1997). Studies without a simple cost/benefit analysis can lead to using incentives that are statistically significant but economically insignificant.

Researchers have addressed many of the foregoing problems and criticisms. The following sections present the results of those efforts and determine if we know more now than we did ten years ago.

Geographically Based Incentives

Researchers have studied the efficacy of incentives associated with enterprise zones more than other incentives. Wilder and Rubin (1996) review the extensive work conducted in this area. The evaluations include a wide variety of data sources and statistical methodologies. Wilder and Rubin call for the debate over the efficacy of enterprise zones to "shift from its rhetorical basis to one more firmly grounded in empirical data" (Wilder and Rubin 1996). Work has been done to begin the shift.

Areas are designated as enterprise zones based on previously established criteria. The criteria require zones to be distinctly different from nonzone areas. The selection process, based on permanent differences in economic and social factors across areas, precludes random assignment to experimental and control groups. These differences can be viewed as permanent over time. Once the nonrandom selection is complete, the economic conditions before and after the selection can be compared across groups. The comparison requires factors external to both zone and nonzone areas to affect both groups identically. This is unlikely. Panel data analysis "controls for external influences over time with aggregate time effects. Moreover, by controlling for nonrandom selection, the data can be used to address the counterfactual question: How did zones perform relative to what their performance would have been in the absence of zone designation?" (Papke 1994). Panel data techniques control for the effects of the selection process and as controls for the geographical heterogeneity among areas.

Papke (1994) applies panel data techniques in her analysis of Indiana enterprise zones. Enterprise zones are approximately the size of a tax district. The tax district, defined by Indiana law, is the unit of analysis. She matches six enterprise zones to six nonzone tax districts on the basis of labor force composition and data availability. Indiana is unusual in that, although tax credits are available for capital and labor, inventories receive the greatest percentage tax credit. She tests the effect of the enterprise zone on machinery and equipment, inventories, and unemployment claims. She uses panel data techniques to estimate various model specifications and finds that enterprise zone designation has a permanent positive effect on inventories (8 percent) and a negative effect on machinery (13 percent). She interprets the net effect to be a change in the composition of capital investment in the enterprise zone and that causes a decrease in the community tax base. Papke also finds the enterprise zone permanently decreases unemployment claims approximately 20 percent within the zone as well in areas adjacent to the zone.

Papke's use of panel data procedures produces improved estimates of the effect of enterprise zones. She suggests similar studies be conducted in other states for comparison purposes.

Boarnet and Bogart (1996) evaluate enterprise zones in New Jersey with the approach taken by Papke. They analyze the effect of enterprise zones on total municipal employment for twenty-eight communities over nine years. Their unit of analysis is city employment and city property values. They find insufficient evidence to support enterprise zones having an impact on municipal employment or municipal property values.

Their study differs from Papke in a critical form. Papke measures the economic effects of the zone at the zone level. Boarnet and Bogart measure the effects of the zone at the city level. The New Jersey enterprise zone typically contains the central business district of the community and includes approximately 30 percent of the municipality's land area (Boarnet and Bogart 1996). They evaluate no explicit measure at the zone level. The implicit theory is that the improvements in economic conditions in 30 percent of the area will be reflected in city-level measures. They have little knowledge of the spatial redistribution of employment that may occur as the result of the enterprise zone.

Man and Rosentraub (1998) and Dye and Merriman (2000) apply similar methodology in the evaluation of tax incremental financing (TIF). They extend Papke's work to the area of TIF by assuming the city's decision to use TIF is endogenous to the selection process. That is, the condition of the area, which TIF is expected to improve, is used as a criterion to designate a TIF zone. Man and Rosentraub evaluate TIF for Indiana cities, and Dye and Merriman evaluate Chicago area cities minus Chicago.

The studies use city-level variables as outcome measures and use comparable econometric methodologies. Both estimate a two-stage model. The first estimates the likelihood of adopting TIF, and the second stage, using results from the first, estimates the impact of TIF on median owner-occupied housing value in the city (Man and Rosentraub 1998) and total municipal property value (Dye and Merriman 2000). Their conclusions contradict each other. Man and Rosentraub (1998) find housing value in TIF cities permanently increases by 11 percent over housing value in non-TIF cities. The adoption of TIF had an overall positive effect throughout the community. Dye and Merriman (2000) find that TIF adoption causes depressed growth rates.

Dye and Merriman compare their work to that of Man and Rosentraub and explain why the studies differ. In addition to using different dependent variables, the two studies are for cities in different states that have different fiscal institutions. Indiana does not require for eligibility that cities demonstrate an area to be blighted. Illinois does. They observe that their study focuses on cities in one metropolitan area rather than across the state. This reduces unobserved heterogeneity.

The four studies in this section address many of the criticisms of the incentive literature. Most attempt to control for geographical heterogeneity. The theoretical models are sound. None conducts a cost/benefit analysis to determine if the statistical findings are economically significant. The different unit of measure varies across studies, as did the locality under study. The researchers contribute valid but contradictory findings to the literature.

Econometric Approach

The use of econometric models to test the efficacy of local economic development incentives is common. The models range widely in their technical sophistication—from simple regression with poorly specified locality growth variables, no treatment of time lags in the growth variable, or fixed-effects controls or endogeneity in the explanatory variables, to considerably more complex models that address most, if not all, of these issues (Fisher and Peters 1997). Anderson and Wassmer (2000) is an example of the considerably more complex models.

Their model addresses many of the problems and criticisms of the literature. They fully understand the theoretical relationships that generate the empirical model and shape their expectations. They are interested in both growth and the quality of the growth. Their outcome measures include the employment rate of residents of the community as well as the poverty rate of the community. They test for the effect of the local incentive on the quality of life for the most disadvantaged as well as the influence of the incentives on public expenditures. They empirically model geographical heterogeneity, endogeneity of incentives as well as other explanatory variables. Demographic characteristics of the community are included as determinates. They also conduct a cost/benefit analysis to determine if the incentives are worth their costs.

Anderson and Wassmer (2000) address the issues of the impact of incentives on firm location, the impact of incentives on the local population, and whether cities compete for development (Sjoquist 2001). They do this by estimating an eleven equation model to explain the impact of local economic development incentives on the employment rate of residents of the community, the poverty rate of the community, community property values, municipal expenditures per capita, and the property tax rates. Their data are for 112 Detroit metropolitan area communities in 1977, 1982, 1987, and 1992.

The model includes city dummies and time dummies to control for fixed effects and to capture the influence of a changing general economy. Fixed effects are factors that cause communities to differentiate from each other and maintain that difference over time. Examples include the distribution of land use, proximity to a regional airport, composition of the labor force, and land use density. These could easily be sources of geographical heterogeneity.

The estimation technique is two-stage, least squares. They use a test proposed by Bound, Jaeger, and Baker (1995) to determine that for each equation the two-stage procedure is appropriate.

The first stage of the two-stage process estimates the equations that explain the adoption of each of the five incentives: tax incremental financing (TIF), downtown development authority (DDA), industrial revenue bonds, manufacturing property tax abatements, and commercial property tax abatements. The decision to adopt an incentive is regressed on local economic conditions, local demographics, use of other local incentives, and policy adoption behavior of neighboring communities. It is in these equations that they test for emulating behavior of communities in the Detroit metropolitan area. The results indicate, "metropolitan Detroit localities are increasingly offering these incentives because other communities are doing the same" (Anderson and Wassmer 2000: 153). This reflects the expected growing competition across jurisdictions.

The second stage uses the results of the first stage to estimate the impact of the selected incentives, controlling for the effect of the local economic and social conditions, economic conditions in surrounding communities, and fixed effects across cities.

The estimated equations are accepted only after being tested rigorously for heteroskedasticity and correcting for it where necessary. If the error terms are *heteroskedastic* (related to a specific variable), then the standard errors derived for the regression's coefficients are biased and the statistical significance of a coefficient cannot be trusted (Anderson and Wassmer 2000: 124).

Upon estimating the coefficients, they conduct a simulation of the impact of each of the incentives. They calculate the efficacy of an exogenous change in each incentive through direct and indirect paths to the numerous outcome measures. The simulation of TIF indicates a decrease in taxable property values. This 38 percent drop in taxable property value in a community results in a 5.29 mill increase in the local property tax rate from the average of 60.57 mills (Anderson and Wassmer 2000: 142). They describe the complete reaction initiated by the adoption of a TIF:

> Holding everything else constant, the offering of a tax incremental finance authority (TIFA) serves its desired purpose and increases commercial activity. The exogenous use of the TIFA also represents an increase in local taste for using more manufacturing and commercial abatements, and for using a DDA. The increase in commercial property value following the use of a TIFA offers local employment opportunities for individuals at the lower end of the income distribution. These opportunities work to reduce the local poverty rate. At the same time, a rise in commercial property value encourages an increase in the number of residents in a community. The end result is that more residents arrive after a TIFA than the number of jobs created by it, and the community's residential employment rate is lower. When the increase in commercial property value and abatements is allowed to influence the local property tax rate, the rate rises to a level higher than before the TIFA. Also, the increase in commercial property value lowers municipal expenditure per capita. (Anderson and Wassmer 2000: 142–43)

Anderson and Wassmer conduct simulations for the other four incentives and use the results of each to conduct a cost/benefit analysis for the respective incentives. The TIF produces higher commercial property values and lower poverty rates but is not cost effective. Only the downtown development authority generated benefits greater than costs. Simple benefit/cost analyses that use the results of these and other simulations indicate that a reasonable case can be made for the benefits of instituting DDA outweighing the costs. A reasonable case cannot be made that the use of the other four local incentives generates local benefits that are greater than local costs (Anderson and Wassmer 2000: 154).

Their model is the current level of sophisticated econometric models used to estimate the effect of local development policies. It addresses many of the criticisms of the incentive evaluation literature. It also continues to wrestle with some of the problems. In his review of the book, Sjoquist reports that Wassmer's and Anderson's results indicate a city that elects to use TIF will increase tax abatements by over $100 million, "which represents an increase of 131 percent, while commercial abatements increase by $8.4 million, or 255 percent" (Sjoquist 2001: 423). More troubling is the effect of the introduction of DDA that reduces manufacturing property tax abatements by over 100 percent. Netzer's (1997) criticism of earlier studies and their unrealistic elasticities applies here.

City dummies control for the geographical heterogeneity across cities but cannot capture the effect of geographical heterogeneity across TIF zones or enterprise zones within a community. A study using data below the city level is necessary to capture such variation.

The Detroit metropolitan area is atypical of many U.S. urban areas. The metropolitan area is one of three out of twenty-two metropolitan areas that experienced a population decline between 1970 and 1992 (Mark, McGuire, and Papke 2000). Detroit city is typical of many central cities in that era that experienced population loss and deindustrialization. It would be worthwhile to estimate the Anderson and Wassmer model using data from a Sunbelt or western metropolitan area.

The study concludes with policy recommendations. Of three options, (1) maintain the status quo and grant local autonomy, (2) ban the use of incentives, and (3) regulate, they favor state regulation. "We believe that fundamental support can come from metropolitan areas within a state if they are just made aware of the non-efficacy of the current system of free local choice and of the social benefits of incentives offered in only targeted communities" (Anderson and Wassmer 2000: 175). It seems unlikely, even knowing of their general ineffectiveness, that state legislators will restrict the use of incentives to targeted communities. Local economic development incentives have more political efficacy than economic efficacy.

Hypothetical Firm Approach

Fisher and Peters (1997, 1998) extend the work of Papke and Papke (1986) and others and use the hypothetical firm approach to evaluate the impact of local economic development incentives on firm income or profit. Standard studies implicitly assume that the incentives have value and only need be offered by local governments. The hypothetical firm approach asks what value the firm places on the incentive and whether the value is sufficient to warrant locating in the accommodating community. In order to accomplish this, the researchers use the Tax and Incentive Model (TAIM), which replicates the operating ratios, balance sheet, and income and tax statements of real, or at least "potentially" real firms (Fisher and Peters 1997: 118). The financial figures for the hypothetical firm are generated using data from annual reports, federal tax statistics, and the Census of Manufacturers (Fisher and Peters 1998: 48).

The hypothetical firm approach addresses many of the criticisms of previous work but not all. Much of the current incentive literature is made up of case studies or limited to one state or a single metropolitan area. TAIM is national in scope and uses individual level data. It uses firm-level and city-level data from firms in industries located in cities of states across the country that have the greatest concentration of employment. The national scope facilitates the generalizability of results. The model is based on impeccable economics (Netzer 1997). The model does not incorporate spatial differentials in factor costs or benefits firms receive from taxes (Fisher and Peters 1997: 120). It includes only manufacturing firms.

They select industries with a positive average growth rate of employment from 1980 to 1990. They exclude industries judged to have an insufficient number of firms or industries that are likely resource based or are producers of military armaments. Ultimately, the data are comprised of six, three-digit Standard Industrial Classification (SIC) industries and two, two-digit SIC industries. The industries are furniture and fixtures (SIC 25), drugs (SIC 283), soaps (SIC 284), miscellaneous plastic products (SIC 308), industrial machinery (SIC 35 less SIC 357), electronic components (SIC 367), motor vehicles and parts (SIC 371), and instruments (SIC 382 plus SIC 384). They randomly assign eight hypothetical small firms and eight hypothetical large firms from each industry to 112 cities in the 24 states that contain 86 percent of the manufacturing employment.

They create a balance sheet for a small hypothetical firm and a large hypothetical firm for each industry, based upon the financial data from the firms in the respective industry. Small firms range in size across industries from $10 million in total assets to $200 million in total assets. Total assets for large firms range from $300 million to $20 billion.

Using historical information to approximate the economic development incentives cities and states are likely to offer, they estimate the return on investment after the application of state and local tax incentives. They then compare the return on investment after incentives to the return on investment without any state and local subsidies. The value of the incentives is the present value of the difference between the return on investment with incentives and the return on investment without the incentives over a twenty-year period.

One objective of the hypothetical firm approach is to determine if the return on investment after taxes and incentives is spatially distributed. Do tax and incentive differentials cause a sufficiently substantial difference in the net return of the project to warrant considering relocation? Their estimates suggest at least a substantive difference between the least profitable cities and the most profitable cities. For the hypothetical small plastics firm, the present value of the twenty-year difference in the least profitable city is $789,037 less than in the most profitable city (Fisher and Peters 1997: 120). This is the smallest difference among small firms. Small firms in the motor vehicle and parts industry have the greatest difference between the least and most profitable cities, $16.9 million (Fisher and Peters 1997: 120). The mean difference between least and most profitable cities for small firms is $3.9 million. The large firm in furniture and fixtures has the smallest difference in project returns between the worst and best cities, $5.5 million, and the large firm in motor vehicles and parts had the greatest difference, $57.8 million. The mean difference between worst and best cities for large firms is $24.5 million.

They conclude incentives are effective when comparing the most profitable cities to the least profitable, but incentives are not effective when comparing closely ranked cities. "Thus it seems reasonable to conclude that, *at least at the extremes*, [their italics] taxes and incentives are potentially large enough to influence location decisions. The worst are substantially worse than the best cities" (Fisher and Peters 1997: 119). They go on to show that the potential dissipates when comparing cities closer in quality. They convert the difference in project return into a wage equivalent. Only large drug firms have a difference in wages that exceeds $1.00 per hour between the worst and the best city: $1.82 per hour. The next largest wage differential is $0.95 per hour in the small drug industry. The mean difference in wage equivalent for small firms and the large firms was $0.78 and $0.86 per hour, respectively. "In hourly wage terms, most cities are separated from the city just above them in rank by less than a penny. We doubt such separation is substantively significant" (Fisher and Peters 1997: 119). Incentives may play a role when comparing cities at the very top or the bottom of the rankings but are ineffective when comparing cities elsewhere in the rankings.

In their subsequent work (Fisher and Peters 1998), they conclude that the tax and incentive regimes of cities in the middle rankings serve mostly to eliminate cities from the location search process. A city with a tax and incentive package that significantly differs, in a negative direction, from the packages of its counterparts, will cause firms to discontinue considering the community. They do qualify that this may not apply to cities that have a unique factor cost advantage. This means a middle-ranked city without the factor cost advantage that offers no incentives is at a disadvantage. It is the paradox believed by most local officials. Not offering incentive packages can hurt you, but offering what everyone else offers or more does not help.

They also explore the impact of nontax incentives and find few cities change rank when nontax incentives were part of the package. "Overall, nontax incentives do not ameliorate, but actually accentuate, the tax differentials between the best and worst cities" (Fisher and Peters 1997: 119). Profitable cities become more profitable.

Finally, they ask if the pattern of incentives is spatially correlated with cities and states of high unemployment. "The end result is a spatial pattern of returns on new investment that bears little or no relationship to the spatial pattern of unemployment" (Fisher and Peters 1998: 212). This is after counterbalancing effects between state taxes and incentives and local taxes and incentives.

The hypothetical firm model uses a distinct approach to evaluate the efficacy of incentives. It requires extensive data and a thorough understanding of the economics that generate the result. They have yet to explicitly include spatial variation in factor costs or some measure of externalities. Shortcomings notwithstanding, it will likely be used extensively in the future.

Conclusion

The studies in this chapter address many of the criticisms of previous research evaluating the efficacy of local economic development incentives. They are well founded in theory, particularly Anderson and Wassmer (2000) and Fisher and Peters (1998). Anderson and Wassmer use the poverty rate as a proxy for socioeconomic outcome measure. Panel data studies attempt to model the geographical heterogeneity across cities.

The studies have various measures for economic development and conduct their research using different units of analysis. Anderson and Wassmer include a cost/benefit analysis. Man and Rosentraub acknowledge that a cost/benefit analysis would improve their study.

What do these studies suggest about the efficacy of the local economic development incentives? The results continue to be mixed but, generally, the incentives play an inconsequential role in the local economic development. Local officials should be cautious and not expect the incentives to improve the overall conditions of the city. The more focused and narrowly defined their use, the more effective they are. Papke finds the enterprise zone incentives are effective with regard to employment but are deleterious to property values. Studies that use a unit of analysis above the zone level generally find that incentives are less effective. The effect of the incentive dissipates as the geographical area under study increases.

The more sophisticated and complex models of Anderson and Wassmer or Fisher and Peters need to be applied at the project level. They offer the greatest potential for integrating the effects of geographical heterogeneity into the process, as well as other relationships at the local level. These techniques will require richer data, but they hold the greatest promise for isolating the effects of incentives.

The efficacy of local economic development incentives literature continues to offer contradictory results and policy recommendations. The models are more soundly based in theory and more sophisticated statistically. The variation in results seems primarily attributable to the unit of measure analyzed and the influence of geographic heterogeneity. Future work should address these two issues. From a historical perspective, we have only recently begun to look seriously at the complex relationships that influence the efficacy of local incentives.

References

Anderson, John E., and Robert W. Wassmer. 2000. *Bidding for Business: The Efficacy of Local Economic Development Incentives in a Metropolitan Area.* Kalamazoo, MI: W.E. Upjohn Institute for Employment Research.

Bartik, Timothy J. 1991. *Who Benefits from State and Local Economic Development Policies?* Kalamazoo, MI: W.E. Upjohn Institute for Employment Research.

Bartik, Timothy J., and Richard D. Bingham 1997. "Can Economic Development Programs Be Evaluated?" In *Dilemmas of Urban Economic Development—Issues in Theory and Practice*, ed. Richard D. Bingham and Robert Mier, 246–77. Thousand Oaks, CA: Sage.

Boarnet, Marlon G., and William T. Bogart. 1996. "Enterprise Zones and Employment: Evidence from New Jersey." *Journal of Urban Economics* 40, no. 2: 198–215.

Bound, John; David A. Jaeger; and Regina M. Baker. 1995. "Problems with Instrumental Variable Estimation When the Correlation Between the Instruments and the Endogenous Explanatory Variable Is Weak." *Journal of the American Statistical Association* 90 (June): 443–50.

Courant, Paul N. 1994. "How Would You Know a Good Economic Development Policy If You Tripped Over One? (Hint: Don't Just Count Jobs)." *National Tax Journal* 47, no. 4: 863–81.

Dye, Richard F., and David F. Merriman. 2000. "The Effects of Tax Increment Financing on Economic Development." *Journal of Urban Economics* 47: 306–28.

Fasenfest, David. 1997. "Commentary: Evaluation Yes, But on Whose Behalf?" In *Dilemmas of Urban Economic Development*, ed. Richard D. Bingham and Robert Mier, 284–88. Thousand Oaks, CA: Sage.

Fisher, Peter S., and Alan Peters. 1997. "Tax and Spending Incentives and Enterprise Zones." The Effects of State and Local Public Policies on Economic Development Symposium, *New England Economic Review* (March/April): 109–30.

———. 1998. *Industrial Incentives-Competition Among American States and Cities.* Kalamazoo, MI: W.E. Upjohn Institute for Employment Research.

Jenkins, Noah Temaner, and Michael I.J. Bennett. 1999. "Toward an Empowerment Zone Evaluation." *Economic Development Quarterly* 13, no. 1: 23–28.

Man, Joyce Y., and Mark S. Rosentraub. 1998. "Tax Increment Financing: Municipal Adoption and Effects on Property Value Growth." *Public Finance Review* 26, no. 6: 523–47.

Mark, Stephen T.; Therese J. McGuire; and Leslie E. Papke. 2000. "The Influence of Tax on Employment and Population Growth: Evidence from the Washington D.C. Metropolitan Area." *National Tax Journal* 53, no. 1: 105–23.

Netzer, D. 1997. Discussion of Fisher and Peters "Tax and Spending Incentives and Enterprise Zones." The Effects of State and Local Public Policies on Economic Development Symposium, *New England Economic Review* (March/April): 131–35.

Papke, Leslie E. 1994. "Tax Policy and Urban Development—Evidence from the Indiana Enterprise Zone Program." *Journal of Public Economics* 54: 37–49.

———. 1997. Discussion of Fisher and Peters "Tax and Spending Incentives and Enterprise Zones." The Effects of State and Local Public Policies on Economic Development Symposium, *New England Economic Review* (March/April): 135–37.

Papke, James, and Leslie Papke. 1986. "Measuring Differential Tax Liabilities and Their Implications for Business Investment Decisions." *National Tax Journal* 39, no. 3: 357–66.

Sjoquist, David L. 2001. "Bidding for Business: The Efficacy of Local Economic Development Incentives in a Metropolitan Area." Book review in *National Tax Journal* 54, no. 2: 417–24.

Wallace, Sherri Leronda. 1999. "A Case Study of the Enterprise Zone Program: EZ Avenue to Minority Economic Development?" *Economic Development Quarterly* 13, no. 3: 259–65.

Wilder, Margaret G., and Barry Rubin. 1996. "Rhetoric Versus Reality: A Review of Studies on State Enterprise Zone Programs." *Journal of the American Planning Association* 62: 473–91.

8

Incentives and Economic Development

The Case of BMW in South Carolina

Donald L. Schunk and Douglas P. Woodward

Introduction

In 1992, Munich-based Bayerische Motoren Werke AG (BMW) announced
it would open an assembly plant in South Carolina. The venture into North
American manufacturing was a major move forward in the global expansion
of BMW. The site along Interstate 85 in Spartanburg County represented the
company's first full assembly plant outside Germany. The venture was also a
milestone in economic development for South Carolina, which had little previous automotive assembly experience prior to BMW. (The Anderson Motor
Company shut down in 1926, as it could no longer compete with mass-
produced Ford models.) Momentarily, the 1992 announcement drew world-
wide attention to the state.[1]

The plant forms part of a burgeoning automotive corridor in the south-
eastern United States, with substantial capital investment and job creation.
Over the 1990s, the South Carolina plant exceeded its initial promise of 2,000
jobs and $600 million in capital investment, with several significant expan-
sions, as new product lines have been developed. By 2001, BMW had invested $1.9 billion in direct investment in South Carolina, employing more
than 4,300 workers.[2] Annual compensation reached $345 million in 2001.
Clearly, the plant substantially augmented the income base of South Carolina. Suppliers invested an additional $2.1 billion (through July 2001), fur-
ther fueling regional growth and development.

As with many automotive ventures since the 1980s, notably the foreign-
owned "transplants," the state's investment incentive package caused some
public concern despite the promised jobs and capital investment (Fisher and
Peters 1998; Glickman and Woodward 1990). In many respects, BMW's location decision typifies the promotion of economic development through

industrial incentives and is worth studying. Furthermore, there have been no comprehensive case studies, including cost-benefit analysis of incentive efforts, with the exception of Haywood's (1998) unpublished report on Toyota's Kentucky investment.

In turn, this chapter will examine state incentives in the context of overall economic development, using BMW as a case study. Prior to BMW's location decision, South Carolina's economy was in transition (Division of Research 1987). The textile industry, which migrated to the area in the late nineteenth century to take advantage of low wages and abundant hydropower found along the region's rivers, formed the manufacturing backbone throughout most of the twentieth century. Since the early 1970s, however, this industry has no longer been a source of net job creation. New businesses have developed in the state, but the manufacturing sector began to erode seriously.

The case examined in this chapter suggests that economic development incentives, when properly designed, can attract significant capital investment, create jobs, and promote regional restructuring and reindustrialization. There may be a role for public policy, especially when it can help establish regional clusters and revitalize regional manufacturing. According to an exhaustive global study of economics linkages, there is a "role for judicious policy intervention to promote the creation and deepening of linkages" (UNCTAD 2001: 209). Many journalists, economists, and policy analysts rightfully question escalating incentives, which are not often subject to careful scrutiny. Yet, when an incentive program helps establish deep economic clustering and contributes net gains for local and state budgets, it may make sense. While the findings presented here focus on an automotive cluster that stretches along Interstate 85 and throughout South Carolina, they carry lessons for regional economic growth in a broad sense.

Specifically, the analysis of incentives examines the BMW case in the following areas:

- the total economic impact of the investment, measuring the extent to which BMW provides employment and income for the local economy;
- the fiscal benefits and costs to the state and to local entities;
- the influence on upgrading and enhancing the manufacturing competitiveness of the region;
- the size and composition of the industry recruitment incentives.

The remainder of the chapter is organized as follows. The next section presents the central evaluation of BMW's investment, beginning with an overview of the methods, followed by a summary of the major findings: the employment and income effects and the fiscal implications for state and local governments. After the cost-benefit results are given, the chapter turns to look at the investment's role in shaping a new industrial cluster. The next section places these results in the wider context of economic development, examining the trend toward restructuring and reindustrialization (mostly in durable goods) in a region hurt significantly by plant closures in the textile and apparel industry (nondurable goods). Following this overview of economic development in South Carolina, the specific incentives used to lure BMW are explored. To be sure, development incentives continue to be a source of great interest and some misunderstanding both among analysts and the public at large. The final section offers a conclusion regarding incentives, based on the case presented here.

BMW's Economic Impact

Most economic impact studies involve estimating the employment and income impacts generated by new plant investment and ongoing operations. The basis for the impact analysis is the economic multiplier concept. Economic impact analysis entails calculating the extent to which the plant spreads employment and income, as well as tax revenue for the local and state governments.

Consider first the direct effects of the BMW investment. Figure 8.1 shows BMW's investment in South Carolina since 1993. Now consider the impact of this investment and the activity generated on jobs and income. The economic impacts begin with the *direct* effects of the automobile plant in Greer, South Carolina. Raising income and employment in South Carolina is a paramount goal for policymakers and an ongoing concern of all citizens. The direct BMW contribution is job creation and economic activity at the plant itself. There was no similar automotive activity before the 1992 announcement, so it has brought entirely new money to the state that would otherwise not exist. Direct employment in the plant has reached more than 4,300 full-time equivalents (2001 figures). The steady growth of direct job creation since 1993 can be seen in Figure 8.2.

To model the *total* effects of spending and income circulating through the economy, the estimates derive from input-output analysis. Input-output analysis gives the total economic impact of the investment. For impact analysis that does not involve major policy changes but rather is focused on the operations of one plant, input-output analysis provides reasonable estimates of employment and income creation. More than six decades after Leontief's first model of the U.S economy, the technique is more widely employed than ever.

In the input-output form of multiplier analysis, the cascading impact of

Figure 8.1   **BMW's Annual Investment in South Carolina**

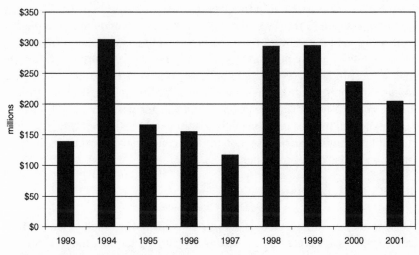

Source: BMW Manufacturing Corp.

Figure 8.2   **BMW's Annual Employment in South Carolina**

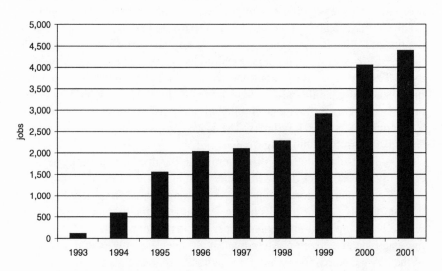

Source: BMW Manufacturing Corp.

spending and income diminishes as it extends deeper into the local economy. In each round of the spending and income cycle, some of the income's impact is dampened as the money is taxed, saved, or used to buy goods and services outside of the community and the state. Hence, there is an extensive "multiplier" effect from BMW's operations and capital investment that continues, but grows smaller, as the spending tapers off, turning into less income, which is then spent as a smaller amount.

Besides direct labor, BMW purchases materials, supplies, and services from local businesses, which create additional jobs and income. BMW's North American supplier network is composed of approximately 120 companies throughout the United States, Canada, and Mexico. South Carolina has 33 of the total companies in this network. In all, BMW's business supports more than 6,700 supplier jobs (2001 figures), creating the first round of employment impacts beyond the direct effects. The income gained by suppliers through BMW contracts is then re-spent. Consequently, suppliers lead to additional *indirect* employment and earnings as their purchases spread into the wider economy.

Beyond BMW's economic ripple effect through suppliers, another chain of activity is touched off by wage and salary payments (Figure 8.3). This income is largely spent in the local economy. In impact analysis, this is the *induced* effect. The induced effect begins with BMW's $345 million in direct personal income paid to employees; subsequently, the employee income is spent at local retail establishments, on various services, and at other businesses, leading to further rounds of spending and income.

The total impact—summing the direct, indirect, and induced effects—accounts for all economic activity that stems from the BMW plant. The direct effects of BMW's impact are obtained from records of BMW's employment, payroll, and input purchases from local suppliers. The total effect is more complicated and involves economic modeling. Given direct information available from the BMW Manufacturing Corporation, the authors used the IMPLAN input-output model to calculate the total impact.

Employment, income, and output effects are the most common metrics for evaluating economic effects or impact. The results of the economic impact analysis reveal powerful effects of a major automotive plant on local employment, income, and economic output. These total economic impacts are displayed in Figures 8.4 through 8.6. Each figure shows the direct and combined indirect and induced effects that make up this total impact.

The figures reveal that, through the multiplier effect, BMW's South Carolina investment supports 16,691 total jobs in South Carolina (about 0.9 percent of the total job base in the state). Given that 4,327 workers are directly employed at the plant, this total job impact yields a multiplier of 3.9. That is,

Figure 8.3   **BMW's Annual Employee Compensation in South Carolina**

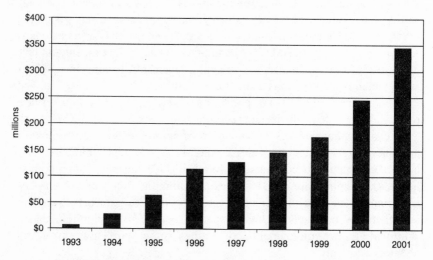

Source: BMW Manufacturing Corp.

Figure 8.4   **BMW's Economic Impact on Employment**

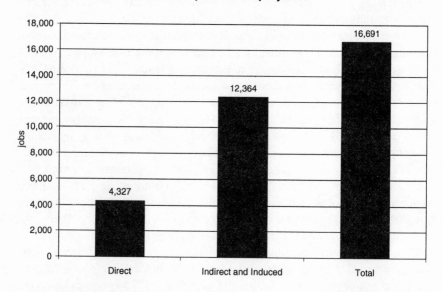

Source: Authors' calculations.

Table 8.1

Employment Impacts by Sector

Sector	Indirect impacts	Induced impacts
Agriculture	13	63
Mining	1	0
Construction	101	116
Manufacturing	3,217	198
TCPU	245	181
Trade	610	2,369
FIRE	141	448
Services	2,345	2,026
Government	40	75
Other	0	176
Total	6,712	5,652

Source: Authors' calculations.

for every direct job in Greer, almost three additional jobs are created elsewhere in the economy. A typical employment multiplier for South Carolina industries and services is closer to two. While most of the direct and indirect jobs are in the manufacturing sector, the multiplier effects support other sectors of the state's economy (see Table 8.1).

The figures also show that the plant generates $691 million in labor earnings for South Carolina (about 1.3 percent of the state's total earnings). The plant itself accounts for $345 million in earnings directly, while indirect and induced effects cause the rest. Dividing the total earnings effect by the total job effect yields income per job of $41,424.

Finally, the input-output analysis yields a total economic output associated with BMW's annual economic activities (2001) in South Carolina of more than $4.1 billion. Economic output is a broader measure than income, measuring the overall value of economic activities associated with BMW in South Carolina. The plant itself accounts for $2.7 billion in annual economic output, and the remainder is determined through its linkages with the economy at large. Although output is often cited as the "economic impact" that results from input-output analysis, personal income and jobs are better metrics of state and local activity in assessing investment for three reasons. First, gross output is not the value-added contribution to the economy. Second, unlike personal income and employment, there is no state and local total that can be used to gauge the magnitude of the impact. Finally, income and employment are useful inputs into fiscal analysis, as discussed in the next section.

Figure 8.5   **BMW's Economic Impact on Labor Earnings**

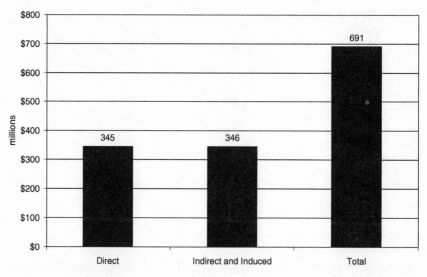

Source: Authors' calculations.

Figure 8.6   **BMW's Economic Impact on Output**

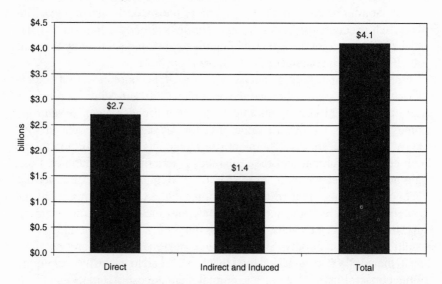

Source: Authors' calculations.

BMW's State and Local Fiscal Effects

Beyond job and income creation, it is important to assess whether an investment supported by state and local governments "pays for itself." Major industrial projects add to a community's tax base, but also place demands on the local infrastructure, service operations (police and fire protection, for example), and the educational system. Public policymakers and local citizens are often concerned about whether the benefits outweigh the costs of new development. Thus, it is important to understand the potential net fiscal benefits—money that can finance new state/local programs and improvements in education, transportation, health, public safety, and other vital government functions.

To assess the net benefits of the plant on South Carolina, the results of the income impact analysis serve as inputs into an assessment of the costs and benefits. The net fiscal effects (benefits less costs) are determined for the state, the county, and the school district.

At the state level, fiscal benefits will be realized through higher sales and individual income tax revenues. Specifically, these benefits will result from the personal income that is supported by BMW's operations via the direct, indirect, and induced income impacts. This income will be taxable directly via the income tax, the amount of which is estimated using state-specific tax information. The after-tax income will be used, in part, for spending on sales-taxable goods within the state. Using appropriate data on household consumption patterns, and sales tax information for South Carolina, the impact on sales tax revenue can be calculated. Meanwhile, the estimated state-level costs include increased education costs to state government, and the costs of the state's Enterprise Program Job Development Credits.

At the local level, the costs examined in this study are driven entirely by the population associated with BMW's direct employment base. Given county-level demographic statistics on, for example, average household size and average number of school-age children per household, the total population impact of BMW's direct employment is estimated.

This population will place additional burdens on the local infrastructure. At the county level, this population will need to be provided with a variety of services, including police, fire, and emergency medical services. The school-age children of BMW's employees will place additional costs on the local school systems. To estimate these various impacts, the fiscal impact model incorporates county and school district information on the costs of providing these services.

The county and school district benefits estimated in this study are the property tax revenues attributable to BMW's employees and BMW itself.

That is, BMW's employees will own homes and cars on which they pay residential and personal property taxes, and BMW itself will pay the fee-in-lieu of property taxes discussed elsewhere. The fiscal impact model utilizes information on the local tax structure, as well as data on median home and automobile values to arrive at an estimate of the property tax revenues paid directly by BMW's employees. Meanwhile, actual nonresidential property tax (fee) payments from BMW are added to this to arrive at the total property tax revenues attributable to BMW and its workers.

These fiscal impacts account for the additional costs of public services and education resulting from BMW's presence. That is, because the benefits are calculated net of costs, they represent incremental funds for improving local government services and education. The analysis assumes that all BMW employees are new residents that place new costs on the local area that otherwise would not have been incurred. (Actually, the overwhelming majority of employees were hired from the local labor pool, so this is a conservative assumption regarding the costs of providing governmental services to BMW employees.)

In Table 8.2, the annual net fiscal benefits are presented for state and local governments. These figures represent annual revenue collections in excess of the additional costs incurred by government. At the state level, the presence of BMW will place additional burdens on, for example, state education costs. However, the substantial earnings impact of BMW results in $27.6 million in tax revenue each year after accounting for the increased state costs.

Local net benefits are presented for the four South Carolina counties most affected by BMW's presence: Anderson, Greenville, Laurens, and Spartanburg. The county benefits are also net of costs of providing services to citizens. Overall, the four counties receive $2.4 million annually in additional net revenue, money that can be spent on meeting the many services that require additional funding. Spartanburg ($1.4 million) and Greenville ($518,000) gain the most, yet Laurens and Anderson also receive over $200,000 in new revenue. The local school districts gain $3.2 million annually.

BMW's Regional Competitiveness Effects

Job and income creation form the basis for economic development. It is crucial to consider how a major manufacturer like BMW has affected economic development more broadly, through enhancing the technological and manufacturing capabilities of the state, particularly through suppliers. This analysis is based on surveys and interviews with BMW personnel and the local suppliers.

Competitiveness factors, probed through interviews with BMW, follow

Table 8.2

Annual Net Fiscal Benefits (dollars)

Local net benefits	County government	School districts
Anderson	214,559	100,593
Greenville	518,310	566,553
Laurens	270,613	200,731
Spartanburg	1,414,250	2,295,819
Four-county total	2,417,369	3,163,636

Source: Authors' calculations.
Note: State government net benefits 27,647,167.

from the well-known case studies on national competitiveness by Porter (1996, 1998, 2000). BMW contributes to regional competitiveness by establishing a stable economic "cluster." An industry cluster is a geographic concentration of industries that drives down costs through proximity to key suppliers, specific labor skills, and other advantages of local networks. Clusters are local webs connecting specialized suppliers and services. Key features of cluster competitiveness include technology transfer and knowledge transfer (including management and production expertise). The industry cluster concept has been widely applied to regions, in which the competitiveness of a region is based on the competitiveness of the industries.

In the cluster framework, competitive economic development is based on firms that continually innovate and respond to market opportunities. Bound together through the economic linkages discussed earlier, a cluster perseveres through continually upgrading managerial and labor force skills and better supplier/customer relations. A cluster's impact shows up through higher productivity, new business formation, and innovation. In short, the local businesses and institutions that constitute a cluster succeed through mutual interests.

The formation of South Carolina's automotive sector after BMW's 1992 announcement is a good example of cluster formation. The cluster enhances the competitive advantages of the state through two major channels: (1) supply linkages and (2) technology, management, and organizational competence. These two features of the automotive cluster in South Carolina are discussed next.

A key aspect in analyzing the benefits of regional clusters is the link between the primary assembler and supplier, although the influence of supplier relations on competitiveness can be difficult to measure.

In general, highly developed supplier linkages create synergies by locating in close proximity (UNCTAD 2001). BMW strongly encourages suppli-

Figure 8.7 **BMW Suppliers in South Carolina**

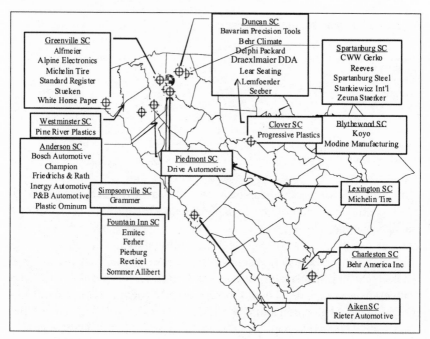

ers to locate near the Greer plant to lower costs. As mentioned earlier, thirty-three BMW suppliers are located in South Carolina. The geographic clustering of suppliers can be seen in the map displayed in Figure 8.7.

BMW's South Carolina facility interfaces with suppliers through two divisions, procurement and logistics. The procurement division is focused on developing BMW's supply base. Logistics is involved in integrating existing suppliers into BMW's supply chain. Both groups work closely with suppliers to ensure that their competencies are aligned with the needs of the plant.

After ten years, BMW's supplier base has mostly stabilized in terms of quality and capacity. For regional competitiveness, a major advantage of BMW's vanguard role in supplier relationships is that it offers spillover benefits for the automotive cluster. Not only is supplier improvement beneficial for BMW, but also it helps suppliers attract contracts from other automotive manufacturers, such as Daimler-Chrysler, Ford, and General Motors. This strengthens the automotive cluster in South Carolina, raising its overall competitiveness in a sector targeted by state economic development promoters.

Through the supplier network and its demonstration effect on other firms, leading foreign investors like BMW transmit globally competitive practices to local economies. Research on foreign investment demonstrates that successful foreign investors must possess firm-specific competitive advantages or core competencies that compensate for their lack of familiarity with the market and production conditions that differ from the home country (Caves 1996). These compensating advantages enable investors to succeed in unfamiliar terrain.

In turn, leading foreign investors serve as conduits for upgrading quality standards throughout a local economy. Hence, a major advantage of investors like BMW is the introduction of new, previously nonexistent, practices and competencies in the host economy.

In South Carolina, one of BMW's major competitive advantages centers around flexible, or agile, production. Much has been written about the vaunted flexible manufacturing techniques of Japanese manufacturers and how their innovations have revitalized U.S. industry. Japanese flexibility is known to have supplanted the mass standardized production that dated back to Henry Ford's assembly-line innovations.[3] Less is known about German competencies in this regard. To be sure, German manufacturers did not invent the just-in-time inventory system, continual improvement, and other features of lean, agile production. Even so, they are adapting and improving the new methods and spreading them globally.

The transfer of know-how and cross-fertilization of skills needed for agile production benefits the local labor force. In South Carolina the production line is organized in self-directed teams. To bolster its labor force skills, BMW has ongoing training initiatives in place. Initially, when the doors to the plant were first opened, the mix of American to German process engineers was 40 percent to 60 percent. Like most complex assembly processes, there were mistakes made and lessons to be learned. American employees learned the German way to assemble and launch a new vehicle. Over time, through a mostly trial-and-error process, the South Carolina production team improved its newly acquired skill set and began to develop its own assembly techniques. U.S. staff members were beginning to replace the German counterparts, and the ratio of American to German process engineers had changed to a 50 : 50 mix. By the time production for the latest BMW model, the X5, had begun, the ratio of American to German engineers had increased to 90 : 10.

Besides innovations in labor practices, BMW has brought other notable agile production competencies to South Carolina manufacturing. The precision and efficiency of the assembly process is notable. An integrated materials handling system has been put in place to move vehicles through the assembly process. Assembly operations begin in the body shop where an overhead conveyor carries parts to workers. Subassemblies are produced here from individually stamped metal parts and components. These subassemblies become BMW bodies when they are welded together and frames, doors, grills, fenders, and hoods are added. A conveyor system then takes the bodies from the body shop to the paint shop. Doors are removed and carried through trim operations by an electrified monorail system. When the bodies arrive at the trim line, they are placed on a conveyor again, which tilts 90 degrees to allow easy access to the underbody. Once in the final assembly area, battery-powered automatic guided vehicles deliver engines. At the same time, a hybrid automatic guided vehicle carries the body. These vehicles feature lift platforms that automatically adjust so workers can comfortably install brake lines, carpets, dashboards, seats, glass, and doors. The body is then transferred to a conveyor where the engine, rear axle, and tires are put in place. Vehicle fluids are added and quality tests performed before associates drive the BMW off the assembly line.

BMW's Greer facility currently employs advanced production techniques, including strategically placed cameras to constantly measure the production line's accuracy, to assemble its Z3 and X5 lines. In addition to quality control systems, BMW designs its products using advanced 3-D modeling programs. This has allowed both engineers in Munich and production experts in Greer to identify assembly problems before they happen. To facilitate the identification of potential production issues, BMW sends several of its South Carolina employees to Munich to participate in knowledge-sharing sessions. In fact, during a nonlaunch year, several South Carolina production staff members may find themselves in Munich two or three times a year.

Another area where BMW is at the forefront of competitive manufacturing in South Carolina is sustainable development and environmental practices. There is a steadfast commitment to environmental protection. For example, the Greer automotive plant is the first in the United States to use a water-based primer matched to base coat paints, which reduces air emissions. Moreover, the plant's wastewater is pretreated and meets the highest standards before discharge into the local treatment plant. In 1998, the plant was awarded ISO 14001 environmental certification for meeting or exceeding international environmental standards.

BMW has had a long history of outstanding environmental performance. At its South Carolina facility, BMW always tries to push proactive environmental policies. BMW's efforts in North America have not gone unnoticed. In December 2000, the Environmental Protection Agency accepted BMW as a charter member of the agency's national environmental achievement tract. So far, BMW is the only automobile company to be included on the EPA's list. At the local level, BMW has been included in South Carolina's environmental excellence program, and the South Carolina Wildlife Federation has presented BMW with its air conservation award.

By adopting such a proactive environmental policy, BMW has been able to increase its flexibility in dealing with capacity issues. Thanks to its conservative approach to emissions, BMW has been able to quickly reconfigure the Spartanburg facility to meet forecasted demand with little EPA intervention. Staying ahead of the curve on environmental issues has not only contributed to the preservation of South Carolina's environment, but it has also helped BMW meet its customer's demands.

In sum, a well-developed supply chain along with the proper competencies must be in place for a regional manufacturing cluster to succeed. A viable cluster depends on a strong supplier network. A full complement of local suppliers helps anchor a cluster in the local economy, allaying concerns about "footloose" investment. The region becomes more competitive as the firms in the cluster transfer knowledge and innovative practices.

BMW's Investment and Economic Development in South Carolina

The location of BMW has enabled the Upstate region of South Carolina to counter a serious deindustrialization trend.[4] After peaking at almost 230,000 jobs in 1973, the textile and apparel employment base has shrunk every year since. The sector most responsible for South Carolina's transition from an agricultural to an industrial state was no longer viable as a source of secure employment. The future of South Carolina's manufacturing sector was uncertain.

By the end of the 1990s, the Upstate South Carolina job base expanded by over 60,000, helping the unemployment rate to fall to 3.0 percent, near full employment. Every county in the region experienced a falling jobless rate during the booming 1990s. Through the 2001 U.S. recession, a major concern in the Upstate region was the tight labor market and lack of available skilled workers. The region's population grew 15.1 percent during the 1990s (in line with the state average), underscoring the need for expanding employment. Migration accounted for about 66 percent of the growth in the Upstate region (well above the state average). About 7,000 of the new residents were international migrants, accounting for 6 percent of the population growth. Meanwhile, in the period 1990 to 1999, the Upstate region's per capita income grew 48 percent, to above the state average.

The investment of BMW, as well as other durable goods producers, injected new life into the state's industrial sector—proving world-class manufacturing can thrive in the Palmetto State. Consequently, South Carolina and the Upstate region have posted employment gains in durable goods industries for the past decade. Today, the Upstate region is still home to about 44 percent of all manufacturing employment in the state. As this section will show, the Upstate region has diversified into durables manufacturing and other nontextile-related industries. As a result, the region has managed to maintain relatively high income growth, while preserving its manufacturing heritage. This section places this recent manufacturing revival in the context of a nationwide decline of manufacturing jobs.

Manufacturing employment in the United States has been diminishing in both relative and absolute terms for decades. Because of rapid job growth in services and trade, manufacturing nationwide has seen its share of total employment fall sharply over the past three decades. In 1970, manufacturing accounted for 27 percent of all nonfarm jobs in the United States. By 2001, this share had fallen to just 13 percent. In terms of absolute employment levels, the U.S. manufacturing sector has been shrinking since 1980. At that time, there was a total of 20.3 million jobs in manufacturing. In 2001, this figure was down to 17.7 million.

These long-term manufacturing job losses can be traced to three primary factors. First, the manufacturing sector has enjoyed productivity gains that have allowed firms to produce more output with fewer workers. That is, the growth of labor-saving technology in U.S. industry has contributed to the manufacturing job losses. It is important to note that this piece of the puzzle implies that manufacturing *output* has not seen the same decline as has *employment*. Second, increased global mobility has played a role by allowing firms to locate outside the United States in search of lower production costs. This is especially true in the case of nondurable goods production and is a major reason for the ongoing loss of employment in the apparel industry. Finally, as U.S. household incomes have grown, there has been a relatively larger increase in the demand for medical, legal, and entertainment services. The share of personal consumption allocated to services has grown tremendously relative to spending on tangible goods.

The absolute job losses seen in the U.S. manufacturing sector have come from both the durable and nondurable goods sectors. Figure 8.8 shows U.S. employment levels in these two industry divisions. Of note here is that for the nation, manufacturing is losing jobs in both nondurable and durable goods production.

In South Carolina and the Upstate area, many of the nationwide manufacturing patterns hold true. In both relative and absolute terms, there have been substantial manufacturing job losses. South Carolina has been among the most manufacturing-reliant states in the country. Therefore, the shift away from manufacturing in the United States certainly had the potential to devastate industry within the state. Because of South Carolina's particular reliance on textile and apparel jobs, the long-term decline in the sector has had a substantial impact on the changing face of the state's economy. In 1970, total

Figure 8.8   **U.S. Manufacturing Employment Levels**

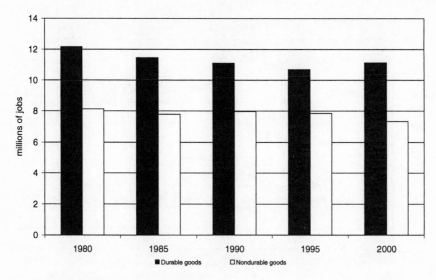

Source: U.S. Bureau of Labor Statistics.

manufacturing accounted for 40.5 percent of all nonfarm jobs in South Carolina. Since then, this share has fallen steadily, reaching 18.1 percent in 2001. Similar to the U.S. pattern, manufacturing employment levels have fallen from 391,900 in 1980 to 332,100 in 2001.

An important difference between the United States and South Carolina's Upstate experiences, and one in which BMW has played a key role, is the strength of the durable goods sector. Between 1970 and 2000, durable goods employment in the United States was essentially flat. The number of jobs in 1970 stood at 11.2 million; during 2000, the figure was 11.1 million. However, employment in the durable goods sector in South Carolina almost doubled over the same period, from 84,400 jobs in 1970 to 160,500 in 2000. This incredible growth in durable goods employment has been vital in stemming the tide of job losses in the state's textile and apparel industries. Despite a net loss of 69,500 nondurable goods jobs between 1970 and 2000, the state's manufacturing sector as a whole actually saw a net increase of 6,600 jobs over the same period because of the influx of durable goods producers.

While the state's durable goods sector has outperformed its national counterpart for decades, the location of BMW in the Greenville-Spartanburg-Anderson metropolitan area in the early 1990s has helped spark impressive growth in that sector. Figure 8.9 shows the trend of durable goods employment between 1990 and 2001 for the United States, South Carolina, and the

Figure 8.9 **Durable Goods Employment Growth Relative to 1990**

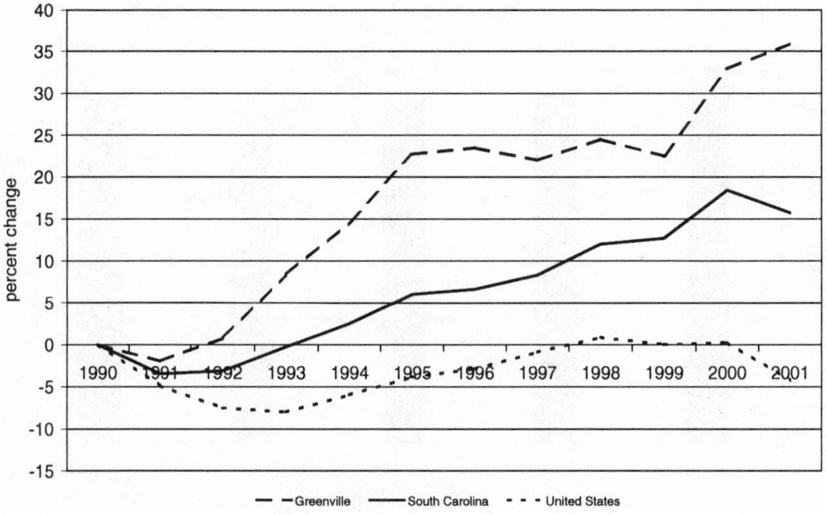

Source: Calculated using data from the U.S. Bureau of Labor Statistics.

Greenville-Spartanburg-Anderson metro area. The percentage change in durable goods employment for these three areas is shown relative to the 1990 levels. This makes it easy to quickly gauge the relative growth rates of durable goods employment among different areas. The figure shows that durable goods employment in the United States has been virtually unchanged since 1990. Meanwhile, South Carolina and the Greenville area, in particular, have enjoyed relatively strong job growth in durable goods.

Development Incentives

The manufacturing growth in Upstate South Carolina is in part the result of public sector promotion of industry. Reindustrialization has remained part of the state's industrial effort, from the administration of Ernest Hollings, who as governor in the 1960s developed the state's technical education system, to former governor Carroll Campbell, who aggressively promoted new manufacturing investment with incentives and was instrumental in helping land BMW in 1992. South Carolina has acted to rebuild the physical capital base, focusing on a strategy to attract industry from both foreign and domestic sources. State and local development missions to foreign countries bore fruit as new plants sprouted where economic activity had been dormant.

This section takes a closer look at the industrial promotion efforts and economic development incentives used to attract BMW. It should be stressed that when states court companies, incentives are only part of the location decision. Companies have many other considerations in determining where to locate. Some of the main location factors include proximate access to market, the presence of a strong manufacturing base, workforce skills and union presence, land and energy costs, and infrastructure like highways, air transport, and ports (Chi and Leathery 1997; Fisher and Peters 1998).

Although not the fundamental location determinant, incentives add to the attractiveness of a site. The large economic impact of automobile assembly plants make them a particular target for industrial recruitment. All recent automotive plant openings have been supported by state incentives. Initial incentive awards used to attract recent automotive plant investments are compared in Table 8.3. Indeed, BMW's incentives were relatively modest, with $130 million in incentives for 1,900 direct jobs promised at the time of the location decision. Alabama's Mercedes assembly plant promised about 1,700 direct jobs at a cost of $250 million in incentives, almost twice BMW's incentive package for significantly less employment.

The $130 million in development incentives offered to lure BMW to South Carolina included tax credits, tax abatements, job training allowances, and infrastructure improvements. Most of the incentives offered were designed to ensure labor and infrastructure quality appropriate to advanced manufacturing. Property tax breaks are designed to make South Carolina competitive with neighbors. Specifically, the state and local BMW incentives were:

- A property tax abatement or set "fee-in-lieu" of taxes (FILOT), valued at over $70 million over twenty years (explained below).
- Labor training through the technical college system valued at $5 million. This is customized job training through the special schools division of the State Board of Technical and Comprehensive Education, which provides training to South Carolinians for new employment made by corporate investment.
- A standard job creation income tax credit ($300 to $1,500 per new job created) valued at $2.85 million per year for up to fifteen years. The state of South Carolina has a 5-percent corporate profits tax. For BMW, the state established a multicounty industrial park (explained below) with a jobs tax credit for every permanent, full-time job created. In five years at $1,500 per job, this would be worth $15 million for 2,000 jobs. Unused credits can be carried forward for ten years. (BMW may not take advantage of these credits.)
- Industrial revenue bonds issued by the state that carry lower interest rates than those offered directly in financial markets.

Table 8.3

Summary of Auto Plant Investments

Company, state, announcement date	Initial job estimate (number)	Initial investment estimate (million $)	Real initial investment estimate 2001 (million $)	Announced incentives (million $)	Real announced incentives 2001 per job	Real incentive cost
Hyundai, Alabama, 2002	2,000	1,000	1,000	118	118	59,000
Toyota, Alabama, 2001	350	220	220	29	29	82,857
Nissan, Mississippi, 2000	4,000	930	944	295	299	74,835
Honda, Alabama, 1999	1,500	400	419	158	165	110,290
GM, Mississippi, 1998	700	500	531	107	114	162,287
Mercedes, Alabama, 1994	1,500	300	343	253	289	192,730
BMW, South Carolina, 1992	1,900	600	715	130	155	81,479
Toyota, Kentucky, 1986	3,000	800	1,166	147	214	71,404

Source: Compiled by author from assorted press coverage of plant announcements.

Notes: Inflation adjustments made using GDP deflator, 2001 and 2002 announcements unadjusted. Incentives include only primary incentive, not additional ongoing incentives. Cost per job figures based on raw data, not rounded figures presented in table.

- A plant site purchased for $25 million and leased to BMW at $1 per year. The land was purchased by the state, the Ports Authority, and Spartanburg County. The government agreed to purchase 900 acres of land near the Greenville-Spartanburg Airport for an estimated cost of $36.6 million; the state committed about $31.6 million, and the local government about $5 million. In addition to land, the state offered site improvements including sewers, utilities, runway expansion at the airport, and roads improvements such as a highway overpass and commitment to widen existing roads along Interstate 85. There was also a $40 million project at the adjacent airport to lengthen a runway to accommodate a fully loaded 747 aircraft.
- $6 million in revenue bonds issued by Spartanburg County to acquire property and improve utilities.
- $10 million allocated for roadwork to improve roads around the plant site.

The largest incentive in monetary terms, and also the incentive least understood by the public, is the property tax abatement. The push for reducing property taxes for businesses goes back to the 1970s when the state's manufacturing employment base began its dramatic decline. Property tax incentives for businesses were deemed to be crucial in luring new plants and expansions. Property tax reductions (through a variety of schemes) were believed to be among the most effective incentives because they would bring the manufacturing assessment down considerably and make South Carolina more competitive with neighboring states.

The FILOT offered to BMW provides a substantial property tax savings, estimated at $70 million for the initial investment. Without the incentive, South Carolina officials believed that the local property tax was not competitive with other states, largely because of a high property assessment ratio placed on manufacturers. It was felt that an amendment to the state constitution, which would allow counties to negotiate a lower assessment ratio, would not stand. Thus, the "fee-in-lieu" was developed as an alternative.

There are distinct advantages to this form of property tax relief for manufacturers. The first is the ability to reduce the statutory manufacturing assessment ratio. The second is the ability to set the millage rate at a fixed level without change over time. Finally, the tax incentive allows for a flexible payment schedule, "as long as the present value of the Company's payments to the County equals the present value of the annual payments that would have been made pursuant to a standard calculation of regular fee-in-lieu payments" (State of South Carolina 1993). The effect of the fee-in-lieu is a major reduction in property taxes for manufacturers wanting to invest in new plants and equipment.

Originally, when the law was first passed in 1987 during Governor Campbell's administration, the incentive was only available to companies investing at least $85 million or more. The logic was straightforward. Large-scale capital investments have huge, positive multiplier effects (as documented in this study) and put less pressure on infrastructure and other state and local expenses than do numerous small projects. This incentive made the state competitive for world-class manufacturers. Theoretically, manufacturing concerns like BMW could locate in many areas, unlike commercial ventures that are tied to the local market. In fact, the FILOT did attract major international investors to South Carolina in the late 1980s and 1990s. Hence, property tax adjustments appear to be justified for large, capital-intensive plants with a national and international market base.

However, the minimum amount of investment for a company to be eligible has been lowered several times since the FILOT law was passed. The minimum investment required has been reduced from the original $85 million, first to $45 million in the early 1990s, and then in 1995 to $5 million. These changes have led to more widespread use of the property tax incentive and have, for most practical purposes, eliminated South Carolina's 10.5 percent assessment on new industrial property. At $5 million, nearly any new capital investment by a manufacturer will be eligible for a FILOT. In fact, a minimum investment of only $1 million is enough to be eligible for incentives in six extremely distressed South Carolina counties. This reduction in the minimum investment level has led to the increased use of FILOT agreements in South Carolina.

The common use of FILOTs makes the original agreement with BMW seem less like an incentive than a de facto tax policy for all manufacturers (recall that it accounts for over half of the original $130 million incentive package). According to data from the South Carolina Department of Revenue, there have been over 320 FILOT agreements negotiated since the law passed in 1987. During the five-year period between 1989 and 1994 (covering the BMW award), about five FILOT agreements per year were negotiated. The average amount of capital investment for these projects was about $157 million, and the average fee paid by these companies in 1998 was about $1 million (much smaller than the BMW agreement). This contrasts dramatically with the four-year period from 1995 through 1998, during which there has been an average of about 75 FILOT agreements negotiated per year. The average amount of capital investment for these 300 or so FILOTs was about $15 million, and the average fee paid by these companies in 1998 was about $130,000.

It should be recognized that the expansion of tax incentives is common among states, although each has its own approach to property tax adjustments. Even though BMW, like most recent investors, pays a set fee-in-lieu of property taxes, it still contributes to the local government finances.

Other incentives offered to BMW besides the tax agreements already discussed should also be placed in the context of economic development. Some incentives such as infrastructure improvements can benefit businesses throughout the area and help develop additional industrial clusters. In particular, BMW's incentive package in South Carolina included improvements for local access roads around the site, lengthening the nearby airport's runway to accommodate fully loaded aircraft, and rail access that would facilitate transportation to the Port of Charleston. These improvements can make it potentially more attractive to prospective businesses considering relocation.

Conclusion

In 1992, during the midst of an economic recession and rising concerns about the "deindustrialization of America," BMW's decision to invest in South Carolina demonstrated that a U.S. manufacturing presence remained essential to global businesses. Subsequently, BMW has been a leading economic development driver in Upstate South Carolina. The operations bring billions of dollars to the region, which circulates through the economic multiplier effect to foment business development. Ten years after the decision, an advanced automotive cluster now spreads across the state, and has created over 16,000 jobs. An automotive cluster is now embedded in the South Carolina economy where none existed a decade earlier.

It could be argued that large investments like BMW would deter further investment, particularly in the automotive sector. Nevertheless, the Upstate region of South Carolina has seen steady growth in the durable manufacturing sector. Ironically, the most vociferous concerns about BMW are no longer about incentives, but rather arise from textile and apparel manufacturers, who see rising wages and salaries as endangering the state rather than showing a sign of progress.

This chapter has offered a comprehensive assessment of the incentive's influence on economic development. The costs and benefits of these incentives are rarely transparent. Through this research, it is clear that the use of incentives in the BMW case has been a success when judged by the following criteria—all suggested by regional economic theory:

- The export-base potential of the investment;
- The overall economic (employment and income) impact;

- The net state and local fiscal benefits;
- The potential for deepening supplier networks and clustering;
- Spillover benefits for other businesses, including infrastructure improvements.

The cost-benefit analysis for state and local governments is critical to any justification for publicly financed incentives. Here we can conclude that the one-time expenses in the incentive package were paid back within the first five years. Using data on BMW's annual operations, the state's portion of the initial incentive package was likely paid off during 1998. As of 1998, the cumulative ongoing net benefits to the state (annual tax revenues less education costs) totaled in excess of $68 million. Even in real terms, this would be enough to cover the state's initial investment of roughly $60 million in the early 1990s. Since 1998, the BMW plant has generated substantial positive returns to the state and local governments each year.

Other investments should be examined according to similar criteria. For automotive investments, which attract some of the largest public support, many incentives programs, like the one offered Toyota in 1986, would appear to be justified (Haywood 1998). It is likely that many investments would not hold up well, and may possibly not be justified on a cost-benefit basis. Indeed, there are cases where plants have closed after little more than a decade. In a case that started the incentive bidding wars for new foreign-owned automotive transplants, Volkswagen's Rabbit plant in Pennsylvania shut down in the 1980s; South Carolina saw Mack Trucks close a plant after twelve years, notwithstanding a large incentive package. Thus, incentive awards ultimately depend on long-term commitments on the part of investors. To some extent, clawback provisions in incentive awards (as discussed elsewhere in this book) can mitigate concerns about employment and capital investment not reaching the promises made at the time of the plant opening. BMW, however, exceeded its promised benefits and appears to be a long-term investor in South Carolina.

Notes

1. See, for example, Sally Solo (1992).
2. See "BMW Plant Background—South Carolina Economic Impact" (2002).
3. For a historical overview of the development of flexible, lean production methods in the automotive sector, see James P. Womack, Daniel T. Jones, and Daniel Roos (1990), and Martin Kenney and Richard Florida (1993).
4. The Upstate region consists of eleven counties that form the traditional textile base of the state: Cherokee, Union, Laurens, Greenwood, McCormick, Spartanburg, Greenville, Anderson, Abbeville, Pickens, and Oconee.

References

"BMW Plant Background—South Carolina Economic Impact." 2002. www. bmwusfactory.com (January 17, 2002).

Caves, Richard E. 1996. *Multinational Enterprise and Economic Analysis*. Cambridge, UK: Cambridge University Press.

Chi, K.S., and D. Leathery. 1997. *State Business Incentives: Trends and Options for the Future*. Lexington, KY: Council of State Governments.

Division of Research. 1987. *South Carolina: An Economy in Transition*. Columbia, SC: Division of Research, Moore School of Business.

Fisher, P.S., and A.H. Peters. 1998. *Industrial Incentives: Competition Among American States and Cities*. Kalamazoo, MI: W.E. Upjohn Institute for Employment Research.

Glickman, Norman, and Douglas Woodward. 1990. *The New Competitors: How Foreign Investors are Changing the U.S. Economy*. New York: Basic Books.

Haywood, Charles F. 1998. "A Report on the Significance of Toyota Motor Manufacturing Kentucky, Inc. to the Kentucky Economy." Lexington, KY: University of Kentucky, unpublished manuscript.

Kenney, Martin, and Richard Florida. 1993. *Beyond Mass Production*. New York: Oxford University Press.

Porter, Michael. 1990/1998. *The Competitive Advantage of Nations*. New York: Free Press.

———. 1996. "Competitive Advantage, Agglomeration Economies, and Regional Policy." *International Regional Science Review* 19, nos. 1 and 2.

———. 2000. "Location, Competition and Economic Development: Local Clusters in a Global Economy." *Economic Development Quarterly* 14, no. 1 (February): 15–34.

Solo, Sally. 1992. "Why Foreigners Flock to South Carolina." *Fortune*, November 2: 48.

State of South Carolina, Office of the Secretary of State. 1993. *Economic Development Incentives in South Carolina Handbook*. Columbia, SC.

UNCTAD (United Nations Committee on Trade and Development). 2001. *Global Investment Report 2001: Promoting Linkages*. New York.

Womack, James P.; Daniel T. Jones; and Daniel Roos. 1990. *The Machine That Changed the World*. New York: Harper Perennial.

9

Revolving Loan Funds

Kelly Robinson

Introduction

Since their inception in the 1970s, revolving loan funds (RLFs) have become a standard tool for local economic development organizations. RLFs provide loans for such varied purposes as working capital, real estate acquisition, new product development, equipment purchases, and environmental investment by businesses. In each case, the role of the RLF in economic development is to provide affordable capital to nontraditional business borrowers who are unable to acquire all or part of what they need from private banks. These nontraditional borrowers may include women, minorities, and residents of distressed communities subject to discrimination. They may also include borrowers with few tangible assets to pledge as collateral, startup firms with uncertain income, and businesses needing loans that are too small to be profitable for private lenders. RLFs provide needed capital and help borrowers to establish a successful credit history, making them more suitable for borrowing from for-profit banks.

Typically, RLFs are organized as public or nonprofit funds capitalized by grants or low-cost loans from governments or foundations. This makes them somewhat different from community development banks and community development credit unions, which are primarily capitalized by deposits from account holders (Williams 1997). Like private sector banks, RLFs are maintained over the longer run by loan repayments. Unlike private banks, RLFs are largely unregulated by federal authorities.

The first federally funded revolving loan fund was created in 1975, when workers of the South Bend Lathe Company sought help from the Economic Development Administration (EDA) to buy their plant in response to its announced closing. However, EDA legislation did not specifically allow the agency to make grants to employees to invest in a for-profit business. The RLF concept arose when the agency determined it could make a grant to a nonprofit employee organization, which could, in turn, loan funds to workers to finance an employee stock ownership plan. Soon thereafter, EDA began capitalizing RLFs with grants as a standard procedure. The Department of Housing and Urban Development (HUD) quickly followed suit, vastly expanding the universe of RLFs when it allowed Community Development Block Grants (CDBGs) to be used for RLF capitalization.

Since that time, RLF use has grown rapidly. Because RLFs are unregulated, highly localized, and active in many different types of lending, there is no single source of statistics for the industry. However, in 1997, the nonprofit Corporation for Enterprise Development (CFED) identified over 600 funds supported by federal agencies such as EDA, HUD, and the U.S. Department of Agriculture's Intermediary Relending Program (USDA/IRP) (Levere, Clones, and Marcoux 1997). These numbers almost certainly underestimate the real size of the RLF industry. For one thing, CFED was unable to account properly for many funds lacking reliable data, including those financed with Small City CDBGs. Furthermore, the industry has continued to grow rapidly since the CFED report was published, with nonfederal funding sources becoming increasingly important. More recent estimates suggest there may be thousands of RLFs, with cumulative assets worth as much as $12 billion (Reznick 2001).

Why Do We Need RLFs?

The effect of firm size on borrowing behavior is striking. Using 1998 survey data, economists with the Federal Reserve Board examined borrowing patterns among "small" firms—defined as businesses with fewer than 500 employees. They found that less than half of those businesses with fewer than 20 employees had any form of bank loan, credit line, or capital lease (Bitler, Robb, and Wolken 2001). These very small businesses make up the vast majority of firms in the United States.[1] For comparison, among firms with between 100 and 499 employees—businesses that are still considered small firms, but are at the upper end of the definition—92 percent used at least one of these financing methods. Keep in mind that this is during the boom years of the late 1990s, when we would expect businesses to be borrowing for expansion. Equally significant, firms with fewer than 20 employees were about twice as likely as firms with 100–499 employees to finance business purchases using high-rate personal credit cards.

Ignoring the possibility of explicit discrimination, there are many reasons why private, for-profit lenders may not lend capital to small businesses, especially in distressed areas. First, these businesses are often risky. As a group, small businesses and startups have significantly higher failure rates than larger established businesses. They also tend to have fewer assets to use as collateral. In the case of startups, it may take a business some time to generate enough income to support significant debt repayment.

Second, even when the businesses are financially sound, it can be difficult for lenders to assess the credit risk of these borrowers. Many first-time business owners have no established credit history. These businesses also tend to have unsophisticated bookkeeping systems without provisions for regular audits. Similarly, small businesses borrow for extremely diverse reasons, making it difficult for underwriters to develop standard risk ratings. When banks cannot assess risk reliably, they will usually either refuse to lend or they will impose tougher terms.

A third reason banks may not loan to small businesses is that it can be expensive. The amount borrowed is typically small, so the fixed costs of underwriting and servicing a loan are large relative to the income generated. Finally, many small business owners are better at "what they do" than at managing their business. Lacking specialized management personnel, these borrowers can require a lot of assistance in applying for and managing their loans.[2]

How They Work

The primary role of most economic development RLFs is to provide the difference between the amount borrowers need and what they can obtain through private capital markets. In some instances, the RLF will be the primary lender. For example, many RLFs today provide "micro" loans that are too small to be worthwhile for traditional banks (Servon and Doshna 1998).[3] Similarly, RLFs often provide startup and/or working capital to small borrowers who cannot qualify for credit from traditional banks. They may also provide venture capital for firms in those sectors and geographic locations neglected by private venture capitalists. Occasionally, RLFs may also provide "bridge loans" that allow a project to move forward quickly by providing a short-term capital source until longer-term bank financing can be arranged.

More often, an RLF will provide a secondary loan to supplement what the borrowers can obtain from a bank. This "gap loan" will typically be structured to ensure that the bank loan is repaid in a timely fashion, with risk transferred to the RLF. Typically, this requires that the RLF take a subordinated position with respect to collateral in the event of default. The RLF may also defer payments until a significant portion of the bank loan has been paid off or until the business is more established and generating sufficient income to repay its debt.

Local banks typically find RLFs to be valuable partners for several reasons. First, RLFs often help prepare borrowers before they actually approach a bank, making the job of the loan officer significantly easier. Second, potential borrowers may not have a viable project without the gap financing provided by an RLF. For instance, the absence of such funding may mean that a proposed investment is too small to generate the income necessary to meet commercial standards for debt servicing. At a minimum, the RLF usually reduces risk to the bank. To give just one example, the additional capital provided by an RLF may allow the borrower to proceed with multiple stages of expansion in a more integrated fashion—eliminating financing gaps that cause inefficient downtime and threaten the project's success. In theory, this reduced risk to the bank should be reflected in better terms for the borrower. Once RLF borrowers have established a record of successful repayment, most go on to rely on traditional banks for future lending.

Underwriting and Servicing Practices

Whereas private banks base loan eligibility mainly on financial characteristics of borrowers, RLFs also consider issues related to their public mission. Many RLFs lend for very specific purposes, and most RLFs lend only to firms within a limited geographic area. Often, potential borrowers must demonstrate that they have been unable to obtain credit from traditional banks. Eligibility rules also vary significantly, depending on the source of funds used to capitalize the RLF. For example, federally funded RLFs are usually not allowed to support activities that cause businesses to relocate from one area to another (since this redistributes national wealth rather than adding to it).

As with any bank, RLFs offer a wide variety of terms on their loans, depending on the situation of the borrower. They may include either fixed or variable rate loans with a range of maturities. However, in contrast to private banks that structure their loans primarily to protect themselves against loss, RLF loans are routinely designed to help the borrower. As an example, the term of an RLF gap loan will often be coordinated with the bank to ensure the bank is repaid and to prevent undue hardship to the borrower. Most RLFs offer below-market interest rates. When variable rates are used, RLFs often impose a cap rate to protect borrowers in the event of large increases in national interest rates. For any given type of loan, RLFs tend to offer longer maturities than their private counterparts, and RLFs are far more likely than private banks to allow deferred payments. Often, RLFs also accept types of collateral not allowed by private lenders. This is especially important to young firms that do not own real estate. In some cases, RLFs may allow loans to be undercollateralized and backed by a personal credit pledge. It is also not unusual for an RLF to take a partial equity position.

RLFs also differ from for-profit lenders in how they monitor and service their loans. RLFs typically go to great lengths to avoid foreclosure, and will restructure or refinance a loan to avoid default. Most RLFs spend a great deal of effort to prevent borrowers from ever reaching this point. Even before the loan is made, RLFs work closely with their borrowers to prepare their applications and structure a loan package that is realistic.

Many loan funds also provide or act as clearinghouses for a variety of technical assistance that can help the business succeed (NADO 1999). This is especially common for RLFs associated with business incubators and those that specialize in lending to microenterprises. For young firms, technical assistance is most likely to take the form of business planning and training in how to run a business (Servon and Doshna 1998). For more mature businesses that have established business plans, technical assistance may take the form of specialized financial counseling, help with auditing and tax reporting issues, and so forth.

Integration with Broader Economic Development Activities

To fulfill its public mission, an RLF must be more than a lender of last resort. It must fund those activities adding most to local economic development. This is not an easy task. First of all, there is an inherent tension in RLF lending between trying to protect the RLF's assets and trying to support those businesses most in need of assistance. When an RLF becomes too risk averse, it may end up supporting activities the private sector would have undertaken anyway. If it becomes too aggressive, the RLF may fund investments with little real chance of success. Second, successful economic development depends as much on how different businesses complement one another as on how they perform individually. RLFs are frequently asked to fund businesses that appear viable but fit poorly with the economic goals of the region.

To balance these conflicting demands, RLF managers need a strong sense of their mission. For most RLFs, the first step in developing such a vision is to prepare a lending plan that explains in some detail how the RLF supports the broader economic development goals of the organization in question. Many funders require such a plan, but these are often treated as a bureaucratic exercise by the RLF management and funder alike. The planning process is better thought of as a tool that provides the RLF operator day-to-day guidance on how to manage their funds most effectively. The types of issues that should be discussed in the lending plan include, but are not limited to:

- A brief description of the community's economic strengths and challenges, including the particular credit gaps confronting local entrepreneurs;
- A description of how the RLF serves to address these challenges in the

short, medium, and long term, including both general goals and specific milestones to be met. This should include references to any other comprehensive economic development plans or strategies in place and how the RLF lending plan relates to those strategies;

- The priority given borrowers and activities given priority. As part of this, the plan should describe other nonprofit lending organizations in the area and explain how the RLF will avoid competing with those organizations;
- The RLF's relationship to local banks;
- Conflict of interest policies (especially important in small communities where borrowers may have personal ties to members of the loan committee);
- How much of the RLF's assets should be loaned out at any given time, provisions for reserve funds, and the like;
- A description of additional services to be offered by the RLF;
- A plan for longer-term capitalization and growth of the RLF, including alternative loss and financial scenarios;
- Policies and criteria for monitoring and evaluating the progress of the RLF in meeting its goal; and
- Principles for revisiting the lending plan from time to time.

The lending plan should not be so specific that it robs fund managers of flexibility. On the other hand, it must be specific enough to provide RLF operators real guidance in how to manage their funds. Obviously, the RLF's lending plan needs to be developed with broad-based local input—including both borrowers and individuals with financial expertise. Again, this cannot be treated as a bureaucratic exercise. Involving potential borrowers is a very practical form of marketing and can help prepare borrowers before they come to the RLF for assistance. Participation by local banks and other nonprofit lenders can ensure that the RLF is doing its best to complement their activities and that it can build partnerships for future projects.

Once a lending plan is in place, the RLF is well advised to develop specific guidelines built on that plan. These can cover operational matters such as:

- Underwriting practices, including interest rate ranges, type of loans offered, preference for fixed or variable rates, and so forth;
- Lending policies or terms to be avoided;
- Policies and criteria for evaluating loan applications; and
- Servicing and foreclosure policies.

Some of this may seem excessively bureaucratic, and an experienced loan officer may be able to make these decisions intuitively. However, the presence of clear guidelines can be especially valuable where staff turnover is high.

In managing their funds, RLF activities and policies will often be constrained by funding agencies. EDA, for instance, requires that RLFs fund activities only in the specific distressed area where the RLF operates—actually requiring the RLF to recall the loan if the borrower subsequently moves out of the area. One of the more important variables affecting how an RLF operates is whether its funding comes from grants or loans. USDA, for instance, capitalizes its RLFs with low-cost loans, whereas EDA gives grants for this purpose. Because USDA is concerned that the federal government gets repaid, it requires its RLFs to hold 15 percent of their assets as a reserve fund to protect against substantial defaults. EDA, on the other hand, requires its RLFs to loan nearly all of their money and precludes them from maintaining cash reserves.

Evidence on RLF Performance

There is a growing body of evidence regarding RLF performance. Unfortunately, these studies look at very different groups of RLFs and often use inconsistent definitions and evaluation methods. Even with these weaknesses, recent studies suggest that loan losses are only slightly higher for RLFs than for private lenders (Table 9.1). For studies done since 1990, default rates are modest—usually under 10 percent. Still, there are wide differences among funds. In its Ohio analysis, for instance, CFED found default rates ranging from 0 percent to 65 percent. Nearly half the funds older than two years had default rates below 6 percent. Most of these studies do not calculate true loss rates, because they fail to account for recoveries of collateral. The exception is research by the National Community Capital Association (NCCA). In a survey of fifty-two member community development financial institutions (CDFIs) lending primarily to businesses, NCCA found loss rates averaging between 4 percent and 8 percent (Lipson 2000).[4]

To be sure, RLF loss and default rates are higher than those for private banks. This is to be expected if RLFs are targeting risky borrowers. Indeed, extremely low loss and/or default rates might indicate that RLFs are making loans to borrowers that could qualify for bank loans. RLF losses may be as low as they are precisely because RLFs provide so much hands-on help to borrowers. This view is supported by CFED's research, which found that microenterprise funds—which involve more direct assistance to borrowers than other types of funds—tend to have lower default rates than other RLFs. Interestingly, CFED's study of Ohio RLFs found that just 14 percent of funds maintained any loss reserves. NCCA's research found the size of these re-

Table 9.1

Past Research on Revolving Loan Fund (RLF) Delinquencies, Defaults, and Losses

Source[a]	Year	Population studied	Key findings
Mt. Auburn Associates	1987	EDA RLFs	Default rate of 9.6 percent on fixed asset loans
Levere, Clones, and Marcoux (CFED)	1997	290 federally funded RLFs	Median default rate of 5.7 percent
		81 Ohio RLFs	Combined delinquency and default rate of 5.1 percent
Rutgers et al.	1997	304 fully loaned EDA defense adjustment RLFs	Default rate of 13 percent
		247 partially loaned EDA defense adjustment RLFs	Default rate of 1.9 percent
NADO	1999	52 rural RLFs	Default rate of 2 percent; 42 percent of RLFs had no defaults at all
Lipson (NCCA)	2000	20 business and microenterprise CDFIs with assets under $2 million	Cumulative loss rate of 7.5 percent
			90-day delinquency rate of 9.4 percent
		17 business and microenterprise CDFIs with assets between $2 million and $6 million	Cumulative loss rate of 4.7 percent
			90-day delinquency rate of 2.6 percent
		15 business and microenterprise CDFIs with assets over $6 million	Cumulative loss rate of 5.7 percent
			90-day delinquency rate of 6.0 percent

[a] See reference list for sources.

serves averaged between 8 percent of total assets for large funds and 12 percent for small ones.

In terms of economic impacts, CFED estimated that the 290 RLFs it studied made more than $560 million in loans and created or saved more than 200,000 jobs at a cost of $5,338 per job. Examining EDA RLFs dedicated to helping communities adjust to defense cutbacks, Rutgers et al. (1997) found that every $1 million contributed by EDA created 304 permanent jobs (an EDA cost of $3,312 per job). The total cost per job was significantly higher because every $1 of EDA funding leveraged an additional $2.50 of private sector funding. Still, the researchers noted that these funds had been making loans for only a few years. Many of the projects being funded were barely under way, with their greatest impacts yet to come. The NCCA study noted that, as a group, the fifty-two business-oriented RLFs it examined (averaging twelve years in age) created more than 42,000 jobs and retained more than 62,000 jobs on a continuing basis. These funds loaned between 83 percent and 93 percent of their funds to for-profit businesses, and between 63 percent and 76 percent of their funds went to firms with fewer than twenty employees (Lipson 2000).

Key Issues Confronting RLFs Today

RLFs today face a variety of challenges, many of which result directly from the maturing and growing sophistication of the industry.

Ongoing Capitalization

In principle, RLFs are self-sustaining; however, there is a variety of reasons why these funds may require periodic infusions of capital. While typical loan losses from RLFs are small, they still erode the capital base. Also, many fund operators divert loan income away from the pool to support administrative costs. Perhaps most important, many RLFs continue to make loans at well below market interest rates. These RLF operators often find that their fund growth does not keep up with inflation. Today, there is a significant debate in the industry regarding the need for subsidized interest rates. A growing number of RLF operators and outside experts believe these losses detract from fund effectiveness and that RLFs can provide capital where it is needed without subsidizing interest rates. Other operators argue that subsidized rates provide a necessary incentive for businesses to invest in distressed areas. Yet another factor contributing to the need for recapitalization is that many RLFs are branching into new types of lending such as microlending and venture capital. Likewise, many local economic development organizations today are redirecting their efforts toward cluster development and other strategies that favor intense investment in small firms.

Many new programs to capitalize RLFs have emerged in recent years. However, it is usually more difficult to recapitalize an existing RLF than to start a new one. In part because RLFs have been marketed as self-sustaining, many funding organizations are hesitant to provide additional support to funds depleted due to loan losses or because loans were made at below market rates. In recent years, funding agencies such as EDA and HUD have experimented with new approaches to recapitalizing RLFs by tapping private capital markets. At this point, three related approaches appear to be most promising: securitization, collateralized borrowing, and the incentives provided by the Community Reinvestment Act (CRA) (Dommel 1995; Robinson 2001).

In its most straightforward form, securitization refers to the pledging of the income stream from an RLF portfolio to back a bond sale. Cash from the bond sale is used to make additional loans, and income from the loans goes to repay bondholders. Currently, the main obstacle to securitization is the hesitancy of RLFs to sell or pledge their loans in secondary markets. Many RLF managers fear they will have to accept large discounts on the sale of their loans (meaning that the RLF receives less than the outstanding value of the loan). They also fear that securitization will limit their ability to work with troubled borrowers. A recent demonstration project by EDA suggests that, while RLFs making below-market loans typically have to accept a discount on the sale of their loans, these discounts are often small. In the EDA demonstration, more than 100 loans were priced for sale. These carried a median interest rate of 7.5 percent, and suffered a discount on sale of just 6.3 percent (Robinson 2001). All of the RLFs participating were able to retain servicing of their loans.

Collateralized borrowing is similar to securitization in that RLF loans are used as security to borrow new capital (usually from local banks). However, there is no security sold, and the loans remain under complete control of the RLF, so there is no discount. Until now, the main drawback of collateralized borrowing has been that participating banks have typically insisted that a large portion (as much as one-third) of the cash raised be set aside as a reserve against possible defaults (Richardson 1996). Although this reserve ultimately reverts to the RLF and may earn income in the meantime, funds in the reserve pool are not available for immediate lending.

The third promising approach to recapitalization is to encourage banks to invest in RLFs in return for CRA credit. To date, the most sophisticated version of this is an approach referred to as "equity equivalent investment" (EQ2), pioneered by NCCA and Citibank with support from the Ford Foundation (Park 2000; Stearns 2001). EQ2 investments are loans that have many similarities to an equity investment. First of all, they have a long initial term (typically ten years). This term is rolling, meaning that it is automatically extended each year unless terminated by the lender. Interest rates on the loan are set independently of the RLF's anticipated cash flows, and no payment on principal is made until the loan is due. Second, the loans are uncollateralized and deeply subordinated. This means, for instance, that the RLF can subsequently pledge its portfolio to back a bond sale. If there is an interruption in repayment, the bondholders would get paid ahead of the EQ2 investors. In return for these very favorable terms to the RLF, the banks receive highly leveraged CRA treatment. Park explains how this works for a hypothetical CDFI:

> Assuming a nonprofit CDFI has equity of $2 million, $1 million in the form of permanent capital and $1 million in equity equivalents provided by a commercial bank, the bank's portion of the equity is 50 percent. Now assume the CDFI uses this $2 million to raise $8 million in senior debt. With its $10 million capital under management, the CDFI makes $7 million in community development loans over a 2 year period. In this example, the bank is entitled to claim its pro rata share of the loans originated, 50 percent or $3.5 million. Its $1 million investment results in $3.5 million of lending credit over two years. (Park 2000: 4)

If there is any weakness to EQ2, it is its complete reliance on CRA. Were CRA to be weakened significantly or become less favorable relative to other investments, the attractiveness of EQ2 would decline accordingly. Likewise, if other forms of CRA investments arise that allow investors to earn a greater profit, EQ2 may become less attractive. However, this is all very speculative.

Growing Pains

RLFs today face a variety of issues that arise from the rapid growth of their industry. First, the industry needs to adopt reporting standards that promote accountability. While most RLFs are audited regularly, these audits are more useful for identifying gross mismanagement than for assessing how well an RLF is pursuing its economic development mission. There is tremendous variation in how RLFs report basic information such as defaults, loss rates, jobs created, and leveraging of private funds. There are even fewer standards for measuring progress in specific types of lending—for instance, capital lent to first-time borrowers or survival rates among startup firms supported. Furthermore, few RLFs report how their loan activities have contributed to achieving the specific goals of their organization. For example, we would like to know if an RLF is making loans to pizza parlors when its parent organization claims to be pursuing a high-tech development strategy. Absent positive action on the part of the industry, there will probably be growing pressure to regulate RLFs more strictly. This could undermine the flexibility that is one of their greatest assets.

RLFs are not intended to behave like banks. However, RLFs need to operate in a fashion that allows them to do business with banks. A good example of this is credit scoring. Given loan records for a large number of standardized borrowers, specialized financial firms are able to develop statistical models that predict the credit risk of individual borrowers with great accuracy, using just a few key characteristics of the borrower. Today, private banks commonly use these "credit scoring" models to underwrite loans. Most RLFs have rejected this approach because they are specifically trying to lend to businesses that would be rejected by private banks. However, credit scoring can still be useful to RLFs. It may, for instance, help RLFs to price their portfolios more efficiently when preparing them for sale in the secondary market. As with many other private banking practices, the RLF manager not only needs to know how credit scoring works, but where it is and is not appropriate, given the mission of the RLF.

Another issue related to rapid growth in the RLF industry is specialization. The most obvious manifestation of this is specialization by type of lending. Thus, for instance, we now see RLFs that specialize in microlending, those that focus on venture capital, and the like. We are also beginning to see specialization in services. Some nonprofits now specialize in providing training for RLF staff, and it is likely that there will soon be organizations dedicated to servicing RLF loans. This can be good for the industry, because specialized service providers can reap scale economies and develop greater expertise than is the case if individual RLFs do everything in house. However, we need to be careful that specific services do not become dominated by a few providers, causing a loss of diversity. Growing specialization will also require that RLF operators become more sophisticated in how they obtain the various services they need.

There are still a number of specialized services that are sorely missing—especially services affecting the industry as a whole. Joint research is a good example. RLFs of all kinds could benefit from better evaluation research, examination of key challenges facing the industry, and information dissemination. Another example would be some sort of internal labor market or "hiring hall." RLFs as a group have a difficult time obtaining and keeping skilled employees. Yet there are not really any industrywide job banks, training standards, curriculums for training, or even standardized job classifications. All of these things could make it easier to develop and place skilled workers where they are needed. To be sure, there are organizations trying to meet these demands, but none of them serves more than a small portion of the RLF community, and they do not integrate their efforts with one another to any significant degree.

For their part, funding agencies also need to become more flexible in order to allow RLFs to operate with greater sophistication. A good example is the requirement that EDA and some other agencies have obliging RLFs to lend a high percentage of their assets at all times. Normally, this is not a problem. However, when traditional banks ease their lending standards, RLFs may find it difficult to make new loans without taking in poor quality borrowers that contribute little to economic development, have higher loss rates, and are expensive to service. This is precisely what happened to many RLFs in the boom of the 1990s, when private banks with large cash reserves loosened their lending standards. In this case, while they were technically prohibited from doing so, many RLFs would have preferred to hold cash in reserve for the inevitable economic downturn when their capital was sure to be needed. A more efficient regulation would allow RLFs to hold cash under such conditions.

Conclusion

In the past twenty-five years, the RLF industry has been remarkably successful. RLF operators are faced with the difficult task of managing their funds prudently while simultaneously directing money where it is needed most. When the first RLFs were created in the mid-1970s, it was not at all certain they would survive. Today, RLFs nationwide have loaned billions of dollars to people left out of private financial markets—creating or saving hundreds of thousands of jobs in the process. By and large, RLFs have done this efficiently—with very small staffs, without large defaults, and without competing with private banks.

The critical challenges the industry faces today are different. RLF operators can no longer operate as freely as they once did. As the level of public investment in RLFs has grown, so has the degree of accountability and financial sophistication expected of RLF operators. These heightened expectations can be seen in nearly every aspect of RLF operations, but especially with respect to their economic development mission. RLFs have shown convincingly that they can make safe loans. It is more difficult to demonstrate that they can react to a changing economy and provide the types of capital needed, when it is needed, for the types of activities most suitable for local development. As with any fast growing industry, the biggest challenge that RLF operators face today is to maintain the innovation that has made them successful so far.

Notes

I wish to thank David Witschi of the Economic Development Administration and Bill Amt of the National Association of Development Organizations Research Foundation for their valuable comments.

1. According to the United States Small Business Administration, more than 99 percent of all employers are small firms (www.sba.gov/advo/stats, dated January 18, 2002). The Federal Reserve statistics indicate that 74 percent of small firms have twenty or fewer employees (Bitler, Robb, and Wolken 2001).

2. According to Bitler, Robb, and Wolken (2001), 90 percent of small businesses are owner-managed.

3. I differ in approach from Servon and Doshna in that I consider microlending to be a specific form of RLF; they see the two as distinct approaches.

4. The term "community development financial institution" (CDFI) can refer either to a generic form of RLF, or RLFs funded under the U.S. Department of the Treasury program of the same name. The generic term usually refers to RLFs that are organized independently of a governmental organization, although they may receive governmental funds.

References

Bitler, Marianne P.; Alicia M. Robb; and John D. Wolken. 2001. "Financial Services Used by Small Businesses: Evidence from the 1998 Survey of Small Business Finances." *Federal Reserve Bulletin* (April): 184–205.

Dommel, Paul. 1995. *Secondary Markets for City-Owned CDBG Loans* (Prepared for the U.S. Department of Housing and Urban Development). Cleveland, OH: Cleveland State University.

Levere, Andrea; Daphne Clones; and Kent Marcoux. 1997. *Counting on Local Capital: A Research Project on Revolving Loan Funds.* Washington, DC: Corporation for Enterprise Development.

Lipson, Beth. 2000. *CDFI's Side-by-Side: A Comparative Guide, 2000 Edition.* Philadelphia, PA: National Community Capital Association.

Mt. Auburn Associates. 1987. *Factors Influencing the Performance of U.S. Economic Development Administration Sponsored Revolving Loan Funds.* Somerville, MA: Author.

National Association of Development Organizations (NADO). 1999. *The Performance and Impact of Revolving Loan Funds in Rural America.* Washington, DC: NADO Research Foundation.

Park, Kyong Hui. 2000. Memorandum to David Witschi, "Information on Equity Equivalent Investments," National Community Capital Association (May 26).

Reznick, Scott. 2001. *Loan Sales and Securitization of Revolving Loan Funds: Demonstration Project Final Report* (Prepared for the Economic Development Administration, U.S. Department of Commerce). Harvey Cedars, NJ: Commonwealth Development Associates.

Richardson, Laurence B. 1996. *A Strategy to Increase Economic Development by Providing a Source of RLF Recapitalization from the Capital Markets through the Utilization of Private Securitization.* Alexandria, VA: Alex Brown and Associates.

Robinson, Kelly. 2001. *Expanding Resources for Economic Development: An RLF*

Demonstration. Washington, DC: Economic Development Administration, U.S. Department of Commerce.

Rutgers University, New Jersey Institute of Technology, Columbia University, Princeton University, National Association of Regional Councils, and University of Cincinnati. 1997. *Defense Adjustment Program: Performance Evaluation, Final Report* (Prepared for the Economic Development Administration, U.S. Department of Commerce). New Brunswick, NJ: Rutgers University, Center for Urban Policy Research.

Servon, Lisa J., and Jeffrey P. Doshna. 1998. *Making Microenterprise Development a Part of the Economic Development Toolkit* (Prepared for the Economic Development Administration, U.S. Department of Commerce). New Brunswick, NJ: Rutgers University, Center for Urban Policy Research.

Stearns, Kathy. 2001. *EDA Secondary Market Demonstration Project for Revolving Loan Funds in South Dakota* (Prepared for South Dakota Rural Enterprise, Inc). Philadelphia, PA: National Community Capital Association.

Williams, Marva. 1997. *Credit to the Community: The Role of CDCUs in Community Development.* Chicago: Woodstock Institute.

10

Financing Neighborhood Businesses

Collaborative Strategies

Beverly McLean and James Bates

American cities enjoyed an economic boom in the 1990s. This was reflected in the nation's lowest peacetime unemployment and inflation rates, the longest period of real wage growth, and highest homeownership rate in twenty years (U.S. Department of Housing and Urban Development [HUD] 1999b). However, if one were to take a stroll through a local business district in an older U.S. industrial city, such as Buffalo or Detroit, one would uncover another story. The once vibrant residential and commercially mixed strips of these cities now contain just the remnants of their lively past—abandoned factories and warehouses, boarded-up houses, vacant lots, and deteriorating storefronts.

Where once automotive and manufacturing industries were dominant employers, today's inner-city neighborhoods offer few well-paid job opportunities. White flight from inner cities to suburbs contributed to a geographic shift in U.S. metropolitan populations and globalization and deindustrialization contributed to the shifting of firms and individuals from urban to ex-urban areas. Subsequently, retail goods and services at the neighborhood level, and low-wage, entry-level jobs disappeared as inner-city retail and service stores closed (Kasarda 1993; Wilson 1996). Consequently, the ability to find entry-level retail and service-sector employment or obtain gainful employment in inner cities decreased markedly for many segments of the population that historically had limited economic advantages: youth, low-income minorities, females, and the less skilled. Concurrent with the disappearance of work in inner cities was the loss of the local provision of basic consumer goods and services—seminal to the quality of life of residents in inner-city neighborhoods.

Urban scholars and public officials view today's inner-city neighborhoods as underutilized and/or unexploited submarkets (HUD 1999a; Porter 1995). Inner-city amenities (developable land, large labor pools, intellectual capital, built-up transportation and communication infrastructures, research and innovation hubs, etc.) are perceived to be underutilized in production processes, and inner-city consumers, with their high aggregate purchasing power and demand for goods and services, go unserved or underserved by local service and retail firms. Michael Porter (1995) in a *Harvard Business Review* article called for a renewed focus on the inner city and inner-city revitalization. For Porter, inner cities offer a strategic competitive advantage, given the aggregate buying power of inner-city residents, the proximity of these neighborhoods to downtown, the existing transportation infrastructure, and clusters of businesses. Porter believes that a private sector that is able to fully realize and exploit these advantages can revitalize the inner city, and that current development strategies that rely on government subsidies and preference programs are ineffective. These strategies, according to Porter, treat "the inner city as an island isolated from the surrounding economy and subject to its own unique laws of competition" (Porter 1995: 55). Past strategies, in other words, simply fall into a trap of redistributing wealth, instead of creating wealth.

Critics of Porter note, however, that his private-sector approach oversimplifies the neighborhood redevelopment process (Bates 1997; Boston and Ross 1997; Harrison and Glasmeier 1997). Boston and Ross point out in the conclusion of their review of Porter's challenge that revitalizing inner cities is more than strategies for dilapidated buildings and worn-out infrastructure. It is also about neighborhood residents—restoring the human potential and reintegration of inner-city communities back into "the economic, political, and cultural life of the surrounding metropolitan areas" (Boston and Ross 1997: 337). Timothy Bates (1997) notes that simply getting the government out of the way will not necessarily stimulate the private investment needed for neighborhood business revitalization. Bates (1997) calls for a more proactive approach—one that moves beyond the charity view of government subsidies and develops private-public sector strategies that seek out and promote firms that have the potential for growth and financial success. For Harrison and Glasmeier, successful neighborhood redevelopment lies in collaboration among all community stakeholder groups (residents, business leaders, and government): "[t]rue collaborations are necessary—and there is considerable evidence they are working, even if the net impact still pales in comparison with the magnitude of the problem" (1997: 36). These collaborations are viewed as helping inner-city residents and business owners build multipronged development paths to address the systemic as well as economic challenges of business and neighborhood redevelopment. Ross Gittell and J. Phillip Thompson (1999) conclude that collaboration can improve inner-city economies as social networks can ultimately increase the social, economic, and political influence of residents that is requisite for comprehensive citizen-driven neighborhood change, and, that may, in due course, lead to the economic improvement of neighborhoods.

This chapter examines collaborative strategies for financing neighborhood business revitalization. First, we present an overview of the barriers for neighborhood business development. Second, we examine the weaknesses and strengths of private-sector financial tools that are available for financing neighborhood business revitalization. Third, we provide case analyses of successful financial collaborative efforts to implement neighborhood business revitalization.

Barriers to Neighborhood Business Development

Barriers to neighborhood business revitalization have been attributed to long-term structural shifts in population, the economy, and residential location (Downs 1981, 1994; Kasarda 1993). Historically, the neighborhood was the building block for inner-city life. Higher inner-city population densities sustained and supported a diverse pattern of service and amenities for its residents (Jacobs 1961). But changes in transportation and communication technologies contributed to substantial population dispersal (Fishman 2000). The central city population growth rate between 1970 and 2000 was 19 percent compared to 60 percent for their suburban rings (Figure 10.1).

A closer examination of these trends reveals that aggregate data mask the geographic imbalance of decline (Table 10.1). Metropolitan areas located in the traditional U.S. industrial heartland had the most significant population redistribution. These metropolitan regions can be grouped by their population trends since 1970: population turnaround in the 1990s, continued population decentralization, and continued regional decline. Central cities, such as Boston and Chicago, experienced overall population decline between 1970 and 2000, but between 1990 and 2000 both cities gained population. Metropolitan regions, such as Cincinnati and Cleveland, Ohio; Milwaukee, Wisconsin; Kansas City, Missouri; Rochester, New York; and Washington, DC-Baltimore, Maryland, experienced substantial population growth in their suburban rings, while their central cities continually lost population. Regions, such as Buffalo, New York, and Pittsburgh, Pennsylvania, experienced not only central city population decline but also regional population decline; however, their suburban rings gained population.

In the 1980s and 1990s, another demographic pattern emerged—black flight from central cities. The proportion of African-American population living in central cities gradually declined (Table 10.2). In 1999, the U.S. Census Bureau estimated that 55 percent of African Americans and 22 per-

Figure 10.1   **Central City Population Trends**

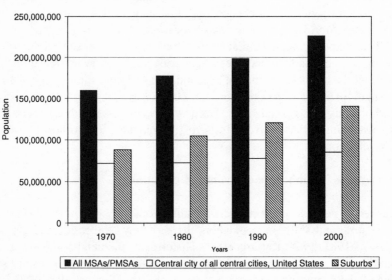

Central city population trends	1970	1980	1990	2000
All MSAs/PMSAs	159,978,725	177,568,121	198,422,153	225,981,477
Central city of all central cities, U.S.	71,804,778	72,679,639	77,770,594	85,343,968
Suburbs*	88,173,947	104,888,482	120,651,559	140,637,509
Percentage population change	1980–1970	1990–1980	2000–1990	2000–1970
All MSAs/PMSAs	11.0%	11.7%	13.9%	41.3%
Central city of all central cities, U.S.	1.2%	7.0%	9.7%	18.9%
Suburbs	19.0%	15.0%	16.6%	59.5%

Source: U.S. Department of Housing and Urban Development State of Cities Database socds.huduser.org/scripts/odbic.exe/Census/Census_Home.htm?
Notes: MSA = Metropolitan Statistical Area; PMSA = Primary Metropolitan Statistical Area.
*All MSAs/PMSAs minus central city of all central cities equals suburbs.

cent of non-Hispanic whites lived in U.S. central cities compared to 56 percent of African Americans and 26 percent of non-Hispanic whites in 1990.

As inner-city populations declined, the population base to support a diverse range of goods and services shrunk. As the data in Table 10.3 indicate, the structural shift in metropolitan economies weakened the ability of neighborhood residents themselves to generate wealth and capital to nur-

Table 10.1

U.S. Central City Population Trends

	1970	1980	1990	2000	2000–1970 (%)	1980–1970 (%)	1990–1980 (%)	2000–1990 (%)
All MSAs/PMSAs	159,978,725	177,568,121	198,422,153	225,981,477	41.3	11.0	11.7	13.9
Central city of all central cities	71,804,778	72,679,639	77,770,594	85,343,968	18.9	1.2	7.0	9.7
Suburbs*	88,173,947	104,888,482	120,651,559	140,637,509	59.5	19.0	15.0	16.6
Trends in metropolitan areas with declining population								
Boston, MA	3,225,828	3,143,108	3,227,707	3,406,829	5.6	-2.6	2.7	5.5
Central city	641,053	562,994	574,283	589,141	-8.1	-12.2	2.0	2.6
Suburbs	2,304,585	2,320,353	2,389,783	2,537,784	10.1	0.7	3.0	6.2
Buffalo, NY	1,349,211	1,242,826	1,189,288	1,170,111	-13.3	-7.9	-4.3	-1.6
Central city	462,783	357,870	328,123	292,648	-36.8	-22.7	-8.3	-10.8
Suburbs	800,813	813,572	799,325	821,870	2.6	1.6	-1.8	2.8
Chicago, IL	7,099,469	7,246,032	7,410,858	8,272,768	16.5	2.1	2.3	11.6
Central city	3,362,825	3,005,072	2,783,726	2,896,016	-13.9	-10.6	-7.4	4.0
Suburbs	3,367,973	3,872,334	4,230,569	4,883,879	45.0	15.0	9.3	15.4
Cincinnati, OH	1,439,857	1,467,664	1,526,092	1,646,395	14.3	1.9	4.0	7.9
Central city	452,550	385,457	364,040	331,285	-26.8	-14.8	-5.6	-9.0
Suburbs	987,307	1,082,207	1,162,052	1,315,110	33.2	9.6	7.4	13.2
Cleveland, OH	2,419,274	2,277,949	2,202,069	2,250,871	-7.0	-5.8	-3.3	2.2
Central city	751,046	573,822	505,616	478,403	-36.3	-23.6	-11.9	-5.4
Suburbs	1,536,080	1,571,173	1,568,462	1,647,863	7.3	2.3	-0.2	5.1

(continued)

Table 10.1 *(continued)*

	1970	1980	1990	2000	2000–1970 (%)	1980–1970 (%)	1990–1980 (%)	2000–1990 (%)
Detroit, MI	4,490,902	4,387,783	4,266,654	4,441,551	-1.1	1.2	4.1	4.1
Central city	1,511,336	1,203,339	1,027,974	951,270	-37.1	-20.9	-7.5	-7.5
Suburbs	2,754,261	2,983,088	3,044,534	3,293,831	19.6	10.4	8.2	8.2
Kansas City-MO-KS	1,383,197	1,449,374	1,582,875	1,776,062	28.4	22.5	12.2	12.2
Central city	507,242	448,159	435,146	441,545	-13.0	-1.5	1.5	1.5
Suburbs	664,986	769,214	896,115	1,059,269	59.3	37.7	18.2	18.2
Milwaukee-Waukesha, WI	1,403,688	1,397,143	1,432,149	1,500,741	6.9	7.4	4.8	4.8
Central city	717,124	636,212	628,088	596,974	-16.8	-6.2	-5.0	-5.0
Suburbs	646,327	710,612	747,103	838,942	29.8	18.1	12.3	12.3
Minneapolis-St. Paul, MN-WI	2,026,715	2,198,190	2,538,834	2,968,806	46.5	35.1	16.9	16.9
Central city	434,381	370,951	368,383	382,618	-11.9	3.1	3.9	3.9
Suburbs	1,282,394	1,557,009	1,898,216	2,299,037	79.3	47.7	21.1	21.1
New Orleans, LA	1,144,130	1,303,800	1,285,270	1,337,726	16.9	2.6	4.1	4.1
Central city	593,471	557,515	496,938	484,674	-18.3	-13.1	-2.5	-2.5
Suburbs	534,367	719,567	764,208	827,357	54.8	15.0	8.3	8.3
Norfolk-Virginia Beach-Newport News, VA-NC	1,056,027	1,200,998	1,443,244	1,569,541	48.6	30.7	8.8	8.8
Central city	307,951	266,979	261,229	234,403	-23.9	-12.2	-10.3	-10.3
Suburbs	196,193	252,102	329,060	419,052	113.6	66.2	27.3	27.3
Philadelphia, PA-NJ	4,878,260	4,781,494	4,922,175	5,100,931	4.6	6.7	3.6	3.6
Central city	1,948,609	1,688,210	1,585,577	1,517,550	-22.1	-10.1	-4.3	-4.3
Suburbs	2,827,100	3,008,374	3,249,106	3,503,477	23.9	16.5	7.8	7.8

Pittsburgh, PA	2,683,853	2,571,223	2,394,811	2,358,695	-12.1	-8.3	-1.5	-1.5
Central city	520,167	423,938	369,879	334,563	-35.7	-21.1	-9.5	-9.5
Suburbs	2,163,686	2,147,285	2,024,932	2,024,132	-6.4	-5.7	0.0	0.0
Rochester, NY	1,020,238	1,030,630	1,062,470	1,098,201	7.6	6.6	3.4	3.4
Central city	296,233	241,741	231,636	219,773	-25.8	-9.1	-5.1	-5.1
Suburbs	724,005	788,889	830,834	878,428	21.3	11.4	5.7	5.7
St. Louis MO	2,461,367	2,419,552	2,498,186	2,603,607	5.8	7.6	4.2	4.2
Central city	622,236	453,085	396,685	348,189	-44.0	-23.2	-12.2	-12.2
Suburbs	1,615,256	1,761,322	1,897,450	2,060,348	27.6	17.0	8.6	8.6
Washington, DC-MD-VA-WV	3,203,542	3,477,873	4,223,485	4,923,153	53.7	41.6	16.6	16.6
Central city	756,510	638,333	606,900	572,059	-24.4	-10.4	-5.7	-5.7
Suburbs	2,234,704	2,643,533	3,386,474	4,089,595	83.0	54.7	20.8	20.8
Baltimore, MD	2,089,092	2,199,531	2,382,172	2,552,994	22.2	16.1	7.2	7.2
Central city	905,759	786,775	736,014	651,154	-28.1	-17.2	-11.5	-11.5
Suburbs	1,153,741	1,381,016	1,612,971	1,866,002	61.7	35.1	15.7	15.7

Source: U.S. Department of Housing and Urban Development State of Cities Database socds.huduser.org/scripts/odbic.exe/Census/Census_Home.htm?

Note: MSA = Metropolitan Statistical Area; PMSA = Primary Metropolitan Statistical Area.

*All MSAs/PMSAs minus central city of all central cities equals suburbs.

Table 10.2

Central City African-American Population Trends, 1980–2000

	White, non-Hispanic			White		
	1980	1990	2000	1980 (%)	1990 (%)	2000 (%)
All MSAs	138,203,564	145,500,961	149,115,432	77.8	73.3	66.0
Central cities	47,373,290	46,371,162	43,826,201	65.2	59.6	51.4
Suburbs	90,830,274	99,129,799	105,289,231	86.6	82.2	74.9

	Black, non-Hispanic			Black		
	1980	1990	2000	1980 (%)	1990 (%)	2000 (%)
All MSAs	21,937,744	25,005,399	29,227,557	12.4	12.6	12.9
Central cities	15,536,971	16,655,699	17,988,454	21.4	21.4	21.1
Suburbs	6,400,733	8,349,700	11,239,700	6.1	6.9	8.0

Source: U.S. Department of Housing and Urban Development State of Cities Database socds.huduser.org/scripts/odbic.exe/Census/Census_Home.htm?.
Note: MSA = Metropolitan Statistical Area.

ture and sustain neighborhood businesses. Economic restructuring from a manufacturing to a service economy resulted in less wealth, as high-wage jobs traditionally held by inner-city African-American high school graduates disappeared (Kasarda 1989; Wilson 1987, 1996) and entry-level, low-wage, retail and service-sector jobs disappeared as inner-city stores closed.

Federal policies and structural racism have also contributed to the current, as well as historical, context of the widening metropolitan wealth disparities (Metzger 2000; Jackson 1985; Wilson 1996). The Federal Housing Administration policies of the 1930s and 1950s restricted home mortgages predominantly to newer suburban housing while refusing to insure mortgages on older, inner-city housing (Bradford 1979). This policy denied inner-city residents the benefits of home price appreciation and neighborhood wealth generation as older inner-city neighborhoods continued to experience population loss and disinvestment—concentrating racial minorities and less affluent households in neighborhoods peripheral to the community development efforts of that time. Further contributing to blight and disinvestment in urban areas was the federal funding of large-scale clearance projects (Fishman 2000).

Commercial lending practices also impeded neighborhood business redevelopment. Studies of commercial lending practices to small businesses have consistently found that African Americans are more likely than other ethnic

Table 10.3

Employed Residents by Occupation (all MSAs/PMSAs)

	1970			1980			1990		
	All MSAs	Central cities	Suburbs	All MSAs	Central cities	Suburbs	All MSAs	Central cities	Suburbs
Professional	9,244,610	4,178,135	5,066,475	12,683,000	5,272,511	7,410,489	17,625,715	6,857,853	10,767,862
Managerial	5,005,825	2,087,823	2,918,002	8,669,740	3,281,109	5,388,631	12,440,390	4,346,834	8,093,556
Sales	4,464,977	1,987,810	2,477,167	8,134,663	3,153,806	4,980,857	11,524,262	4,138,622	7,385,640
Administrative	11,301,406	5,644,805	5,656,601	14,440,705	6,147,112	8,293,593	16,105,027	6,226,055	9,878,972
Precision	7,968,479	3,146,996	4,821,483	9,806,160	3,425,394	6,380,766	10,257,641	3,335,966	6,921,675
Machine tools	7,423,456	3,270,629	4,152,827	6,789,546	2,716,856	4,072,690	5,728,587	2,207,816	3,520,771
Transportation	2,135,529	966,872	1,168,657	3,251,792	1,233,471	2,018,321	3,534,067	1,263,476	2,270,591
Material handler	2,421,364	1,143,360	1,278,004	3,330,226	1,390,994	1,939,232	3,486,663	1,360,892	2,125,771
Farming	830,002	78,147	751,855	1,287,696	265,832	1,021,864	1,514,184	377,680	1,136,504
Services	6,444,128	3,335,724	3,108,404	9,621,156	4,407,069	5,214,087	11,851,155	5,206,759	6,644,396
Private household	787,269	438,260	349,009	450,674	240,746	209,928	421,643	215,429	206,214
All occupations	58,027,045	26,278,561	31,748,484	78,465,358	31,534,900	46,930,458	94,489,334	35,537,382	58,951,952

	1980–1970			1990–1980		
Percentage change	All MSAs	Central cities	Suburbs	All MSAs	Central cities	Suburbs
Professional	37.2	26.2	46.3	39.0	30.1	45.3
Managerial	73.2	57.2	84.7	43.5	32.5	50.2
Sales	82.2	58.7	101.1	41.7	31.2	48.3
Administrative	27.8	8.9	46.6	11.5	1.3	19.1
Precision	23.1	8.8	32.3	4.6	−2.6	8.5
Machine tools	−8.5	−16.9	−1.9	−15.6	−18.7	−13.6
Transportation	52.3	27.6	72.7	8.7	2.4	12.5
Material handler	37.5	21.7	51.7	4.7	−2.2	9.6
Farming	55.1	240.2	35.9	17.6	42.1	11.2
Services	49.3	32.1	67.7	23.2	18.1	27.4
Private household	−42.8	−45.1	−39.9	−6.4	−10.5	−1.8
All occupations	35.2	20.0	47.8	20.4	12.7	25.6

Source: U.S. Department of Housing and Urban Development State of Cities Database http://socds.huduser.org/scripts/odbic.exe/Census/Census_Home.htm?

Table 10.4

Median Rent, Housing Value, and Income, by Geographic Area

Median household gross rent in 1999 dollars	1970	1980	1990
All MSAs/PMSAs	485	507	602
Central city of all central cities, U.S.	459	477	561
Suburbs*	537	552	656

Median household owner's value in 1999 dollars	1970	1980	1990
All MSAs/PMSAs	79,865	104,529	113,319
Central city of all central cities, U.S.	70,419	89,163	90,884
Suburbs*	85,876	113,830	124,026

Median family income in 1998 dollars	1969	1979	1989
All MSAs/PMSAs	45,422	47,133	49,447
Central city of all central cities, U.S.	42,247	41,659	42,217
Suburbs*	47,270	49,881	53,141

Source: U.S. Department of Housing and Urban Development State of Cities Database, socds.huduser.org/scripts/odbic.exe/Census/Census_Home.htm?.
Notes: MSA = Metropolitan Statistical Area; PMSA = Primary Metropolitan Statistical Area.
*HUD Household gross rent calculations exclude single-family units in 10 acres of land or more.

groups to have their business loans denied (Bates 1993; Ando 1988). Ando's study of commercial lending found a much lower acceptance rate for African Americans (72 percent) compared to other ethnic groups (Ando 1988). Bates (1993) expanded on the Ando study by examining the effect of neighborhood location on acceptance rate and found even more evidence of redlining based on whether the business was located in a minority neighborhood. According to Bates (1993), the black business community suffers from "an endless cycle of economic drain" (1993: 89).

As Table 10.4 indicates, the consequence of these trends was a decline in inner-city neighborhood capital accumulation through store closings and institutional disinvestment. Pockets of decline, however, coexist with pockets of new residential housing. It is not uncommon to find one or two houses in disrepair, abandoned houses, and unkempt vacant lots located adjacent to a new, inner-city development project or infill houses. In other words, many older central cities are not landscapes of total despair, but rather landscapes of "creeping blight." Ironically, it is the creeping blight process that presents an opportunity for neighborhood business revitalization.

Despite the deficits described above, urban policymakers and the business sector have begun to view inner-city neighborhoods in terms of their assets and potential for development and profit. Driving most of the current private-sector interest in inner-city neighborhood consumer markets is a perceived urban retail gap. The urban retail gap is the difference between the aggregate retail purchasing power of inner-city residents and the amount of potential revenue that can be captured by local retailers. Even though individual income levels are lower in U.S. inner cities, the aggregate purchasing power in most U.S. cities is considered to be high because of the higher population density of cities in comparison to sprawling suburbs. The U.S. Department of Housing and Urban Development estimates that the retail purchasing power in U.S. inner cities is approximately $331 billion. There is, however, substantial "outshopping" from these neighborhoods. This is, in part, because of the dearth of shopping opportunities (especially grocery stores) in these neighborhoods and the poor quality mix of inner-city retail establishments. Since needed goods and services are unavailable in inner-city areas, residents are forced to shop for these items in other areas. HUD estimated a retail gap in forty-eight inner-city areas, or, in their terms, new market areas, totaling approximately $8.7 billion. HUD calculated the retail gap using Claritas data and focused on what they defined as new market areas—census tracts in which median family income was 80 percent or less of the greater metropolitan area or census tracts in which the poverty rate was 20 percent or more. In the city of Chicago alone, HUD estimated the retail gap to be approximately $2.3 billion (HUD 1999a).

Private-Sector Tools for Neighborhood Business Development

Historically, public managers and analysts viewed business-lending programs as the cornerstone of an inner-city business development strategy (Bates and Fusfeld 1984). Loans were generally used for financing either long-term debt such as mortgages for commercial real estate purchases or short-term debt for construction, equipment purchases, and working capital. Conventional bank loans were not generally used for business-startup. Urban scholars contended that the lack of capital or access to capital (debt or equity) was the main impediment to business startup and growth (Ando 1988; Fratoe 1988). Two popular theories that define this condition and the underlying assumptions of current public-sector intervention are that: (1) the underwriting standards of mainstream lenders unduly penalize poorly collateralized entrepreneurs in the loan origination process, and (2) commercial lenders redline businesses choosing to locate in low-to-moderate income areas. While great strides have been made by the public and private sectors to increase opportunities for would-be entrepreneurs vis-à-vis increased enforcement of fair lending laws and growing grassroots participation in Community Rein-vestment Act activities, state and local government lending activities con-tinue to fuel many of the physical improvements and business startup activities in urban neighborhoods. Even with the growth of a formal public-sector role in financing neighborhood business development, most loan programs still only empower entrepreneurs through access to credit.

According to Nunn (2001), financial resources for inner-city businesses are just one of many tools needed to revitalize inner-city neighborhoods and foster neighborhood business redevelopment. Inner-city businesses need to marshal tools that will enable them to address the economic, political, and social conditions within their neighborhoods. Nunn concludes from his analy-sis that Porter's prescription ignores the realities of inner-city business con-ditions. In Indianapolis, the Retail Trade Association explained its unwillingness to locate in inner-city, low-income neighborhoods as a func-tion of higher operating costs. Or, as Nunn (2001), summarizes—their reluc-tance comes from too much "theft, labor problems associated with hiring and keeping reliable employees, general disorder, and unpredictable foot traf-fic into and out of stores, and different cultural practices in inner-city neigh-borhoods" (Nunn 2001: 170).

The shortcomings of lending programs and the applications of the Porter model suggest that future neighborhood business development initiatives will actually require higher levels of involvement from local government. Harrison and Glasmeier (1997) point out that Porter overlooks the supportive role the government plays in facilitating cluster development and networking. Often local public officials are the brokers, the financiers, and the facilitators in the early stages of a regional take-off: some examples include the Silicon Valley, the Silicon Forest (Willamette Valley in Oregon), and Austin, Texas, the re-search triangle. Most of these successes have come from visionary local of-ficials and citizens fighting against "the entrenched business interest to push a moribund local economy into a new trajectory" (Harrison and Glasmeier 1997: 31–32). This is even more evident in the case of the defense-led suc-cesses documented by Markusen, Hall, Campbell, and Deitrick (1991) in *The Rise of the Gunbelt.*

Collaborative Financing for Neighborhood
Business Redevelopment

How can the lessons of financing these regional successes be applied to fi-nancing neighborhood business development? Gittell and Thompson (1999) illustrate the success of this type of approach in their analysis of the Neigh-borhood Entrepreneur Program (NEP). NEP is a private-sector initiative that blends market incentives with community interests. It complements the private-sector activities with governmental activities such as rent subsidies and participation guidelines. It leverages local government agencies to provide neighborhood services, and it intermediates between the New York City Housing Partnership, low-income residents, the unemployed, and neighborhood residents (who are predominantly minority). NEP serves as the link for potential entrepreneurs and bank loans. In addition, NEP provides technical assistance for nurturing "niche" entrepreneurs by involving neighborhood residents in stabilizing distressed neighborhood housing projects. In sum, NEP illustrates that financing neighborhood business development in distressed neighborhoods involves not just the financing of a project, but a synergy among the financial tool, the neighborhood business, the private sector, the neighborhood, and an intermediate agent that serves as the bridge between neighborhood entrepreneurs and the broader community.

Another example of regional actors marshaling an array of resources for small business development is the Regional Alliance for Small Contractors. The Regional Alliance believes its role is to provide a confluence of services and relationships that serves to create a viable alternative to the "old-boy" network that has traditionally excluded Women/Minority Business Enterprise firms. To accomplish this objective, the Regional Alliance serves not only as a broker between small contractors and large construction projects, but leverages resources for small contractors. Its Financial Small Contractor program is a loan program for small contractors to prepare applications for loans and bonds. Its Managing Resources program offers professional training focused on practical applications to problems frequently encountered on construction projects. Its Loaned Executive Assistance program provides consulting service on construction and business management. And its opportunity marketplace acts as an informational clearinghouse for disseminating information that links small contractors to public development agencies and major construction firms regarding opportunities for large construction projects. Through this collaborative approach to business development, small contractors located in underserved neighborhoods gain not only access to finance and bonding, but access to expertise and resources from both public- and private-sector agencies.

While anecdotal, as rigorous research on these programs is limited, several neighborhood business development collaborative initiatives have produced noteworthy accomplishments. These programs share the distinctions of requiring a citizen driven/community context for proposed neighborhood redevelopment activities, and serving as an intermediary or bridge between entrepreneurs and service providers (lenders, government, technical assistance providers, regulatory bodies, etc.).

The following four case studies illustrate how collaborative financing strategies can be utilized to finance neighborhood business development strategies. We outline a statewide neighborhood business initiative for targeting neighborhood redevelopment (State of Maryland Neighborhood Business Development Program), a national intermediary program (LISC [Local Initiative Support Corporation] Neighborhood Main Street Initiative), a locality-based initiative (Nuestra Communidad Development Corporation), and a community-banking initiative (South Shore Bank).

Case 1

State of Maryland Neighborhood Business Development Program

Over the past five years, Maryland's Department of Housing and Community Development has invested nearly $30 million in Federal Community Development Block Grant funding in older distressed neighborhoods located throughout Maryland. Financing for this neighborhood initiative comes through the state's Neighborhood Business Development Program (NBDP) (Baynes 2001).

Maryland state officials and planners regard older distressed areas, known as "designated neighborhoods," as places in most need of social and physical revitalization, and, therefore, in most need of concentrated public-sector financial investment and planned intervention. In order for a neighborhood to qualify as a "designated neighborhood," it must first be a residential and commercially mixed area that is identified and declared eligible by the local government, and then approved by the secretary of the Department of Housing and Community Development. If the secretary reviews and approves the declaration, the neighborhood is placed on the state's "designated neighborhoods" list and is then eligible for funding. The state provides funding to for-profit and not-for-profit businesses locating or expanding in designated areas.

To date, nearly 75 percent of the $35 million in financial assistance has been used to assist for-profit enterprises locating or expanding in designated areas, and 25 percent of the funds have been used to assist not-for-profits. For-profits are able to access financial assistance in the form of loans, and not-for-profits, in the form of grants. Proposed projects must have at least three of the following characteristics in order to qualify for financial assistance:

• Plans for significant exterior improvements;
• Commitment to first floor commercial or retail space use that generates street-level activity;
• Plans for improvements to a vacant/underutilized building or site;

- Plans to bring currently unavailable or inadequate goods or services to the neighborhood; and
- Job creation.

In addition to NBDP investments, Maryland coordinates community and economic development programs that target the "designated areas." These activities include a pilot program that provides home-buying incentives for business owners and employees wishing to live near their workplace (Live Near Your Work Program) and specialized tax incentives that encourage public/private partnerships (Neighborhood Partnership Program) to support neighborhood-related activities that focus on such things as:

- Community services, including child care and recreational services;
- Redevelopment assistance supporting physical improvements to upgrade the area;
- Employment training and job placement services;
- Education and literacy training; and
- Community crime prevention (Baynes 2001).

The critical aspect of NBDP is its connections to the state of Maryland's Smart Growth initiative to stimulate investment in Maryland's older communities. The priority is to finance projects that strengthen neighborhood commercial districts and are part of a revitalization strategy. The state of Maryland actively reviews other state programs to coordinate ongoing efforts within the locally designated "neighborhood revitalization areas." NBDP aggressively promotes the use of its state community development block grants as a resource tool to leverage the use of state grants, loans, and tax credits to promote business development in neighborhood commercial districts.

Case 2

Neighborhood Main Street Initiative

The National Trust's National Main Street Center and Local Initiative Support Corporation established the Neighborhood Main Street Initiative (NMSI) in 1996 as a demonstration program to assist community development corporations (CDCs) to create and implement comprehensive business district revitalization strategies. Target business districts are located in Lansing, Michigan; Tacoma, Washington; Oakland, California; Richmond, Virginia; Philadelphia, Pennsylvania; and Providence, Rhode Island. NMSI provides technical assistance, workshops, and networking opportunities to program

Table 10.5

National Main Street Initiative Economic Development Summary

	Net new businesses	Net new jobs	New investments
1999	166	653	$21,454,442
2000	175	710	$26,772,882
Increase	9	57	$5,318,440
Percent increase	5.4	5.4	25

Source: LISC National Main Street Initiative (2001).
Note: Five-site assessment of LISC National Main Street Programs: Tacoma, WA; Providence, RI; Lansing, MI; Oakland, CA; and Philadelphia, PA.

participants to assist their efforts to revitalize neighborhood commercial districts that are considered visible, results-oriented, inclusive of neighborhood stakeholders, and comprehensive. Some short-term goals for neighborhood programs may involve façade improvement, coordinated event marketing, and public and streetscape improvements. Some long-term activities may involve market analysis, and business attraction and retention initiatives. As Table 10.5 indicates, between 1999 and 2000, NMSI leveraged over $26 million to finance new investment in target communities, created 175 businesses, and created approximately 710 new jobs (Marketek 2001a). The resultant financial investments in neighborhoods are not made by NMSI but by other entities (public and private). An example of NMSI collaboration is Fruitvale in Oakland, California. According to LISC:

> Fruitvale consists of mostly low- to moderate-income families with a large proportion of residents living below the poverty line. Nearly 1/5 of residents lack basic English skills. The housing stock is in poor condition and overcrowding is common. Of the neighborhood's 53,000 residents, over half are Latino, and over a quarter are Asian American, with significant African American and Native American populations (LISC). (Marketek 2001b)

NMSI activities in Fruitvale focused on promotions, neighborhood crime prevention, tax and loan workshops, façade improvements, and market analysis studies. LISC reports that Fruitvale has attracted over $4 million in public and private funds, improved over 100 building façades, and facilitated 36 business startups.

Initial financing for NMSI projects came from Pew Charitable Trust and Key Bank. Although the demonstration program ended on April 30, 2000, LISC and NMSC have continued to collaborate on the project and have added additional sites to NMSI. These additional sites, known as expansion sites, are eligible to receive an array of services:

- Program assessments;
- Work plan development;
- Visioning workshops; and
- Introduction to event marketing and market analysis.

Members may also attend group-training sessions and participate in other networking opportunities. The program now has a network of twenty-eight sites and focuses program activities on four primary areas: design, organization, economic restructuring, and marketing promotion (Marketek 2001b).

As an intermediary, LISC is a broker between the neighborhood-initiated main street project and private financiers. The local neighborhood stakeholders are the ones that bring the results-oriented vision for transforming their neighborhood business district. LISC simply acts as an intermediary agent that brokers relations, provides technical assistance, and connects with funding agencies.

Case 3

Nuestra Communidad Development Corporation

Nuestra Communidad Development Corporation (NCDC) is a grassroots Community Development Corporation founded by residents of Boston's Dudley neighborhood. The CDC was established to assist residents to reclaim their community by controlling land acquisition and housing development, and to leverage community resources—financial, technical, political, human, and physical—in order to make the Dudley neighborhood more livable. The Nuestra Communidad CDC deploys several programs ranging from real estate and business development to community organizing to support its neighborhood and community development activities (Nuestra Communidad 2001).

While community organizing and real estate development are major thrusts of Nuestra, the agency has implemented several collaborative economic development initiatives to increase employment opportunities for low-to-moderate-income neighborhood residents. These initiatives include the Neighborhood Business Development Center, Village Pushcarts Program, and Kitchen Incubator Initiative.

Neighborhood Business Development Center

Nuestra operates the Neighborhood Business Development Center (NBDC) in partnership with several local housing and community development corporations, including Codman Square Neighborhood Development Corporation, Quincy-Geneva Housing Corporation, Urban Edge Housing Corporation, Dorchester Center for Adult Education, Tent City Corporation, and Roslindale Board of Trade. The primary activities of NBDC are to provide hands-on technical assistance to entrepreneurs needing business startup and planning assistance, loan packaging assistance, skills training, and networking. Partnering agencies provide many of the NBDC's entrepreneurial assistance services. NBDC activities are focused toward the Roxbury, Dorchester, Mattapan, the South End, and Roslindale sections of Boston. Between 1992 and 2001, NBDC secured $4,182,288 in funding for a total of sixty-seven loans with an average loan size of $62,422. Over 88 percent of the businesses were women and minority owned with an average of 4.7 jobs per establishment. The program has had a 0.11 percent default rate. NBDC provides business loan packaging services for various financial institutions, including banks, Boston Local Development Corporation, CDC Tax Credit, and the JVS-SBA Micro Loan Program.

Village Pushcarts

Nuestra's Village Pushcarts Program, a microenterprise initiative, is designed to teach entrepreneurial skills to low-to-moderate-income residents of Roxbury and Dorchester. Residents are assisted to engage in small-scale retailing via pushcarts in the Dudley Square MBTA Bus Station, the Boston Common, and Downtown Crossing location. The goal of this nine-month program (April to December) is to teach low-income, low-skilled, inner-city residents the necessary skills to allow them to obtain high-paying skilled positions in retail management and/or to start a small retail business. No prior experience is required to participate in this training program. Residents pay a monthly fee of $200 to $700 to rent Village Pushcarts. Rents vary by location. For this fee, residents receive liability insurance, nearby storage space, comprehensive one-on-one technical assistance, entrepreneurial training, small business loans and grants, marketing assistance, and a highly visible demand location for business operation. Since 1998, the program has assisted thirty-four entrepreneurs using only nineteen pushcarts.

Kitchen Incubator Initiative

The Kitchen Incubator Initiative evolved from the Village Pushcarts program, as low-income entrepreneurs, interested in selling food on their carts, needed certified kitchen space and storage space for food and carts. The Kitchen Incubator, located in Jamaica Plain at the Brewery Development Corporation, the Old Samuel Adam's Brewery, is expected to provide commercial kitchen space for entrepreneurs interested in the food business whether it is catering, bodega ownership, or restaurants. Entrepreneurs can use the space to prepare salable food. Program operators anticipate that the Kitchen Incubator will create up to forty jobs per year in low-income areas (Nuestra Communidad 2001). The program was just launched in 2001.

Driving NCDC's mission is a commitment to a community-driven process to promote self-sufficiency and neighborhood revitalization. Key to NCDC's success is the emergence of local neighborhood stakeholders with a vision for revitalizing their neighborhood business district and a desire to collaborate with local businesses and other community-based organizations. A key aspect of every project is an emphasis on training, cooperative work, mobilizing and leveraging resources from a broad array of institutions (local banks, the Massachusetts State Department of Housing and Community Development, Metropolitan Boston Housing Partnership, local banks, and Community Development Block Grants).

Case 4

South Shore Bank (Shorebank Corporation)

Shorebank Corporation was established in 1973 to revitalize the South Shore neighborhood of Chicago. South Shore grew out of the response of federal regulators not giving permission to the bank to pull out of the neighborhood. South Shore Bank was subsequently purchased with capital from charities and investors who simply desired to do good (Grzywinski 1991).

Initially, the program focused on generating community wealth by attracting retail and service businesses to 71st Street in Chicago. The rationale was straightforward: "resident demand for local jobs and local wealth creation opportunities must be met. Residential communities will require local jobs to maintain the fabric and amenities of their communities" (Houghton 1995: 3). The underlying premise for this initiative is that the best strategy combines a social mission with the hard discipline of business.

Shorebank's major innovation was to reverse the direction of the outflow of human and financial capital from a distressed neighborhood. Prior to opening the South Shore Bank of Chicago, most South Shore residents made deposits in financial institutions located in Chicago's loop. The neighborhood itself provided the foundation for future success with its solid working-class base and a cadre of residents committed to turning it around.

Shorebank formed several subsidiaries to move its projects forward. City Lands was formed to invest in real estate projects. The Neighborhood Institute was formed to help find government grants for rehabilitation projects. The strategy was to find one of the biggest eyesores on a block, put together a financial package to reverse the decline, turn it around to make the street look better, and thus encourage others to fix the smaller buildings with loans from Shorebank.

Shorebank's initial success came from knowing to whom to loan and knowing what the neighborhood needed. From the beginning, South Shore Bank profiled and monitored the residents. The bank managed to make home mortgage and business loans to clients when no one else would. In addition, Shorebank staff met with neighborhood residents and landlords to determine what retail and services the neighborhood needed. Its current subsidiaries include:

- Shorebank Neighborhood Initiation: job training and placement services, entrepreneurship development, wealth creation, and youth development.
- Shorebank Development Corporation: property management and affordable and mixed-income development projects in Shorebank's target neighborhoods.
- Shorebank Advisory Services: consulting services on community development finance issues.
- Neighborhood Market Intelligence: new proprietary market intelligence products for businesses that need assistance in understanding and finding market opportunities in underserved communities. It provides businesses with accurate neighborhood information, business criteria for making neighborhood comparisons, and business models for site selection and marketing (Shorebank Corporation 2001).

Findings

Each of the above initiatives illustrates how the collective ability of localities can transcend current paradigms about inner cities and community economic development systems. Whereas initiatives that focus their funding on business creation, retention, or expansion fail to systematically transform neighborhoods and empower people, the case studies reviewed illustrate the degree to which different program missions, designs, and services created to revitalize inner-city businesses require comprehensive, community-driven strategies.

The specific development tools varied substantially:

- Financing startup and expanding retail, service, and manufacturing businesses;

- Developing mixed-use facilities, consisting of street-level commercial space with accompanying residential housing;
- Funding community services, including literacy, job training, mental health services, childcare, crime prevention, and recreation;
- Supporting physical improvements to upgrade areas;
- Organizing the community;
- Enforcing code;
- Providing commercial and industrial technical assistance;
- Providing design review committees;
- Providing joint marketing efforts area promotion; and
- Providing strategic visioning.

Nevertheless, our case studies reveal that, even though neighborhood business initiatives differ, they share common elements that contributed to their success: (1) multifaceted orientation (offering a range of programs and services); (2) locality-based assets orientation; (3) results-driven orientation (setting benchmarks and monitoring, documenting, and evaluating outcomes in terms of benchmarks); and (4) collaboration between neighborhood visionaries, community-based organizations, governmental agencies, private-sector financial institutions, and intermediaries. Each program evolved from the recognition that the neighborhood stakeholders know best their strengths and assets. Intermediary agents brokered connections to financial resources and leveraged resources for technical assistance, training, and physical revitalization and façade improvements.

In the case of the Maryland initiative, the initiative itself was the intermediary agent for leveraging neighborhood commercial district revitalization. The LISC Neighborhood Main Street Initiative illustrates how a national intermediary can serve as a broker for leveraging financial and technical assistance resources for locally driven neighborhood initiatives. Nuestra Communidad Community Development Corporation serves as an example of how neighborhood residents themselves can leverage and mobilize financial resources for neighborhood business development. The South Shore Bank provides an example of how a private-sector institution can reverse the outflow of capital from a distressed neighborhood and provide the financial infrastructure for neighborhood residents to revitalize their neighborhood.

The lessons learned from each of these experiences are the importance of collaboration, the presence of "brokers," and the community-driven process. Collaborative processes ensure that communities leverage the greatest amount of available resources for long-term neighborhood revitalization. Measurable impacts of these initiatives are still predominantly anecdotal. Continued research into bridge building and community collaboration is vital to inform and guide the financing of neighborhood business practice and add to the knowledge and insight about cultural, social, and political variation in financial strategies for neighborhood business redevelopment.

References

Ando, Faith. 1988. "Capital Issues and the Minority-Owned Business." *Review of Black Political Economy* 17 (Spring): 77–109.

Bates, Timothy. 1997. "Response: Michael Porter's Conservative Urban Agenda Will Not Revitalize America's Inner Cities: What Will?" *Economic Development Quarterly* 11, no. 1: 39–44.

———. 1993. *Banking Black Enterprise.* Washington: Joint Center for Political and Economic Studies.

Bates, Timothy M., and Daniel R. Fusfeld. 1984. *The Political Economy of the Urban Ghetto.* Carbondale: Southern Illinois University Press.

Baynes, Kevin. 2001. State of Maryland Housing and Community Development, Interview with authors, August.

Boston, Thomas D., and Catherine Ross. 1997. *The Inner City: Urban Poverty and Economic Development in the Next Century.* New Brunswick: Transaction.

Bradford, Calvin. 1979. "Financing Home Ownership: The Federal Role in Neighborhood Decline." *Urban Affairs Quarterly* 14, no. 3: 313–35.

Downs, Anthony. 1981. *Neighborhoods and Urban Development.* Washington, DC: Brookings Institution.

———. 1994. *New Visions for Metropolitan America.* Washington, DC, and Cambridge, MA: Brookings Institution and Lincoln Institute of Land Policy.

Federal Housing Administration. 1936. *Underwriting Manual; Underwriting and Valuation Procedure Under Title II of the National Housing Act.* Washington, DC: U.S. Government Printing Office.

Fishman, Robert. 2000. "The American Metropolis at Century's End: Past and Future Influences." *Housing Policy Debate* 11, no. 1: 199–214.

Fratoe, Frank. 1988. "Social Capital of Black Business Owners." *Review of Black Political Economy* 17 (Spring): 33–50.

Gittell, Ross, and J. Phillip Thompson. 1999. "Inner-city Business Development and Entrepreneurship: New Frontiers for Policy and Research." In *Urban Problems and Community Development,* ed. Ronald Ferguson and William Dickens, 473–520. Washington, DC: Brookings Institution.

Grzywinski, Ronald. 1991. "The New Old-Fashioned Banking." *Harvard Business Review* (May–June): 87–98.

Harrison, Bennett, and Amy Glasmeier. 1997. "Response: Why Business Alone Won't Redevelop the Inner City: A·Friendly Critique of Michael Porter's Approach to Urban Revitalization." *Economic Development Quarterly* 11, no. 1: 28–38.

Houghton, Mary. 1995. "Lessons About Economic Development Interventions." Paper presented at Association of Collegiate Schools of Planning annual meeting, Detroit, Michigan (October).

Jacobs, Jane. 1961. *The Death and Life of Great American Cities.* New York: Random House.

Jackson, Kenneth T. 1985. *Crabgrass Frontier: The Suburbanization of the United States.* New York: Oxford University Press.

Kasarda, John. 1989. "Urban Industrial Transition and the Urban Underclass." *Annals of the American Academy of Sciences* 501 (January): 26–47.

———. 1993. "Inner-City Concentrated Poverty and Neighborhood Distress: 1970 to 1990." *Housing Policy Debate* 4, no. 3: 253–302.

Marketek Inc. 2001a. Economic Impact Assessment of National Main Street Initiative. New York: Local Initiative Support Corporation (LISC). Unpublished documents.

———. 2001b. Program Impact Assessment of National Main Street Initiative. New York: Local Initiative Support Corporation (LISC). Unpublished documents.

Markusen, Ann; Peter Hall; Scott Campbell; and Sabina Deitrick. 1991. *The Rise of the Gunbelt: The Military Remapping of Industrial America.* London: Oxford Press.

Metzger, John. 2000. "Planned Abandonment: The Neighborhood Life-Cycle Theory and National Urban Policy." *Housing Policy Debate* 11, no. 1: 7–40.

Neustra Communidad Development Corporation. 2001. Program Brochure and Description. Boston: Author Unpublished Documents.

Nunn, Samuel. 2001. "Planning for Inner-city Retail Development: The Case of Indianapolis." *Journal of the American Planning Association* 67, no. 2: 159–72.

Porter, Michael. 1995. "The Competitive Advantage of the Inner City." *Harvard Business Review* 73 (May–June): 55–71.

Regional Alliance of Small Contractors. 2002. "The Regional Alliance of Small Contractors: Building Tomorrow's Partnership Today." www.regional-alliance.org (January 28, 2002).

Shorebank Corporation. 2001. "Shorebank Corporation About Shorebank." www.shorebankcorp.com/main/history.cfm (September 17, 2001).

HUD (U.S. Department of Housing and Urban Development). 1999a. *New Markets: The Untapped Retail Buying Power in America's Inner Cities.* Washington, DC: Office of Policy Development and Research.

———. 1999b. *Now is the Time: Places Left Behind in the New Economy.* Washington, DC: Office of Policy Development and Research.

Wilson, William J. 1996. *When Work Disappears: The World of the New Urban Poor.* New York: Knopf.

———. 1987. *The Truly Disadvantaged: The Inner City, the Underclass, and Public Policy.* Chicago: University of Chicago Press.

Part 4

Special Situations

11

Urban Tourism and Financing Professional Sports Facilities

Ziona Austrian and Mark S. Rosentraub

Introduction

Virtually every community or region with at least 300,000 residents has entertained proposals for the development of a facility to be used by a professional sports team. Although some ballparks used by minor league or lower division baseball teams involve relatively modest investments, the premier facilities in North America's largest cities have cost in excess of $400 million. Moreover, in several regions, the public and private sectors have combined to invest more than $1 billion in professional sports facilities.

While the past decade saw a number of new facilities built, those communities that were not part of this initial boom period now find themselves evaluating planned stadiums or arenas. The building frenzy began with Oriole Park at Camden Yards in 1992. The city of Baltimore, seeking another jewel for a downtown revitalization program emphasizing tourism and entertainment, built the first of a wave of "retro" parks, designed to evoke memories of facilities that existed in the 1940s and 1950s while at the same time replete with the latest amenities that generate substantial levels of revenues. These revenues promised new wealth for team owners and players, if taxpayers paid part or all of the costs for the facility.

Baltimore was not the first, or the last, city to focus on sports facilities for economic development and revitalization. Today, "retro" facilities are a staple of the downtown development and regeneration programs of dozens of cities. In all of these plans the sports facility is seen as essential for enhancing a community's identity, linking various elements in a tourism or entertainment economic development policy, and attracting new jobs through an enhanced quality of life (Austrian and Rosentraub 1997).

The proposal for development of a new ballpark, stadium, or arena in a downtown area should be received with extraordinary anticipation. Projects of this nature bring construction jobs to a community, and the vast majority of the new facilities have added to the luster and skylines of most North American cities. However, the enthusiasm generated is frequently diminished by debates concerning the financing for the facility. Virtually every proposal for a new facility across the past two decades has been described as a public/private partnership, in which each sector is responsible for a share of the building's costs but teams retain all or most of the income. The division between a city and the team of a facility's cost and the produced income streams is the core element of each public/private partnership. Every community must evaluate the appropriate level of investment relative to the public and private benefits produced by a team's presence. Developing a framework for understanding the financial instruments actually used and those that would be appropriate requires a review of the issues and pressures that shape the possible and politically realistic financing options.

To develop this framework and help economic development leaders evaluate the different factors that shape a financing plan, this chapter is divided into four sections. Following this introduction, the second section focuses on the issues that define the framework for any financing program for a professional sports facility. The third section reviews the financing tools actually used by cities for the facilities built during the past decade, and the fourth and final section presents our conclusions.

Factors Influencing Financing Plans for Sports Facilities

There are five factors that shape the division of responsibilities for financing a sports facility. The first of these, an assessment of the private and public benefits produced by a team's presence, will vary from community to community. Others, such as the structure of the sports business world (do professional sports operate in competitive or regulated markets?), the status of sports in society, the differences among sports facilities, and the team owners and their goals, cannot be controlled by local communities but define critical elements of the negotiation process (Rosentraub and Swindell 2002).

The Private and Public Benefits from Professional Sports Teams

At first glance it would appear that the entertainment or benefits provided by professional sports teams should be considered as classic private goods with consumers expected to pay the full cost for the benefits they enjoy. The owners of teams can easily exclude those who are unwilling to pay, so that only those purchasing tickets (or listening to advertisements) enjoy the entertainment. Under this model, a professional sports team is seen as no different from any other form of entertainment where it is easy to exclude nonpayers.

Team owners would be expected to charge an appropriate price for seats (and broadcast rights) and realize a sufficient return to pay labor, build the needed ballpark, and earn a profit. If professional sports provides private goods, there is no need for public financing other than the provision of infrastructure (transportation, water, safety, etc.) that supports all forms of development.

While there is no debate about the conclusion that professional sports teams produce private benefits, proponents of public participation in the financing of sports facilities point to three different sets of potential externalities (or public consumption benefits) that would make professional sports a good or service deserving taxpayer support. *First*, relative to economic development, several constituencies have argued that new facilities attract investment in related businesses, provide an amenity that retains businesses and attracts other firms, and help revitalize downtown areas. *Second*, teams generate intangible benefits that accrue to both users (fans attending games) and nonusers or the residents of a community, including the excitement created by teams and the luster added to a city's reputation by a team's presence. In societies that place a high value on sports, hosting a team or winning a championship game generates substantial levels of interest, excitement, and prestige. *Third*, sport teams unify the region's fans. Supporting sports teams provides a common denominator among people of different ages, race, income levels, and ethnic backgrounds. Some of these assertions are valid.

For decades sports teams in North America thrived playing in privately financed facilities. The basic premise was that professional sports teams generate substantial benefits for consumers, and team owners could easily administer a fee for the benefits received and sell the right to broadcast descriptions and images of a game or event. Later, when different cities decided to build ballparks, stadiums, or arenas, teams were charged rent. The public sector's role in financing of facilities in an effort to attract or retain teams and to foster economic development, civic pride, or an enhanced image is a phenomenon of the past fifty years.

However, in terms of the economic benefits from a team's presence, there is an extensive and growing body of empirical work indicating that facilities and teams are not associated with regional economic development and growth (Rosentraub et. al. 1994; Baade 1996; Noll and Zimbalist 1997; Rosentraub 1997; Rosentraub 1999; Humphreys 2001; Rappaport and Wilkerson 2001). These studies confirm that there is no positive externality or public goods benefit for redevelopment emanating from sports facilities or teams. Consequently, public investments to revitalize an area cannot be justified in terms of anticipated regional growth.

This does not mean that there are no externalities generated by a team's presence. Teams, facilities, and events add to the quality of life in a community. In addition, teams enhance the image of a community in the minds of residents and increase the pride people have in their communities. These benefits exist even for those residents who do not attend sporting events or who do not describe themselves as fans (Swindell and Rosentraub 1998). In a society where sports are an essential, if not defining, element of contemporary culture, the presence of a team does create a benefit or status that is valued by people. This value will vary from community to community. For example, Los Angeles, secure in its identity and place in the world's economy chose not to provide the public support necessary to attract a National Football League team. In contrast, Nashville and St. Louis provided extraordinary subsidies to ensure their city would have a team. These differences in the proportion of costs a community was willing to accept for building a stadium is a measure of the value of the intangible benefits. Hamilton and Kahn succinctly stated this case in their analysis of the subsidy provided for the building of Oriole Park at Camden Yards:

> . . . the state and its subdivisions lose approximately $9 million a year on (Oriole Park at) Camden Yards. This is approximately $12 per Baltimore household per year; the public subsidy to the stadium is justified only if the public consumption benefits of the Orioles are at least this large. (Hamilton and Kahn 1997: 274)

Relative to the issue of civic pride and the excitement generated by a team's presence, Jacobs Field and Gund Arena in Cleveland, built in 1994, now attract more than 4 million people to a part of the downtown area avoided for years. As a result,

> Downtown Cleveland is a far more-lively place today than it was five years ago. There is a contagious vitality and excitement that should not be discounted or ignored. . . . Will this new recreational nexus create a great many jobs? No. Will the sports facilities encourage a substantial or significant change in development patterns? No. Is downtown Cleveland a more exciting place? Is there a greater sense of excitement and civic pride? Are people who long ago gave up on downtown returning for recreation? The answer to each of these questions is yes. . . . Are these benefits or returns worth the hundreds of millions of dollars spent by taxpayers to subsidize sports? . . . The investment in sports amounts to less than $10 per person per year. . . . Did Cleveland and Cuyahoga County get good or adequate value for their investment? In a city with a full set of urban challenges, is the new image created by these public investments worth the commitments if there is no direct economic impact? . . . Those

are questions only the residents of Cleveland and Cuyahoga County should answer. (Rosentraub 1996: 26–27)

The recognition that positive externalities or public consumption benefits are produced by teams does not lead to the immediate conclusion that broad-based taxing instruments or other forms of public support should be used to pay for sports facilities. As important as the presence of public consumption benefits from sports is the distribution of these externalities. Communities must be careful to assess who enjoys the public consumption benefits from sports. If these benefits are unevenly distributed and concentrated only among the fans who attend games or higher income individuals, then the use of broad-based taxes to support a sports facility is inappropriate. For example, if fans attending games also report the highest levels of enjoyment of public consumption benefits, then increasing ticket prices or user fees would be the appropriate way to finance the facility required to ensure the presence of the benefits. Similarly, if higher income households report enjoying more of a team's externalities, then a taxing or finance instrument that assesses the costs of financing a facility against these households is warranted. Regardless of the distributional issues, however, what this discussion discloses is that it is appropriate for the public sector to make an investment in a sport's facility in terms of the externalities generated. The appropriate amount to be supported by public investment depends on two factors: the proportions of the benefits that are private and those classified as public consumption and the distribution of public consumption benefits. This assessment must be made community by community and will vary, leading to different partnerships.

Do Professional Sports Operate in Competitive or Protected Markets?

Even if teams generate substantial levels of intangible benefits that warrant public sector investments in facilities, if teams are provided with market protections to reflect these benefits, then communities may not be required to provide additional incentives. Team owners and league officials describe the market in which they operate as highly competitive, seeking to attract consumers who could attend other entertainment or recreational events. Teams must play well and attract and retain popular, skillful, and entertaining athletes capable of winning games, or else fans/consumers will spend their disposable income on other entertainment options. If teams exist in a very competitive market, then taxpayer support for the positive externalities produced is appropriate. However, there is evidence that the leagues created by team owners are cartels that control the supply and distribution of teams.

The four major sports leagues in North America (Major League Baseball, the National Basketball Association, the National Football League, and the National Hockey League) have unfettered control over the supply and location of teams. Market forces, defined as the demand for teams in a particular sport, do not determine how many teams or franchises will exist or how many teams can play in a particular market area. Piraino describes professional sports as

> one of the last refuges of unchallenged monopoly power in America. Most monopolies have been forbidden by regulation or judicial decree from abusing their market power. However, Major League Baseball, the National Football League, the National Basketball League, and the National Hockey League each have been able to acquire, maintain, and exercise their monopoly power with little judicial or regulatory oversight. . . . The owners have successfully conspired to keep the number of franchises substantially below that which would exist in a free market. (Piraino 1996: 1677–78)

The most recent example of the leagues' monopoly power involves baseball and northern Virginia. The residents of northern Virginia have expressed considerable interest in hosting a Major League Baseball team, and information provided to Major League Baseball even indicates that there would be substantial financial support from area businesses for the team (Rofe 2001). Despite this interest, there is no plan to expand or to place a team in the area for at least two years. There are also other communities that want teams, and they too have to wait until Major League Baseball agrees to expand (Leonhardt 2001).

Control over the supply of teams has led to a system where communities that want teams are forced to pay subsidies or higher prices to secure the needed good. Since the early 1950s, taxpayers and fans have been paying premiums to attract teams; these extra charges or fees represent the higher cost of hosting a team that would likely be absent or reduced if sports were forced to operate in a truly open and competitive market. As the nation's population and wealth have increased, more cities could successfully host a team. With more cities pursuing teams, leagues realized that if they artificially constrained the supply of teams such that there were always more cities than franchises, those communities that wanted a team would offer extraordinary subsidies in the form of accepting larger responsibilities for the cost of building and maintaining ballparks, arenas, and stadiums. These amounts exceed the value of public consumption benefits that would exist in a completely open market for the supply of teams.

A series of court decisions and congressional acts have protected the leagues in their control over the supply of teams (Rosentraub 1999). With so many cities desiring teams, and the leagues slowing expansion of the number of available franchises, the size of inducements offered to secure teams has rapidly increased. In several instances a community paid the entire cost of a new facility and then permitted teams to retain all of the generated revenues, thus increasing the profitability of any team.

The Status of Sports in Society

Are teams and sports just another form of recreation competing for consumer attention, or do particular sports, and team sports in general, occupy positions of value in society that make them unique without any realistic substitute? When team owners and league officials point to the excitement created for a community as a result of a winning team or a championship, they implicitly acknowledge that sports generate something quite different from other forms of recreation. For example, while communitywide celebrations and parades are frequently held when a team wins a championship, such public displays or outbursts are absent from other forms of entertainment. There is also a pronounced tie between sports and politics that is absent from other forms of entertainment. Before every team game in the United States, the national anthem is played. This rarely occurs before a concert or movie. Beyond these simple examples, there are several studies that highlight the importance of sports for societies (Michener 1976; Wilson 1994; Rosentraub 1997). Sporting events have also been repeatedly incorporated into political messages. National leaders regularly appear at championship games, and greeting champions is also part of the political ritual associated with sports. Hence, a baseball, football, or basketball team can be considered a substitute for another form of recreation only if one chooses to ignore the political value of being at the center of celebrations and events that attract the political and social attention of a society.

If sports are an integral aspect of societies, as many have claimed, then there are concerns when control over this important resource is placed in the hands of small groups of entrepreneurs. If sports are a defining element for a society, it is reasonable to consider a role for the public sector in terms of determining the supply of teams. In addition, if it is decided that the private sector should have unilateral control of an asset that is of extreme value to society, should the public sector be able to regulate the price that is charged in exchange for this control?

If so, then it might be possible to use a public utility framework to look at the issue of financing the facilities used by professional sports teams.

For example, suppose an effective rate of return for a business with the market protections afforded the four major sports leagues was found to be 10 percent or 15 percent. After analyzing expenditures for player salaries and other expenses, regulatory agencies using business and accounting firms from the private sector could analyze the capability of teams to reach established profit levels while still paying for the cost of a ballpark, arena, or stadium. If there was insufficient revenue to field a competitive team, earn an acceptable profit rate, meet other costs, and build a facility, then a recommendation for a subsidy could be made and approved. Such a procedure would eliminate the very high returns some owners have realized on their investments after receiving a subsidy (Rosentraub 1999) and build considerable support for the public provision of resources to build facilities. However, when reports of excessive profit levels abound (Office of the Controller, City of Philadelphia 2000), it is difficult to maintain extensive public support for the use of tax dollars to build a sports facility.

Facility Types: Ballparks, Stadiums, and Arenas

Financing plans also vary by the type of facility developed; arenas can host more events and thus have more revenue potential than a football stadium or a ballpark. Another issue that has perplexed voters is why communities cannot continue to build just one facility for baseball and football teams, as they do for hockey and basketball teams.

Relative to the issue of one facility for a football and baseball team—a popular strategy in the 1960s and 1970s—it is important to realize that the space within which most of the action takes places in football and baseball is quite different. The majority of the action in baseball occurs within the infield diamond; hence, most fans want to sit surrounding that area. In football the action takes place across an area that is more than 100 yards in length. As a result, seating should be constructed in a much different pattern, requiring a differently shaped facility. For football, it is possible to build a facility seating 70,000 fans and provide each fan with a good view of the field. For baseball, it is not possible or desirable to squeeze that many fans into the space over which most of the action takes place. As a result, the most successful baseball facilities typically have seats for fewer than 45,000 fans. Sports entrepreneurs have learned that people will pay higher prices for seats that have excellent views of the action on the field. As a result, smaller baseball facilities have resulted in higher revenue levels for teams.

The arenas used for basketball and hockey games have the greatest number of opportunities to earn revenue, since they can be the location for numerous events. While smaller in scale, approximately 20,000 seats, arenas can host concerts, shows, conventions, and a variety of sporting events (e.g., arena football, tennis, boxing, wrestling). As a result, the most successful arenas can host upward of 200 different events in a year, and while the seating capacity is far less than that of a ballpark or stadium, arenas cost less to build and can become very profitable venues. The ability of these facilities to earn revenues from other entertainment events also means there are other financing options available to help pay for the facility. It is possible to host events at baseball and football facilities, but the fear of damaging the playing surface often means that events cannot be held during the season. As a result, one still finds very few events held at ballparks or football stadiums.

Owners and Their Goals

The last factor that needs to be considered in terms of understanding the financing plans that emerge are the goals and objectives of individual owners. Sloan (1971) was among the first students of the economics of sports to argue that owners, unlike other business entrepreneurs, could have both pecuniary and nonpecuniary objectives. While it is clear that some owners seek to maximize their profits from a team, those with other sources of wealth may be willing to spend more of the income generated by a team for players and needed facilities. Some owners could also be described as more "public regarding" and consider their ownership of a team to be an obligation and commitment as one might make for any form of arts, culture, and entertainment in a region (Kennedy and Rosentraub 2000). Finally, some owners are able to utilize their team to complement sales from other businesses. For decades, the St. Louis Cardinals were used to establish and enhance the market position of Anheuser-Busch and its breweries. Ted Turner was able to use the Atlanta Braves to help build his successful media business. These owners may also be willing to pay a larger share of the cost of a facility as the profits they earn from other businesses depend on a successful image from their sports teams.

Financing Tools

The financing tools available to the public sector to support a sports facility include broad-based or general taxes, specific consumption taxes, user fees, tax increments, sports taxes, tourist taxes, and lottery or gaming revenues. The selection of the instrument used to finance the bonds negotiated is tied to the framework adopted (as described above) and the political environment in the community that is considering a new facility. Some taxing instruments are more politically acceptable than others. Bonds are always negotiated, but each community needs to decide on the best revenue instruments to be used to collect the revenues needed to meet the annual bond payments.

General or Broad-based Taxes

There are two basic sets of commitments that the public sector can make to retire bonds. A specific tax can be identified, or the public sector can add the annual payments required to retire a bond to all other obligations it has to fund. When a government pledges its full faith and credit to repay a bond, it is encumbering its general revenues and therefore using a broad-based tax, or a tax paid by all residents of the area and those who visit the community. Communities that place a high value on public consumption benefits from sports, and those that believe sports teams and their facilities generate economic development have used general taxing powers and taxes that apply to purchases or property to finance their share of a facility's cost. For example, Arlington, Texas, voters approved an increase to their local sales tax to finance their share of the costs for the Ballpark in Arlington.

Specific Consumption Taxes

It has become increasingly common to find governments interested in pledging revenues from specific acts of consumption to pay for sports facilities. For example, several communities have used "sin taxes," or extra taxes paid for the consumption of alcohol and tobacco products. Other communities have used parking taxes and taxes on consumption of food and beverages in restaurants. There have also been taxes placed on stays in hotels and on car rental, but these are considered taxes on tourists. Taxes that are seen as "voluntary" or paid by nonresidents have enjoyed more political support as many citizens do not consider taxes of that nature as a general burden.

User Fees

The imposition of user fees refers to payments made by fans or spectators for the construction or maintenance of a facility. In Philadelphia, Pittsburgh, and Indianapolis, entertainment taxes are collected on the sale of every ticket to events held in the facilities used by professional teams. These funds are then used to support the public sector share of the facility's cost. Another form of a user charge is an extra fee for parking in areas adjacent to a facility. Any fees assessed for advertising within a facility or for consumption of food and beverages inside a facility (extra sales tax) would also be classified as a user fee, as the fans attending games or events pay these charges.

Tax Increments

Some communities have established base levels of taxation and then pledged the increments or extra tax dollars generated by a facility's presence. These plans are similar to tax incremental financing programs used for development in numerous states. A base level of taxes, primarily income and sales taxes, is specified based on what would be generated if a team were not playing in the facility. The taxes collected above this base are considered the increment and then used to repay the loan. The real issue in the use of tax incremental financing for a facility is the extent to which the taxes are actually an increment. For example, if, in the absence of a team, people still spent the same money for recreation but in other parts of a community, then there is no real increment.

Sports Taxes

Sports taxes are those paid by the athletes. In states that assess income taxes, if there were no team in the area, then visiting as well as home athletes would not pay income taxes. As a result, several communities pledge these revenues, as they are considered a complete increment. Again, this logic may be flawed if fans' spending is offset by less consumption of other forms of entertainment. The lower level of consumption of other forms of entertainment would lead to lower wages and thus lower taxes collected at the other sites of recreation and entertainment. One example is Indianapolis, which has created a sports district tax, combining the income tax paid by athletes and those who work at the facilities with all the sales taxes paid in the region. This plan has a degree of political attractiveness in that those who do not want to pay for the facility can simply consume services in other parts of the community and thus never pay the tax.

Tourist and Gaming Taxes

Numerous communities use taxes on visitors to the area (hotel usage, short-term car rental) to pay for sports facilities. These are politically attractive, as surveys indicate that residents prefer assessments that do not appear to be paid by residents (Swindell and Rosentraub 1998). Some communities have used the revenues from lotteries to pay for sports facilities. This is a form of revenue generation used in many European countries and is frequently seen as some sort of a "sin tax."

Theory into Practice: Public Sector Financing of Sports Facilities

The public sector's level of responsibility varies by type of facility. With arenas able to host numerous nonsports events, the owners of basketball and hockey teams can frequently enjoy revenue streams that are not available to owners of football and baseball teams. Fear of damage to the playing surfaces in ballparks and stadiums and scheduling problems limit the revenues that can be produced from nonsports events. Thus, with these additional profits for the owners of basketball and hockey teams, the public sector's share of the construction costs has generally been smaller (see Table 11.1).

The Boston Celtics/Boston Bruins paid for the new arena they use, as did the Washington Wizards/Washington Capitals, and the Toronto Raptors. The Philadelphia 76ers/Philadelphia Flyers also play in a facility that was largely paid for by the private sector. The Los Angeles Lakers, Los Angeles Kings, and Los Angeles Clippers play in the Staples Center, which was also largely paid for by the private sector.

The public sector provided most of the support to build or remodel sixteen out of the eighteen ballparks built since 1989. The public sector paid 100 percent of the cost of remodeling the home of the Chicago White Sox, and the Atlanta Braves paid only $50 million to remodel the Olympic Stadium built for the 1996 games. The Olympic Stadium was built by the Olympic Organizing Committee and was a public asset. The team was then permitted to use it as their home. In relation to many other facilities for Major League Baseball teams, the number of tax dollars involved in the construction of the Olympic Stadium (now called Turner Field) was far less. But there was a real opportunity cost in the sense that the asset (and the land involved) could have had other uses that generated tax dollars or created income for the city through the sale of the land. The public sector played a major role in other facilities: At least 75 percent of the construction costs of five other ballparks were funded by the public sector, while nine additional teams play in facilities where the public sector paid between 50 percent and 74 percent of the construction costs.

Similar patterns are found in funding the construction of stadiums used by football teams. Five stadiums were fully financed by the public sector, while nine more football teams play in facilities where the public sector contributed funds to pay for more than half of the cost of construction. There are three exceptions to this pattern. The Washington Redskins paid

Table 11.1

Construction Costs and the Public Sector Share

Team	Type of facility[a]	Opening year	Total	Percent public	Percent private
			Cost of construction		
Major League Baseball					
Anaheim Angels	1	1998	100	30	70
Arizona Diamondbacks	1	1998	355	71	29
Atlanta Braves[b]	1	1997	235	100	0
Baltimore Orioles	1	1992	235	96	4
Chicago White Sox	1	1991	150	100	0
Cincinnati Reds	1	2003	361	83	17
Cleveland Indians	1	1994	173	88	12
Colorado Rockies	1	1995	215	75	25
Detroit Tigers	1	2000	395	63	37
Houston Astros	1	2000	266	68	32
Milwaukee Brewers	1	2001	322	66	34
Philadelphia Phillies	1	2003	346	50	50
Pittsburgh Pirates	1	2001	233	71	29
San Diego Padres	1	2001	411	57	43
San Francisco Giants	1	2000	306	5	95
Seattle Mariners	1	1999	517	72	28
Texas Rangers	1	1994	191	80	20
Toronto Blue Jays	1	1989	388	63	37
National Basketball Association					
Atlanta Hawks	4	1999	214	91	9
Boston Celtics	4	1995	160	0	100
Chicago Bulls	4	1994	150	7	93
Cleveland Cavaliers	2	1994	152	48	52
Dallas Mavericks	4	2001	325	38	62
Denver Nuggets	2	1999	165	3	97
Houston Rockets	2	2003	175	100	0
Indiana Pacers	2	1999	175	41	59
Los Angeles Clippers	4	1999	375	10	90
Los Angeles Lakers	4	1999	375	10	90
Miami Heat	2	1999	241	59	41
Philadelphia 76ers	4	1996	206	11	89
Phoenix Suns	2	1992	90	39	61
Portland Trail Blazers	2	1995	262	13	87
San Antonio Spurs	2	1993	186	100	0
Seattle SuperSonics	2	1995[c]	110	100	0
Toronto Raptors	4	1999	180	0	100
Washington Wizards	4	1997	260	0	100
National Football League					
Atlanta Falcons	3	1992	214	100	0
Baltimore Ravens	3	1998	229	87	13
Buffalo Bills	3	1999[c]	63	100	0
Carolina Panthers	3	1996	248	0	100
Cincinnati Bengals	3	2000	458	95	5
Cleveland Browns	3	1999	306	70	30

Denver Broncos	3	2001	364	73	27
Detroit Lions	3	2002	225	36	64
Green Bay Packers	3	2003 [c]	295	58	42
Houston Texans	3	2002	402	71	29
Jacksonville Jaguars	3	1995 [c]	135	90	10
Miami Dolphins	3	1987	115	10	90
New England Patriots	3	2002	350	0	100
Philadelphia Eagles	3	2003	395	21	79
Pittsburgh Steelers	3	2001	244	69	31
Seattle Seahawks	3	2002	430	77	23
St. Louis Rams	3	1995	300	100	0
Tampa Bay Buccaneers	3	1998	190	100	0
Tennessee Titans	3	1999	292	100	0
Washington Redskins	3	1997	251	28	72
National Hockey League					
Atlanta Thrashers	4	1999	214	81	19
Boston Bruins	4	1995	160	0	100
Carolina Hurricanes	2	1999	160	87	13
Chicago Blackhawks	4	1994	150	7	93
Colorado Avalanche	4	1999	165	3	97
Columbus Blue Jackets	2	2000	150	0	100
Dallas Stars	4	2001	300	42	38
Florida Panthers	2	1998	212	87	13
Los Angeles Kings	4	1999	375	10	90
Minnesota Wild	2	2000	130	100	0
Montreal Canadiens	2	1996	156	0	100
Nashville Predators	2	1997	144	100	0
Ottawa Senators	2	1996	136	21	79
Philadephia Flyers	4	1996	206	11	89
Phoenix Coyotes	2	2001	180	0	100
Washington Capitals	4	1997	260	23	77

[a]Type of facility: 1 = ballpark, 2 = arena, 3 = stadium, 4 = shared arena. [b]The Atlanta Braves facility was built for the 1996 Olympic Games. The Braves paid $50 million to convert it into a baseball stadium. [c]Renovated.

the full cost of their stadium's construction, while the public sector was responsible for paying for the needed infrastructure (which amounted to 28 percent of total cost). It has been argued that the very lucrative market for football in the Washington, DC, area made such an arrangement feasible. Years before, a similar cost-sharing plan was used for the home of the Carolina Panthers, even though this was an expansion team playing in an area with far less wealth than is found in Washington, DC. The values and interests of owners account for some of the differences noted. The New England Patriots are also paying virtually all of the costs for their new home with the public sector providing funds for the needed infrastructure. The lucrative nature of the Boston/Providence market supported this deal, even after the owner sought permission from the National Football League (NFL) to accept a far better proposal from the state of Connecticut and the city of Hartford. The NFL and its television partners did not want the Patriots to abandon the lucrative Boston market and refused to permit the move. The NFL could have permitted the team to move and then placed a new or expansion franchise in the Boston region, but the market for this team was seen as too close to the market area of a Hartford team to support the notion of an expansion.

Financing Tools Used by the Public Sector

In most cases where the public sector funds some or most of the construction costs of sports facilities, bonds are issued by the public sector to repay their investment. The real issue for students of public finance, then, is the taxing instrument used to repay the obligations. In some instances revenues from more than one source are used. This section describes who issued the bonds and how bonds were repaid by using examples from the building of ballparks.

In several of the most recent construction projects, the public sector was involved through all three levels of government: city, county, and state. These include the Milwaukee Brewers, Philadelphia Phillies, the Pittsburgh Pirates, and the new ballpark proposed for the St. Louis Cardinals. In each of these instances, the public sector is paying for more than 50 percent of the cost of the new facility. For example, in building Miller Park for the Milwaukee Brewers, the infrastructure costs ($72 million) were shared by the city, county, and state. In addition, Wisconsin issued $160 million in tax-exempt bonds that are paid through a five-county, one-tenth-of-a-cent sales tax increase. In the case of the Phillies, in November 2000, the Mayor's Office in Philadelphia announced an agreement with both Major League Baseball and the NFL to build two new stadiums at a cost of $1 billion. Under the agreement, the city will issue $304 million in bonds to finance its share; the money will be paid back by new tax revenue created by the stadiums and the new 2 percent tax on car rental. The state of Pennsylvania will grant $170 million, and the teams will provide $482 million.

It is also important to note that for some ballparks built in the 1990s, nonprofit organizations created by the public sector were established to deal with the financing, construction, and maintenance of the facilities. For example, in Cleveland, the Gateway Economic Development Corporation was created to build a city sports complex, including a ballpark for the Cleveland Indians and an arena for the Cleveland Cavaliers. The nonprofit organization issued bonds to fund construction and owns the facilities. Another example is the Denver Metropolitan Major League Baseball Stadium District, which owns the Colorado Rockies facility, Coors Field. Covering the six counties surrounding Denver, the district was created by the Colorado legislature; it

Table 11.2

Financing Tools Used by the Public Sector to Build Baseball Facilities

	Hotel/ motel taxes	Sales tax	Car rental tax	City reserve funds/ general revenues	Sales tax on restaurants and bars
Major League Baseball					
Anaheim Angels	*			*	
Arizona Diamondbacks	*				
Atlanta Braves					
Baltimore Orioles					
Chicago White Sox	*				
Cincinnati Reds		*			
Cleveland Indians					
Colorado Rockies		*			
Detroit Tigers	*		*		
Houston Astros	*		*		
Milwaukee Brewers		*			
Philadelphia Phillies			*		
Pittsburgh Pirates	*	*			
San Diego Padres	*				
San Francisco Giants					
Seattle Mariners		*	*		*
Texas Rangers		*			
Toronto Blue Jays					

issued bonds and levied a one-tenth of 1 percent sales tax in the six-county area to fund the ballpark.

Table 11.2 illustrates the different taxes utilized to repay bonds. The tax instruments most commonly used involve sales (all consumption), hotel and motel use, and car rental use. The public sector used at least one of these taxes to pay back debt for construction of new facilities for thirteen of the eighteen teams. Both hotel/motel and car rental taxes are used to pay back debt for the facilities of the Detroit Tigers and the Houston Astros. To pay for Comerica Park in Detroit, revenues from casinos operated by Native Americans (a gaming tax) were also utilized. Sales taxes, usually at the county level, are being used to pay for facilities of seven teams. But in the case of the Ballpark in Arlington, a sales tax in one city, Arlington, was used to retire the bonds used by the public sector and a "sin tax" helped to pay for Jacobs Field.

Unique financing tools have also been used to supplement the tax revenues pledged to retire bonds. For example, fees from commemorative license plates are being used to build Safeco Field, the home of the Seattle Mariners. These contributions, as well as a 0.017 increment in the state sales

External facility advertising	Facility-generated revenues	Sports lottery tickets	Sin tax on alcohol and cigarettes	Tax incremental financing (TIF)	Commemorative license plates	Admission taxes/ticket surcharge	Indian gaming revenues
*							
*							
	*						
		*					
						*	
*							
		*					
	*			*	*		
					*		

tax and proceeds from the sale of sports lottery scratch games, are all part of Washington State contributions. It should be noted that unique revenue sources are frequently viewed with caution by the bond market as reliable sources for repayment of obligations. As a result, a more traditional revenue source, such as a sales tax, has to be part of most bond packages. If a more traditional tax is not involved, interest rates will be higher and the market may well "demand" bond insurance (in case of insufficient revenues to make payments) before the bonds are purchased. Another financial tool is a facility's admission tax or ticket surcharge. This is being used to pay for part of the cost of the facilities for the Seattle Mariners and the Texas Rangers, where a one-dollar surcharge was imposed to help pay for some of the cost of the Ballpark in Arlington.

Relationship Between the Share of Public Funding and Selected Economic Variables

When communities analyze providing different levels of support for a sports facility, it is critical that the impact on the wealth of a team's owner is considered. In terms of establishing the appropriate share for both the public sector and the team, the issue of the possible increase in the team owner's wealth may need careful consideration.

The examples presented here are all taken from Major League Baseball, although other sports were examined, too. We have examined lagged as well as present and future relations between the public sector's share of funding new construction and several economic variables relating to the teams and their markets.

Figure 11.1 describes the relationship between the public sector share and team values two years before completion of the new facility. In general, baseball teams with higher team values prior to building a facility received relatively less public support. In other words, teams with smaller values depend on a larger public share to build their ballparks. One team that highlights this relationship is the San Francisco Giants; the team had the third highest team value at $213 million, and the public sector contributed only 5 percent of total costs. An exception to this negative relationship is the Baltimore Orioles, where the public sector paid for 96 percent of building Oriole Park at Camden Yards, although the team was valued at a high of $200 million two years prior to the opening of new facility.

Another interesting relationship is that between the share of the public sector and a team's total revenues one or two years prior to the opening of the new facility. Figure 11.2 shows this relationship for baseball teams. It illustrates that a negative relationship exists between the two variables. The lower the team revenues prior to the new construction, the higher the role the public sector played in financing the new facility. One exception (outlier) to be noted in the figure is the Atlanta Braves, where the team's revenues, $79.1 million, were relatively high, and the public sector paid all of its facility cost. However, as noted, Turner Field was built for the 1996 Summer Olympics and was later converted for baseball by the Braves.

In theory, the market size in which a team plays also has an impact on the public sector role. We would expect that teams in the larger markets could pay a larger share of the cost, hence requiring a smaller share of the public sector. Several market size variables were tested, including percent of household with high incomes and number of large firms. Figure 11.3 presents the relationship between the share of the public sector and number of large companies in the market.

The figure points to a negative relationship between the public sector share and the market size, although several exceptions suggest a less apparent relationship. The exceptions include the San Francisco Giants with a relatively small market size and small public sector participation. On the other extreme are the Chicago White Sox and the Baltimore Orioles, both with large mar-

Figure 11.1 **Public Sector Share and Team Value**

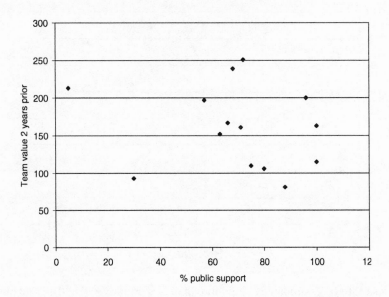

Figure 11.2 **Public Sector Share and Team Total Revenue**

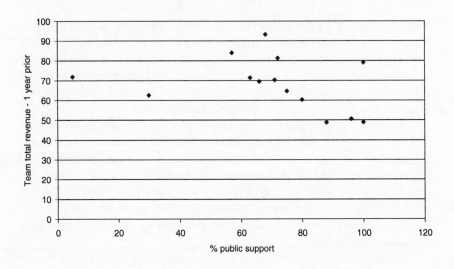

Figure 11.3   **Public Sector Share and Size of Market**

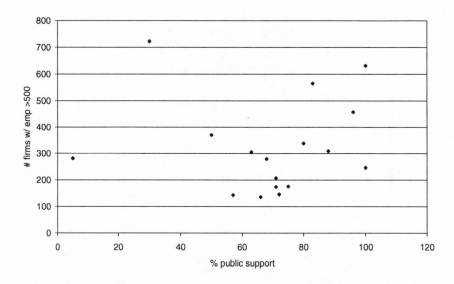

kets (458–632 companies with more than 500 employees) and a large public sector share (83–100 percent) of financing for their ballparks. The White Sox, however, are not supported to the same extent as are the Cubs, and their owner threatened to move the team unless a large subsidy was provided.

Conclusions

The public sector's share of the costs for building and maintaining a professional sports facility should be proportionate to the share of benefits classified as positive externalities or public consumption benefits. The return to the team owners in terms of the franchise's increased value should also guide proposals for public/private partnerships, as should the ability of the facility to generate revenue from other entertainment activities.

Community leaders are restrained from selecting the desired portion of a financing plan that should be borne by the public sector because of the leagues' control over the supply of teams. As a result, if an owner rejects a proposed partnership, the threat of the team leaving an area is frequently seen as too real for some communities to risk. Thus, it is not uncommon to find that that public's share of the expenses of building a facility are larger than would be suggested from an empirical assessment of the benefits received by the public and a team's owner.

To repay the bonds used by local governments to pay for a facility, there is a pronounced tendency to use sales tax instruments. In some cities, taxes that do not impact local residents have been the favored choice (taxes on hotels, motels, and car rentals) while in other areas increments to the general sales tax have been used. Taxes on the sale of alcohol and tobacco products have also been used in some areas to avoid increases in the general sales tax. Politically, gaming revenues are also seen as a desirable source of funding, but in some instances these resources have to be supplemented with other taxes to ensure the existence of a sufficient pool of revenue to repay the public's debt.

References

Austrian, Ziona, and Mark S. Rosentraub. 1997. "Cleveland's Gateway to the Future." In *Cities, Sports, and Taxes*, ed. Roger Noll and Andrew Zimbalist, 355–84. Washington, DC: Brookings Institution.

Baade, Robert. 1996. "Professional Sports as Catalysts for Metropolitan Development." *Journal of Urban Affairs* 18, no. 1: 1–18.

Hamilton, Bruce W., and Peter Kahn. 1997. "Baltimore's Camden Yards Ballparks." In Noll and Zimbalist, eds., *Cities, Sports, and Taxes*, 245–82.

Humphreys, Brad R. 2001. "The Myth of Sports-Led Development." *Economic Development Commentary* 21, no. 1: 28–33.

Kennedy, Sheila, and Mark S. Rosentraub. 2000. "Public-private Partnerships Professional Sports Teams, and the Protection of the Public's Interests." *American Review of Public Administration* 30, no. 4: 436–59.

Leonhardt, David. 2001. "The National Pastime Falls Behind the Count." *The New York Times*, August 12, Section 3: 1, 10.

Michener, James A. 1976. *Sports in America*. New York: Random House.

Noll, Roger G., and Andrew Zimbalist. 1997. "The Economic Impact of Sports Teams and Facilities." In Noll and Zimbalist, eds., *Cities, Sports, and Taxes*, 55–91.

Office of the Controller, City of Philadephia. 2000. "Analysis of Stadia Proposals": www.philadelphiacontroller.org.

Piraino, Thomas A., Jr. 1996. "The Antitrust Rationale for the Expansion of Professional Sports Leagues." *Ohio State Law Journal* 57, no. 5: 1677–1729.

Rappaport, Jordan, and Chad Wilkerson. 2001. "What Are the Benefits of Hosting a Major League Sports Franchise?" *Economic Review* 86, no. 1 (Kansas City: Federal Reserve Bank of Kansas City): 55–84.

Rofe, John. 2001. "Norfolk Biz Would Spend $38M on MLB." *Street and Smith's Sports Business Journal* 4, no. 16 (August 6–12): 4.

Rosentraub, Mark S. 1996. "Does the Emperor Have New Clothes?" *Journal of Urban Affairs* 18, no. 1: 23–31.

———. 1997. *Major League Losers: The Real Cost of Sports and Who's Paying for It*. New York: Basic Books.

———. 1999. *Major League Losers: The Real Cost of Sports and Who's Paying for It*. Revised edition. New York: Basic Books.

Rosentraub, Mark S., and David Swindell. 2002. "Negotiating Games: Cities, Sports, and the Winner's Curse." *Journal of Sports Management* 16, no. 1: 18–35.

Rosentraub, Mark S. et al. 1994. "Sport and Downtown Development: If You Build It Will Jobs Come?" *Journal of Urban Affairs* 16, no. 3: 221–39.

Sloan, Peter. 1971. "The Economics of Professional Football: The Football Club as a Utility Maximizer." *Scottish Journal of Political Economy* 17, no. 2: 121–45.

Swindell, David, and Mark S. Rosentraub. 1998. "Who Benefits from the Presence of Professional Sports Teams? The Implications for Public Funding of Stadiums and Arenas." *Public Administration Review* 58, no. 1: 11–20.

Wilson, John. 1994. *Playing by the Rules*. Detroit: Wayne State University Press.

12

Financing Redevelopment of Brownfields

Peter B. Meyer and Kristen R. Yount

In the past decade, urban brownfield redevelopment has emerged as both a major economic development and environmental priority in the United States (Bartsch et al. 1991; U.S. Conference of Mayors 1998, 1999, 2000). Brownfields are defined by the Environmental Protection Agency (EPA) as "abandoned, idled or underutilized industrial and commercial facilities where expansion or redevelopment is complicated by real or perceived contamination" (Kaiser 1998).

Some of these complications arise from the nature of the sites themselves (their size or shape); others from the types of settings in which the sites are located (poor neighborhoods, inadequate infrastructure, and the like). Yet more arise from actual contamination or from the stigma associated with a site that just might be contaminated and a very large percentage from the regulatory and financial environment facing such redevelopments. Despite these potential problems, there is great interest in reusing these sites because (a) from a private sector perspective, their location may offer exceptional profits from successful reclamation and reuse; and (b) from a public sector perspective, their regeneration may contribute to both the economic and community development goals of the municipalities in which they are located.

The EPA focuses on land and water pollution in defining brownfields, but brownfield redevelopment involves an array of other factors retarding regeneration: "contamination" by crime, by crowding, by old infrastructure, and, given the undeniable presence of racism, by high concentrations of minority populations. The earliest federal study of the problems facing brownfield regeneration efforts, in fact, found that nonenvironmental factors were at least as important as the presence of contamination and costs of cleanup in inhibiting developer interest (Urban Institute 1998). Unlike the physical problems caused by pollution on specific sites, these nonenvironmental elements of "contamination" may not be amenable to piecemeal solution by individual development projects.

Recognition of these broader factors has led to new public policies that have become more supportive of brownfield redevelopment efforts. At the state level, geographically targeted economic development programs emerged first in the explosion of state enterprise zones (Meyer 1991). Specific area foci more recently have taken root in broader programs to support individual investments in targeted economic areas that are, more often than not, linked to zones of known brownfield concentrations (Bartsch, Collaton, and Pepper 1996). The growth of state and local efforts to limit sprawl and promote downtown redevelopment has improved the competitive position of brownfields along with other central city sites (National Governors Association 2000; Wells 1999). Most significant, forty-seven of the fifty states now have specific programs designed to ease the regulatory burdens brownfields face, and most also offer targeted economic development incentives (Bartsch et al. 2001; Meyer 2000a).

This chapter begins with an overview of "the brownfield problem"—both the physical conditions and the regulatory context that discourages investment—and the recent improvements in the legal climate. We describe the major federal financial support for brownfield projects and summarize state brownfield investment stimulus policies. We conclude with enumeration of a range of financing options and approaches available to redevelopment agencies and describe the growth of the environmental insurance industry, a private response to reducing the exceptional risks and uncertainties associated with brownfield investments.

The Brownfields Problem

For the proactive municipality, local development agency, or other economic development organization (EDO), brownfields redevelopment may be a central concern. Some municipalities simply have no other available land, while others have contaminated sites in strategically critical locations. Reuse of such sites also may be desirable because the public sector costs of building and maintaining infrastructure are lower in built-up areas (Meyer and Deitrick 1998).

Plant closings and downsizing that began in the 1970s have left potentially contaminated sites underutilized in most communities (Bartsch and Collaton 1996). Spatial restructuring in local economies has added other sites—abandoned dry cleaners, gas stations, repair and metal working shops and other small service facilities—to the mix. The sheer number of these sites, estimated to be at least 500,000, attests to their importance (Council for Urban Economic Development 1999; Simons and Iannone 1997). Growing environmental concerns fuel the belief that sites that were used for industrial operations prior to 1980 are dangerously contaminated, but this accepted "fact" has not been verified (Davis and Margolis 1997; Gerrard 1998).

Federal Law: Liability and Uncertainty

When Congress enacted the Comprehensive Environmental Response, Compensation, and Liability Act (CERCLA or Superfund) in 1980, it intended to facilitate reclamation of acutely contaminated, but neglected sites. Unfortunately, while CERCLA has had many beneficial environmental impacts, court interpretations have led to unintended negative impacts on economic development efforts (Coffin and Shepherd 1998; Ryan 1998; Schwab 1997). The problem generated for economic redevelopment under CERCLA lies in the fact that the current land owner (as well as all past land owners) may be held responsible for any environmental problems (and are considered to be "potentially responsible parties" or PRPs) on a site even if the contamination occurred before the current owner purchased the property. The redevelopment difficulties arise less from cleanup requirements than from the complex legal liability questions that arise from the principles of "strict" and "joint and several" liability embedded in the act.

"Strict" liability does not require the demonstration of any wrongdoing. This means that even if the contamination actions taken were legal at the time they were done, a party may still be held accountable for the costs of cleanup and environmental damages. This liability is also retroactive, meaning that even if the pollution occurred prior to the passage of CERCLA in 1980, one may still be held accountable. "Joint and several" liability comes into play when there are several PRPs. CERCLA creates three general classes of responsible parties: generators of the hazardous substances found at the site, owners and operators of the site, and transporters who have the authority to select the site for disposal. The courts have held that any of these three classes of parties may be held liable for the entire cost of site cleanup, unless it can be shown that the harm is "divisible" (e.g., where there are two or more physically separate areas of contamination).

This ambiguous potential liability has resulted in situations in which even those who in no way caused the contamination, or who acquired title when they did not want to (as in the case of loan defaults, inheritances, and tax delinquencies) experienced exposure to some risks (Bartsch, Collaton, and Pepper 1996). For example, while CERCLA contained a "secured creditor exemption" that provided liability protection for lenders, in the early 1990s, the courts found that lenders could lose their liability exemption by foreclosing on a property or by participating in the daily management of a business. These legal decisions severely depressed brownfield lending (Yount and Meyer 1994).

Changes in the Regulatory Climate

The 1996 Asset Conservation, Lender Liability, and Deposit Insurance Protection Act provides protection for some of the "bona fide new purchasers" (parties who have had nothing to do with the existing pollution) and others who may have acquired title as the result of processes over which they have no control, such as inheritance or legally required tax foreclosures. The act also protects lenders who foreclose and take title only to sell to recover on loan defaults.[1] Unfortunately, even five years later, it appears that many potential market participants do not know the extent of the protections this act has provided to them. A further issue is that the relief offered by the act is limited to protection from federal government actions. The act does not address possible liability associated with claims that may be pursued by private parties for property damage and bodily injury associated with brownfield properties and actions on them. Nevertheless, EDOs can play a very important role in providing information on the protection provided, and, in so doing, may reduce the need for economic development subsidies to attract investors to brownfield sites.

There is a growing recognition that brownfields reclamation provides widespread benefits. The economic value of turning brownfields into parks is recognized by organizations as diverse as the Urban Land Institute and the Trust for Public Land (Garvin et al. 1997; Trust for Public Land 1999). Other major planning and economic development associations also recognize that there are broad economic benefits available from redevelopment of idle, but possibly strategically located, lands (NADO 1999; American Planning Association 1999).

The Council for Urban Economic Development (1999) recently examined 107 very diverse types of completed projects. They found that cleanup costs averaged only 8 percent of total project costs, median public costs per job created were $14,003, and every $1 of public-sector funds invested leveraged an additional $2.48 in private funds (with half the public money coming from nonlocal sources). In short, brownfields appear to offer good EDO investment opportunities. The Council for Economic Development also examined the skills needed to undertake brownfields redevelopment. Critical capacities include site assembly (where there are many small parcels of land), and the ability to package the financing, using federal and state funds as well as attracting private investment. These, of course, are skills central to any EDO, and suggest that EDOs can make an important contribution to cost-effective local brownfields redevelopment efforts.

Property Valuations and Capital Access Problems

All the public efforts to promote brownfield redevelopment are dependent on the flow of private sector capital to the projects. To the extent that redevelopers are reliant on debt capital, their access to funds depends on the standards for commercial bank real estate lending. Such lending, in turn, is affected by the valuation of assets offered as collateral, often the very brownfields slated for redevelopment. Bank lenders, subject to regulations limiting their risk exposures, control their default risk by offering loans only up to some predetermined maximum loan-to-value ratio. Real estate appraisers become the key institutional gatekeepers for such financing, by virtue of their roles in defining the "value" on which banks, insurance companies, and other large lenders rely in setting loan maxima (Stack and Jacobsen 1999).

The problems facing appraisers when they are asked to determine probable market prices for brownfield sites are extremely complex. The *Appraisal Journal* suggests that, unfortunately, their responses tend to the simplistic and extreme exaggeration of the effects of stigma on property values.

One approach embodies assumptions about the applicability of market values of "comparables" that are virtually indefensible in light of the extreme diversity of types of contamination, costs of cleanup, and possible liabilities across properties (Arens 1997). The alternative relies on forecasts that downgrade future income streams through the use of exaggerated discount rates on the basis of possible costs that may arise in the event of "reopeners" of approved cleanups, although virtually no such regulatory demands have ever occurred (Chalmers and Jackson 1996; Dotzour 1997).

Despite the availability of environmental insurance that can provide extensive coverage for the exceptional risks of brownfield redevelopments, the appraisal community appears unready to incorporate such risk transfers in their downward adjustments to brownfield property values (Meyer 2000b). EDOs working to promote redevelopment of brownfields can thus ease developers' access to capital to the extent that they can work with local appraisal professionals on their valuation practices.

Public Programs to Stimulate Brownfields

Federal Initiatives: Public Brownfields Redevelopment Funds

Federal recognition that brownfields redevelopment is more than just an environmental issue resulted in the 1995 launch of the Brownfields Economic Redevelopment Initiative, under which, by July 2000, the EPA had awarded pilot grants to close to 400 state, local, and tribal organizations for projects to stimulate cleanup and redevelopment of brownfields. The Federal Interagency Working Group on Brownfields, created in 1997 to better integrate national support for brownfield reclamation, involves fifteen different federal government agencies (U.S. EPA 1995, 1997). While individual pools of funds may not suffice for particular local projects, the programs of different agencies do complement each other, so EDOs have the opportunity to generate a portfolio of federal support for projects.

Environmental Protection Agency

- *Brownfields Assessment Demonstration Pilots:* These grants, generally known as Brownfields Pilot Projects, were motivated by the fact that many local redevelopment agencies were writing off large portions of their land assets as irretrievable. The diverse experience of more than 400 Pilots shows that funds have been used for individual site assessments, areawide brownfield database development, and special programs to involve community members in brownfield site redevelopment planning (U.S. EPA 2001).
- *Brownfields Cleanup Revolving Loan Funds*: Federal grants can capitalize such funds with up to $500,000; they allow state, local and tribal agencies to make loans to developers that facilitate cleanups (U.S. EPA 1999). These funds help fill a financing gap created by the fact that many commercial lenders remain hesitant to provide funds using brownfields as collateral, unless the sites have been given a state agency approval of cleanup. Such nontraditional sources of debt capital to pay for cleanup may remain essential, even for projects with very attractive risk-adjusted returns on investment.
- *Job Training and Development Demonstration Pilots:* The EPA also provides up to $200,000 over two years for projects to address the environmental justice and economic inequality issues presented by brownfields. Grants may be used for environmental employment and training for community residents to increase the local benefits of brownfield redevelopments.

Department of Housing and Urban Development (HUD)

- *Community Development Block Grant (CDBG) Program:* Both CDBG and Section 108 Loan Guarantee Program funds have long been used for brownfield projects. This use was formally defined as eligible in 1998, and HUD has provided guidance to grant and loan guarantee recipients on the benefits to be gained from targeting brownfields for regeneration (Research Triangle Institute 1998).

- *Brownfields Economic Development Initiative (BEDI):* This program has provided a growing volume of funds (starting with $25 million in fiscal year 2000) targeted for local efforts to regenerate brownfields. BEDI applications must be accompanied by a request for new Section 108 Loan Guarantee authority and must advance one or more of the CDBG program objectives of benefiting low- and moderate-income persons, preventing slums or blight, or addressing imminent threats and urgent needs.

Department of Commerce, Economic Development Administration (EDA)

The Economic Development Administration provides various assistance to help communities develop and implement local economic development strategies, all of which could be used for brownfields. This use has been encouraged since 1997.

- *Planning Program:* This ongoing EDA funding for economic development planning for 320 Economic Development Districts and 70 Tribal Planning Organizations may be used to integrate brownfields redevelopment into broader economic strategies known as Comprehensive Economic Development Strategies (CEDS).
- *Public Works and Economic Development Program:* These funds may be used to provide infrastructure for a site, rehabilitate buildings after a site is cleaned, or other similar "bricks and mortar" activities. Typically, EDA has not funded environmental remediation activities.
- *Economic Adjustment Program:* These funds target areas suffering from long-term distress such as economic restructuring or shorter-term challenges such as plant closings and natural disasters. They may be used for bricks and mortar activities, planning, and for funding locally administered revolving loan funds.
- *Local Technical Assistance:* These small grants can fund feasibility studies (including environmental site assessments), market analyses, and similar small projects necessary to support site redevelopment.

Other Federal Programs and Resources

- *National Oceanic and Atmospheric Administration (NOAA) Coastal Zone Management Program:* Monies from this program are not general shore-

line economic development funds but are targeted to areas that may
have contamination threatening coastal waters. They can support land
acquisition and mitigation activities for sites adjacent to waterways or
coastal areas.

- *Department of Health and Human Services (DHHS) Social Services
  Block Grants:* These funds can provide for job training related to
  brownfield cleanup efforts in empowerment zones and enterprise communities. DHHS funds programs such as the health studies on environmental exposures conducted by the Agency for Toxic Substances and
  Disease Registry and the environmental job training available from the
  National Institute of Environmental Health. The delivery of services
  that benefit residents near brownfields may be important in obtaining
  support and participation of local communities, even if DHHS cannot
  pay for site assessments or mitigations.
- *Department of Transportation:* Both the Federal Highway Administration and the Federal Transit Administration provide funds specifically
  for brownfields redevelopment. The resources available under the Transportation Equity Act for the 21st Century (TEA-21) can be integrated
  with other support to improve transportation access and infrastructure
  near brownfield sites.
- *U.S. Army Corps of Engineers:* The Corps responds to requests from
  local EDOs or governments and can provide engineering assistance to
  communities in four broad areas associated with brownfields: site assessment, remediation, property redevelopment, and sustainable reuse.

Federal Initiatives to Attract Private Capital to Brownfields

- *Community Reinvestment Act:* Private banks can claim credit for lending on brownfield projects in low- and moderate-income neighborhoods.
  Many banks remain unaware of the 1995 regulatory change by the Office of the Comptroller of the Currency to support brownfields redevelopment (Kaiser and Bennett 1999). Local EDOs and governments may
  be able to increase the flow of bank lending to brownfields simply by
  making sure local bank lending decisions take the availability of these
  credits into consideration.
- *Brownfields Tax Incentive:* This tax provision passed in 1996 allows
  investors to expense brownfield site mitigation costs on their income
  taxes in the year in which they are incurred, rather than depreciate them
  over time. The value of this tool has been limited by two provisions: (a)
  requirements that sites be located in impoverished areas that have trouble
  attracting capital; and (b) recovery of expensed costs in the event of

resale before the expiration of the normal depreciation period. The tool is thus of use mainly to firms who want to redevelop a brownfield for their own use or otherwise remain owners (U.S. EPA 1999).

Pending Legislation

Congress has attempted to pass legislation to stimulate brownfield redevelopment for the past decade. Brownfields reform has, however, been held captive by those pursuing "Superfund reform"—largely efforts to eliminate the "polluter pays" responsibilities under CERCLA. With the support of the Bush administration, however, there appears to be a renewed prospect for new brownfield legislation, pushed hard by the EPA with approval from the White House. The new proposals include hundreds of millions more in federal aid to local government brownfield programs and funds for state enforcement of brownfield standards and maintenance of state-level registries of brownfield sites. Both are part of efforts to devolve federal regulatory enforcement and create new liability protections for innocent purchasers and nearby landowners that may be affected by migrating contamination from brownfield sites. The prospect is for more liability relief for demonstrably innocent parties, and for increased federal-state cooperation, with more standard-setting and enforcement powers given to the individual states.

State and Local Brownfield Stimulus Programs: An Overview

Five broad classes of direct intervention by state and local governments have the potential to promote cleanup and reuse of brownfield sites, although not all were promulgated specifically for that purpose.

Regulatory Relief

Most state brownfield programs extend federal provisions for "risk-based corrective action" that permit the extent of site mitigation to vary with the intended use of a site, and that authorize "engineering controls" to contain contamination rather than remove all the pollution. Authorization for retention of some pollutants on site is generally accompanied by state requirements for "institutional controls" on future uses of the property (which can be deed restrictions, deed notices, easements, and constraints on specific actions, such as well-digging and the like). Strategic use of these controls can reduce cleanup costs substantially while providing adequate protection at sites with residual contamination.[2] Regulatory relief is also offered by state mechanisms for provision of greater certainty. These mechanisms include written cleanup standards, timetables for decisions by regulatory bodies, and other measures that, while not affecting standards or undermining state powers, raise expected investment returns simply by eliminating some of the need to make allowances for uncertainty.

Liability Reduction

The state programs also offer some limits on prospective liability to brownfield mitigators that complete a state-approved cleanup or containment plan and meet other requirements. In general, the relief takes the form of a "Covenant Not to Sue" that the state offers, assuring it will not demand further mitigation effort, or a "No Further Action" letter, assuring that it considers the mitigation to be complete. The availability and extent of relief available varies among states on two key dimensions: (a) eligibility for relief—which is not available to PRPs in some states; and (b) extent of relief—which may or may not include protection from suits from nongovernmental claimants, even if it protects the project from further state action. All the state assurances, however, include some form of "reopener" clause, permitting action to be demanded in the event that the mitigation is found to provide inadequate protection, due either to new scientific findings on risks or evidence of some remedy failures.

Direct Financial Support

Subsidies for regeneration of brownfields may just be targeted traditional economic development efforts such as loans, grants, or tax relief, but they also can take the form of assistance for brownfield-specific transaction costs: environmental assessments, and cleanup or containment efforts. Local level public participation in financing appears to provide a needed "comfort level" for developers, who feel that the threat of future enforcement actions, or the costs to them of liability suits, may be reduced if they have a public "partner" (Urban Institute 1998).

Public Site Reclamation

In some instances, it may pay for a municipality, a region, or some public-private agency to deliver a "clean" property to market for private developers. Such public action may remove most of the uncertainties associated with a cleanup. Thus, even if the dollar costs of land acquisition and site preparation are recovered upon sale, a developer may undertake a project on a cleaned site because the projected return on investment need not include a risk premium to cover the uncertainties associated with mitigation efforts. The public return to such an effort may come from the impact of the project for the development potential of an entire area, not just the individual parcel (Meyer 1998).

Constraints on New Developments on Greenfield Sites

Any policies that raise the costs of real estate investment on land that competes with brownfields can help stimulate private redevelopment efforts. Any urban growth or service boundaries, development exactions, public facilities requirements, minimum density controls, special-use zoning and limits on permitted types of greenfield development, road pricing schemes that raise costs of commuting, constraints on parking or driving in cities, and the like may all stimulate investor interest in brownfields. They should be considered part of an overall financing program.

Tools for Implementation of Brownfield Redevelopments

Many of the traditional tools used by EDOs over the past decades are applicable to brownfields. They appear to be underutilized, due in part to emphasis on the unique features of environmentally impaired sites. Brownfield regeneration has also been made easier by the growth of the environmental insurance industry.

Local Brownfield Redevelopment Tools

Local EDOs have extensive experience with financing techniques that can promote brownfield redevelopment. Many of them are discussed in other chapters in this volume and do not need to be described in detail here. However, it appears that the heightened focus on individual sites that results from concerns about contamination is a barrier to application of these techniques.

Brownfield reclamations are, after all, real estate development projects. Thus, any of the many actions that could be taken to improve the market attractiveness of particular parcels could increase investor interest in them. Brownfield redevelopment generates economic benefits beyond those from reuse of a single site, since stigmatized sites can undermine the market value of whole areas. Three traditional tools, in particular, are worth mentioning.

- *Tax Incremental Financing (TIF):* TIF, as described in chapter 3, can provide public capital to support site assessments and mitigations, based on the revenue gains made possible by the removal of the negatives associated with brownfield status.

- *Off-Site Investments:* Projects on noncontaminated sites that improve a neighborhood or other area attractiveness can also make brownfields more attractive to investors. Whether it is new housing or commercial activity in an area or infrastructure investments that make sites more attractive for industrial use, the potential returns on nearby brownfields can be enhanced.
- *Site Assembly:* The majority of brownfield properties are reputedly under a half an acre in size. The assessment and mitigation expenses are a higher proportion of total project costs for small brownfields than is the case for larger projects (Yount and Meyer 1999). Assembling either a group of brownfields or one brownfield and adjacent "clean" sites can create a parcel that would attract a larger investment and dilute the environmental expenses as a proportion of total project costs.

Insurance Coverages Available for Brownfields

There are three environmental insurance coverage classes that are directly applicable to the problems of risk management and transfer and the broader issue of reducing uncertainty in efforts to bring contaminated sites back into more active use. In addition, other environmental insurance products, available to consultants, engineers, and contractors, can play a role in brownfield redevelopment. The three major coverages are: (a) Pollution Liability Policies, (b) Cleanup Cost Cap Policies, and (c) Secured Creditor Policies (Yount 1999). Because there is no "standard" package, akin to homeowners or car insurance, each policy is "manuscripted" (specially designed) to meet the particular need of each individual project. Each buyer thus must have the capacity to identify the specific mix of coverages needed and to negotiate with the underwriters.

Pollution Liability Policies

These coverages address the damages to health, the environment, or economic prospects that may be caused by contamination. They protect insured parties against costs that can arise after a completed mitigation, so a redeveloper can use them to provide protection to a subsequent user or buyer of a brownfield for the exceptional risks associated with past contamination. They incorporate three distinct elements:

1. Protection against the costs of third party bodily injury and property damage claims that may arise, regardless of compliance with governmental mitigation requirements;
2. Protection for the insured against the costs of further remediation

and related expenses, if required after initial compliance with governmental mitigation requirements, due to exercise of regulators' "reopener" clauses; and

3. Protection against legal defense costs associated with the first two elements.

Cleanup Cost Cap Policies

This form of coverage is intended to limit the uncertainties associated with the possibility that additional contaminants may be found during a cleanup, requiring unanticipated remediation effort. The insurer pays the excess costs above a deductible amount (usually a percentage of the estimated cleanup cost). Engineers' prior estimates of cleanup effort and cost required are key to the cost and coverage of such policies, so developers need to invest in such engineering work before buying the coverage.

Secured Creditor Policies

These coverages are written to benefit lenders, not developers or subsequent users of a site. By reducing lenders' risks, they may ease developer access to debt capital. They reimburse lenders for their losses and/or costs in cases of borrower defaults associated with a pollution condition, and act, in effect, as loan guarantees for environmental risks.

The fact that small sites make up the majority of the universe of brownfield parcels limits the possible utilization of this insurance for individual projects. The cleanup costs on these sites are usually so low that individual insurance coverage for them is not cost effective (Meyer and Chilton 1998; Yount 1999; Yount and Meyer 1999). Moreover, the development firms attracted to such small sites are not likely to be of such a size that they have the capacity to negotiate for the types of insurance coverage that would best serve their risk-management needs. Thus, on grounds of both premium cost and coverage-negotiation efficiency, EDOs may be able to increase investor and developer interest in reclamation of the small sites that comprise the majority of the brownfields problem by providing insurance coverage for small sites.[3]

While insurance products are commonly used in large-scale, private brownfield projects, entities such as EDOs face exceptional difficulties in obtaining needed coverages.

1. The level of public and nonprofit sector knowledge is low with respect to environmental insurance in general and the value of coverage to brownfields projects in particular.

2. Brownfield policies are complex, and the need for manuscripting coverages means that EDO programs cannot simply replicate private sector programs. They contend with both publicly and privately owned sites, must provide for both small- and large-scale projects, and may be subject to special legal requirements dictating insurance purchases.

3. Relatively few brokers have brownfields expertise, and most of these are fully occupied with private sector developers, so the needed specialists may not be available to serve EDOs' needs. Exceptional effort, thus, is needed to design the state- and local-level brownfield insurance programs that could spur reclamation and redevelopment.

Final Caveats and Observations

The negative publicity associated with brownfields has led many local development groups to ignore such sites in their economic regeneration efforts. The emergence in the past five years of a growing group of private for-profit developers and investors specializing in brownfields demonstrates that, despite their history, these sites *do have a basic market appeal to the private sector* under some conditions (Meyer and Lyons 2000; Theriot 2001). The potential appeal of brownfields does not, however, make the decisions facing EDOs interested in their development any easier.

On the one hand, the private actions reinforce the claim that brownfields can be economically attractive. On the other, the very fact that some private brownfield redevelopments occur suggests that, in some instances, EDO subsidies to brownfield regeneration projects may be inefficient uses of local economic development effort and dollars. Moreover, some brownfield investors avoid involvement with publicly owned sites, because they fear constraints on their redevelopment options and possible stigma associated with the apparent "need" for public involvement. EDOs thus need to avoid involvement with sites that could sell themselves and to concentrate on the many brownfields that do not have market appeal to large, generally nonlocal, investors but that could, with a small public incentive, become attractive. The tools to provide the subsidies and facilitation exist, but the selection of targets remains difficult.

Notes

1. While the 1996 act clarified the actions lenders could take to avoid liability as owners if they foreclosed, two primary concerns about loaning on brownfields still remain: (a) A borrower's ability to repay a loan may be jeopardized if unexpected and

expensive cleanup costs should occur. (b) Lenders fear that if they do have to foreclose, environmental problems might lower the value of their collateral.

2. In practice, these controls have been found to present problems with regard to enforcement, funding, regulatory authority, monitoring, and implementation (ASTSWMO 1996; Gaspar and Van Burik 1998; ICF Kaiser, Inc., and E.P. Systems Group, Inc. 1999; Wernstedt and Hersh 1998).

3. This sort of coverage is precisely what the Commonwealth of Massachusetts arranged in 1999 for small-scale brownfield projects in that state. Other states continue to examine the appropriateness of the Massachusetts model for their purposes, but cities and counties are also looking to find new ways to promote brownfield regeneration and infill in their areas (Massachusetts 2001).

References

American Planning Association. 1999. *Planning Communities for the 21st Century*. Special Report of the APA's "Growing Smarter" project. Chicago: Author.

Arens, S.B. 1997. "The Valuation of Defective Properties: A Common Sense Approach." *Appraisal Journal* 65 (April): 143–48.

Association of State and Territorial Solid Waste Management Officials (ASTSWMO). 1996. *Survey of States on Institutional Controls at Federal Facilities*. Washington, DC: Author.

Bartsch, C., and E. Collaton. 1996. "Industrial Site Reuse and Urban Redevelopment—An Overview." *Cityscape: A Journal of Policy Development and Research* 2, no. 3: 17–61.

Bartsch, C.; E. Collaton; and E. Pepper. 1996. *Coming Clean for Economic Development*. Washington, DC: Northeast-Midwest Institute.

Bartsch, C.; B. Dorfman; and R. Deane. 2001. *Brownfields "State of the States": An End-of-Session Review of Initiatives and Program Impacts in the 50 States*. Washington, DC: Northeast-Midwest Institute: www.nemw.org/brown_stateof.pdf (November 21, 2001).

Bartsch, C.; C. Andress; J. Seitzman; and D. Cooney. 1991. *New Life for Old Buildings: Confronting Environmental and Economic Issues to Industrial Reuse*. Washington, DC: Northeast-Midwest Institute.

Chalmers, J.A., and T.O. Jackson. 1996. "Risk Factors in the Appraisal of Contaminated Property." *Appraisal Journal* 64 (January): 44–58.

Coffin, S., and A. Shepherd. 1998. "Barriers to Brownfield Redevelopment." *Public Works Management and Policy* 2, no. 3: 258–65.

Council for Urban Economic Development. 1998. *Brownfields Redevelopment Manual*. Washington, DC: Author.

Council for Urban Economic Development [Gilliland, E]. 1999. *Brownfield Redevelopment: Performance Evaluation*. Washington, DC: Author.

Davis, T.S., and K.D. Margolis, ed. 1997. *Brownfields: A Comprehensive Guide to Redeveloping Contaminated Property*. Chicago: American Bar Association.

Dotzour, M. 1997. "Groundwater Contamination and Residential Property Values." *Appraisal Journal* 65 (July): 279–85.

Garvin, A.; G. Baren; and C. Leinberger. 1997. *Urban Parks and Open Space*. Washington, DC: Urban Land Institute.

Gaspar, C., and D. Van Burik. 1998. *Local Government Use of Institutional Controls at Contaminated Sites.* Washington, DC: International City/County Management Association.

Gerrard, M.B., ed. 1998. *Brownfields Law and Practice: The Cleanup and Redevelopment of Contaminated Land.* New York: Matthew Bender.

ICF Kaiser, Inc., and E.P. Systems Group, Inc. [Meyer, P.B.]. 1999. *State Initiatives to Promote Redevelopment of Brownfields: An Assessment of Key Features.* Washington, DC: U.S. Department of Housing and Urban Development.

Kaiser, S.-E. 1998. "Commentary: Brownfields National Partnership." *Public Works Management and Policy* 2, no. 3: 196–201.

Kaiser, S.-E., and E. Bennett. 1999. "The Federal Role in Financing Brownfield Revitalization." In *Financing Brownfield Reuse,* ed. C. Bartsch, 53–56. Washington, DC: Northeast-Midwest Institute.

Massachusetts, Commonwealth of. Governor's Office for Brownfields Revitalization. 2001. "Brownfield Redevelopment Access to Capital (BRAC) Program": www.state.ma.us/massbrownfields/State_Subsidized_insurance_program.htm (November 21, 2001).

Meyer, P.B. 1991. "Meaning and Action in Local Economic Development Strategies: A Comparison of Policies in Britain and the United States." *Environment and Planning C: Government and Politics* 9, no. 4: 383–98.

———. 1998. Accounting for Differential Neighborhood Economic Development Impacts in Site-specific Area-based Approaches to Urban Brownfield Regeneration. Paper presented at Annual Conference, Association of Collegiate Schools of Planning, Pasadena, CA, November.

———. 2000a. *An Assessment of State Brownfield Initiatives.* Washington, DC: U.S. Department of Housing and Urban Development, Office of Policy Development and Research.

———. 2000b. "Accounting for Stigma on Contaminated Lands—The Potential Contributions of Environmental Insurance Coverages." *Environmental Claims Journal* 3, no. 3 (Spring): 33–55.

Meyer, P.B., and K.M. Chilton. 1998. *Environmental Insurance for Brownfields Redevelopment: A Feasibility Study.* Washington, DC: U.S. Department of Housing and Urban Development. Available at: www.huduser.org/publications/econdev/envins.html.

Meyer, P.B., and S. Deitrick. 1998. "Brownfields and Public Works." *Public Works Management and Policy* 3, no. 2: 202–9.

Meyer, P.B., and T.S. Lyons. 2000. "Lessons from Private Sector Brownfield Redevelopers: Planning Public Support for Urban Regeneration." *Journal of the American Planning Association* 66, no. 1: 46–57.

National Association of Development Organizations Research Foundation (NADO). 1999. *Reclaiming Rural America's Brownfields.* Washington, DC: Authors.

National Governors Association. 2000. *New Mission for Brownfields: Attacking Sprawl by Revitalizing Older Communities.* Washington, DC: Author.

Research Triangle Institute. 1998. *Redeveloping Brownfields: How States and Localities Use CDBG Funds.* Washington, DC: U.S. Department of Housing and Urban Development, Office of Policy Development and Research.

Ryan, K.-L. 1998. "Toxic Turnabouts: News from the Brownfield Front." *Planning* 64, no. 4: 20–23.

Schwab, J. 1997. *Redeveloping Brownfields.* PAS Memo. Chicago: American Planning Association.

Simons, R.A., and D.T. Iannone. 1997. "Brownfields Supply and Demand." *Urban Land* 56: 36–38, 78.

Stack, W.J., and T. Jacobsen. 1999. "Diminution in Property Value Arising from the *Stigma* of Environmental Contamination: A Phantom Injury in Search of Actual Damages." *Environmental Claims Journal* 11, no. 2: 21–47.

Theriot, C. 2001. "Hello, Good Buyer." *Brownfield News* 5, no. 5: 12–14.

Trust for Public Land. 1999. "20 Cases of Brownfield Conversions to Parks." Washington, DC: Author: www.tpl.org/tier3_cdl.cfm?content_item_id=904&folder_id=729 (November 21, 2001).

Urban Institute [Walker, C.; P. Boxall; C. Bartsch; E. Collaton; P.B. Meyer; and K.R. Yount]. 1998. *The Impact of Environmental Hazards and Regulations on Urban Redevelopment.* Washington, DC: U.S. Department of Housing and Urban Development, Office of Policy Development and Research.

U.S. Environmental Protection Agency (EPA), Office of Solid Waste and Emergency Response. 1995. *The Brownfields Economic Redevelopment Initiative—Application Guidelines for Demonstration Projects.* Washington, DC: Author: www.epa.gov/swerosps/bf/pilot.htm (November 21, 2001).

———. 1997. *Brownfields National Partnership Action Agenda.* Washington, DC: Author: www.epa.gov/swerosps/bf/97aa.htm (November 21, 2001).

———. 1999. *Deliberations of the EPA National Brownfields Tax Incentive Roundtable.* Chicago, March 5.

———. 2001. *Brownfields Cleanup Revolving Loan Fund Pilots.* Washington, DC: Author: www.epa.gov/swerosps/bf/rlflst.htm (April 17, 2000).

U.S. Conference of Mayors. 1998, 1999, 2000. *Recycling America's Land: A National Report on Brownfields Redevelopment.* Vols. 1, 2, 3. Washington, DC: Author.

Wells, B. 1999. *State Investment Strategies to Save Open Space and Steer Development.* Washington, DC: National Governors Association Center for Best Practice.

Wernstedt, K., and R. Hersh. 1998. "Urban Land Use and Superfund Cleanups." *Journal of Urban Affairs* 20, no. 4: 459–74.

Yount, K.R. 1999. "Environmental Insurance Products Available for Brownfields Redevelopment, 1999." Washington, DC: U.S. Environmental Protection Agency, Office of Solid Waste and Emergency Response. Available at www.epa.gov/brownfields/pdf/insrep99.pdf.

Yount, K.R., and P.B. Meyer. 1994. "Environmental Concerns and the Social Psychology of Risk." *Economic Development Quarterly* 8, no. 4: 338–44.

———. 1999. "Project Scale and Private Environmental Decision-making: Factors Affecting Investments in Small- and Large-Scale Brownfield Projects." *Urban Ecosystems* 3, no. 2: 179–93.

13

Financing Public Investment in Retail Development

William M. Bowen, Kimberly Winson-Geideman, and Robert A. Simons

Justifying Public Investment in Retail Development

The stated purpose of public sector economic development projects is usually to achieve one or more of several outcomes, including job creation, tax base enhancement, higher levels of income, greater income stability or a more equitable income distribution within a given geographical region, often in a local urban jurisdiction. In addition, though usually unstated, the appearance of development activity is usually popular with voters, and elected officials hope to cash in on this at reelection time as tangible evidence of their success. These projects often entail direct or indirect public expenditures to enhance the efficiency, productivity, or extent of the factors of production—land, labor, capital (e.g., real estate) and technology—within the region. Furthermore, public expenditures are typically intended to induce subsequent investment by the private sector, thus "leveraging" public funds, and, in turn, further achieving the desired outcomes.

Retail development clearly fits in its own way within the preceding characterization. Public investments in retail shopping centers or their underlying anchor tenants usually occur as a means of catalyzing the establishment of shopping centers in new or newly recognized retail nodes. Alternatively, investments are intended to fuel the growth of retail firms that otherwise would not become established locally, or else to induce a firm or firms to establish themselves locally when otherwise they would remain (or go) elsewhere. Project success depends upon whether the center or firm can eventually sustain profitability on the private market, and this, in turn, depends upon its having the appropriate size, access, visibility, and character and whether it is located in close enough proximity to a sufficient number of residential households with adequate spending power to support the new retail space.

The potential benefits of public investment in retail are generally recognized to include increased numbers of jobs, increased tax revenues, and increased convenience for local residents who (once more retail businesses are located nearby) need not travel so far to satisfy their demands. Retail centers in urban areas that have experienced economic decline can also at times be strategically important, notably when they help stem population loss by stabilizing or revitalizing urban services, a key component of which is access to convenience shopping (e.g., supermarket-anchored neighborhood and community shopping centers). Benefits can also be attributed to retail development in urban central cities and other subregional geographic areas if it stabilizes local services, or attracts or retains developed shopping centers within a specific urban municipal jurisdiction. Since public funds are expended, public officials as well as the general public must continually decide if it is worthwhile for the local public sector to make the investments.

Depending largely upon how well conceived any such investment is initially, it can potentially have either beneficial or detrimental effects, or, as is probably more often the case, some largely idiosyncratic mixture of both. To the extent that it stimulates economic growth that brings the sorts of jobs and resources needed to improve the quality of life throughout the region, it is clearly beneficial. But as anyone who has attempted to put together even a highly simplified model of a regional economy can readily attest, even very modestly sized regional economies are complex and have many highly interrelated elements. It is, therefore, usually difficult, at best, to anticipate all the implications of the investment, much less to determine formally whether the net benefits exceed those of the next best alternative course of action.[1] As a consequence, the number of times that public investments are made in retail development considerably exceeds the number of times that such investments are thoughtfully conceived and reasonably well justified.

In general, conducting studies that justify public investment in economic development and assess its costs and benefits are controversial because the methods used to do so are often poorly understood by the public at large, and they can be easily manipulated to appear to the untrained eye to provide the desired outcome. Therefore, relying on available theory and published methodologies is key in justifying and analyzing the expenditures.

Suppose, for example, that a public investment is made, thus attracting a new retail firm to anchor a retail center, and that firm brings numerous new jobs. On its face this could be interpreted as completely beneficial and desirable insofar as it increases the overall level of income and the tax base within the region. But upon closer scrutiny, there are some confounding factors. First, whether or not the expenditure of public funds was necessary to attract the firm—whether otherwise the firm would not have been established there (especially when the location is a highly profitable one)—is always open to debate. Second, there is the question of potential for the firms' success. A high percentage of newly established businesses fail, and if the new firm fails, at least as many jobs as are initially created are likely to then be eliminated. Third, because retail businesses tend not to export their goods and services, their multiplier effects tend to be minimal, whereas their expansion potential is limited by the size of the local market. Insofar as the same funds could quite possibly be otherwise expended for new export-oriented jobs, they could bring far greater return on investment to the region. Fourth, especially if the additional jobs are relatively low paying ones without health and other job benefits, they could bring the range of potential problems associated with increased variance in the regional income distribution (Thompson 1965: 178–88), especially at the lower end. Fifth, a larger, more efficient store with lower prices might displace several small stores that have higher prices, numerous employees, and strong local ties to their clientele. The net gain in employment may be close to zero. In short, unless the additional jobs turn out to have net benefits that are relatively greater than those for an alternative feasible use of the public investment, the net effect on the regional economy could amount to an overall decrease in the quality of life for many of the region's inhabitants.

In theory, there are two widely accepted, broad, and overarching theoretical justifications for any investment of public funds in our U.S. economy. The first is when private markets fail, in which case the investments are justified on *efficiency* grounds (Friedman 1984). In other words, when in an economic transaction private markets fail, for whatever reason, scarce resources are not used to their best advantage. One reason this can happen is when "spillovers," or what economists call "externalities" occur. That is, markets fail when there are indirect benefits (or costs) to society that are not accounted for in the pricing of a good or service. More specifically, when *indirect costs* are involved, the externalities are negative. A good example of a negative externality is the cost of environmental pollution, which is typically not accounted for in the pricing of the production of the good. For instance, if there is a cost paid by society to dispose of tires in a landfill when they are used up, then for the private market to function successfully the true cost to the consumer of tires should acknowledge this. The public sector strategy for fixing negative externalities is to internalize them, for example, by including a fee for tire disposal in the purchase price. On the other hand, when there are *indirect benefits* involved, the externalities are positive. A good example of a positive externality is the indirect benefit to surrounding property values that occurs when real estate development of new houses brings up property values in the immediately adjacent area. The immediately adjacent homeowners benefit through increased property values, and, to some extent, all of the city residents benefit from corresponding increases in property tax revenues. The key point here with such indirect benefits is that they are consumed collectively by people who do not actually make the investment—that is, those who do not assume the costs of the development—while, at the same time, the developer, who does assume the cost, cannot exclude these others from sharing in the resulting benefits. The public sector strategy for fixing positive externalities is to subsidize them, for example, by making public sector investments in retail development projects. Spillover effects in retail development can potentially occur if a local retail firm stimulates and becomes the focus for further development of adjacent retail development, new apartment buildings, movie theatres, skating rinks, miniature golf courses, industrial parks, or other economic activities in the immediate area (Jackson and Johnson 1991).

Another main source of market failure is the absence of adequate information. For example, in urban retail markets, household income (the prime demand factor for retail real estate) is often underreported due to in-kind government programs and the underground economy. Failure to correct this imperfect information will lead to the conclusion that the local market area has a spending power that is substantially below the actual level. For a more complete accounting of inner-city retail niche markets and their market failure problems, see Simons and Brennan (1996).

The second justification for making an investment of public funds in retail development occurs when society does not consider the distribution of purchasing power (wealth and income) acceptable or "fair," in which case the investments are justified on equity grounds.[2] A current situation ripe for public investment in inner-city retail development justified on equity grounds is described in some detail below. For now, suffice it to say that ideally, when violations of equity occur, finance of public investments occurs at the most geographically expansive level of government that is politically feasible. The attempt of a local government, for instance, to redistribute wealth or income increases mobility incentives for low-income families to migrate in to take advantage of the program and higher-income families to move out to avoid the corresponding tax burden.

In practice, investments in economic development projects most often occur without theoretical justification along either of these lines, and are based instead upon one of three largely ad hoc concepts (Leven 1985). The first, *the economic base concept*, is demand-driven in that it attaches primary importance to exports as the causal factor in regional economic growth. The implied tactics for economic developers are to attract and retain export activities and to help them to grow and prosper within the region. The second, the *aggregate production function concept*, emphasizes supply-side economic development strategies in that the economic developer's tactics are to help increase the region's aggregate production levels through investments designed to improve the marginal efficiency of private capital investment or of local components of the production process. Examples include investments to enhance the region's infrastructure, human capital base (Mathur 1999), or environment. The third, *import substitution*, can justify public sector investment in economic development projects when it can be shown that rather than increasing exports public investments can help establish local production of goods and services that otherwise would have been imported from outside the local economy.

Starting to put all of these thoughts together, with the exception of positive spillover effects and occasional instances of imperfect information, in our judgment it seems reasonable to assume that adequately competitive market conditions will obtain in most local retail trade. In this regard, to understand and thoroughly take into account efficiency considerations is a key to successful public investment in retail development. In the absence of market failure, local public sector investments in economic development projects are likely to waste resources. To this extent, the appropriate role for the investment of public funds in retail development projects is quite small (Blair 1995: 11). Only if the benefits attributable to the positive spillovers— increased tax revenues, numbers of jobs, and convenience for local residents who, once more retail businesses are located nearby, need not travel so far anymore to satisfy their demands—outweigh the corresponding costs, is the investment justified on strong theoretical grounds related to externalities.[3] Investments made on such grounds are likely to be economically successful.

Past this point, specific application of the three ad hoc concepts to retail, despite their seeming appeal, is limited. In terms of economic base theory, the emphasis is on the importance of exports. Since most consumer demands satisfied by retail are local (or regional) in orientation, the export base concept, as a rule, is not applicable. One notable category of exceptions would be festival shopping centers and others, such as the Mall of America in Minnesota, that are large enough to attract tourists or consumers from outside the region. Similarly, the aggregate production function concept is, as a rule, not applicable to retail, primarily because the bulk of retail sales go to satisfy final consumer demand and so do not discernibly tend to help increase the region's aggregate production levels. Moving on to the concept of import substitution, it usually pertains to local industries that supply major local businesses (Persky, Ramney, and Wiewel 1993). Insofar as retail firms are usually not in this category, the concept is not applicable. There is a sense, however, in which a slightly modified form can be used to help describe (and prescribe a public sector response to) the related phenomenon known as "retail leakage." Retail leakage occurs when retail dollars generated from within an area for convenience shopping are spent in another region outside the trade area. Examples of this include supermarket-anchored local goods and services where prices are generally constant and time to the shopping center is most important, comparison shopping including big-ticket items like durable goods, clothing, furniture, and other goods found at regional department stores in anchored shopping malls, or automobile sales. This leakage denies the local economy the tax base and jobs that would normally accompany this type of development. The appropriate public sector response to retail leakage would be to establish the relevant retail firms locally, thus presumably helping to keep the previously exported retail dollars circulating in the local economy.

To summarize, publicly assisted retail projects can theoretically be justified on the ground of efficiency, usually by the occurrence of spillovers or imperfect information, or on the ground of equity, which will be discussed below. Weaker justifications based upon the three ad hoc concepts can also be used. The export-base concept is applicable primarily insofar as retail projects create tourist-related shopping centers. The aggregate production function concept is, as a rule, not applicable at all. A slightly modified version of the concept of import substitution is applicable primarily insofar as retail projects help to meet the local populations' service needs, thus stemming retail leakage to other economic areas.

Types of Financial Instruments (Tools) Available

Whereas the number of times that public investments are made in retail development considerably exceeds the number of times that such investments are thoughtfully conceived and reasonably well justified, there are nevertheless instances in which such investments are justified. In such cases, it is important for the economic developer to be cognizant of the types of financial instruments available for the purpose.

When a local public investment in retail development has been deemed justifiable, several types of financial instruments (financing tools) designed to fill the financing gap between private debt financing and private equity are available. Funds are provided for financing new and expanding retail businesses, usually targeting those that create new jobs. Often the instruments are not specifically directed to retail development. Some have a much broader use base, typically industrial, extending all the way to far-reaching considerations such as brownfield redevelopment (brownfields are previously developed lands that are, or are perceived to be, contaminated with environmentally objectionable substances). Financial inducements for retail development projects typically assume one of four forms: loans, bonds, grants, or tax incentives. The following defines the four forms of financial inducements that are available and also provides examples of each.

Loans

State, association, local, and commercial loans are available to many developers for funding retail development projects. Many of these loan programs can offer creditworthy companies no- or low-interest loans, effectively increasing the amount of money available for projects. Loans usually have shorter repayment schedules than bonds. Many times the available amount of publicly subsidized loans are capped to allow the community to fund as many projects as possible. Project creditworthiness is assessed according to:

• Current level of debt
• Source of funds to repay debt
• Developer's past experience in obtaining and repaying loans
• Current socioeconomic conditions
• Management capabilities

The city of Pittsburgh, Pennsylvania, for example, offers low-interest loans through their Urban Development Fund (UDF). This program allows the city to loan up to 50 percent of total project cost (not to exceed $250,000) for commercial real estate projects. These funds can be used for the purchase of land and/or for building and related costs. The rate is fixed at 80 percent of prime, and the term is not to exceed thirty years.[4]

Many of these loan programs are revolving funds. For example, the city of Cleveland, Ohio, has a Small Business Revolving Loan program that provides low-cost loans for the acquisition of fixed assets (land, buildings, and equipment) and/or construction. The loans are funded with Federal and State Urban Development Action Grants, Community Development Block Grants, or EDA repayment revenues. Loans are available to any Cleveland business that will retain or create jobs. These loans are limited to $15,000 times the number of jobs retained or created with a limit of 40 percent of project financing, not to exceed $500,000. For example, a firm that is fixing up an old building for a new retail outlet that will have fifteen full-time employees could qualify for a $225,000 loan on its $600,000 rehab project. The rate on these loans is 75 percent of prime, although this is subject to negotiation (City of Cleveland Department of Economic Development 2001).

Bonds

Bonds, promissory notes sold by local governments or utilities, may be used to raise funds for large construction projects, possibly including retail. Bond interest rates are usually higher than federal or state-sponsored low-interest loans, but lower than commercial loan rates. In general, bonds issued by communities with more stable socioeconomic conditions and successful debt management track records will be more attractive to buyers than those with weaker circumstances (Standard and Poor's 1998). Bonds are purchased by investors and repaid through tax receipts or user fees.

The most common types of bonds are General Obligation and revenue bonds. First used in New York City in the early 1800s, General Obligation (GO) bonds are regarded by many as the safest possible investment next to U.S. Treasury bonds. For decades they were routinely secured by the full faith and credit of municipalities, and backed by the entire amount of taxable property within these communities. The proceeds were generally used for an uncontroversial public purpose. GO bonds can be issued by a municipal or county government to fund capital projects, such as street improvements. They are secured by the jurisdiction's general taxing power, and if planned revenues, such as property and/or income taxes, fall short of the amount needed to meet payments, the jurisdiction may raise taxes to generate the needed revenue. Revenue bonds, sometimes referred to as water/sewer bonds, are issued by the community and are backed by user fees or service charges paid by system users. These types of bonds may be used to extend or replace existing utilities in an effort to spur economic growth. These bonds are regarded as riskier investments, since they do not convey the full faith and credit of the municipality.

Recently, the use of revenue bonds has become more common. When using revenue bonds to help finance a project, the local government lends its tax-exempt interest rate to the project thus enabling potentially large debt service savings to the borrower. However, the loans are not secured by the municipality, but by the real estate build-out that the bonds help initiate. Use of Tax-exempt Revenue Bonds has been limited (capped on a modest per capita expenditure level) for over a decade. Because of its desirability, this tool is often allocated competitively.

As an example, the state of Connecticut's Department of Economic and Community Development provided a $1 million grant to the Greater Dwight Development Corporation in 1997 to help finance a New Haven shopping plaza with a Shaw's supermarket as the anchor store. The chronically depressed, inner-city neighborhood had been without a major supermarket for many years. This grant was provided through the state's Urban Action Bond

Program that is funded through state-issued bonds. While not specifically designated for retail development, the urban action bonds can be used for retail/supermarket projects. They may be authorized for any community and economic development projects. In addition to the state grant, the $14.7 million project was financed through a U.S. Department of Housing and Urban Development grant, an equity investment from the Local Initiatives Support Corporation's Retail Initiative, and $11 million in market-rate bank loans. The anchor opened in June 1998 and employs 175 people. Four smaller businesses use about 20,000 square feet in additional retail space.[5]

Grants

Limited grant money is sometimes available for retail project costs. At most, grants should be considered a component of an overall funding strategy. This is because they are typically too small to fund an entire project and have specific stipulations on how the money must be used. Since grants are often awarded competitively, they are an inherently unreliable source of funding for individual projects. As an example, the state of Pennsylvania offers grants to financially disadvantaged communities to prepare and implement business development strategies within municipal enterprise zones. Amounts vary based on the use of the funds. Planning and basic grants are awarded in amounts up to $50,000, and competitive grants are available in amounts up to $250,000.[6]

Tax Incentives

Tax incentives are available primarily as either abatements or credits. Abatements allow a partial to full reduction of property taxes for a fixed period of time. Generally, abatements apply only to buildings and exclude tax on land. They often include a recapture provision, allowing the taxing authority full repayment of all abatements in the event the recipient defaults on the terms contained in the agreement.

Tax credits serve as a percentage reduction in tax liability. They are typically based on a specific criterion, such as the Historic Preservation Tax Credit offered by the federal government. This program allows for a 25 percent tax credit of the total cost and expenses of rehabilitation for a historic property—provided that the costs exceed the total basis (pre-rehab value) in the property and the rehabilitation meets the standards consistent with the Standards of the Secretary of the U.S. Department of Interior for rehabilitation. Tax credits may be carried back three preceding years and carried forward for the next ten, to be used to offset taxable income. Sites must be certified historic structures and listed individually on the National Register or they may be located in a certified historic district listed in the National Register of Historic Places.

The city of Toledo provides an excellent example of tax incentives, specifically abatements, available for businesses locating in their Community Reinvestment Area (CRA). CRAs were created by the Ohio Community Reinvestment Area Program legislation, effective as of November 1977. This program allows cities to designate CRAs in which real property tax exemption can be granted for an increased property valuation that results from improvements or new construction in the designated areas. CRAs are typically economically depressed and suffer from blight. In Toledo, the city offers up to fifteen years of tax abatement for all new construction locating in the CRA. The amount of the abatement is based upon the increase in property valuation resulting from improvements, subject to agreements with the designated school district and wage requirements.[7]

Tax credits are also often granted to employers of low-income or minority workers under such programs as the various enterprise zones.

Innovative Funding Sources

The key to successful funding for retail development is often not to look only at financial arrangements that have the word "retail" attached to them but to keep the end goal of retail development in mind. This is especially true for inner-city site assembly.

Many localities have used innovative strategies for funding retail and other economic development projects. For instance, in the mid-1990s, the city of Cleveland received a $40 million dollar lawsuit settlement. Rather than put it in the general operating budget, the administration chose to create the Neighborhood Development Investment Fund (NDIF). Unique to this city, the fund is structured to provide gap financing for large-scale economic development and housing ventures. The NDIF is also used to finance the acquisition and site preparation costs associated with industrial and commerce park developments. The minimum loan amount is $500,000, up to 25 percent of project financing but no more than $2 million. The loans have a standard rate of 4 percent fixed, subject to negotiation. The loan is recorded as a lien position on a fixed asset (the subject property or other property owned by the borrower), subordinated to first position financing. The first position in the queue is typically an acquisition or construction loan issued by a lending institution (City of Cleveland Department of Economic Development 2001).

Other types of less direct and often very innovative financial inducements are available to reduce the costs associated with the development of retail projects. Communities may create a special taxing district for the purpose of tax incremental financing (TIF) (see chapter 3, in this volume). A TIF allows the increase in tax revenues raised from new development, as assessed by the net increase over the existing property tax base, to be earmarked to fund capital improvements, such as streets, sidewalks, lighting, water, and sewers (Miles, Haney, and Berens 1996). TIF is closely related to revenue bonds and is incompatible with tax abatement because the stream of property taxes is allocated to debt repayment rather than the borrower's bottom line.

Also available in some cases are programs that subsidize the cost of land acquisition, some of which can at times be used for retail development. For instance, the city of Cleveland implemented a land bank program that has been in existence for over thirty years. Over time, this program has allowed the city to acquire numerous parcels of land through tax delinquency. It now offers this land to potential retail developers at amounts significantly below the market value.

In some cases loans, grants, and tax incentives available for cleanup and redevelopment of brownfields can be of use for retail development. For example, the Wisconsin Department of Commerce offers millions of dollars in grants to businesses and other parties for the redevelopment of brownfields, some of which may be used for retail projects. Similarly, the Cook County, Illinois, property tax incentive allows the real estate tax classification of a property to be changed while remediation and redevelopment are taking place. This can result in significant savings by directly reducing the property's assessment rate. The Illinois EPA must approve the eligibility of remediation costs for this credit, and the credit must be claimed in the same taxable year the approval is granted. If the property is sold, the credit may be transferred to the buyer. The tax credit is 25 percent of the unreimbursed eligible remediation costs.

As communities continue to provide innovative financing opportunities that adequately subsidize the costs associated with retail development, developers will exercise every option to access them. Without these subsidies, some areas lack the economic viability to use a strictly market-based method of attracting new or expanding development. When they do use subsidies, financial inducements and funding strategies can become very important to providing basic local services to residents in the form of shopping centers and retail establishments.

Public Investment in Retail to Achieve Greater Efficiency or Growth

When a market failure is used to justify public expenditures for retail development, a fully conceptualized justification rests not only upon its presence, as opposed to absence, but, furthermore, upon the expectation that the net benefit (i.e., benefits-costs) of the public expenditures will be positive.

Setting aside a host of perplexing issues regarding the measurement problems of benefits and costs, as well as those dealing with the determination of which constraints to consider exogenous or unalterable, the overall approach is:

1. determine which costs (loans, grants, land, tax abatements, etc.) and benefits (tax revenues, jobs, increased tax base, votes in the next election etc.) are to be included for each year in the analysis;
2. select a discount rate that reflects the community's relative evaluation of benefits and costs this year and benefits and costs in the future, so that all can be stated in comparable terms; and
3. obtain an aggregate, discounted present value of the project.

The key elements in making the determination of whether to invest are a listing of all the major outcomes anticipated to come from the project, a listing of all parties affected by these outcomes, and then a valuation of the effect of the outcomes upon their welfare, as it would be valued in money terms by them. A number of excellent textbooks can be found in which the procedures are considered in detail (e.g., Layard and Glaister 1994). For an example of benefit cost analysis in the housing context, see Simons and Sharkey (1997).

Public Investment in Retail to Improve Equity

It was mentioned previously that public sector investments in retail development projects are theoretically justified also by considerations related to neighborhoods and social equity (Wiewel, Brown, and Morris 1989; Nowak 1997). Specifically, investments in retail development can be theoretically justified on equity grounds when inequities in the retail sector arise and are acknowledged by society. Sometimes these factors are also lumped into the "social benefits" or intangibles category in an efficiency-based, benefit-cost framework.

In this regard, a fairly common complaint made by disadvantaged inner-city residents today is that the large retail stores at which the greatest selection and best prices are found tend to be located far away in the suburbs. An example of this is supermarkets. The complaint is that large supermarkets tend to locate in the suburbs rather than the inner city or in neighborhoods near the downtown. The residents, therefore, have to buy their groceries from small-scale corner grocery stores, where the range of options is considerably lower and prices are considerably higher. Similar complaints are made in relation to other nondiscretionary retail goods, such as are found in general-purpose discount stores. In a nutshell, the argument is that the spatial distribution of these retail firms is such that a disproportionately low number of the ones offering the best buys on nondiscretionary items are located in disadvantaged areas in the inner city. Thus, those living in disadvantaged inner-city neighborhoods that can least afford to pay higher prices for nondiscretionary retail goods are also those that by virtue of the location decisions of retailers have the fewest options.

Moreover, there would seem to be little, if any, economic rationale that would explain the locational decisions of the retail firms in this regard. Indeed, given the population densities in many inner-city neighborhoods, even in those with low per capita incomes, there is a sufficient number of clientele with sufficient purchasing power within a very short distance to support an array of large-scale retail stores. When such arguments can be substantiated by careful market-data analysis, they can be used to help justify public sector investments in retail development on the equity-related grounds of income and resource redistribution. They can also have local job creation implications. Especially in urban retail markets, these problems often are related to the aforementioned lack of information about household income in the area.

On purely economic efficiency grounds, there is little, if any, reason to expect large-scale retail firms not to locate in disadvantaged inner-city neighborhoods. To the extent that startup, expansion, and/or locational decision processes of retail firms are economically rational, and therefore more likely to succeed in the marketplace, they tend to be based upon tradeoffs among locational features needed for the firm to generate profit. These include factors such as transportation costs, taxes, accessibility to clientele, proximity to the appropriate workforce, availability of the necessary infrastructure, and site and energy costs (Blair 1995). While the particular tradeoffs considered by firms will vary with firm and situation, in general, the economically rational firm selects the location at which the particular mix of factors promises the greatest net revenues (profits minus costs).

To the extent that retail location is determined by accessibility to clientele, specifically the aggregate distance from the consumers to the retail store, one would expect a tendency for higher concentrations of retail stores in the inner city. Greater accessibility is assured there by greater population density and minimum aggregate distance to consumers from throughout the region. Of course, the tendency for retail to concentrate downtown would be expected to be offset somewhat by the longstanding tendency in the United States toward urban decentralization of population and industry. Especially since the middle of the twentieth century, this tendency has included a trend toward the suburbanization of retail business, along with the appearance of large, planned shopping centers (Cadwallader 1996: 113). One would expect retail development also to be found at the intersections of major transportation routes, where increased land values stimulate increased development.

One way to use market analysis to help determine whether public sector investment in retail projects can be justified by equity considerations is to look at the spatial distribution of definite categories of retail activity in relation to sociodemographic data. The idea is, in essence, to evaluate how close members of given social groups are to given categories of retail activities. The process begins by first, at a conceptual level, selecting a category of retail activity, such as "major supermarkets," for which geocoded data are available. Then one counts how many times particular supermarkets can be found located within a given unit area, such as a census tract, and how many members of the given social groups (e.g., low-income families) are located within that area. If the numbers of members in the social group are high where the numbers of major supermarkets are low, then this indicates a disproportionately low distribution of supermarkets in neighborhoods characterized by residents belonging in those social groups. If, in relation to a comparison area, a significantly lower level of proximity is found for minorities, low-income and other disadvantaged populations, this is normally taken as empirical substantiation for the claim of disproportionate distributions, thus helping to substantiate the existence of inequities. Finally, demographic market studies that rely on available census data often understate the buying power of local residents, a form of information market failure. More refined methodologies are required to tease out actual spending power to justify market demand (Simons and Brennan 1996).

Summary and Conclusion

On balance, probably the economic developer's most important task is to make sure that a suitable proportion of regional employment is in industries whose products are in heavy demand from outside the region. Most retail jobs are not export oriented, and so investment in retail is a second-best alternative that, as a rule, makes sense only when investments in export-oriented jobs are not feasible.

Past this point, the success of a public-sector investment in a retail project is likely to depend heavily upon how well it is initially conceived and justified. Theoretically, there are two overarching reasons for making such an investment, one based upon efficiency and the other on equity. On efficiency grounds, the public investment piece, usually a lever to access private funds, can be justified by market failure from spillover effects (positive externalities) and/or lack of adequate information about certain (e.g., urban) retail market areas. If the market fails for either of these reasons, and, furthermore, the net benefits minus costs are positive, the expenditure can be fully justified. In practice several other ad hoc concepts are also used to justify expenditures, but with the exception of the couple of limited sets of circumstances mentioned above, these concepts are not applicable to investment in retail. Otherwise, in some cases, there can be a justification found in equity considerations.

When it is determined that public investments in retail are to occur, there are a number of financing instruments that can be used, and these were introduced and briefly described above. Given the range of funding sources, including the innovative ones, the key to success, in our view, is to focus on the broader goal of finding the necessary financing, rather than restricting oneself to funds designated specifically for retail.

In terms of benefit-cost analysis, the key point, in our view, is that the preponderance of retail development projects have a somewhat idiosyncratic mixture of beneficial and detrimental effects, and that, therefore, even in the presence of a market failure, unless a thorough benefit-cost analysis is done, the net effect of the investment could be to decrease the quality of life in the region. We briefly introduced the technique and suggested one of several excellent sources that can be used for guidance when implementing it.

Notes

1. Net benefits refer to the value of the full range of benefits minus their corresponding costs. The costs are the value of the alternative benefits that would have been available had the resources used to support the project not been thus used.

2. An excellent and simply presented analysis of the relationship between efficiency and equity, clearly illuminating the role of the public sector, can be found in Schreiber and Clemmer (1982: 82–88).

3. The only other strong theoretical justification we can imagine is when, in the presence of imperfect information, the benefits from gathering more and better information outweigh the corresponding costs. For example, as is suggested in the section in this chapter on public investment in retail to improve equity, a complaint often made by disadvantaged inner-city residents today is that the large retail stores at which the greatest selection and best prices can be found tend to be located far away in the suburbs. One of the reasons for this is imperfect information used in estimating the purchasing power of residents in those areas. The relatively large underground economy there, in combination with other factors, can lead to significant underestimates of residential purchasing power. If it could be shown that the benefits to the region that would follow from the accurate information exceed the costs of gathering it, this would theoretically justify the expenditure of public funds to gather the information. For instance, if a large retail store were to locate in the area, it might decrease the demand for buses needed for local residents to travel to and from the suburbs to avail themselves of such stores. At the same time, air quality could be improved, bringing significant benefits. Similarly, because small, local stores tend not to have the same cleanliness standard as do the large retail stores, if a large retail store were to locate in the area, it might decrease the demand for public health inspectors. Furthermore, the perceived quality of life in the vicinity could be greater, making it easier to attract

residents, thus increasing tax revenues. If all such positive factors could be delineated and their value estimated, and if the corresponding benefits were to outweigh the costs of gathering the information needed to improve purchasing power estimates, this would constitute a strong theoretical justification for the public investment.

4. For further information, see www.ura.org/busdev2.htm.

5. For more information, see www.state.ct.us/ecd.

6. For further information, see www. dced.state.pa.us/PA_Exec/DCED/business/f.ez.htm.

7. For further information see: www.ci.toledo.oh.us/index.cfm/dept=dept3nav&page=page1252.

References

Blair, John P. 1995. *Local Economic Development: Analysis and Practice.* Thousand Oaks, CA: Sage.

Cadwallader, M. 1996. *Urban Geography: An Analytical Approach.* Upper Saddle River, NJ: Prentice Hall.

City of Cleveland Department of Economic Development. 2001. http://www.city.cleveland.oh.us/government/departments/econdev/edsbrlprog.html.

Friedman, Lee. S. 1984. *Microeconomic Policy Analysis.* New York: McGraw-Hill.

Jackson, E., and D. Johnson. 1991. "Geographic Implications of Mega-Malls, with Special Reference to West Edmonton Mall." *Canadian Geographer* 35: 226–32.

Layard, Richard, and Stephen Glaister, ed. 1994. *Cost-Benefit Analysis.* 2d ed. Cambridge: Cambridge University Press.

Leven, Charles L. 1985. "Regional Development Analysis and Policy." *Journal of Regional Science* 25: 569–92.

Mathur, Vijay. 1999. "Human Capital-Based Strategy for Regional Economic Development." *Economic Development Quarterly* 13, no. 3: 203–16.

Miles, Michael; Richard Haney, Jr.; and Gayle Berens. 1996. *Real Estate Development: Principles and Process.* Washington, DC: Urban Land Institute.

Nowak, Jeremy. 1997. "Neighborhood Initiative and the Regional Economy." *Economic Development Quarterly* 11, no. 1: 3–10.

Persky, Joseph; David Ranney; and Wim Wiewel. 1993. "Import Substitution and Local Development." *Economic Development Quarterly* 7, no. 1: 18–29.

Schreiber, Arthur F., and Richard B. Clemmer. 1982. *Economics of Urban Problems.* 3d ed. Boston: Houghton Mifflin.

Simons, Robert A., and John Brennan. 1996. "Development and Issues of Inner-City Retail Niche Markets." In *Megatrends in Retail Property*, ed. John Benjamin, 295–313. Boston: Kluwer.

Simons, Robert A., and David. Sharkey. 1997. "Jump Starting New Urban Housing Markets: Do the Fiscal Benefits Justify the Public Costs?" *Housing Policy Debate* 8, no. 1: 143–72.

Standard and Poor's. 1998. *Public Finance Criteria.* New York: Standard and Poor's.

Thompson, Wilbur. 1965. *A Preface to Urban Economics.* Baltimore: Johns Hopkins University Press.

Wiewel, Wim; Bridget Brown; and Marya Morris. 1989. "The Linkage Between Regional and Neighborhood Development." *Economic Development Quarterly* 3, no. 2: 94–110.

14

Rural Economic Development

John Magill

Introduction

Economic development in rural America occurs within both the market realm and a wider community context with numerous challenges to economic growth and wealth creation similar to those in more densely populated places. The magnitude of those challenges, however, requires a clear goal to achieve measurable economic development in a rural community, and that goal is more difficult to achieve as the distance from population centers increases. A brief review of the nature of rural development, associated planning activities, and identification of the resources available highlights the importance of evaluating options, if rural communities are to reap the benefits of new economic activity. Rural economic development is likely to succeed only with a combination of understanding and a vision for a specific place, applied to the policies and resources available to rural areas of America.

America stretches from its largest cities to isolated towns in the mountains, with economic activity as varied as its landscape and people. Economic development flows across this landscape in an uneven pattern. Development occurs in many places with limited direct financial assistance from government and nonprofits. But in rural America, economic development often needs assistance because of the limited economic tools—human capital, financial assets, and natural resources—available there. Rural America, where approximately one in four Americans lives at the turn of the twenty-first century, lags behind metropolitan areas in many statistical categories. Rural Americans reside in a vast land area, which in some Plains States dwarf the metropolitan communities. Long-lasting economic and community development in such places will not occur without recognition of the expanse of land and the importance of each individual.

Background

Rural America is remote from the major metropolitan areas that contain most of the wealth and the faster growing employment sectors that exist in almost every state. Rural areas are defined by a variety of agencies and organizations at the federal level from the U.S. Bureau of Census, to the Office of Management and Budget, to the U.S. Department of Agriculture. Each agency relies upon its own vocabulary about places in America: rural and urban places, metropolitan/nonmetropolitan, and rural-urban continuum (Fluharty 2001). According to the 1990 census, 24.8 percent of the nation lived in a rural area (U.S. Census 1990). By all measures rural areas lag behind in many economic statistical categories, and their citizens do not participate fully in the economic development seen in metropolitan areas. Incomes and economic growth rates lag behind the nation and metro areas within individual states (Drabenstott and Shaeff 2001).

Defining economic development is a difficult, awkward, and time-consuming task. For the purpose of this discussion, economic development occurs when wealth is created for citizens, businesses, and government. Each part supports the opportunities of the other. Citizens purchase goods and they work at firms. Businesses provide jobs and pay taxes. These activities enable citizens to maintain an improving standard of living, resulting in government support of the services necessary to sustain a community over the long term.

Today, in many places in rural America, fading business and stagnant wage rates prevent the accumulation of wealth by households and smaller firms. Large manufacturers with lower-skill jobs and large discount retailers may provide employment and consumer choice, but they do not bring rising wage rates or long-term, sustainable development by themselves.

Successful rural economic development needs the private sector and government to cooperate to enhance the local marketplace, so individuals and businesses have the opportunity to flourish. Government at all levels, through the prudent use of expenditures and policies, lays out the parameters in which economic development occurs. Government, though, is unable and ill suited to determine the businesses that succeed or fail in the marketplace.

Rural economic development strategy begins with the recognition that successful development results in a measurable improvement in the economic and social conditions of individual citizens and communities. Economic development requires the same combination of elements, regardless of location—people, resources, and capital. Yet in rural America, two of the three ingredients, people and capital, are often difficult to locate and are limited in nature. Thus, the challenge for rural development is to identify the economic opportunities able to leverage the community's competitive advantages. If successful, the use of leverage leads to changed local conditions.

Many rural areas remain dependent on only one form of economic activity, be it agriculture, manufacturing, or natural resource extraction. In each case, changes in market demand coupled with increased global competition and the commodity nature of many goods inhibits rural communities from capturing economic growth at the pace they desire. The alternative they must consider is a major change in the local economic structure.

Economic development predominantly takes three forms: large-scale, new, capital investment, often a manufacturing or warehouse facility; expansion of local businesses; and entrepreneurship. Entrepreneurship may have the potential for the greatest return for a rural place, but it remains the most difficult to accomplish with many new small businesses failing in their first years.

Don Macke of the Nebraska Community Foundation identifies five uniquely rural hurdles to be overcome by an enterprise in rural America: "Distance to markets, independent spirit of rural populations, capital availability, economies of scale and absence of entrepreneurial networks" (National Association of Development Organizations Research Foundation 2001). Four of the five hurdles can be lowered through policy and effort. Only distance to market cannot be changed; it remains a physical fact.

Scott Loveridge, Director of the Regional Research Institute at West Virginia University, would add lack of information and business services to the row of hurdles rural development faces (Loveridge 2000). Without accurate economic information, rural business often fails to act in a timely manner and becomes less competitive over time. Strong business services in the form of accounting and legal assistance provide a foundation upon which a business can develop. A number of rural communities are using development finance tools to help attract and sustain these services and others, such as telecommunications and printing. Community Development Corporations (CDCs) and other nonprofits also act to fill this void and assist with accounting and business planning to help improve the chances a business can overcome the hurdles confronting rural economic development activity.

Many states still pursue in-migrating businesses as the primary economic development strategy rather than striving to help local entrepreneurs and businesses succeed. It is reasonable to assume at this juncture that the search for new, large-scale investment produces one winner and many losers. A diversified strategy of helping local firms expand, retaining and creating jobs in conjunction with increased entrepreneurial activity, may be a more successful and lasting economic development strategy. This two-pronged strategy serves existing concerns and sows the seeds for future employers, creators of wealth, for the benefit of the rural community.

Places beyond the metropolitan limits easily recognize that true economic growth comes from attracting capital to itself from beyond the micro region through exports of goods and services. Smaller populations and lower income levels necessitate this strategy as rural America lacks both population density and wealth. Business activity in rural areas is often inhibited by both lack of available private capital and higher capital costs due to a lack of competition among private lenders. It is possible to witness a difference of as much as two percentage points between a local bank in a rural area and a larger lender able to mitigate the danger of weaker loans in its portfolio.

Government investment in businesses and communities in rural America operates to offset real or perceived market imperfections inhibiting development opportunities. The investments by different levels of government attempt to bring capital into places where there is a mismatch between a high demand and low supply of capital to finance public and private goods. Grant and low-interest loan dollars spent for infrastructure assist communities unable to enter the bond markets due to income constraints or ability to carry debt. Rural communities with less intrinsic wealth are constantly challenged in financing these public goods by the inability to generate adequate revenues to support the amortization of bonds and notes.

Financing

Financial resource searches begin for many communities with the pursuit of monetary grants. Federal dollars are the most common, with each state having access to Small Cities Community Development Block Grant (CDBG) funds. The dollars are directed by legislation to benefit low-moderate income citizens and their communities. Many states use some portion of these funds for economic development activity.

Ohio sets aside approximately 22 percent of its annual CDBG allocation for economic development activities. This percentage equaled $8 million for economic development in fiscal year 2002 (Office of Housing and Community Partnerships 2002). The program provides below-market-rate-interest loans, with the ability to take a second or even third collateral position to businesses, and infrastructure grants to communities to support business development. Rural Ohio communities able to identify a business with growth potential are able to leverage substantial private investment using CDBG funds as the key subsidy in a project. Williams County in Northwest Ohio obtained a $400,000 grant from the state, of which $239,000 was spent on water and sewer infrastructure and $151,000, as low-interest loans for machinery and equipment. The firm, Custom Molded Plastics, was able to attract $5.2 million in loans. The anticipated result is sixty-two new jobs, with forty-four being made available to low-moderate income individuals. Custom Molded Plastics is a locally owned startup firm looking to capture market share in plastics related to the automobile and manufacturing sectors (Office of Housing and Community Partnerships 2000).

In June 1990, the Federal Reserve Bank of Boston hosted a conference, "Is There a Shortfall in Public Capital Investment?" to discuss infrastructure financing and its importance to economic performance. Alicia Munnell, senior vice president of the Federal Reserve Bank of Boston, with the assistance of Leah M. Cook, wrote of the positive relationship between public infrastructure investment and private investment and employment growth: "The conclusion is that those states that have invested more in infrastructure tend to have greater output, more private investment, and more employment growth" (Munnell 1990). For the purposes of rural development this translates into placing infrastructure development at the forefront of public expenditures rather than tax and workforce incentives.

Beyond CDBG funding the federal government offers Rural Development, Appalachian Regional Commission, and Community Service Block Grant (CSBG) funds, to name a few. The federal process for funding relies upon appropriations from Congress to supply states and agencies with funds to support infrastructure, community building, and social delivery services. Communities and nonprofit organizations can apply for these funds from either the state or federal agencies to support their activities. The dollars are made available through a combination of grants and loans. Many poorer rural communities rely upon the grant dollars to fund the needed improvements in their communities. Unfortunately, the composition of today's funding provides more dollars in low-interest loans than in grants. A decade ago, the Department of Agriculture, through the Farmers Home Administration, now Rural Development, provided financing with more than half in grants; today the maximum level of grant assistance is in the range of 40 percent.

Rural communities wishing to provide needed infrastructure for economic or even community development now need to gather the disparate pieces into one funding scenario. Often a community will obtain a combination of CDBG, Rural Development, and local dollars to build centralized water and sewer services without an economic development project, but rather as necessary community investment. To obtain this financing, many communities must have their combined water and sewer rates at 2.5 percent–3.0 percent of median income. For example, in rural southwestern Indiana, Gibson County, with a median annual household income of $36,764 (U.S. Census 1998) a combined monthly bill could be at the level of $76.60. Any new or improved infrastructure service makes the community more competitive for future economic development investments. Economic development activity should lead to an increase in community wealth to help offset the costs of having important services spread over a small rate base.

This change in funding requires communities to rely upon their visioning and planning process to help guide their decisions. The relationship between sound planning and appropriate financing is direct. Successful projects and communities moving forward use the financing to support planned investments. The investments in the form of infrastructure, industrial parks, and housing can help a small town nurture incremental growth or respond quickly to a large-scale development opportunity.

Infrastructure investment followed by specific resources and opportunities to support private investment are a logical next step for rural America. As the economy changes, entrepreneurship is more important. Reports differ on the role of small business to overall microeconomic performance; however, "75% percent of rural firms have fewer than 20 employees" (National Association of Development Organizations Research Foundation 2001). This large group of firms and their success are one determinant of wealth creation in rural places.

Access to capital is an ongoing, long-term concern for rural entrepreneurs. Small Business Development Centers and other nonprofits, including CDCs, now partner with emerging entrepreneurs to develop a complete business plan and to help obtain capital. The plan is able to fully describe the business and its financial needs for capital in the form and language desired by lenders, private and public. A well-prepared business plan gives the entrepreneur a greater likelihood of success with a loan decision than does a free flowing discussion.

The federal government through the Small Business Administration, Department of Housing and Urban Development, Department of Commerce, Economic Development Agency and dollars in other agencies and departments is a large mover in the market to provide small-business financing and infrastructure assistance to benefit business. These government products often involve a direct lending component of subordinated lending providing below-market-rate-interest loans and acceptance of a secondary or even tertiary collateral position. It is believed that public dollars with these characteristics are able to give greater security and likelihood of repayment for private investment. The dollars are normally applied to fixed asset financing—bricks and sticks.

Revolving loan funds (RLFs) are a locally controlled financier of small businesses in rural America. One source of capitalization for RLFs is CDBG funds granted to communities for lending to private businesses with repayments returning to the local communities. As the RLF industry ages, however, more individual RLFs are being capitalized with bank and other private investments.

In 1997, the Corporation for Enterprise Development (CFED) undertook a detailed national study of the RLF industry, "Counting on Local Capital." CFED gathered in-depth data from six states, including Washington, California, and Ohio. Two years later, CFED wrote that, nationally, RLFs had total assets of $8 billion (Levere and Wingate 1999). For rural places, RLFs can be crucial to economic development. In 1999, it was estimated that 6 percent of all jobs in Vinton County, Ohio, with its population of approximately 12,000, were directly created by RLF-assisted businesses. The businesses ranged from the only grocery store in the county to a microenterprise loan for a shitake mushroom farmer (Magill 1999).

The CFED study provided a glimpse of the type of lending activity that may be occurring in rural areas. Loans average in size from $51,725 to $77,162. At a cost per job between $5,388 and $6,476, each loan resulted in the creation of eight to fifteen jobs. Most funds do not have policies regarding the types of businesses eligible for assistance. The loans are given as a subordinated note at a below market rate. RLFs in general had delinquency rates of approximately 6 percent (CFED 1997).

Individual states, depending upon their priorities and financial health, support grant and low-interest loan programs with general revenues to help businesses in rural communities. Ohio, for example, developed its Rural Pioneer Loan Program with the following criteria: "Businesses must demonstrate that they will create new jobs for Ohio citizens in rural areas. Loans may be used for acquisition of land and buildings, new construction, renovation and expansion of existing buildings and acquisition of machinery and equipment" (Connect Ohio 2002). This program structure is similar to what exists in many other states involved in rural development financing.

Education

Knowledge, innovation, and applied higher skills are the foundation of an emerging global economy driven by new products, processes, and information. The nature of the economy ensures that a premium is paid for noncommodity goods. Rural areas are often populated by less-educated individuals, and they lack the worker skill sets required to produce the quality, value-added goods demanded by consumers and firms prospering in a knowledge-innovation-driven economic system.

The 1998 Census estimates of the educational attainment among individuals eighteen years or older found a gap of 8.6 percent for those with the bachelor degree or more between the metropolitan (22.2 percent) and nonmetropolitan (13.6 percent) areas. The gap between metropolitan and nonmetropolitan attainment rates was smaller at the high school graduate or more level with metro areas seeing 82.1 percent of the population at this level, while the nonmetro areas have 77.7 percent (Bureau of the Census 1998). There exists a reasonable correlation between the higher educational attainment rates and incomes seen in metropolitan vis-à-vis rural areas.

A possible solution for policymakers concerned with rural economic development is to provide additional economic opportunity for greater numbers of educated individuals to stay in rural America. Unfortunately, the reality in labor markets in rural America, according to rural sociologists Molly Sizer Killian and Lionel J. Beaulieu, is fewer opportunities for higher educated individuals, resulting in fewer economic reasons for these individuals to stay (Killian and Beaulieu 1995). For example, rural economists and researchers on behalf of the Economic Development Administration demonstrated that manufacturing firms in rural areas see their location hindering the recruitment of management and professional staff necessary to the operation of a modern plant (Gale, McGranahan, Greenberg, and Teizeira 1999).

Rural America thus witnesses fewer high-wage jobs attractive to younger, more highly educated individuals, leading to a slow decline in human capital and lower economic development over time. Pennsylvania State University education researchers Debra Blackwell and Diana McClaughlin, relying upon data collected by the Bureau of Labor Statistics, analyzed the educational goals of rural youth, the future workforce and creators of wealth for their communities. Blackwell's and McClaughlin's (1998) findings highlight that the lack of higher value economic activity occurring in poorer rural places and this realization of lower economic opportunity often leads to the abandoning of rural areas by those best able to lead.

Increased funding for education in rural America may be necessary for any long-term economic improvement. "If rural areas are to attract high technology manufacturing and producers services, their fundamental educational systems must produce a workforce with excellent basic communication and computational skills, plus an ability to respond to the rapid technological changes associated with these industries," according to agricultural economist Glen C. Pulver (1995). School funding, though, remains a highly charged issue in many states. The issue involves numerous stakeholders and competing objectives, such as levels of expenditure and means of revenue generation. While the stakeholder demands generate headlines, the lack of current educational resources and assets likely ensures that any expansion in entrepreneurial activity and infrastructure investment will not yield the anticipated economic returns.

New investment to generate returns relies upon individuals with the skills to use the investment to build and sustain business development. Noted economist John Kenneth Galbraith goes further by describing relationships between a growing economy and education: "The modern economy requires a well-prepared adaptable labor force. The expanding sectors—production based on technology and the arts and design, the great and growing travel, cultural and entertainment industries and the professions—all must have an educated workforce" (Galbraith 1996).

Conclusion

Seeking financial resources for important development initiatives aimed to move the community forward may strain its leaders as they try to bring a vision of economic development to a market reality. The public coffers are dwindling for many rural communities, and there is limited access to the private capital markets based upon current demand (Mikesell and Wallace 1996). Rural development becomes difficult to accomplish without the finances to pay for necessary infrastructure improvements or provide incentives to retain or locate business.

Participants in rural development efforts run the gamut from the federal government to small CDCs focused on a small sector or group of clients. These local and regional organizations look to fill particular needs in the community and help build capacity to accomplish long- and short-term goals. While federal dollars can be an important part of any development effort, long-term successful economic development begins and ends with local leadership and local organizations taking responsibility on a day-to-day basis.

CDCs in rural areas often fill roles generally taken by government in more populated areas, areas with the financial resources to support a larger bureaucracy (Tyndall 2000). CDCs choose to be contributors to the rural community confronting the same basic need as any business and government in rural America, finding the right people. These individuals, sought by all, possess skill sets able to identify resources, generate support, and implement programming to facilitate development. Some CDCs direct their efforts to specific goals, ranging from housing to social services to economic development, by choice or funding sources. Rural economic development strategies may look to draw upon the appropriate CDC for specific work and upon their staffs to support local business and the larger community effort.

Even with government assistance and local support, the markets for goods and services produced by rural enterprises do not promise any businesses success or community prosperity. Each entrepreneur and place must produce a product or quality of life customers and local citizens desire.

Rural economic development is a complex struggle relying upon a limited number of individuals and organizations. Unfortunately, community wealth creation is unlikely for many places without continued support for these dedicated individuals as they strive to improve rural America. Dollars alone will not achieve the desired goals unless there are people with the educational background and experience to apply them properly.

References

Blackwell, Debra L., and Diana K. McClaughlin. 1998. "Do Rural Youth Attain Their Educational Goals?" *Rural Development Perspectives* 13, no. 3: 37–44. Available at www.ers.usda.gov/publications/rdp/rdp1098/rdp1098e.pdf.

Bureau of the Census, U.S. Department of Commerce. 1998. *Education Attainment of Persons 18 Years Old and Over, by Metropolitan and Nonmetropolitan Residence, Age, Sex, Race and Hispanic Origin.* Washington, DC: Government Printing Office.

Connect Ohio Business Resources. 2002. www.connectohio.com/bus_resources/econ_dev/bus_dev.asp.

Corporation for Enterprise Development (CFED). 1997. *Counting on Local Capital: A Research Project on Revolving Loan Funds.* Washington, DC.

Drabenstott, Mark, and Katharine Shaeff. 2001. "Looking to the States for New Rural Policies." *Main Street Economist* (June): 1–5.

Fluharty, Chuck. 2001. *Critical Rural Data and Definitions Issues: Why All This Matters to Rural Communities!* Washington, DC: Congressional Rural Caucus, National Rural Network, and Rural Policy Research Institute.

Galbraith, John Kenneth. 1996. *The Good Society: The Humane Agenda.* Boston: Houghton Mifflin.

Gale, H. Fredrick; David A. McGranahan; Elizabeth Greenberg; and Ruy Teizeira. 1999. "Rural Competitiveness: Results of the 1996 Rural Manufacturing Survey." Food and Rural Economics Division, Economic Research Service, U.S. Department of Agriculture, Agricultural Economic Report, no. 776.

Killian, Molly Sizer, and Lionel J. Beaulieu. 1995. "Current Status of Human Capital in the Rural U.S." In *Investing in People: The Human Capital Needs of Rural America,* ed. L.J. Beaulieu and D. Mulkey, 27–40. Boulder, CO: Westview Press.

Levere, Andrea, and Dave Wingate. 1999. "Counting on Local Capital: Evolution of the Revolving Loan Fund Industry." *Community Investments Newsletter.* Federal Reserve Bank of San Francisco. Available at: www.frbsf.org/publications/community/investments/cra99–1/page1.html.

Loveridge, Scott. 2000. "Introduction: Successful Rural Business." In *Small Town and Rural Economic Development: A Case Studies Approach,* ed. Peter Schaeffer and Scott Loveridge, 239–41. Westport, CT: Praeger.

Magill, John. 1999. "Office of Housing and Community Partnerships July 1999 Revolving Loan Fund Semi-Annual Report Summary." Unpublished manuscript, Department of Development, Office of Housing and Community Partnerships, Columbus, Ohio.

Mikesell, James J., and. George B. Wallace. 1996. "Are Revolving Loan Funds a Better Way to Finance Rural Development?" Food and Rural Economics Division, Economic Research Service, U.S. Department of Agriculture, Agriculture Information Bulletin, no. 724–05.

Munnell, Alicia H., with Leah M. Cook. 1990. "How Does Public Infrastructure Affect Regional Economic Performance?" In *Is There a Shortfall in Public Capital Investment?* ed. A.H. Munnell, 69–103. Boston: Federal Reserve Bank of Boston.

National Association of Development Organizations Research Foundation. 2001. "Taking Care of Business: The Role of Regional Development Organizations in Promoting Rural Entrepreneurship." Washington, DC.

Office of Housing and Community Partnerships, Ohio Department of Development. 2002. Economic Development Program. Available at: www.odod.state.oh.us/cdd/ohcp/edpn.htm.

———. 2000. "FY 2000 CDBG Economic Development Program Applicant Profile." Columbus, OH.

Pulver, Glen C. 1995. "Economic Forces Shaping the Future of Rural America." In *Investing in People: The Human Capital Needs of Rural America*, ed. L.J. Beaulieu and D. Mulkey, 49–64. Boulder, CO: Westview Press.

Tyndall, Margaret. 2000. "Rural CDCs: Building the Capacity of Success." *Community Dividend*. Minneapolis, MN: Federal Reserve Bank of Minneapolis, no. 1.

U.S. Census. Census Bureau, U.S. Department of Commerce. 1998. *County Estimates for Median Household Income for Indiana*. Table C98–18. Available at: www.census.gov/hhes/www.saipe/stcty/c98_18.htm.

———. 1990. *Summary of General Characteristics: 1990*. Washington, DC: U.S. Government Printing Office.

Part 5

Private Finance

15

Use of Bank Credit to Finance Small Businesses

Timothy Bates

Over 50 percent of the startup funding used to launch new small businesses nationwide comes from borrowings. The largest single source of those borrowings is mainstream financial institutions, largely commercial banks. As businesses move beyond startup and they mature, their reliance upon mainstream financial institutions for financing increases heavily. Among mature small firms, financial institutions provide over 90 percent of their borrowed capital.

Bank loans have become increasingly accessible to small businesses over the past two decades. Proliferating forms of consumer credit—credit cards, home equity loans, overdraft accounts—have been finding their way into small business finance. If one is denied a small-business loan, the alternative is likely to be one of these popular forms of consumer credit. The folklore of small business is that bank financing is difficult to obtain if one is launching a new firm. In fact, such financing is widely available.

As bank credit has become more widely available, have borrowing constraints largely disappeared for small businesses? The unambiguous answer is "no." Assembling sufficient financial capital to start and operate a small business is a minor issue for some firms and a major issue for others.

Access to financing is a barrier that businesses must overcome if they are operating successfully: For some the barrier is high while for others the financial capital barrier is low. This chapter seeks to explain how financing barriers impact small firms and to identify common circumstances in which businesses are apt to encounter serious barriers when they seek credit and capital. Financing barriers, in fact, are most often constraining at the point when one attempts to start a new business.

Limited Access to Financial Capital Constrains Startups and Young Firms

Existing scholarly literature in the economics and business fields identifies three primary ways that constrained access to financing stunts the formation and development of new small businesses. First, some potential entrepreneurs never take the plunge because they are unable to assemble sufficient financial capital to launch their businesses. This "discouraged-entrepreneur" phenomenon is most pronounced in capital-intensive fields, such as manufacturing. Second, since the amount of financial capital invested at startup is a powerful determinant of firm size, limited financial capital often translates into stunted (undercapitalized), overly small, young firms. Third, since overly small firms often generate insufficient revenues to pay the bills and provide the owners with a decent livelihood, very small, poorly capitalized businesses often close after a few years of operation. Reducing financial capital constraints, by implication, would alleviate all three of these problems and substantially increase the size and scope of the nation's small business community. Each of these three types of financing constraints is discussed in detail below.

Discouraged entrepreneurs, by definition, are those nascent entrepreneurs whose dreams of creating a firm are frustrated by their inability to raise sufficient capital: their small businesses are stillborn. Evans and Jovanovic (1989) used data from the National Longitudinal Survey of Young Men to estimate the incidence of discouraged entrepreneurs among white males, aged twenty-four to thirty-four. Absent financial capital constraints, Evans and Jovanovic estimated that 5.1 percent of the young white men would have become entrepreneurs over a two-year period; in fact, only 3.8 percent became entrepreneurs (1989: 824). They conclude that, "the liquidity constraint deters 1.3 percent of the population from trying entrepreneurship" (Evans and Jovanovic 1989: 824). Extrapolating their findings to the overall economy, the authors estimate that 300,000 people annually are discouraged entrepreneurs.

Supporting evidence from Great Britain was derived from a random survey of employees who were asked, "How seriously have you considered being self-employed?" Of the 17 percent who responded "very seriously," 451 were asked the follow-up question, "Why did you not become self-employed?" Over 51 percent gave as their reason "for not setting up a business that they could not obtain the necessary capital. It was the most common reason" (Blanchflower and Oswald 1998: 44).

Broadly mirroring the findings of Evans and Jovanovic, Reynolds and Miller indicate that roughly one in thirty of all adults active in the U.S. labor force "appear to be involved in a new firm startup at any point in time" (1992: 405). Many of these nascent firms, once again, are found to be stillborn. Greater household wealth lessens the likelihood that one's business creation plans will be undermined by financial capital constraints, and this is why high net-worth individuals—across the board—are more likely to start firms than others.

Would receiving an unexpected lump sum of cash increase the likelihood of pursuing entrepreneurship? The answer, according to Holtz-Eakin, Joulfaian, and Rosen (1994), is unambiguously "yes." They examined the labor force status of 3,023 people who were not self-employed in 1981 but who all received inheritances in 1982 or 1983. By 1985, nearly 20 percent of them were self-employed: the larger the inheritance, the greater the likelihood of establishing a business. Just as capital constraints kill planned businesses, the evidence suggests that business formation flourishes when the constraints ease.

The second type of capital constraint impacts firms that actually do begin operations, but they do so in an undercapitalized state. A survey of firms by the National Federation of Independent Businesses found that small businesses in operation for three or fewer years reported that, on average, only 50 percent of their initial loan request was met (Scott and Dunkelberg study, cited in Evans and Jovanovic 1989). Issues of uncertainty and moral hazard, according to Blanchflower and Oswald (1998), underlie consistent patterns of banker underfinancing found in small business startups relying upon borrowed funds to begin operations. The underfinanced firms need capital to buffer them from the liabilities of newness. New firms, observe Cooper et al. (1994), are struggling to establish administrative procedures, define their institutional identity, and gain credibility with customers and suppliers. This "process of experimentation is characterized by iterations of trial and error" (1994: 372). Greater financial capital availability at startup and in the early years of operation helps firms to survive this process of experimentation and learning; undercapitalization, in contrast, limits the new firm's ability to withstand unfavorable shocks and to undertake corrective actions. More initial capitalization, in brief, buys time while the entrepreneur learns how to run the business and overcome problems.

Among young firms, it is the larger operations that are most likely to survive (Bates 1993). Given this widely observed fact, it is important to know which factors most decisively determine whether a young firm will survive and grow to a viable size. Controlling for firm industry of operation, I found that traits of startups most strongly determining firm size in early years of operation were owner human and financial capital resources invested in the startup (Bates 1993). Specifically, the larger, young firms were headed by college-graduate owners who worked full-time in the business and invested significant financial capital in the venture. Of these traits, the one most decisively determining young firm size (measured by sales revenues) was the dollar amount of financial capital invested at startup. Undercapitalized startups were severely penalized, experiencing much lower sales revenues and higher rates of firm closure and failure than better capitalized young firms (Bates 1993).

Table 15.1

Comparison of Startup Capitalization Among Active, as Opposed to Discontinued, Small Firms, 1991, Nationwide Statistics

	Active	Closed down
1. Nonminority-owned firms		
Total financial capital at startup (mean)	$36,301.00	$17,434.00
Percent started with zero capital	20.2%	35.7%
Leverage at startup (debt divided by equity)	1.29	1.03
Percent using borrowed funds to finance startup	39.4%	24.6%
2. Black-owned firms		
Total financial capital at startup (mean)	$16,454.00	$8,013.00
Percent started with zero capital	26.1%	36.6%
Leverage at startup (debt divided by equity)	1.09	0.76
Percent using borrowed fund to finance startup	30.1%	25.4%
3. Asian-American-owned firms*		
Total financial capital at startup (mean)	$62,246.00	$15,914.00
Percent started with zero capital	14.0%	26.1%
Leverage at startup (debt divided by equity)	1.04	0.50
Percent borrowed funds to finance startup	48.6%	35.9%

Source: U.S. Bureau of the Census, Characteristics of Business Owners Database. *This subset contains immigrant owners only and is therefore not directly comparable to the data on Asian-American-owned firms contained in Tables 15.2 through 15.4.

Thus, the struggling young firm that is undercapitalized introduces us to the third major impact of constrained access to financing—the heightened likelihood of firm failure and closure. Irrespective of the mix of debt and equity capital that financed business startups, the greater the dollar amount of invested capital, the greater the likelihood that the young firm will remain in operation (Bates 1990). The classic small-business failure is the bankrupt venture, the firm closing with unpaid bills. As Gimeno et al. (1997) point out, initial capital endowments serve as a buffer, heightening the young firm's ability to overcome operational problems and withstand periods of poor business performance. Lacking an adequate buffer, poorly capitalized firms may be forced to close down during difficult periods, due to illiquidity problems creating an inability to pay the bills.

My analysis of a large, representative group of young white-owned small businesses compared the startup capitalization patterns of active firms to those that had gone out of business during the 1987 through 1991 period. Using U.S. Bureau of the Census small business data, the surviving firms had average startup capital of $36,301, over twice the $17,437 reported by the closures (Table 15.1). These figures include firms launched with zero financial capital: 35.7 percent of the closed firms started out with no capital versus

20.2 percent of the surviving firms (Bates 1997a: 194). This study used two criteria to define small businesses: (1) firms under consideration all submitted income-tax returns to the federal government in 1987, as either proprietorships, partnerships, or corporations; and (2) their gross sales revenues in 1987 were at least $5,000. Firms not meeting this $5,000 threshold were dropped.

Surviving firms stand out as active borrowers: Mean startup debt was $20,414 for those still in business, versus $8,866 for the firms that had shut down. Survivors, as well, were more likely to borrow than closed firms, and their average leverage (debt divided by equity capital) was higher. Active borrowing at startup disproportionately typifies the larger-scale, more viable small businesses.

The Dissenting View: Barriers to Obtaining Startup Financing Are Not a Problem

Not all scholars agree that limited access to financing is a problem for small-business startups. Light and Rosenstein (1995) assert that discriminatory lending practices by banks are not a barrier to startup and business operation; the notion that such financial-capital barriers retard firms is a "myth." They support their position on the irrelevance of financial-capital barriers, in part, by noting that entrepreneurs often start firms with little or no financial investment.

Firms do, indeed, often start out with little or no financial capitalization, but firms thus capitalized are also heavily overrepresented among the firms that close down a few years after startup (Bates 1997a). Firms (borrowers as well as nonborrowers) that closed down over the 1987–91 period are compared, in Table 15.1, to small businesses that continued in operation. This comparison of continuing firms versus closures highlights the fact that borrowing to launch one's firm is strongly associated with remaining in operation. The firms that closed down were disproportionately the ones started with less financial capital; they were less active borrowers than the surviving firms (Table 15.1). For each of the racially defined firm groups, more active borrowing and higher leverage are associated with enhanced business survival prospects (Bates 1997a).

Less active borrowing is most characteristic of the black-business group. Capitalization differences, in turn, are enduring causes of disparities between black- and white-owned small businesses. Poorly capitalized firms, whether minority or nonminority owned, generate low sales volumes; tiny firms often generate insufficient net revenues to produce a decent livelihood for the owner; poorly capitalized, tiny firms disproportionately go out of business during the early years of operation (Bates 1997a).

Light and Rosenstein (1995) support their position that launching a firm requires little or no capital, by citing a 1988 study by Fratoe. Since Fratoe's study relies upon the only comprehensive source of data on startup financing, the Census Bureau's Characteristics of Business Owners (CBO) database, reconciling his findings with the facts (taken from the CBO database) cited in this chapter is straightforward. "One of the most interesting facts disclosed by the CBO study is that the majority of all business owners initiated their enterprises with little or no financial capital" (Fratoe 1988: 39). Fratoe defines a "small business" as anyone who generated gross sales of at least $50 from self-employment in 1982 and filed a schedule C (proprietorship) form with his or her 1982 federal income tax return. About 40 percent of proprietorships thus defined generated gross self-employment sales of less than $5,000 in 1982; that is, most of these proprietors were wage or salary earners who earned small amounts of self-employment income. Indeed, most of these tiny small businesses were started with little or no capital.

Fratoe, Light, Rosenstein, and I certainly agree that one needs little or no financial capital to generate gross self-employment revenues of several hundred, or even several thousand, dollars per year. But we disagree about whether this constitutes a small business. Throughout this chapter, casual self-employment activity has been delineated from small-business ownership: a $5,000-revenue cutoff has been applied whenever CBO data are used, and small businesses are defined as only those meeting the $5,000 cutoff (see Bates 1997a, for additional information on the CBO database). To Fratoe and Light, anyone who held a Tupperware party that produced sales of $100 is a small-business proprietor. In this chapter, the Tupperware seller was engaged in casual self-employment but has not started a small business. Limited access to financial capital is indeed a barrier to those seeking to launch substantive small businesses.

High Barriers or Low Barriers?

Financing barriers, in fact, are less likely to inhibit the tiny, zero-employee young business operation than the larger-scale employer firm. Among the small-business groups described in Table 15.1, black-owned firms utilized the least financial capital to launch their new ventures. Most of those firms had no paid employees. Among young black businesses employing ten or more workers, in contrast, average startup capitalization was $134,753 (Bates 1998: 127). Raising capital for a very small operation may indeed be easy for most business owners; adequate capitalization may nonetheless be difficult to raise for owners launching more substantive ventures.

Regarding the black business community specifically, low levels of borrowing do not imply minimal financial capital constraints. Rather, limited access to loans, reflecting supply-side constraints, may hold down borrowing in situations where loan demand is high. In this case, less active borrowing is likely to coexist with discouraged entrepreneurs and overly small, underfinanced firms. Light and Rosenstein assume that lack of demand for loans holds down borrowing among new businesses. In the case of black firms, however, borrowing levels reflect lack of supply. Evidence documenting steeper barriers facing loan-seeking black-owned firms is summarized later in this chapter.

Businesses started in different industries typically have widely different capitalization requirements. Nationwide, Asian Americans report higher mean household net-worth holdings than any other racially defined group, and this fact eases financial capital barriers for those contemplating starting a small business (Bates 1997a). A popular area of firm creation is skilled-services industries, including finance, insurance, professional services, and other skill-intensive fields. Examining Asian-American startups in skilled services, average capitalization was $30,542, and 22.4 percent of the new owners borrowed money to launch their businesses (Bates 1997a: 127). The second most popular startup field for Asian Americans was retailing. Average capitalization in this industry was $68,885, and over 58 percent of the new owners borrowed money to launch their firms (Bates 1997a: 127).

Services, across the board, generally have low startup-capitalization requirements, suggesting relatively minor financing barriers for most prospective owners contemplating establishing a business. Retailing is considerably more capital intensive, raising the relevance of the financing barrier to prospective creators of new firms. Manufacturing and wholesaling stand at the top of the small business hierarchy regarding capitalization requirements: startups often require over $100,000 to begin operations. The higher the capitalization requirements, the more likely the business is to rely upon a bank loan to get under way. Overall, lower financing barriers typify the smaller business startups in service industries, and higher barriers constrain the larger ventures starting out in the more capital-intensive trade and manufacturing industries.

Financing Small Business Startup

Data collected by the U.S. Bureau of the Census since the late 1980s have provided the first comprehensive portrait of small-business startup financing. For small firms started nationwide, business owners have tapped three major sources of debt capital to finance their new operations. These are, in order of importance: (1) financial institutions, (2) family members (one's

Table 15.2

Financing Small Business Formation, Nationwide Statistics

	Percentage of startups using		
	Borrowed funds	Equity capital only (no debt)	No financial capital
Nonminority-owned firms	37.2	39.1	23.7
African-American-owned firms	28.8	42.3	28.9
Asian-American-owned firms	40.4	43.4	16.2

Source: U.S. Bureau of the Census, Characteristics of Business Owners database.

parents, most often), and (3) friends. Borrowings from financial institutions, in aggregate, exceed the funds borrowed from all other sources combined.

A study of young businesses that were operating in 1987 utilized Census Bureau data to generate a broad overview of startup financing (Bates 1997a). Different small-business groups, defined by owner race, exhibit differing startup financing patterns, but their similarities tend to be more prominent than their differences (Table 15.2). Well over half of the small-business startups described in Table 15.2 used no debt financing whatsoever to start their operations. Indeed, quite a few started out with no financial capital. Nearly 88 percent of the firms (Table 15.2) were started by nonminority white owners, and 24 percent of these startups began operations with zero financial capital. These zero-capital startups were largely tiny, zero-employee firms, and they were concentrated in services industries.

Another 39 percent of the nonminority startups that began operations with financial capital used no borrowed funds: The firms were launched using equity capital only, and most of this equity capital came from the personal resources of the owner. Only 37 percent of the nonminority startups described in Table 15.2 used borrowed money to begin operations, but these firms stand out as the larger-scale businesses. Most of the young employer firms are launched using a combination of borrowed funds and owner equity capital to finance startup. Among the young nonminority firms, the greater size of startups beginning with borrowed funds stands out when mean annual sales revenues for 1987 of borrowers versus nonborrowers are compared: The average borrowing firm had annual sales of $268,373, versus $112,459 for the nonborrower, nonminority-owned business (Bates 1997a). It is also noteworthy that borrowing firms are more likely to remain in operation than nonborrowers. For nonborrowing firms active in 1987, 26.6 percent of the young nonminority operations had gone out of business by late 1991; for the borrowers, the corresponding figure was 16.6 percent.

Given the greater viability of young firms that borrow, one might conclude that more loan availability would produce increases in small business viability independent of other characteristics of firms and their owners. It probably would. Yet a word of caution qualifies this inference. Debt and equity capital are complements at startup: The borrowing firms have greater owner investments of equity capital than do nonborrowers. Borrowing owners, furthermore, tend to be more highly educated and are more likely to work full-time in their business, relative to nonborrowers.

On balance, greater borrowing access would benefit many firms, but it is no cure-all (Bates 1993). Just as debt and equity are complements, so are the owner's human and financial capital. No serious empirical study to date has demonstrated that expanded loan access can overcome deficiencies in the owner's human capital (Bates 1997a). Greater loan access, instead, is most likely to benefit those possessing the skills, education, and experience that constitute the bedrock of small-firm viability.

Asian-American owners stand out as the group starting firms possessing the highest average capitalization. In addition to their large equity investments, Asian-American owners actually used borrowed funds more often than nonminority owners—40 percent of the Asian-American startups were launched with borrowed money, versus 37 percent of the nonminority ventures (Table 15.2). Black-owned businesses relied less on borrowed funds— 29 percent of these startups began with zero financial capital while another 29 percent borrowed; meanwhile 42 percent began with equity-capital financing only (Table 15.2). For the universe of black-business startups, mean capitalization was under $15,000; looking solely at the borrowing firms, average startup capitalization was higher at $35,842.

The fact that firms starting out using borrowed money are the larger-scale firms accounts for over half of the aggregate small-business startup capitalization being debt capital. Debt as a percentage of aggregate startup capital is 56 percent for white-owned firms, 51 percent for black businesses, and 50 percent for ventures launched by Asian Americans. The balance of startup financing is equity capital, predominantly from owner personal resources. Where does debt capital come from?

Table 15.3 lists the frequency with which startup firms tapped the three major sources of debt that finance small businesses. All of the racially defined small-business borrower groups received startup financing more often from financial institutions than from the second most important debt source (family). Indeed, the order of importance of sources of debt—financial institutions are most important, family is second, and friends rank

Table 15.3

Source of Borrowed Financial Capital Used by Small-Business Startups, Nationwide Statistics on Borrower Firms (as percent)

	Financial institutions	Family	Friends
Nonminority-owned firms	65.9	26.8	6.4
African American-owned firms	59.1	21.2	11.3
Asian American-owned firms	52.6	37.6	21.9

Source: U.S. Bureau of the Census, Characteristics of Business Owners database.
Note: Some firms borrow from more than one source.

third—is the same for all of the borrower groups, minority as well as nonminority.

Although financial institutions dominate small-firm startup financing across the board, there are important differences in financing sources for racially defined groups. White-owned firms rely most heavily upon financial institutions (66 percent borrowed from this source) while Asian Americans (53 percent) were least reliant. Similarly, friends were an important source of startup financing for Asian Americans (22 percent tapped this source) and a minor source of debt capital for white-owned firms (6 percent). Asian owners were over three times more likely to finance business entry with loans from friends than were nonminorities.

Considering average loan size by borrowing source (Table 15.4), in conjunction with borrowing frequency by source, the importance of financial institutions in startup financing comes into clearer focus. Much larger loans extended by financial institutions add up to a dominance of startup financing by this loan source.

Are Barriers to Obtaining Startup Financing Disproportionately a Problem for Minorities?

A well-established and growing scholarly literature shows that minority-owned businesses have less access to loans from financial institutions than do similar firms owned by whites (Cavalluzo et al. 1999; Blanchflower et al. 1998; Bates 1997b; Ando 1988). Note that data summarized in this chapter are broadly consistent with this prevailing conventional wisdom. Among firms described in Table 15.2 above, 25 percent of all white-owned startups borrowed from financial institutions, versus 21 percent of Asian-American

Table 15.4

Characteristics by Source of Loan, Nationwide Statistics for Small Businesses That Borrowed to Finance Startup

	Financial institutions	Family	Friends
A. Average loan size (dollars)			
Nonminority-owned firms	56,784.00	35,446.00	30,907.00
African American-owned firms	31,958.00	18,306.00	16,444.00
Asian American-owned firms	67,299.00	39,137.00	34,255.00
B. Leverage (debt, equity ratio) by source of loan			
Nonminority-owned firms	3.10	2.32	2.03
African American-owned firms	2.69	2.22	2.15
Asian American-owned firms	2.23	2.07	2.06

Source: U.S. Bureau of the Census, Characteristics of Business Owners database.

startups, and 17 percent of black-owned business startups.

Most of the evidence to date concerns the capital constraints facing black-owned businesses. Average startup capitalization for young black firms nationwide that were operating in 1992 was $14,108, and median capitalization was under $10,000, according to Census Bureau data; the corresponding figure for the average nonminority firm was $40,065.

In 1992, the Roper organization polled 472 black-business owners nationwide to gauge how they viewed their own firms, as well as black businesses generally. Asked why there were so few black-owned firms in the nation, 84 percent responded that "black-owned businesses are impeded by lack of access to financing" (Carlson 1992: R16). Asked to cite specific problems impeding operations in their own firms, 61 percent indicated that "obtaining sources of capital" was a major problem; 54 percent listed "access to credit" as a major problem. These were the two most common major problems identified by the surveyed black-business owners (Carlson 1992: R16).

The Federal Reserve System conducted a survey of 4,637 small businesses in 1993, and this survey collected extensive information about firms that had sought loans over the three previous years (just over 2,000 of the surveyed firms had sought loans). These data are known as the National Survey of Small Business Finances (NSSBF). The major issue stressed by studies using NSSBF data is summarized by Cavalluzzo et al. (1999: 189): "Businesses owned by African Americans were two-and-one-half times as likely to be denied credit on their most recent loan request than were businesses owned by white males." This study also noted the higher rejection rates experienced by Asian and Hispanic small-business owners, particularly the former group, who were 13 percent more likely than white males to have been denied credit.

The fact that black-owned firms have less access to financing than whites is well established and not controversial (Pierce 1947; Bates 1973; Bates 1997b). The interesting question is whether black-owned firms possessing identical firm and owner traits (other than race) have less access to bank credit than their twin white-owned firms. Recent studies based upon the NSSBF data reinforce past findings; the result is a group of studies, all of which demonstrate that the answer is yes: Blacks have less access to financial institution loans than twin white-owned firms (Cavalluzzo et al. 1999; Blanchflower et al. 1998; Bostic and Lampani 1999). The recent NSSBF studies also begin to fill a void in the knowledge about the borrowing patterns of Asian and Hispanic-owned firms, but small sample size problems do crimp the usefulness of NSSBF data for analyzing these subgroups of loan applicants.

Common findings across the three studies that utilize the 1993 NSSBF data—Blanchflower et al. (1998); Cavalluzzo et al. (1999); and Bostic and Lampani (1999)—are twofold. First, financial institutions are extraordinarily important sources of credit for small businesses, accounting for the vast majority of debt financing flowing to small firms, whether minority or majority owned. Second, black-owned firms have significantly less access to that debt financing than do white-owned firms.

In their analysis of bank loan approval using all of the most recent loan applicants, Bostic and Lampani (1999) find that blacks are only 45 percent as likely as whites to have their applications approved. This is the approval differential remaining after controlling statistically for owner traits, business characteristics, and broad loan application characteristics, including the history of the relationship of the applicant to the institution evaluating the loan. Noting that "lenders are concerned about local conditions when evaluating firm loan applications" (1999), Bostic and Lampani analyze the impact of fifty-three banking market and local geographic characteristics upon loan approval patterns, including neighborhood median household income, poverty rate, unemployment rate, home values, and dozens of others. They end up with the same large and statistically significant black/white differences as the Blanchflower and Cavalluzzo studies regarding loan approval patterns.

An analysis of loan applicants, finally, understates the problem of credit barriers disproportionately handicapping minority business enterprises (MBEs) because, as Blanchflower et al. (1998) observe, "Black and Hispanic-owned firms are much more likely to report that they did not apply for a loan, even though they needed credit, because they thought they would be rejected" (22). Overall, black and Hispanic firms included in the Federal Reserve System's NSSBF database were 40 and 22 percentage points more likely *not* to file a loan application—fearing denial—than were white-owned firms (Blanchflower et al. 1998). Attributing part of this differential to the greater credit risk typifying MBEs, the Blanchflower study proceeded to control statistically for these risk factors—such as credit rating, size, profitability, and so forth. Borrower credit risk thus controlled for, they found that "Nevertheless, a gap of 26 and 15 percentage points still exists between black- and Hispanic-owned firms, respectively, compared to white-owned firms" (Blanchflower et al. 1998: 23). Fear of rejection reduces credit availability above and beyond the differential created merely by actual denial of MBE business loan applications.

Using different data generated by the Community Reinvestment Act monitoring efforts of bank regulatory agencies, Immergluck (1999) has shown that minority areas in Chicago suffer from lower bank lending rates than higher-income and white neighborhoods, after controlling statistically for firm size, industrial mix, and other traits.

The conclusions of individual studies of minority business loan access are not decisive because each has its own peculiarities, rooted in differing methodologies and databases. The collective findings gain credibility because (1) they were conducted at different points in time, (2) they utilized databases from varying sources, and (3) despite their differences, extremely consistent findings are forthcoming, particularly regarding large black/white gaps in access to small-business financing.

The broad trend, since the late 1960s, has been toward growing minority-business access to loans from financial institutions. In his 1944 survey of black businesses, Pierce (1947) found that 3 percent of them had gotten startup financing from banks. The 17 percent of black firms reporting to the Census Bureau that they received startup financing from financial institutions represents progress from the era Pierce described. But it does not represent equal access (Bates 1999; Cavalluzo et al. 1999).

Financing Small-Business Creation with Consumer Credit

A valid analysis of financial institutions' lending to small firms cannot focus narrowly upon availability and terms of business loans because a broader range of financing alternatives—particularly consumer credit—is being tapped by the small-business community. If one applies for a business loan and is turned down, consumer credit alternatives are numerous. Perhaps reflecting their restricted access to mainstream business loans, black-owned businesses have been particularly active in using consumer credit to finance their startup operations (Bates 1997b). CBO data identify two important forms of consumer credit—home equity loans and credit cards—that are used to finance business creation. Note that these types of loans are treated as loans from financial institutions in the CBO database.

Among white business startups described in this chapter that started out using borrowed funds, 18 percent relied upon home equity loans or credit cards for their business financing. In contrast, 30 percent of startup black business borrowers used these types of consumer credit. Among borrowers that are otherwise identical regarding firm and owner characteristics, the borrower utilizing credit cards to finance startup received a significantly smaller loan, relative to those getting other types of loans from financial institutions (Bates 1997b). Black business borrowers were over twice as likely as whites to rely upon credit card financing.

There is an obvious interrelatedness in financial institution lending patterns that depresses homeownership and small-business creation. If small business loans are unattainable, the potential home-owning black entrepreneur has the option of using a home equity loan to finance a business startup. Home equity loans are tough to obtain for someone who does not own a home: "Minorities were two to three times as likely to be denied mortgage loans as whites. In fact, high-income minorities in Boston were more likely to be turned down than low-income whites" (Munnell et al. 1996: 25).

Other Trends in Bank Financing of Small Businesses

Comprehensive data sources describing small-firm borrowing patterns are few. Beyond Census Bureau data, the 1993 (NSSBF), produced by the Federal Reserve System, in conjunction with the U.S. Small Business Administration, ranks as a valuable source of small-firm financing data. While the Census Bureau's CBO data describe startup financing, the NSSBF data describe firms that are older and larger, on average, than the universe of small businesses (Bates 1999). Where do these larger, more mature firms do their borrowing? "Over 80 percent of the most recent small business loans came from commercial banks, and 96 percent came more generally from some financial institution" (Cavalluzzo et al. 1999: 190). Overall, slightly under 1 percent of the firms described in the NSSBF data borrowed from families or other individuals.

An interesting trend in small-business finance is the apparent decline of relationship banking, which is being squeezed by the rise of credit-scoring techniques to make lending decisions. Being in the in-group, according to Uzzi (1999), increases one's access to business loans and reduces borrowing costs. Owners of small businesses having social, noncommercial attachments with their bankers are the ones benefiting from this in-group status. While not proved empirically, an obvious implication of the nature of relationship banking is that owners lacking in-group status (most black business owners) receive the opposite treatment: less credit access and more onerous loan terms.

The growing application of credit scoring to the small-business lending process has the potential to level the playing field somewhat for the beneficiaries and victims of traditional relationship lending patterns. Evidence on this topic is just beginning to accumulate, but it appears that credit scoring may be producing more of a meritocracy in business lending, perhaps to the detriment of the old boy's network. The findings of a study by the Federal Reserve Bank of Atlanta indicate that "institutions that credit score small business loans are more likely to lend more in low-income areas than nonscorers." (Padhi et al. 1999: 605). Bankers that do not credit score loans, furthermore, tend to concentrate their lending geographically, favoring nearby borrowers, while credit scorers "are more likely to lend further away from where they have a physical presence" (Padhi et al. 1999: 605).

One possible long-run outcome of the rise of credit scoring to evaluate small-business loans is the lessening of the distinctions between consumer loans (where credit scoring is nearly universal) and small-business lending. In the process, traditionally underserved clienteles—low-income areas, minority borrowers—may experience increased access to the loan products offered by mainstream financial institutions.

Concluding Remarks

Financing constraints are not a problem for many types of small businesses. Very small firms operating in labor-intensive industries often have minimal borrowing needs. Well-established, profitable firms generally find that the banking system stands ready and willing to fund their loan requests. Financing constraints are most often a problem for business startups, particularly when new ventures are entering capital-intensive fields like manufacturing. Substantive new firms being created in capital-intensive industries normally draw their financing from a combination of equity capital, invested by owners, plus debt capital. The major source of borrowing for these firms is bank credit. Startup loans are often forthcoming, as well, from family and friends, but bank loans are both larger and more frequent sources of debt for new firms.

Absent access to loans, potential entrepreneurs may be forced to abandon their plans, particularly when the envisioned firms were to be established in capital-intensive lines of business. While the tiny, zero-employee new venture may be unharmed by limited loan access, the larger-scale employer firm may be severely hurt. While financing constraints cause some to abandon their business startup plans, others proceed with inadequate financing. Such undercapitalized firms are vulnerable to failure during their early lives: The negative cash flow phase that is common among young firms is often fatal to the venture running out of cash prior to achieving viability.

Black- and Hispanic-owned firms face higher barriers than white-owned firms of similar size and scope when they attempt to finance small-business startup. These capital access constraints clearly linger as the firms mature, causing many minorities to tap consumer credit forms—such as credit cards—to finance business operations.

A banking system geared toward financing the needs of small firms is vitally important to the viability of the nation's small-business community. Expanded credit availability is particularly important to the health of the youngest firms, the larger-scale, more capital-intensive ventures, and the nation's minority-owned businesses.

References

Ando, Faith. 1988. "Capital Issues and Minority-Owned Business." *Review of Black Political Economy* 16, no. 4: 77–109.

Bates, Timothy. 1973. *Black Capitalism: A Quantitative Analysis.* New York: Praeger.

———. 1990. "Entrepreneur Human Capital Inputs and Small Business Longevity." *Review of Economics and Statistics* 72, no. 4: 551–59.

———. 1993. *Banking on Black Enterprise.* Washington, DC: Joint Center for Political and Economic Studies.

———. 1997a. *Race, Self-Employment, and Upward Mobility.* Baltimore: Johns Hopkins University Press.

———. 1997b. "Unequal Access: Financial Institution Lending to Black- and White-Owned Small Business Startups." *Journal of Urban Affairs* 19, no. 4: 487–95.

———. 1998. "Job Creation through Improved Access to Markets for Minority-Owned Businesses." In *The Black Worker in the 21st Century: Job Creation Prospects and Strategies*, ed. Wilhelmina Leigh and Margaret Simms, 125–45. Washington, DC: Joint Center for Political and Economic Studies.

———. 1999. "Available Evidence Indicates that Black-Owned Firms Are Often Denied Equal Access to Credit." In *Business Access to Capital and Credit* , ed. Jackson Blanton, Alicia Williams, and Sherrie Rhine, 167–76. Washington, DC: Federal Reserve System.

Blanchflower, David; Philip Levine; and David Zimmerman. 1998. "Discrimination in the Small Business Credit Market." Working Paper. Washington, DC: National Bureau of Economic Research.

Blanchflower, David, and Andrew Oswald. 1998: "What Makes an Entrepreneur?" *Journal of Labor Economics* 16, no. 1: 26–60.

Bostic, Raphael, and Kenneth Lampani. 1999. "Racial Differences in Patterns of Small Business Finance," In *Business Access to Capital and Credit*, ed. Jackson Blanton et al., 149–79. Washington, DC: Federal Reserve System.

Carlson, Eugene. 1992. "Battling Bias." *Wall Street Journal*, April 3.

Cavalluzzo, Ken; Linda Cavalluzzo; and John Wolken. 1999. "Competition, Small Business Financing, and Discrimination: Evidence from a New Survey." In *Business Access to Capital and Credit*, ed. Jackson Blanton et al., 180–266. Washington, DC: Federal Reserve System.

Cooper, Arnold; Javier Gimeno-Gascon; and Carolyn Woo. 1994. "Initial Human Capital and Financial Capital as Predictors of New Venture Performance." *Journal of Business Venturing* 9: 371–95.

Evans, David, and Boyan Jovanovic. 1989. "An Estimated Model of Entrepreneurial Choice Under Liquidity Constraints." *Journal of Political Economy* 97, no. 4: 808–27.

Fratoe, Frank. 1988. "Social Capital of Small Business Owners." *Review of Black Political Economy* 16, no. 4: 33–50.

Gimeno, Javier; Timothy Folta; Arnold Cooper; and Carolyn Woo. 1997. "Survival of the Fittest? Entrepreneurial Human Capital and the Persistence of Underperforming Firms." *Administrative Sciences Quarterly* 42: 750–83.

Holtz-Eakin, Douglas; David Joulfaian; and Harvey Rosen. 1994. "Sticking It Out: Entrepreneurial Survival and Liquidity Constraints." *Journal of Political Economy* 102, no. 1: 53–75.

Immergluck, Daniel. 1999. "Intraurban Patterns of Small Business Lending." In *Business Access to Capital and Credit*, ed. Jackson Blanton et al., 123–38. Washington, DC: Federal Reserve System.

Light, Ivan, and Carolyn Rosenstein. 1995. *Race, Ethnicity, and Entrepreneurship in Urban America.* New York: Aldine and Gruyter.

Munnell, Alice; G. Tootell; L. Browne; and J. McErney. 1996. "Mortgage Lending in Boston: Interpreting HMDA Data." *American Economic Review* 86, no. 1: 25–53.

Pahdi, Michael; Lynn Woosley; and Aruna Srinivasan. 1999. "Credit Scoring and Small Business Lending in Low- and Moderate-Income Communities." In *Business Access to Capital and Credit* , ed. Jackson Blanton et al., 587–624. Washington, DC: Federal Reserve System.

Pierce, Joseph. 1947. *Negro Business and Business Education.* New York: Harper Bros.

Reynolds, Paul, and Brenda Miller. 1992. "New Firm Gestation: Conception, Birth, and Implications for Research." *Journal of Business Venturing* 7, no. 5: 405–17.

Uzzi, Brian. 1999. "Embeddedness and the Making of Financial Capital: How Social Relations and Networks Benefit Firms Seeking Financing." *American Sociological Review* 64, no. 3: 481–505.

16

Business Angels

Adam J. Bock

Introduction

Finding capital to jump-start a small business, especially a technology-based business, requires determination, creativity, boundless energy, and patience. Funding for research, development, and operations may require years of effort and millions of dollars of investment capital. A few entrepreneurs have the resources to make this happen, but most will need to find other sources of funding.

Angel Capital: Early Stage Financing for High-Risk Companies

Angel capital is usually the second stop in the external financing search. Most entrepreneurs first utilize their own savings and assets, and then tap "friends and family" to launch the company. These funds, most often in the $10,000 to $100,000 range, may help cover legal, accounting, and other "startup" costs associated with creating a corporation and initiating operations. Generally this will only fund preliminary activities; it is rarely enough to fund research and development (R&D) or market entry. For many entrepreneurs, the next source of capital is wealthy individuals: private investors capable of taking significant risks and investing anywhere from $10,000 to $1,000,000 each. These are the "angels."

An "angel" or "angel investor" is an individual meeting certain minimum net worth or income criteria who invests in a startup company in which he or she has no previous involvement. *Angel capital* or *angel financing* is the money invested by angels. The generic term "venture capital" may be used to include angel capital. Angel investments may be referred to as the "seed round" or the "angel round," depending on the circumstances and the size of the investment. For example, if the founders invested $250,000 of their own money, this will usually be called the "seed round." If angels then invest $750,000, this will usually be called the "angel round."

Not all angels invest in high-risk, high-technology companies. Some angels invest in small, family-run businesses like restaurants, hardware stores, and small service firms. It is our experience, however, that these investments are usually less than $250,000, and that the most common angel "type" investing in these opportunities is "friends and family" or an immediate associate. In many situations, traditional bank financing (guaranteed or secured loans) may be available based on the near-term prospect for revenues and profits.

Financing high-tech startup companies, however, is usually a different story. Bank financing sources are generally inaccessible because there is no collateral to secure loans to cover research and development. In addition, the prospect for profits, or even revenues, may be years away. Many estimates suggest that angels are the primary source of financing for early stage high-tech ventures, funding 60 percent of tech firms seeking less than $1 million (Van Osnabrugge and Robinson 2000). The financing needs of these businesses usually exceed the resources of the entrepreneur and "friends and family." Therefore, our focus in this chapter will be on the high-risk technology startups seeking $250,000 to $2 million in angel financing, where the angels do not have a prior connection to the entrepreneur.

Risk Capital for Startup Companies: Filling the Financing Gap

We often hear about the lack of early stage financing for high-risk, high-growth companies. Entrepreneurs struggle to find $250,000 to $750,000 for product development, sales and marketing, and general administrative expenses. Banks rarely secure this type of investment, and institutional investors, like venture capitalists, do not find it economically viable to research deals this small (Mason 1996). Alvarez et al. (1997) show that this "financing gap" exists primarily for entrepreneurial firms trying to raise less than $500,000.

For this type of early stage investment, the angel investor may be an entrepreneur's best option. Individual investors have the time and the interest to study deals one at a time, and to provide the financing that technology-based startup companies need to become viable. Unlike professional lenders or managed funds, angel investors have a high enough risk tolerance to make investments at the earliest stage of company development—often before there is a prototype or even a clearly identified market need. Angels generally expect a high return on their investment to justify the higher risk.

Freear, Sohl, and Wetzel (2000: 50) utilize a relatively simple definition for an *informal investor* (i.e., an angel investor) originally provided by Ou: "any individual who provides risk capital directly to a business for the purpose of asset appreciation and who is minimally involved in the day-to-day operation of the business at the time of the investment." In reality, no single definition perfectly matches the activities of every angel in the United States. Some invest based on a long-term portfolio perspective; some invest purely for the excitement of being involved in high-tech development. As a group, however, angels fill a critical role in the financing process by making the high-risk, high-return investments that help fuel technological innovation and development.

Impact of Angels and Startup Financing

There is a common misconception that jobs are created primarily by Fortune 500 companies. The reality is very different. In *Angel Investing*, Van Osnabrugge and Robinson (2000: 9) note: "most new jobs are created by entrepreneurial firms, firms growing at a rate of at least 20 percent per year. Since 1979, more than 75 percent of net new jobs have been created by around 8 percent of small businesses." To put it in numerical terms, while the payrolls of Fortune 500 companies fell by 4 million jobs between 1979 and 1995, entrepreneurial firms generated 24 million new jobs (Freear et al. 2000: 47).

Angels are one of the most important sources of finance for the small, entrepreneurial firms that are generating new jobs. In fact, angels have generally been a larger, more broadly distributed source of financing for early stage firms than professional venture capital companies. "The truth is that angel investors, rather than formal venture capitalists, make the most venture-capital-style investments to young entrepreneurial firms. Business angels—the invisible segment of the venture-capital markets—fund thirty to forty times as many entrepreneurial ventures as do venture capitalists, the market's visible segment" (Van Osnabrugge and Robinson 2000: 10).

A "venture capital" firm ("VC" or "venture capitalist) is a professional organization that manages a pool of money or "fund" and invests in high-risk companies, often with new technologies. A VC may have billions of dollars under management, investing anywhere from $500,000 to $50,000,000 in portfolio companies. The first financing provided by a VC (or a similar "institutional investor") is often referred to as the "first round," despite the fact that there may have already been a seed round, an angel round, or both.

Some estimates suggest that there may be as many as 2.5 million angels in the United States, investing in tens of thousands of ventures each year. As much as 80 percent of these funds go to startup companies in the earliest rounds of external financing (Singer 2000). "The National Venture Capital Association (NVCA) has suggested that angels may actually invest around $100 billion annually." This is reinforced by the fact that since 1995, only 9 percent to 11 percent of the companies funded by venture capitalists have been at the seed stage (Singer 2000: 55).

Deal Size and Number of Investments

VC financing has grown dramatically in recent years, from $22.6 billion in 1998 to $59.2 billion in 1999 and $103.8 billion in 2000.[1] NVCA statistics suggest that total investments in 2001 will likely be closer to the $60 billion level. This appears to follow the general growth and decline trend of the technology-heavy NASDAQ over the past five years. It is unclear whether total angel financing has followed a similar trend, because no nationwide data are available. We would tend to assume that the trends have been generally similar.

The impact of deal size, however, shows the breadth of the angel investing process. The average VC investment is generally greater than $10 million,[2] while our experience shows that the average angel investment round is generally in the $250,000 to $750,000 range. If we assume that total VC funding and angel financing are approximately the same order of magnitude, the disparity in deal size suggests that angels invest in ten to one hundred times as many ventures each year as professional venture capitalists.

Success Anecdotes

Major success stories drive angel investing. Perhaps the most well-known example is Apple Computer. Apple was started with $91,000 in angel funding in 1977. It is estimated that the value of this investment at exit for the angels (i.e., after the IPO[3]) was $158 million just a few years later.

A more modest example is PanVera Corporation in Madison, Wisconsin. This biotechnology company was started in 1992 with $100,000 of founder money, and subsequently raised two rounds of angel funding totaling $4 million. PanVera did not receive financing from venture capitalists. In 2000, the announced merger of PanVera with Aurora Biosciences (NASDAQNM: ABSC) put a stock-based value of PanVera at approximately $90 million.[4] This example also demonstrates that groups of angels working together can put together significant rounds of financing to accelerate a business.

Obviously, these examples are the *exceptions*. Most estimates suggest that as many as eight or nine out of ten high-tech startup companies will fail. But angels continue to invest based on the promise of enormous returns and the opportunity to be part of a market-changing technology. The portfolio-based angel investor hopes that the "home run" companies will more than pay for the investments that fail.

Angels and Altruism

Angel investing is predominantly a local phenomenon, although some national networks do exist.[5] In our experience, most angels have strong preferences for investments that support the local economy. Logistics play a factor:
It is easier to research and monitor a business within driving distance. But
angels often exhibit strong "hometown" loyalty, and may want the money
they invest to help the local economy by creating jobs and generating growth.
This is a positive externality to the angel investing process, but it is something that most angels take seriously.

What Is an Angel?

Legal Description

The term "angel" is a pseudonym for an individual who qualifies as an "ac-
credited investor" as defined by the Securities and Exchange Commission
(SEC). Specifically, it refers to individuals that are not corporate insiders
(i.e., they are not directors, officers, or partners in the business), who meet
one of the following criteria:

1. "Any natural person whose individual net worth, or joint net worth
   with that person's spouse, at the time of his purchase exceeds
   $1,000,000," or
2. "Any natural person who had an individual income in excess of
   $200,000 in each of the two most recent years or joint income with
   that person's spouse in excess of $300,000 in each of those years
   and has a reasonable expectation of reaching the same income level
   in the current year."[6]

   In other words, an angel is someone who can afford to make, *and lose*, an
investment in a high-risk venture. The original Regulation D requirements
for private offerings date back to 1933. The definition may seem arbitrary,
but it can protect vulnerable individuals from risking their life savings on
high-risk deals. The theory is that the people most qualified to make these
investments are those who can afford to lose every penny they invest.[7]

De Facto Angels

In reality, more than 2 million Americans meet the $1,000,000 net worth
minimum requirement; one out of every sixty people between the ages of

thirty-five and eighty-five qualifies as an angel. Again, our anecdotal experience suggests that *active* angels, those looking to make early stage, high-risk investments as part of their overall portfolio of assets, tend to have a net worth significantly higher than the $1,000,000 minimum.[8]

Silver (1997) suggests that many currently active angels are typically "wealthy entrepreneurs or business executives." In the past five years, there has been discussion of "a new breed of private investor . . . cashed-out entrepreneurs who have the money and the know-how."[9] Our experience suggests that this has changed as well. Many active angels do tend to have previous business experience, whether in senior management, corporate finance, corporate law, or other aspects of direct business management or professional business services. But the economic boom of the past ten years has brought significant numbers of nonexecutives into angel investing circles. We regularly speak with physicians, small-business owners/managers, attorneys, college professors, and college and government administrators who have the resources and the interest to be business angels.

The odds are that these individuals will be "passive angels." Many enthusiastic investors with limited expertise in entrepreneurial ventures look toward other, more experienced angels for direction. They can benefit from participation in formalized angel networks and syndicates, where deals are identified and researched in a standardized process.

We have not seen obvious trends in angel investing amounts. As Silver (1997) notes, individual angels will "often put as little as $25,000 to $50,000, and rarely more than $1 million, into a deal." In putting together financing deals for groups of angels, we have seen individuals invest as little as $5,000 and as much as $2,000,000. Although we expect that invested amounts are likely to be based on some rough correlation to an angel's liquid assets, we have not noted other patterns of investment size based on angels' background or employment. We have seen angels with successful entrepreneurial ventures choosing to make a few large investments in opportunities they get involved in, while many angels with nonbusiness backgrounds often spread small investments around to numerous ventures. This would be an interesting area of research.

Super-Angels

"Super-angel" is a term we have begun to hear within the past few years. This refers to an individual with the financial resources to make investments of $1,000,000 or more in a single company. We assume these are individuals whose net worth exceeds $10,000,000. In addition, we find that these angels often have a very specific focus for their investments, either in a given geographical area, industry, or *type* of deal (such as a roll-up or a turnaround). These angels can single-handedly propel a venture from startup through the early growth phase. In most cases super-angels demand and receive special terms and considerations for their investment, including participation in management or even voting control.

A biotech company with gene analysis technology developed at the University of Wisconsin received a multimillion-dollar angel investment from a super-angel. This helped accelerate the company's development cycle, and has led to significant follow-on venture capital investments.

Angel Networks

An angel network is any informal or formal arrangement in which angels examine opportunities together. Our anecdotal information suggests that most angel networking is still done on an informal basis. Numerous entrepreneurs have commented that access to a single angel can lead quickly to a "web" of potential investors. Angels prefer to receive leads on investments from trusted friends and associates. Angels have good reason to maintain a low profile; high-profile angels can find themselves solicited by dozens of entrepreneurs seeking financing.

A formalized angel network is usually designed to help a group of individuals streamline their efforts to identify high-potential investment opportunities. In some cases, one or two of the angels will lead the group, identifying and researching deals. In others, the angels may decide to hire staff for this purpose. When deals are identified, each angel has the ability and legal responsibility to decide whether or not to make an investment, and how much to invest. The angel group may choose to form a separate legal entity to make the investment. For example, the angels could form a new limited liability corporation (LLC), and have the new entity invest in the startup company. This simplifies the reporting and documentation requirements for the startup company, but may have complicating factors for the angels with regard to income accounting.

The most formalized angel network is the "angel fund" or "angel venture capital" group, in which angels pay into a pool to create a small-scale venture fund. For example, a group of twenty angels might invest $100,000 each to create a pool of $2,000,000. The fund would likely identify an individual to perform the research and analysis, with the expectation that the "fund" will invest in five to ten deals over the course of a few years. Final decision-making authority still rests with the angels in some form of majority vote for any given investment. Increasing the level of formalism in the network has advantages and disadvantages. The network has increased negotiating power and can more effectively leverage its presence in the community. It should also be able to identify and research deals more efficiently than angels working independently. On the other hand, the individual angels will have less influence over what types of deals are considered; in the case of the "fund" example, angels might end up funding deals they vote against (and vice versa).

Singer provides a narrative summary for the continuing evolution of angel networks:

> First, the angels went from investing individually to pooling their money and investing through formalized networks—groups ranging from the well-known Band of Angels, in Silicon Valley, to the Nashua Breakfast Club, in Nashua, N.H., and from the CommonAngels in Boston, to the Capital Network, in Austin. Then, rather than following a strict sequential order for their investments (that is, the angels providing the seed money, and the VCs kicking in for later rounds), the angels started piggybacking onto VC deals, with the entrepreneurs sometimes bringing the parties together in a round that would raise $1 million to $3 million. And most recently, angels have begun establishing small limited-partnership funds fed by individual investors, such as the San Francisco-based Venture Strategy Group, which closed its first, $25-million vehicle last year. Angels are also teaming up with VCs to contribute to traditional VC funds or to participate in arrangements like those designed by Venture Investment Management Co. (VIMAC), in Boston. (Singer 2000: 56)

From the VC perspective, the resources involved in researching and closing a $5,000,000 deal are about the same as for a $500,000 deal. VCs struggle to justify the effort required to make seed-level deals. Over time, angels have adapted to formalize and streamline their investing processes. By mimicking the VC infrastructure while retaining decision-making control, groups of angels have found ways to make the seed-level investments that VCs may not pursue.

Creating or Joining an Angel Network

Forming an angel network can be as simple as bringing together a group of investors over coffee to discuss opportunities and listen to presentations, or as formal as setting up an investment company and funding it with upfront capital. In either case, we recommend that individuals consider the following steps and sample questions:

I.   Identify the goals of the network:
     Is the network applying a portfolio approach to angel investing?

Is the network primarily a social activity?

What level of returns do the angels expect?

Does the network intend to focus on a specific type of company or industry area?

What size investments do participants wish to make?

How much in total do the angels plan to invest per year?

II.   Understand the strengths and weaknesses of the network:

What experience do the participants have?

In what aspects of general management are the angels most competent and comfortable?

Does the group have legal, financial, and accounting expertise?

III. Consider the operational mechanics:

Will the angels invest as individuals or as a group?

Will there be a legal entity involved in managing the process?

Will there be a designated researcher?

How will the group learn about opportunities?

Will there be a formal office?

How often will the group meet?

What are the operating expenses of the entity, and the likely costs to each angel?

IV.   Agree to the level of involvement:

Will investors be taking board seats on portfolio companies?

Will investors stay active in company activities?

Will investors consider follow-on investments?

Will the angels actively participate in due diligence analysis?

Will there be one or two angels who nominally lead the group?

V.   Develop deal flow:

Create connections to access opportunities (law firms, accounting firms, other angels, other angel groups, local VCs, financial institutions, local and regional government).

Establish a relatively standardized evaluation process based on tapping the expertise of the group and trusted associates.

Work with other investment groups and financiers to improve the due diligence process and share information when appropriate.

VI.   Make investments:

Stick to your investment goals; make the investments that meet your criteria.

Support your portfolio companies as best you can.

If the investment results are not satisfactory, review the investment process.

What Is an Angel Deal?

Industries

One of the classic rules of angel investing is: "Invest in what you know." Many angels make local investments in companies related to their previous business experience. These are often family-run, closely held businesses where the angel expects to receive a share of the yearly profits and the possibility of a significant return if the company is sold.

Most angels expect extremely high returns from their early-stage investments. Some invest specifically in areas of explosive market growth, even if these are unfamiliar industries and technologies. In the past few years, the most promising industries with high year-to-year growth rates have been information technology, biotechnology, and telecommunications. The first two formal angel networks in Wisconsin focused on these areas: one researching information technology companies, and the other investigating life sciences technologies.

Robinson and Van Osnabrugge (2000: 16) refer to an article by Chan (1999) suggesting that "U.S. angels fund 60 percent of all young technology firms looking for $1 million or less in start-up funds." And nearly two-thirds of the angel matching services in the United States believe that "their angels prefer high-tech investments (Van Osnabrugge and Robinson 2000: 262).

Our own experience provides supporting evidence. Many angels are looking for businesses that require a moderate to significant amount of startup funding to cover early losses. Classic examples of this could be software or pharmaceuticals, where extensive development costs are eventually paid off by the low variable cost of providing a software download or a single drug dose. Once the market accepts the product, the firm obtains extremely high margins on each additional sale.

This does not address the issue of whether the company is viable in the long run. But most angels hope to get their investment returns in a three- to seven-year period. With this in mind, an acquisition (or the rarer IPO) is a very satisfactory result.

Company Characteristics

Smart angels investigate many aspects of a startup business. But many angels consider the entrepreneur and the management team to be the most important factor.

According to University of Wisconsin Professor Bob Pricer, most angels live by the rule of "Better an 'A' management team and a 'B' product than a 'B' management team and an 'A' product."[10] This sentiment has been repeatedly echoed in our discussions with angels. Former DEMCO CEO and active angel Greg Larson has stated, "In the end, I'm betting on the entrepreneur—after all, I'm giving him my money." Tom Terry, a former senior associate with the Capital Group in Los Angeles explained, "I have to have a strong level of trust with the management team. I don't want to spend all my time interrogating them to get information. It needs to be more than just an investment—it needs to be a relationship."

This is a consistent theme. "You seem to think we invest in businesses. We do not. We invest in people (Seglin 1998), suggests one angel. "Nicholas Negroponte, a founder of the MIT Media Lab and an avid angel who is involved in at least forty companies, insists, 'I also bet on the jockey, not just the horse'" (Seglin 1998). Robinson and Van Osnabrugge (2000) provide survey results about the investment criteria that angels use in making decisions. Four of the five top criteria focus on the entrepreneur.

Academic research provides an explanation for angels' focus on the trustworthiness of the entrepreneur. Freear et al. (2000: 56), note: "Business angels tend to rely upon the entrepreneur to protect them from losses due to market risk. Consequently, they are more concerned with agency risk than market risk. Venture Capital funds are more concerned with market risk because they have learned to protect themselves contractually from agency risk using boilerplate contractual terms and conditions." In other words, VCs use the legal documentation to limit risk, while angels tend to rely on their judgment of the entrepreneur.

The research suggests that most angels' secondary focus is the market. A large and growing market gives the company a better chance to reach the size necessary to generate the returns angels are seeking. Seglin (1998) adds: "It wouldn't hurt if your business was built around some leading-edge proprietary technology in a market no other company dominates. And, of course, it's always nice if you can offer your prospective benefactors a clear exit strategy—since they'd like to cash in on their investments in, oh, say, five years."

It is interesting to note, however, that in the survey results provided by Van Osnabrugge and Robinson (2000), exit strategy is not mentioned as one of the top ten investment criteria. Neither is competition. This is probably one of the most crucial differences between angels and venture capitalists. For a venture capital company, understanding the competitive environment, and the potential for another technology to "leap-frog" the market, is crucial. For many angels, however, it is simply too early to predict the competitive situation. The venture capitalist must also actively consider exit strategies, because there are shareholders or limited partners to report to. Angels are more lenient in considering exit strategies because of the high probability of numerous rounds of financing between investment and exit.

From anecdotal experience, we suggest that the following represent reasonable expectations demonstrated by angels in considering opportunities:

1. Fundamental technology should be beyond proof-of-concept stage;
2. Management team should be capable and functional, but is unlikely to be able to take the company through significant growth without additions/changes;
3. Preliminary market research should demonstrate that there are customers willing to pay for the new product/service;
4. Founders and/or managers should have already committed sweat equity and cash;
5. Financing needs should be based on achieving a key milestone; and
6. Entrepreneurs seeking angel financing should know enough about finance to have a reasonable understanding of valuation and have thought about potential exit strategies.

Deal Size and Staging

Much of the literature on angel financing focuses on situations where a single angel provides the first $50,000 to allow an entrepreneur to complete the research phase of a new technology or product. It is, therefore, useful to differentiate between two types or stages of angel deals: the "friends and family" deal and the "unassociated angel" deal.

"Friends and Family"

According to Professor Pricer, over 90 percent of American startups are initially funded by friends and family.[11] For most technology-based startups, this is not sufficient to support the company's R&D efforts.

"Unassociated Angels"

Once a company has demonstrated proof-of-concept, the costs associated with development can grow quickly. The company may need to apply for patents and/or trademarks, or even negotiate for access to intellectual property. Accounting and legal expenses add up, and since most technology companies have limited revenue opportunities early on, these businesses often expect to show significant losses for the first few years. For example, a medical software company must complete the product and receive FDA approval *before* it can begin marketing the product. These costs must be funded externally.

In these cases, many technology companies widen their search for money and look to "unassociated angels," or angels who were not previously connected to the entrepreneurs. They might have friends or family who are linked to the entrepreneurs, but the subjective degree of separation precluded them from the initial "friends and family" round.

Our experience shows that this "seed" round of financing can range significantly—from $250,000 to well over $2,500,000. The average appears to be between $500,000 and $750,000. Our anecdotal estimate of the length of time before the company uses up this financing appears to be between nine and sixteen months.

Down Rounds

In the past two years, numerous companies "burned through" seed-round financing, but failed to reach breakeven or to attract venture-capital financing. These companies may consider a "down round," in which new financing is sought at a valuation below one or more of the previous rounds. In this case, early investors will be diluted—their investment value will fall and their ownership stake may drop dramatically.

This poses a dilemma for everyone: the entrepreneur, the seed-round financier, and potential new investors. The seed-round financier is likely to be struggling with the "sunk cost" dilemma. Rational analysis requires that the investor ignore her previous investment and focus on the merits of the company at the current time; this is an exercise only for the most stoic and analytical angel. Potential new investors are understandably wary about putting new money into a business that has not met its goals—if the seed round investors are not reinvesting, this will be an extremely difficult sell. For some entrepreneurs, rapidly shifting financial markets may have discounted a normally attractive deal. But for many entrepreneurs, optimistic projections simply were not met. The company must choose to battle on in the face of ever-increasing skepticism, or to give up, despite some progress.

Expectations for Returns

Expectations for returns appear to range widely across angel groups. Most angels regard financial projections provided by startup companies as questionable at best. "To many angels, the rate of return is hypothetical; they just aim for something better than what they could get from a bank. Other more professional angels, especially in angel syndicates, may make efforts to guess-timate return" (Van Osnabrugge and Robinson 2000: 204).

There does, however, appear to be some consensus that angels look for opportunities with rates of return in excess of 30 percent. Of course, if we consider this the desired rate of return for a portfolio of startup investments, where the likely failure rate is anywhere from 30 percent to 80 percent, we would expect to find angels looking for the potential return on any one in-vestment to be 70 percent annualized, or even higher. Many venture capital-ists look for individual deals with potential return rates above 50 percent annualized, and it is not unreasonable to consider angel investing to be riskier than venture capital.

Typical Term

In most deal discussions, a document is created that outlines the general arrangement for an investment.[12] This document is often referred to as the "term sheet." It may be as short as one page, but can be much longer. Usu-ally, the term sheet is not the investment document, but is simply the record of the "terms" or agreed-upon details of the investment. This will usually contain information such as the amount of the investment (including if there is a minimum and/or maximum amount allowed), whether the invest-ment will be equity or debt, and any special considerations that have been agreed to.

Despite numerous publications to the contrary, our experience suggests that there is no such thing as a set of "typical terms" for an angel deal. We submit the following factors as possible causes:

1. Many angels do not codify their specific objectives and investment criteria;
2. Many angels are not familiar with all of the legal and financial as-pects of a term sheet and/or shareholder agreement;
3. Many angels find the prospect of negotiating from scratch to be un-appealing; and
4. Many angels make investments based on the recommendations of friends and associates, and a sense of trust developed with an entre-preneur; under these circumstances, some angels consider the ac-tual term sheet to be a formality.

We have seen some general terms developed that are worth mentioning. These can be grouped into a few specific categories: instrument type, board representation, control, exit, and other.

Instrument Type

Equity. Most angels seem comfortable with common or preferred stock. Convertible preferred stock is standard for VCs, and many angels are finding it to be an effective instrument for protecting an investment while retaining upside potential. At the same time, the selection of instrument may be mitigated by the expectation that VC funding will be sought in the near term. When a VC gets involved in negotiations for a new round of financing, they will be in the driver's seat.[13]

Debt. Many angels are willing to accept, or even prefer, straight debt instruments, or debt investments with warrants. Warrant deals often cannot be valued as easily as traditional equity deals, but there may be significant advantages to the angel for protecting the investment. At the same time, VCs are generally uninterested in making investments when there is a requirement for the company to pay off previous investors.

Automatic Conversion. If angels accept preferred stock or debt, they usually demand automatic conversion to common stock in the case of an exit event.

Dividend/Interest Provision. Our experience suggests that angels are generally willing to forgo dividends or interest payments while a company is completing technology and product development. At the same time, angels usually want to make certain that they have dividend and interest rights similar to those of founders.

Board Representation

Board Seats. Angels with relevant experience can make excellent board members. Angel networks and syndicates often bring to the table both the demand for board representation, and the implicit promise that the board member will add expertise and credibility to the team.

Control

Voting Control. In the case of high-technology startups, it is our experience that angels do not expect to receive voting control of the business through stock ownership. In some cases, however, angels may demand supermajority vote, or even veto power over certain issues, such as significant corporate transactions (merger, dissolution, etc.). It is our experience that angels expect to assist companies, rather than run them.

Board Control. In our experience, it is rare for angels to request increasing board representation in the case of nonperformance by the company.

Exit

Exit Participation. Angels expect to participate in any exit event. In most cases, angels expect to have rights with regard to an exit event similar to those of the founders. We have seen situations in which angels have negotiated for a *preferred* exit—for example, if the management initiates an exit event advantageous to management but disadvantageous to the angels (based on relative ownership), the angels would receive their original investment plus a predetermined return before the management gets paid out.

Registration Right. Many angels look to identify their registration rights for an IPO event.

Other

Legal Costs. Our experience suggests that angels are generally comfortable bearing their own legal costs, especially when the company has already prepared investment documentation.

Key Person Insurance. Angels generally require companies to obtain key person insurance on senior managers and/or critical scientific staff.

Noncompete/Nondisclosure Agreements. Angels generally require companies to commit to obtaining noncompete and nondisclosure contracts for employees.

Antidilution/First Right to Purchase. Angels often request a first right to purchase additional securities offered by the company. Although some angels also request antidilution rights, it should be noted that venture capitalists may consider antidilution clauses as deal-killers.

Reserved Shares. Most angels are comfortable with some amount of shares set aside in the form of stock options for key employees.

Purchase Agreement/Shareholder Agreement. Angels expect some type of purchase agreement and/or a shareholder agreement that clearly identifies the various rights and responsibilities of shareholders.

How Do Angels Behave?

Identifying Deals

For any angel or angel syndicate, the key is deal flow. Venture capitalists invest in less than 2 percent of companies they consider, whereas some research suggests that angels invest in as many as one out of every five deals they consider (Van Osnabrugge and Robinson 2000: 146). Our experience seems to match that of the other angel networks in Wisconsin, which suggests an investment rate more comparable to that of venture capitalists. Since inception in March 2001, Early Stage Research has investigated over 250 companies, and has invested in four. Wisconsin Investment Partners has researched over 150 opportunities, and has invested in five.[14]

Regardless of the numbers, an angel's investments are only as good as the companies considered. Some individual angels receive business plans on their front doorstep. Most angels, however, rely on business associates and friends to identify opportunities.

The angel networks in Wisconsin have received publicity in the past two years, and have subsequently received a significant number of proposals for investments. Numerous Web sites exist to attempt to match angel networks with entrepreneurs, although in general the quality of the opportunities varies dramatically.

In the case of Wisconsin Investment Partners, Managing Partner Dick Leazer is the ex-managing director of the Wisconsin Alumni Research Foundation and maintains very close ties with the research community at the University of Wisconsin-Madison. Our experience suggests that a network of business associates is still the best source of deal opportunities.

Researching Deals

Due diligence is a time-consuming process. Many venture capitalists have established procedures for researching investment opportunities and the resources to be somewhat efficient. For individual angels, and angel networks, the process is often more freeform. Angels rarely have access to information databases, industry reports, or travel budgets. It may be difficult for an angel to identify or pay an industry expert to provide an opinion on a given technology or market.

Our experience with angels and entrepreneurs has led us to focus on a fairly standard set of factors when evaluating a deal.[15] These usually include questions about the management team, business viability, the market or industry, competition and barriers to entry, and exit strategy.

Management Team

- Does the team have expertise in the specific technology?
- Does the team have general management expertise?
- Has the team ever started a company before? Was there an exit event?
- Has the team made personal investments in the company ("sweat equity" and/or cash)?
- Does the team show a willingness to bring in experienced talent as well as to grow talent internally?

Business Viability

- Does the business opportunity show a clear path to operating as a profitable business?
- Does the business have a clear development plan to bring the technology to market?
- Is there a sustainable competitive advantage?

Market

- Has there been confirmation from customers that the product is viable in the current marketplace? Will it generate premiums over other products? Can it be produced more cheaply than other products?
- Is the market large enough to support a new entry? How will market dynamics change when the new product arrives?
- Is the product targeted at a specific niche, or at a broad-based segment?
- Is the market growing? What is the relevance of the product life cycle to current market conditions?
- What market share can be reasonably expected?

Competition and Barriers to Entry

- What is the relevant competitive environment? Is competition consolidated or fragmented?
- What is the likely competitor response to the new product?
- Are there significant barriers to entry within the industry? Can the company create or take advantage of these or new barriers?

Exit Strategy

- Is there a reasonable exit strategy for the business?
- Are the entrepreneurs interested in an exit strategy, or are they hoping to run the business as an operating company?
- What exits have occurred in the market space?

Sources of Information

Angels use numerous sources of information to understand an opportunity. A partial list includes:

1. The company's business plan/offering memorandum;
2. Interviews and discussions with the entrepreneurs;

3. Literature searches (newspapers, magazines, electronic databases, SEC filings);
4. Interviews with industry experts (college professors, consultants, current industry members);
5. Competitor research;
6. Financial forecasting tools (pro forma projections, valuation analyses);
7. Discussions with other angels, angel groups, or institutional investors;
8. General Web-surfing for information; and
9. Customer interviews.

The single most common regret expressed by angel investors with regard to how they would invest differently is "More due diligence" (Van Osnabrugge and Robinson 2000: 211). As Van Osnabrugge and Robinson (2000: 212) state, "To be a successful private investor in an entrepreneurial firm, it pays to be more like the professional venture capitalist by conducting thorough due diligence, forming a detailed investment contract, and lending a helping hand to the venture once a deal has been made."

Investing in Groups

There is little doubt that investing in groups can provide angels with significant advantages. Initially, a group provides individual angels with access to more deals, but it can also offer a more efficient process for researching and evaluating opportunities, increased negotiating power, improved ability to monitor and assist investments, and the value of pooled expertise and contacts.

At the same time, investing in groups can lead to unexpected dynamics. There may be unusually influential members of the group (such as a successful entrepreneur or an industry expert), or there might be a tendency for the group to invest only when every member is interested. This is complicated by the fact that some, if not most of a group's investments will fail. In fact, since the failures will probably be identified long before the successes pay out, it is very important that expectations are managed appropriately. In the case of angel networks where individuals have final say over their investment decisions, it should be understood that personal responsibility for decisions is crucial. In a syndicate or fund where decisions are made by majority vote, angels must be comfortable not second-guessing the group. The goal should be to keep the companies in front of the angels after the investment so each member can see the progress and problems firsthand.

Angel Investing Advice

Discussing the realities of angel investing can be daunting. The following list of "Angel Investing Tips"[16] is a useful starting point for dialogue with both active and potential angels:

1. This is "High Risk Capital." Be prepared to lose everything.
2. Take a portfolio approach:
    a. Allocate a certain amount of capital over a set period, and
    b. Allocate it among a number of opportunities.
3. Most winners will be sale of the business—not IPOs.
4. These are mid- to long-term investments.
5. Selecting investments:
    c. Invest in management teams you know well, and
    d. Invest in industries where you intuitively understand the value proposition.
6. Look skeptically at hockey-stick financial projections.
7. Assume additional capital will be necessary.
8. Understand the purposes of angel capital.
9. Worry about financial dilution—not percentage dilution.
10. Have fun!

Working with Angels

Finding Angels

There are numerous ways to identify and approach angels. At the same time, angels often carefully guard their exposure to limit solicitation. As one commentator suggests: "So how do you find angels? Well, mostly you don't. They find you" (Seglin 1998).

While not always the case, this is a consistent response from angels, entrepreneurs, and various service providers. Many angels are very active in seeking out opportunities. "Negroponte finds some of his investments through former Media Lab students. And Walnut finds its investments through 'a deep referral network of entrepreneurs, venture capitalists, and former Harvard Business School students'" (Seglin 1998).

There are numerous ways to make the first connection to angels. In most cases, the key is to have a very clear, concise explanation of the opportunity. Some angels will "self-select" out of the process because they are not interested in a given industry or a type of deal. The process of reaching angels can be time-consuming; entrepreneurs should not waste time on angels who will not be interested.

Once the message is focused, spread a wide net initially. Discussions with any number of people and groups may obtain results. The potential sources include: friends and family, the company's accounting firm, the company's law firm, the company's bank, other small business managers, local business consultants, faculty and staff at the local business school, connections through university alumni programs, listings from local chambers of commerce, local angel networks and investment clubs, and other entrepreneurs.

Getting an Angel's Attention

Private investors often have limited time to consider opportunities. Angel networks and syndicates are equally busy. For most entrepreneurs, there is a serious tradeoff between preparing materials versus actually running the business. With that in mind, we have some suggestions for entrepreneurs trying to figure out what information to provide to angels.

As a general rule, we do not recommend gimmicks or stunts. We simply suggest that the entrepreneur provide the minimum information necessary to convince the angel to investigate further. As noted previously, the connection utilized to provide the information is nearly as important as the information itself. An executive summary coming from a trusted source will be read.

Executive Summary

A clear, well-written executive summary may be the most effective way to engage an angel's interest. We recommend an executive summary of two or three pages. It should be written in a professional style and should: explain the product or service, provide brief bios on the management team, describe the target market, clearly identify the company's sustainable competitive advantage, and note any current business partners or customers.

If possible, it is useful to mention competition and provide very simple financial projections (if historicals are available, include summary information). Many executive summaries are five pages long; this is not a problem, as long as the message is conveyed clearly. In theory, the executive summary should be the first part of a complete business plan. Since we recommend more concise business plans, we also recommend concise executive summaries.

Some angel groups require the submission of a formal document, where information is provided in a highly specified format. This allows the reviewers to check quickly to see if the business opportunity meets criteria of special interest.

Business Plan

Many entrepreneurs mistakenly believe that the business plan needs to explain every aspect of the business. Many also believe that packaging helps their plan stand out. It is our opinion that the following factors are most likely to be marks of an effective business plan:[17]

1. *Physical appearance:* length of fifteen to twenty-five pages, single-spaced, plain font, diagrams and graphics where appropriate, plain white paper, no special bindings.
2. *Transmittal:* MSWord, Adobe PDF file or equivalent so that the file can be transferred easily by e-mail (note: this excludes large, complex graphics that can turn a ten-page text document into a 5Mb e-mail).
3. *Cover page:* name of the company, contact information, and one sentence describing the business concept.
4. *Financials:* Unless otherwise specified, historical profit and loss statements, historical balance sheet information, and historical cash flow statements must be provided if available. Pro forma projections should include at least three years of projections, but no more than five years of projections. Yearly profit and loss statements, balance sheet information, and cash flow statements should be included. Monthly profit and loss/cash flow for the first projected year may be appropriate. Financial information can be included in an appendix and should be about five pages total.
5. *Topics:* required information includes a description of the product or service, an explanation of any underlying technology, an overview of the market, relevant information about competitors, information on the revenue model, background of the management team, and expected use of funds for the financing round. It may be useful to provide additional data on possible exit strategies, sales and operational plans, and other information on related technologies or opportunities.

Management Information

As noted previously, many angels place a significant amount of importance on the entrepreneur or the management team. A partner at a venture capital firm once commented that when he gets a business plan, he turns immediately to the financial section; our angel investors usually turn immediately to the management resumes. If the management team is small, it is appropriate to include complete resumes in the business plan. For space considerations, it may be necessary to limit management information to short biographies. It is recommended that managers state the names of previous employers, as well as the various positions held. If the biography is not specific, most angels will ask. Gruner (1996: 86) adds, "Entrepreneurs should also be prepared to supply a seemingly endless list of references."

Presenting to Angels

Most angels have strong natural curiosities. Angels are excited to learn, especially about new technologies and new products. Many angels will go out of their way to find time to listen to and participate in presentations about totally unfamiliar businesses. Our experience suggests that many angels are tolerant of mediocre or even poor materials, and will often agree to meet with entrepreneurs just to learn more about the company.

At the same time, it is also our experience that the presentation is one of the most difficult and easily botched activities in obtaining angel financing. Many angels are strongly influenced by their rapport with an entrepreneur; a bad presentation can be the end of the process. Of course, every opportunity and situation is different, and no single set of rules can guarantee success or even prepare an entrepreneur for every eventuality. At the same time, we have a limited list of suggestions for consideration in presenting to angels:[18]

Short Presentation

Angels are generally not interested in lengthy PowerPoint presentations. We recommend having five to ten slides prepared that very quickly establish the business concept, the qualifications of the team, the market and competitive environment, and the financing goal.[19] The slides should be clear and uncluttered—visuals may be useful but complex diagrams are likely a mistake. Having backup slides can be useful, but the presenter should not anticipate using them, much less speed through the presentation to cover them.

Questions and Answers

In reality, it is unlikely that the presenter will get through even a five-slide presentation without fielding questions, some of which may diverge significantly from the presentation. It is our recommendation that the entrepreneur be willing to let the angels determine the course of the dialogue. The presenter can remind the angels of the time constraint and redirect the group to the presentation to ensure that the major concepts are covered. We suspect, however, that an angel who feels that he got answers to his questions and wants to learn more is a better prospect than an angel who feels he was led down a predetermined path. This is also why we recommend only the "bare bones" presentation—it gives the presenter a straightforward yet extremely flexible agenda for making sure that key issues are mentioned but that discussion can be wide-ranging.

Format and Handouts

In the small group setting, we actually recommend that presenters consider a "handout presentation" rather than utilize a projector. Providing a handout with printed slides gives the angels a convenient note-taking format, allows them to look ahead to see where the presentation is going, encourages dialogue and sharing among the group, and generally ensures that the angels will leave the meeting with the critical information about the company. In addition, it alleviates the need to have the lights turned off, and encourages the angels to look at the entrepreneur rather than a screen or the wall.

Demonstrations

We strongly recommend the use of a demonstration whenever appropriate. We can only remind entrepreneurs that a successful demonstration is a powerful selling tool, but an unsuccessful demonstration is nearly always a deal-killer. Set up and test the demonstration before the meeting even begins.

Attitude

Perhaps one of the most important factors in the presentation is the presenter's attitude and persona. The best recommendation we can make is to be *enthusiastic* but *levelheaded* and *open-minded*. Respond to every question succinctly and factually, do not take anything personally, and admit your ignorance if you really do not know. The single most important, and most difficult recommendation, is to listen to the questions and comments and *hear* what the angels are saying. Angels rarely ask "trick" questions, but it's still easy to hear one question and inadvertently answer another. Be open to what the angels are saying, and try to be aware of the difference between criticism and brainstorming. Respond to criticism when appropriate, and try to turn brainstorming to your advantage by encouraging the angels to help you improve the business. There may be no more effective way to elicit an angel's interest than to find a way for him to help.

After the Investment

The real work will come after the investment is made. For companies obtaining angel financing, getting the money in the bank is just the first of progressively higher hurdles in building a successful business. Angel investors should take an extremely proactive stance in working with the company. Angels should demand a clear set of reports and updates. We recommend quarterly (unaudited) financial reports, specifically profit and loss statements, as well as some type of report on product development or potential customer pipeline. It can be difficult to balance the concerns between the entrepreneur's time and the need to stay in contact. We recommend monthly meetings, such as breakfast meetings, to stay informed. Our experience suggests that these interactions help keep entrepreneurs on track.

In some cases, angels look for active involvement. According to Freear et al. (2000: 54), "In 75 percent of the angel-backed firms, at least one private investor held a seat on the board of directors."

In many cases, the entrepreneur hopes the angel can provide assistance with financial issues, including additional financing. Freear et al. (2000: 55) report the results of a study by Ehrich showing that "entrepreneurs seek expertise through their investors generally in the areas of staffing and financial management." Although many angels can help companies identify additional financing sources, we believe that the most useful assistance that angels can provide will come in the form of business networking and general business expertise.

Summary

We have tried to provide an introduction to the world of angel financing for high-tech startup businesses. The breadth of angel investing is so diverse that no summary can encapsulate it. Angels invest in high-technology ventures as well as local retail stores. Angels invest in real estate developments and low-profit urban redevelopment projects. Angels invest for monetary returns, and for personal and altruistic returns.

Angel investing has always been one of the most dynamic, high-risk areas of finance. It is a key driver of the U.S. economy, providing an irreplaceable source of early-stage capital for innovators, scientists, and entrepreneurs. Angels often invest *before* professional venture capital firms get involved— in effect, angels take the risks that the VCs avoid. In the final analysis, the angel investor has always been the key step in early-stage corporate finance— the leap of faith bringing together the entrepreneur and the necessary capital to get companies off the ground.

Notes

The author would like to thank: Dick Leazer (manager, Wisconsin Investment Partners, LLC) for his wisdom, advice, and expertise; Sal Braico (associate, Early Stage Research, LLC) for his assistance with research, analysis, and editing; and Mark van Osnabrugge (Marakon Associates) and Robert Robinson (Harvard Business School) for permission to use information from their book, *Angel Investing*, as well as their thoughtful suggestions and critiques. Finally, the author would like to express his continuing gratitude to Professor Bob Pricer at University of Wisconsin-Madison, who has tirelessly and selflessly promoted the cause of small business and entrepreneurship.

1. www.nvca.com/.

2. www.nvca.com/.

3. An IPO (initial public offering) is the event that allows the stock of the company to be traded publicly on a major exchange (such as the NASDAQ or the New York Stock Exchange).

4. Aurora has since been acquired by Vertex Pharmaceuticals (NASDAQNM: VRTX).

5. Additionally, the advent of the Internet has led to numerous Web sites that attempt to provide long-distance connections between angels and entrepreneurs. See www.vFinance.com/; www.UniversityAngels.com/; www.BusinessPartners.com/.

6. www.sec.gov/divisions/corpfin/forms/regd.htm.

7. It is not the author's intent to either support or detract from the legitimacy of the Regulation D requirements. The author is noting that this may be the simplest mechanism to reduce the risk of scams and frauds perpetrated on the vulnerable, specifically those with limited assets and little or no business experience.

8. Based on anecdotal information, we estimate that the majority of angels we interact with have a net worth of $3,000,000 to $10,000,000.

9. Jeffrey Sohl, director of the University of New Hampshire's Center for Venture Research, quoted in Stephanie L. Gruner, "Conversations with Angels," *Inc Magazine*, October 1, 1996.

10. Personal interview of Robert Pricer by Adam J. Bock, 1999.

11. A common, but less complimentary term is "Friends, family, and fools."

12. Some of the terminology used in this section may not be familiar to every reader. It is not possible to provide a complete explanation in this chapter, so the author recommends that readers visit www.entreworld.org/Content/Glossary.cfm, which provides a glossary of standard investment terms, as well as links to other sites of interest.

13. One Chicago venture capitalist commented, "There are three parties at the table: the entrepreneur, the angels, and me. My primary concern is myself. After that, I'm most concerned about the entrepreneur—if he doesn't have incentives to succeed, I may as well write off the investment now. Clearly, if I have to beat someone down to get the deal done, the angel is the most vulnerable" (Panel discussion at Garage.com event, Chicago, 2001).

14. As of July 2001.

15. Again, the reader is referred to www.entreworld.org/Content/Glossary.cfm for assistance with terminology.

16. Informal list, presented in spring 2001, used courtesy of Frank Ballantine, of Sachnoff and Weaver, Ltd., Chicago.

17. We are referring to business plans only for companies seeking seed financing from angels.

18. This set of rules refers to opportunities to present to individual angels or a small group of angels (less than fifteen). Presentations to large groups of angels require a different approach.

19. This is, in fact, a visual version of the business executive summary.

References

Alvarez, F., et al. 1997. "Financing Issues in the Twenty-First Century." Kauffmann Foundation Research Conference Paper, Babson College, April 16–19.

Chan, G. 1999. "Manna Makers: 'Angel Investors' Bestow Precious Investment Capital on the Chosen Few." *Sacramento Bee*, April 26, 1B1.

Freear, J.; J. Sohl; and W. Wetzel, Jr, 2000. "The Informal Venture Capital Market: Milestones Passed and the Road Ahead." *Entrepreneurship 2000*, ed. D. Sexton and R. Smilor, ch. 3. Chicago: Upstart.

Gruner, S.L. 1996. "Conversations with Angels." *Inc Magazine* (October 1): 86.

Mason, C.M. 1996. "Informal Venture Capital: Is Policy Running Ahead of Knowledge?" *International Journal of Entrepreneurial Behavior and Research* 2, no. 1: 4–14.

Seglin, J.L. 1998. "What Angels Want." *Inc Magazine*: www.imc.com/magazine/19980515/1121.html (May 15).

Silver, Jonathan. 1997. "ABCs of Venture Capital and Angel Investors." *Nation's Capital*: www.bizjournals.com/washington/stories/1997/03/17/smallb3.html (March 14).

Singer, Thea. 2000. "Where the Money Is." *Inc Magazine* (September 1): 52–57.

Van Osnabrugge, M., and R.J. Robinson. 2000. *Angel Investing*. San Francisco: Jossey-Bass.

17

Venture Capital

David E. Arnstein

Introduction

Venture capitalists are professional investors who specialize in funding and building young, innovative enterprises. The venture capitalists, in harmony with the entrepreneurs they fund, are an important catalyst in the continuous growth of the new economy. Venture capital (VC) is a large and vital financing source, with 693 venture funds in the United States managing $210 billion (NVCA 2001a). In 2000 alone, a National Venture Capital Association (NVCA) study showed U.S. companies originally backed by venture capital created 5.6 million new jobs, and these companies represented $956.8 billion in revenue. Venture capital is commonly referred to as the first "institutional" funding round, after a "friends-and-family" and/or "angel-financing" round. Together, venture capitalists and entrepreneurs enable job creation, medical advancements, and technological breakthroughs that continuously exceed our greatest expectations.

Important Distinction: Debt Versus Equity Financing

To understand the nature of VC, it is useful to begin by comparing the characteristics of a typical venture capital investment to those of a traditional debt financing. Debt generally has a limited upside (defined by the interest rate), but also seeks to limit the potential downside through some general or specific claim on company assets, as well as a specified time for repayment. For any given borrower, the more senior the claim on the borrower's assets, the safer the debt instrument will be.

An equity investment, by contrast, represents an ownership stake in the company and has potentially unlimited upside. But it also has much greater potential for loss, since equity is a residual claim on the value of the company—the "low man on the totem pole"—whose value consists of whatever is left after all debt holders are paid off in order of the seniority of their claim. Hence, there is a tradeoff whereby equity investors take on much greater risk than debt investors (lenders) but demand correspondingly higher returns as compensation for the greater risk. This principle applies to all equity markets—public stock exchanges like the NYSE or NASDAQ, as well as private equity markets, which include early-stage VC. However, for private equity investors there is additional risk associated with the lack of a liquid market to facilitate the easy trading of securities. And for early-stage VC investors there is also all the risk related to a small, startup venture that may have unproved technology and products, untested management, market uncertainties, and other challenges and major development milestones lying ahead.

VC: Highly Specialized Risk Capital

Venture capital is an organized pool of high-risk capital. VC investments are made where the investor believes there is an opportunity to participate in young, growing companies that have the potential for significant economic returns. The pool of capital available to venture capitalists, or "VCs" (the *managers* of these pools of high-risk capital), is generally drawn from limited partners, "LPs" (the sources of this investment capital). VCs will form an investment fund by gaining the commitment of a group of limited partners, each of whom will supply a specified dollar amount over the life of the fund. These LPs include private and public pension funds, endowment funds, foundations, corporations, wealthy individuals, foreign investors, and the venture capitalists themselves. Successful venture capital investments, while having the opportunity to be financially and personally rewarding for all parties involved, present unique challenges relative to other asset classes.

The business of venture capital involves the process of not only adequately financing companies, but also building companies, sometimes from scratch. This requires the VC to work hand-in-hand with the entrepreneur to make good decisions to build a company that will grow in value and attract more investment dollars from new investors in the future. The venture capitalist generally plays an important role in building the right management team, projecting the correct financing needs, outlining obtainable milestones and helping management execute them, and deciding the most appropriate exit strategy, among many other strategic issues.

The responsibility that comes with this active investor role requires extreme patience, the ability to deal with setbacks, and the ability of the venture capitalist and the entrepreneur to work together as a team. Post-funding, the venture capitalist and the entrepreneur are an informal partnership that must continuously act with aligned interests for the company to succeed. While each individual VC fund may focus on a different stage of investing and/or industry segments, the underlying mission is consistent across all funds—to provide exceptional returns to all stakeholders.

VC Investment Stages

Venture capital is commonly divided into two overall financing stages, early-stage financing and expansion financing. Most VC funds focus on one of these overall financing stages. Funds that invest in the earlier stages of a company's life cycle are investing at a point of higher relative risk and consequently will require higher returns than later-stage investors. In 2000, early-stage companies received 23 percent of all investments and later-stage companies received 20 percent, while over 54 percent of venture capital disbursements were invested in expansion-stage companies (NVCA 2001b). The fund I am associated with, Venture Investors LLC, located in Madison, Wisconsin, concentrates on early-stage investments.

In order to determine the appropriate funding stage, the entrepreneurial management team and its advisers must decide the type of investment that is most suitable. Since no two venture capital funds operate in the exact same manner, it is incumbent on the company seeking funding to analyze their needs and choose the appropriate funds to approach for financing. There are many resources available to assist the entrepreneur in finding the right venture capital fund. A well-known resource, *Pratt's Guide to Venture Capital 2001*, lists an index of venture capital firms by stage-of-investment preferences, geography, and investment type (Kwateng 2001). Web-based search engines are increasingly useful in obtaining information about the VC community and linking to individual funds' Web sites.

Below is a summary of common terminology used by the venture capital industry to describe investment stages and preferences. It should be understood that the investment stages described below roughly correspond to measurable milestones, which correspond to opportunities for companies to seek additional outside financing.

Early-Stage Financing

- *Seed Financing* (less than $1 million): For high-technology ventures, seed financing normally provides the initial funds for preliminary research and development, early proof of concept, and prototype development. In cases where R&D efforts are expensive and protracted, development stage financing, or R&D financing, could be required beyond typical seed financing. A critical risk exposure at this point is the risk of unsuccessful product development efforts (Smith and Smith 2000: 32).

- *Startup Financing* ($1 to $2 million): Provided to companies completing product development and initial marketing to begin revenue-generating activities (Levin 1998: 7). The companies may be in the process of building a management team or they may already be in business, but normally have not sold any commercial products. Usually such firms have made market studies, assembled some key management, developed a business plan, identified key customers, and are ready to do business.
- *First-Stage Financing* ($2 to $6 million): Provided to companies that have expended their initial capital (often developing and market testing a prototype), and require additional funds to initiate full-scale manufacturing and sales (Kwateng 2001: 10). Although these companies have typically eliminated the technology and engineering risks, they now have to execute the business fundamentals of production, sales, and marketing.

Expansion Financing

- *Second-Stage Financing* ($2 to $15 million): Working capital for the initial expansion of a company that is producing and shipping, and has accounts receivable and inventories. Although the company has made progress, it may not yet be showing a profit. When a VC investment is in a more mature company seeking expansion financing, the investment risks and potential gains are generally lower than in a startup (Levin 1998: 8).
- *Third-Stage Financing* or *Mezzanine Financing* ($10 to $40 million): Provided for major expansion of a company whose sales volume is increasing and is breaking even or profitable. These funds are normally used for plant expansion, marketing, working capital, or development of an improved product (Kwateng 2001: 10).
- *Bridge Financing* ($1 to $20 million): Needed at times when a company is approaching a major round of financing or is planning to go public in the next six months to a year. Often, bridge financing is structured to be folded into the next round of VC funding or, in the case of an initial public offering (IPO), to be repaid from the proceeds of the public offering. It can also involve restructuring of major stockholder positions through secondary transactions. Restructurings are undertaken if there are early investors who want to reduce or liquidate their position or management has changed and the stockholdings of the former management team are being bought out (Kwateng 2001: 10).

Table 17.1

Investment Horizons Returns as of December 31, 2000 (as percent)

Fund type	One year	Three years	Five years	Ten years	Twenty years
Early/seed	51.2	93.7	65.5	35.8	23.8
Balanced	33.2	61.5	42.9	27.0	17.5
Later-stage VC	19.9	31.7	31.1	25.2	18.3
All venture	37.6	64.8	48.0	29.9	19.9

Source: NVCA (2000a).

While some of the stages have the possibility of overlapping, it is important to realize that each investment stage occurs at a specific time in the company's overall growth cycle. As a company meets milestones and creates value, it also moves along the food chain of what type of investment stage it seeks. Since there is the highest degree of risk within the early/seed-investment stage, there is also a higher return required at this stage. Venture capitalists receive a higher amount of equity ownership in a company with an early-stage investment, compared to an investor at a later stage investing the same amount of dollars. While the early investors' ownership percentage will get diluted over time as new investors are brought in, their cost basis will still be low enough to provide a higher return at this investment stage as long as the value of the company increases relative to the total capital investment. The early-stage investor must believe in the idea that a small percentage of a large pie is more attractive than a large piece of a small pie. Table 17.1 is an analysis of returns across different investment stages (NVCA 2001a). Although a number of companies in a typical fund's portfolio will fail completely or earn very low returns, a few big winners will often generate returns that are more than sufficient to offset these losses and drive the overall portfolio returns to a level commensurate with the high risk taken on by the VC investor.

VC Industry Preferences

In addition to seeking a particular stage of investing, many venture capitalists focus on particular industry sectors. Because of their focus on one or a few specific sectors, VC funds are generally not diversified over a range of industries. However, this lack of diversification and the resulting concentration of risk can be offset with a depth of knowledge and experience in the targeted industry sectors, and diversification across different companies within that sector. Furthermore, the limited partner investors in funds can achieve sector diversification by investing in several VC funds.

Figure 17.1   **Venture Capital Disbursements in 2000 by Sector**

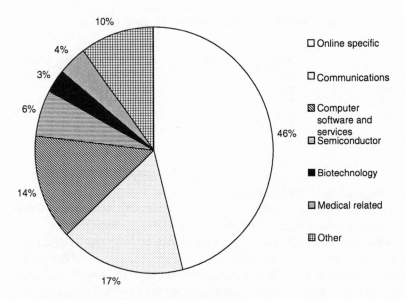

Source: NVCA Annual Report 2000.

In addition to any specific knowledge a venture capitalist may possess that determines which sectors are targeted, there are also external market forces that play into this decision. At different times, particular industries may be more attractive to venture capitalists based on new technology developments, overall market need, and public market performance. The attractive industries in recent times include biotechnology, medical devices, telecommunications, the Internet, and computer software and services. While attractive industries have changed over time—and the investment returns have varied over a broad range from one industry to another—the general foundation of these attractive industries has not. A common theme among historical VC investments is new fundamental technology and innovation. Venture capitalists serve a very important function in commercializing new technologies by acting as a screening device for new innovations, products, and services, and as a facilitator of their development.

Disbursements by venture capital funds reached an all-time high in 2000. The amount invested in 2000 was $103.5 billion, and that was distributed to 5,412 companies (NVCA 2001c). While the investment pace slowed considerably in 2001, investment continues, more in line with the historical level of 1999. The types of companies that received funding in

2000 are shown in Figure 17.1 (NVCA 2001c). It's important to note that the industries that receive funding have two common characteristics: they are technology companies and they address large market opportunities.

VC Geographic Concentration

VC investments are highly concentrated in areas on the east and west coasts of the United States. The area well known as the birthplace of venture capital is Silicon Valley, located in California. It is an area that is located on the San Francisco, California, peninsula, and radiates outward from Stanford University. Silicon Valley was conceived when college pals Bill Hewlett and Dave Packard started in a Palo Alto garage sixty years ago what is known as Hewlett Packard. With a mere $538 in startup capital, they started what is now commonly referred to as the "high-tech revolution" (www. netvalley.com 2001).[1]

As a result of the successful birth of Hewlett Packard, many venture capital funds were formed in Silicon Valley. Venture capitalists, as a general rule of thumb, prefer to invest in companies that are geographically close to the fund. This is particularly true of early-stage investors, where taking an active role is more important, and being nearby facilitates the high level of involvement required. The largest geographic concentrations of funds are in California and New England (the greater New York and Boston areas), respectively, and, therefore, the largest numbers of startup companies are located in these areas. Although this concentration still exists today, the competition for deals and the large increase in available capital has forced funds to look elsewhere for new deals.

While this concentration has been true historically, regions such as the Rocky Mountains and the Great Plains have seen a significant increase in venture investing in recent years. Although other markets have been underserved, venture capitalists are recognizing the potential in these areas. One example of this trend is Madison, Wisconsin, located in the Midwest. Madison is home to the third-largest research institution in the United States, the University of Wisconsin-Madison. Venture capitalists now recognize the potential for commercializing new technologies coming out of large research institutions now located on the east and west coasts. Third Wave Technologies, one of a few biotech initial public offerings in 2001, was founded on technology commercialized out of the University of Wisconsin-Madison. Third Wave made its debut at an IPO valuation of approximately $420 million, with $86 million of venture capital already invested in the company. Third Wave Technologies, along with other successful biotech startups, has attracted local venture firms Mason Wells and Baird Venture Partners, as

Figure 17.2   **Disbursements per Fund by State Region, 2000** ($ billions)

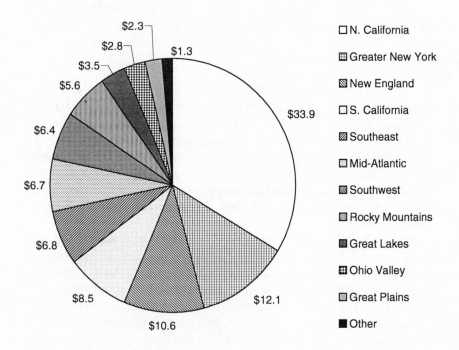

Source: Pratts Guide 2001.

well as several large coastal and international funds. They, along with exist-ing fund Venture Investors LLC, are providing increasing amounts of new capital to the Madison area.

The National Venture Capital Association and sources such as *Pratt's Guide to Venture Capital* and others annually track the geographic distri-bution of VC investments. The Rocky Mountains, the Great Plains, and New England posted the greatest percentage gains in terms of dollars in-vested with growth rates in 2000 of 137 percent, 114 percent, and 103 percent, respectively. Despite this percentage growth, the Great Plains re-mains at the bottom of the list in absolute dollars. However, this increase may be attributed to the increased efficiencies in the VC market in these areas, as investors began recognizing an abundance of quality opportuni-ties relative to the amount of capital available. This allowed more compa-nies the opportunity to access capital, resulting in the higher growth rates in these regions. Figure 17.2 summarizes the geographic distribution that occurred in 2000 (Kwateng 2001: 15).

VC Impact on Economic Development

VC has a significant impact on the economic landscape of communities where investments are made. Successful VC-backed companies normally grow jobs quickly, create high-paying jobs, and push the technology envelope. Venture-backed companies traditionally have a larger percentage of engineers, scientists, and managers in the workforce than the average company. A study commissioned by the National Venture Capital Association, and conducted by Wharton Economic Forecasting Associates (WEFA), revealed that U.S. companies originally backed by venture capital in 2000 created 5.6 million new jobs. Those companies also generated $956.8 billion in revenues to go along with the new jobs created. In addition, according to the study, VC companies represented 2.3 percent of the nation's total jobs and 7.4 percent of the gross domestic product in 2000.

As stated earlier, an example of economic impact on a community is Madison, Wisconsin. The successful evolution of Third Wave Technologies from a venture-backed enterprise to a publicly traded company has affected Madison in a very favorable way. One area of impact is increased awareness of startups and a more active entrepreneurial environment. Researchers, scientists, and entrepreneurs who have witnessed the success of a local company now have the motivation and resources available to attempt to emulate the recent success. In addition, the liquidity offered by the Third Wave IPO has allowed first and second generation companies to be started by former Third Wave employees. In order to invest in these new enterprises and not miss out on the next big opportunity, more VC funds have been attracted to the area, adding additional investment capacity. The above example shows that "success breeds success," and VC can have an immediate and long-lasting effect on the economic foundation of a community.

VC History

The concept of venture capital investment is not new.[2] Venture capitalists often relate the story of Christopher Columbus. In the fifteenth century, he sought to travel westward instead of eastward from Europe to reach India. His far-fetched idea did not find favor with the King of Portugal, who refused to finance him. Finally, Queen Isabella of Spain decided to fund him, and the voyages of Christopher Columbus are now recorded in history. Along with the funding of Christopher Columbus, venture capitalists are also credited with financing the American railroad industry in the early 1800s.

The modern VC industry can be traced back to the days after World War II. In 1946, the first VC firm was formed, American Research and Development Corporation (ARD). The founder of ARD was General Georges Doroit, a French-born military man often referred to as "the father of venture capital." In the 1950s, he taught the importance of risk capital as an available financing source at Harvard. ARD is best known for its investment in Digital Equipment Corporation (DEC). In 1946, ARD invested $70,000 in DEC, and, in 1959, the investment had a market value of $37 million. This extremely large return instantly made venture capital an attractive and visible market, with many new funds being formed in the late 1960s.

As venture funds began to form at record rates, there were many venture-backed companies that launched an initial public offering of stock in the 1960s. This favorable IPO market allowed many funds to achieve quick liquidity, with over 1,000 venture-backed companies going through IPOs in 1968. Although things looked favorable in the late 1960s, the abundance of companies flooding the market all at once created a prolonged slump in the public markets. VC investors, as well as public market investors, were frustrated and disappointed with this protracted bear market. As a consequence, the VC industry had a big setback in 1974, when Congress voted to outlaw all investments from pension funds into these high-risk investments, contending that venture capital was an abuse of pension fund money. The outcome of this legislation was an impossible fund-raising market for venture capitalists, resulting in nominal returns to investors.

In the late 1970s, the future for VC began to look bright once again. There were two legislative initiatives in 1978 that greatly enhanced the fund-raising environment. First, Congress slashed the capital gains tax rate to 28 percent from 49.5 percent. Next, the Labor Department issued a clarification that eliminated the Pension Funds Act as an obstacle to venture investing. The clarification was issued on the Employee Retirement Income Security Act prudent-man standard. Under this standard, the statutory duty to act "as would a prudent man" will be satisfied with respect to a particular investment if the fiduciary has thoroughly considered the investment's place in the whole portfolio, the risk of loss of opportunity for gain, and the diversification, liquidity, cash flow, and overall requirements of the pension plan. This clarification made sense on the basis that VC investments should not be judged individually, but rather as an asset class. The VC asset class has a low correlation with other asset classes, thus improving overall portfolio diversification risk. These two new initiatives, in conjunction with a strong IPO market led by companies like Federal Express and Apple Computer, reignited interest in VC investing. Thus, the 1980s began an extended period of growth for venture capital fund raising and investing.

This growth in VC fund raising also marked the institutionalization of venture investing. No longer were the primary sources of funds wealthy

Figure 17.3 **Venture Capital Investments, 1990–2001** (September 30, 2001)

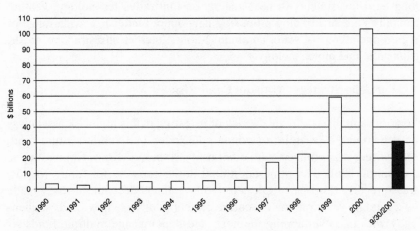

Source: NVCA Web site.

individuals and private investors, but rather pension funds and other institutional investors became the key sources of capital. With this shift to
institutions, VC funds had access to a much greater pool of investor capital and faced a more efficient fund-raising process. Annual invested capital soared from $4 billion in 1987 to over $17 billion in 1997, finally
peaking at $100 billion in 2000. This large amount invested in 2000 cre-
ated an environment of too much money chasing the available deals. At
the same time, as fund raising grew, the public markets were in an un-
precedented period of growth. These two forces combined to once again
flood the market with IPOs, some of which had no sustainable business
model and others that were simply overvalued, ultimately causing the
high valuation bubble to burst. The end results were that many investors
incurred substantial losses and many portfolio companies found themselves being "reevaluated" by the market.

A positive lesson learned from this recent experience is to back entrepreneurs with strong business models, the vision and ability to execute, and the
tenacity to see their ideas through. Current trends in the VC industry point to
more sustainable levels of fund raising and investing. Through September
30, 2001, $30.9 billion has been invested compared to $81 billion for the
same period in 2000 (NVCA 2001b). Although down relative to 1999 and
2000, activity in 2001 represents an increase from 1998, the year immediately preceding the bubble. The long-term trend continues to be strong and
steady in the upward direction, with 1999 and 2000 emerging as a temporary
and unsustainable bubble (see Figure 17.3). As VC and public markets return

to more sustainable growth rates, venture capitalists continue to look for long-term investments in next-generation innovative technology. Venture capitalists are still finding promising new opportunities in a wide range of sectors including software, communications, Internet infrastructure, medical/health, and biotechnology.

VC Portfolio Strategy: Mitigate Fund Risk

Venture capitalists mitigate the risk of investing in this high-risk asset class by developing a portfolio of young companies in a single venture fund. Many times they coinvest with other professional VC firms. Coinvesting is a common method to bring additional dollar capacity for future rounds, and to receive third-party validation to investment decisions already made by a fund. In addition, many venture partnerships raise new funds sequentially with one overlapping the next, and thus manage multiple funds simultaneously. Doing so allows the venture capitalist to continuously invest in new companies while nurturing those investments made previously, thus improving the ultimate chances of success by expanding the size of their portfolio.

An important part of this diversification strategy is for venture capitalists to invest in companies that fit the expertise of the fund. When considering an investment, VCs carefully screen the technical and business merits of the proposed company. VCs only invest in a small percentage, less than 1 percent, of the businesses they review, so each investment is crucial to the overall success of the fund. Most funds will have readily available criteria describing the types of companies they invest in, what stage of investment they consider, and what value and expertise they can bring to the investment. This allows a fund to invest in a number of companies within its particular expertise, thereby increasing the likelihood of success.

Characteristics of Attractive VC Investments

Venture capitalists are long-terms investors who typically take a very active role in their portfolio companies. When a venture capitalist makes an investment, he or she expects to realize a return on that investment in a three- to seven-year time horizon, on average. The initial investment is just the beginning of a long relationship between the venture capitalist and the entrepreneur. VC investments are made in young and innovative companies with the potential for explosive growth.

There are five characteristics that can be applied across the spectrum of venture funds that make companies seeking VC investments attractive:

1. A company seeking VC financing must have a proprietary product or service that offers a distinct competitive advantage sustainable over time. The competitive advantage should be a quantifiable economic advantage, such as better, cheaper, or faster. This is crucial because a venture capitalist needs to understand what problem in the market the product is solving and what economic incentive there is for the customer to buy it. Venture capitalists look for meaningful barriers to competitive entry, so that the advantage can be sustained over time. Such barriers may include: patent, trade secrets, or other intellectual property protection, a unique team and/or industry relationship, regulatory barriers, and occasionally first-mover advantage with some substantial switching cost that allows the innovator to capture the value of being first to market over its competition. The competitive landscape is an important part of the due diligence review while contemplating an investment decision.

2. To achieve the targeted return, an investment must have the potential for a significant increase in investment value in five to seven years. The ultimate increase in value will in part be a function of the stage of investment in the company. With this high return expectation, venture capitalists do not expect every investment to be a "grand slam." Instead, the likely scenario is that one out of ten investments will be a "grand slam," and this investment will net high enough returns to withstand the other portfolio company failures. Given the high rate of failures, each and every VC investment has to have the *potential* to be a grand slam at the outset. Without this upside potential going into each VC investment, a venture capitalist cannot make the portfolio model work.

3. The founders of the company have relevant industry and/or technical experience, and are solely focused on the opportunity. The founder's ambition and commitment should be a compelling reason to invest in their product or service. Entrepreneurs who have worked in an industry for many years, have significant accomplishments, and have a stellar reputation are most likely to receive venture financing. The founding team is one of the most important considerations when venture capitalists make financing decisions.

4. Another characteristic is that the entrepreneur shares the fund's long-term objective of building a company and ultimately taking it to a liquidity event, such as an initial public offering or the sale of the company. This characteristic is vital for the VC fund to provide returns and liquidity to its limited partners, which is the fundamental mission (and fiduciary responsibility) of the fund. Entrepreneurs who are intent on keeping a company closely held, or saving it for the next family generation are not candidates for VC financing. While some may view an IPO as the more "glamorous" exit vehicle or the alternative offering the greatest potential returns, a majority of

venture-backed companies are exited through a merger or acquisition that can also be very lucrative.

5. A final characteristic of venture-backed companies is that the founders recognize the areas of their greatest strength and weakness. Ideally, the founders should have a desire to build a team of skilled professionals to complement their own capabilities. This may include recruiting a CEO who is a seasoned veteran of a specific industry and has different skill sets than the founders. Along the same lines, it is important to work with entrepreneurs who also view investors and board members as valuable resources, and are receptive to input. An entrepreneur who meets the above criteria will have a significantly increased chance of funding and building a successful business.

VC Business Plan Expectations

While the ultimate decision to invest will not rest solely on the quality of the business plan, to attract initial interest a sound business plan is crucial.[3] Preparing a plan that meets the venture capitalist's expectations is challenging and time consuming. *Pratt's Guide to Venture Capital* offers guidelines to entrepreneurs who are preparing the business plan. Also, many VC fund Web sites offer advice on what is expected in the plan. While there is no exact road map for preparing a business plan, it is generally recommended that a full business plan be no longer than forty pages plus financial statements, and an executive summary (the only thing most VCs read initially) be around five pages or less. The sections to follow are a summary of the important points that must be addressed in order to attract sufficient interest from a venture capitalist.

Executive Summary

The executive summary is the most important section in the plan and it should be written last. In two to five pages, the summary must provide a compelling story about what your company does and why it is unique and valuable. It should paint a picture of the large opportunity in the marketplace, why it is not presently being served adequately, your company's unique capabilities or products, and its unfair competitive advantage that will enable it to capture the value over its competitors and generate superior growth and margins. Provide an explanation of how you will efficiently reach the customer through your marketing and sales program. Define the required management skills and describe the qualifications of the existing key managers. State the amount of capital that is required to implement the plan, the planned uses of the funds (including specific development milestones that will create value and reduce risks), the timing of your capital requirements, and projected financial results.

Business History

Naturally, the business history should include the date the business was founded and the form of the organization (C Corporation, S Corporation, Partnership, LLC, etc.). Any material investments into the company or changes in ownership or business focus should be discussed. The current breakdown of ownership should be provided.

In addition, the business history should briefly tell the story of why the company came into being. Define the chance discovery, the unique perspective, or ideal combination of experiences that enabled the company to identify the superior solutions to the market's problems rather than someone else. The business history should provide a brief insight into why the founders were in the right place at the right time with the right skill sets to seize the opportunity.

The Product and/or Service

This section should provide a detailed description of current products (or services) and products that are under development. For technology-based businesses, include a discussion of the product development strategy, the R&D efforts planned to support it, and the technological hurdles to be addressed along the way. Most investors consider a broad range of opportunities and many may not have a deep technical background. These factors may prevent them from having an intimate understanding of the status of technical developments in the industry. Keep it brief and avoid a highly technical description filled with undefined industry jargon, especially in an industry niche that is not widely known or understood.

The Market

This section should provide a broad overview of the market sector and the specific segments being targeted. Discuss the overall market size and growth, significant industry trends, and major opportunities and constraints presently facing the industry. Ideally, this information should be supported by reference to trade journal articles, industry studies, industry experts, and government sources that publish supporting historical data and industry forecasts.

The Competition

Too often business plans fail to acknowledge the presence and potential of all forms of competition. Identify the existing competitors in the market with a discussion of their particular strengths and weaknesses. Provide an estimate of their market share and basic information about their financial performance and resources, if available. Specifically discuss the products that you will be directly and indirectly competing against. Discuss the relative price, performance, and other characteristics of these products from a customer's perspective. Discuss the trends in their price/performance tradeoff. It is very helpful to include a competitive matrix or table that provides a summary comparison of each product on each important attribute. Who are the key rivals and why are they of particular concern?

The section should also discuss competitive responses to your product offerings, both those that have occurred and those that are anticipated. Provide a rationale for the expected responses from the competitors, both current and long term.

In addition to existing competitors, the section should discuss possible new competitors that may emerge. What are the barriers to entry for new competition? Also discuss potential substitutes (which include doing nothing and maintaining the status quo) for your product or service with a particular focus on those that have a superior price/performance tradeoff.

Marketing and Sales

The business plan is a strategic document, presenting a comprehensive picture of a market opportunity and how a company plans to exploit it. The marketing section should not only describe the strategy, it must also go a step deeper and present tactical details. It is not sufficient to say, for example, that you plan to spend the industry norm of 15 percent of revenues on marketing, which will enable you to get a mere 1 percent of a $10 billion market, resulting in $100 million in sales. Rather than showing how sales will drive a marketing budget, show how the actions detailed in the marketing plan will drive your projected sales. The key components of a comprehensive marketing plan include promotion, sales, distribution, and service.

Manufacturing and Operations

What are the manufacturing, assembly, and shipping requirements? Discuss the current facilities and manufacturing capacity. Are there any new investments in capacity required? If it is an early-stage company with a new product, what are the critical issues and risks in scaling up the manufacturing process? If subcontractors are used, discuss how they are selected and their performance is relied upon for success. If there is a sole source of any critical input that impacts the price and performance of your product, address the risk of that input becoming unavailable or unreasonably expensive and how those risks will be mitigated.

Management

Investors often have the rule of thumb that they would rather invest in grade A managers with a grade B product than a grade B manager with a grade A product. The management team is perhaps the single most important criterion in the selection of an investment opportunity. Provide a complete resume of each of the senior managers (including all relevant work experience, education, patents and technical publications, and professional certifications) and an organization chart.

Early-stage companies typically have incomplete teams. In these cases, investors want to understand the particular strengths of the current team, and the skills and attributes required to complete the team. Describe how you expect the roles of the present team to evolve and provide a recruitment schedule to fill key positions as the organization grows.

Also include background information on any board members, shareholders, or advisers who provide added expertise and credibility for the company. Include a description of how active they are within the organization and any expected changes in their roles.

Significant Risks

VC investments are inherently high-risk investments. Many of the risks are the ordinary risks faced by every new business (i.e., no established customer base and a lack of liquidity for investors). Sophisticated investors are already familiar with these risks. Your attorney will insist on disclosing these risks if you draft the document as a private-placement offering, but it is not necessary to state the obvious in a business plan. Investors are primarily interested in your perception of two kinds of risk: internal risk and external risk. Internal risk includes all risk factors associated with the company's ability to execute its plan and achieve its objectives. The external risks are those that may undermine your ability to be successful even if you flawlessly execute your plans. Discuss in depth the steps you are taking to mitigate these significant risks.

Exit Alternatives

VC investors typically expect to be shareholders in your company for three to seven years. They are patient, long-term investors, but eventually they need liquidity to return capital to their investors. Briefly discuss how you expect to create liquidity for your investors.

Financial Projections

Historical and projected financial information is required to enable investors to understand the rough magnitude of the opportunity: the entrepreneurs' assumptions in drafting the plan (how realistic are they?), planned uses of capital, the current and potential value of the company, and tradeoffs between risk and return for the investment. The business plan authors have to find the balance between the optimistic outlook that conveys the potential of the opportunity and the conservative forecast that makes the numbers both credible and achievable. Delivering on its promises and meeting investors' expectations are important, if a company hopes to maintain continued access to financing in the future.

At a minimum, this section should include:

1. Current year-to-date and annual income statement, balance sheet, and cash flow statement for the past five years (or since inception if the company is less than five years old).
2. Projected income statement, balance sheet, and cash flow on an accrual basis for the next five years. First-year projections should provide a monthly breakdown (and annual totals) with enough detail to provide investors information on head counts and compensation levels. Year two should provide monthly, or at least quarterly detail. Years three through five require only annual projections and do not require the same level of line item detail. Projections should also refer to any assumptions used in calculating the numbers.

VC Due Diligence Process

While some VCs will meet with entrepreneurs without a complete business plan, most funds will not enter the important due diligence process without a business plan. The due diligence process begins when the venture capitalist has gained sufficient interest to look closer at an investment opportunity based on the business plan, presentations, and discussions with the founders. Since venture capitalists invest in less than 1 percent of the deals they see, reaching the due diligence stage with a VC fund is a significant event for the entrepreneur. Although a fund may be in diligence with a company, this does not mean an investment is for certain. An investment will be determined only after satisfactory completion of the fund's diligence process.

The diligence process typically lasts thirty to ninety days as a minimum, and is very time consuming for both the fund and the entrepreneur. During this process, the fund will thoroughly examine everything about the company, the technology, the industry in which it operates, and the team. Research will be done on the market size, industry trends, competitive landscape, and any intellectual property claims. Any beta customers, potential customers, industry contacts, or other potential coinvestors will be contacted to gain insight into the opportunity. The VC fund will make reference calls on key management and founders to gain comfort that a long-term partnership is viable. The time and research involved in the VC due diligence process is one main difference between a VC investment and an angel investment.

Upon satisfactory completion of the due diligence process and affirmative support of the venture fund partners and advisory board, a "term sheet" will normally be generated to propose parameters for an investment in the company. The term sheet spells out the investment amount, terms and conditions, and valuation for the company. Some funds will present a term sheet before engaging in a full-blown due diligence process, although most do so after wrapping up the process. In either case, the investment is normally subject to final completion of the diligence process. Valuation is often the most difficult area to gain consensus between the fund and the entrepreneur.

VC Term Sheet

In most VC deals, there are common terms that VC investors will present, often contained in a nonbinding term sheet. A well-prepared term sheet will avoid "deal killers." It will contain not only a proposed valuation but also the key financial and legal terms of the transaction. A term sheet is assembled with the expectation that it will be discussed and negotiated between the fund and the entrepreneur. However, since the term sheet becomes the road map for the definitive investment documentation, it is very important for the entrepreneur to understand the standard terms in a VC term sheet. The failure of the management team and entrepreneur to appreciate the objectives of the VC investors can lead to early breakdowns in what might otherwise have been fruitful discussions and negotiations. As a result, it is critically important for the entrepreneur team to utilize the services of counsel experienced in venture capital financing.

Since venture capital is typically a minority investment in a company, a properly structured term sheet will also help neutralize the prerogatives of control, hence aligning the interests of the investors and entrepreneur. It is apparent that the owner of a controlling interest in a company enjoys some very valuable rights. Many factors, however, may limit a majority owner's right to exercise many of the prerogatives of control normally associated with majority ownership. Examples of the prerogatives of control are the ability to elect directors and appoint management, determine management compensation, acquire or liquidate assets, or register the company's stock for a public offering. The ability to limit the majority's ability to make unilateral decisions on the above examples gives the minority investor the ability to neutralize these important prerogatives of control.

With preferences contained in the terms that venture capitalists receive, it is vital that the entrepreneur select a fund that brings more value to the table than just money. This value can be in industry knowledge, industry contacts, strong follow-on financing relationships, and a stellar reputation. It is just as important for the entrepreneur to choose the right venture capitalist as it is for the venture capitalist to choose to invest in the right company.

Below is a brief outline of common points in a typical VC term sheet (Sjoquist and Feigen 2000). Keep in mind that appropriate structuring of a transaction cannot make a bad investment good; it can, however, influence the results of investments that are not meeting the initial expectations. Obviously, there are many other legal terms with which an entrepreneur will need to get comfortable, usually with the assistance of counsel when structuring an investment.

Instrument Type

Venture capitalists expect to participate in a company's equity growth. The venture capitalist will generally purchase a senior security that is convertible into common stock or comparable equity. This convertible senior security affords a measure of downside protection by virtue of its liquidation preference in the event the company fails. The liquidation preference allows the investors to receive their investment back first when a liquidation event occurs, such as the sale of the company. Convertible preferred stock has become the investment vehicle of choice for venture capitalists due to its flexibility, its ability to neutralize the prerogatives of control in the event of agreed-upon deviations from anticipated performance, and its flexibility in tailoring the vehicle to the critical issues involved in the company. The preferred stock, or its equivalent, often contains redemption provisions to enable the investor to recover the investment, if the enterprise fails to achieve anticipated levels of success.

Conversion

Preferred stock is almost always convertible into shares of a company's common stock at the discretion of the holder. In addition, preferred stock may provide for automatic conversion upon the occurrence of certain events, usually the completion of an IPO or the prior conversion of a prearranged percentage of outstanding preferred stock. Typically, preferred stock is convertible on a one-to-one ratio, subject to adjustment for the diluting events described below.

Antidilution

Convertible preferred stock frequently contains provisions that protect against dilution from stock splits, stock dividends, consolidations, and other corporate restructuring. Furthermore, the terms protect against the diluting effect of a sale of common stock at per share prices lower than those paid by the investor group. The common antidilution protection found in venture capital investments is referred to as "price protection." Price protection formulas are typically either on a "full-ratchet" basis, where the effective purchase price is adjusted all the way down to the lower price at which subsequent shares are sold, or on a "weighted-average" basis, where the magnitude of the adjustment depends on how many new shares are sold at the lower price (more shares sold at a lower price means more dilution, making the adjustment for existing investors greater). It is common for antidilution provisions to carve out an exception for some number of shares reserved for issuance under an employee stock option plan.

Liquidation Rights

In the event that the company is liquidated, holders of preferred stock typically have a priority claim relative to other classes of equity, but a junior position relative to debt. The liquidation preference equals some specified multiple of the original purchase price (typically one to three times) plus accrued but unpaid dividends. Participating preferred has become the standard in VC transactions, providing preferred holders with pro-rata participation on an as-converted basis after receiving their liquidation preference.

Registration Rights

If the company attains its goals of high growth and value creation, and becomes a viable IPO candidate, registration rights help assure the VC investor access to liquidity in the public market under certain conditions.

Voting Rights

Preferred stock issued in VC investments traditionally has voting rights similar to those of common stock (on a converted basis), plus additional voting rights where certain key events require majority or super-majority of preferred stock (or certain series) voting as a class. Generally, any major strategic initiatives or decisions such as selling/merging the company, going public, or selling securities to investors requires the approval of preferred stockholders voting separately from common stockholders.

Board Representation

Holders of preferred stock normally have the right to elect some number of directors of the company. The common holders elect the remaining directors, or there may be mutually elected directors. The investment agreement usually allows the preferred holders to elect a majority of the board of directors upon the occurrence of certain events, such as failing to meet agreed-upon milestones or violating covenants.

Summary

Venture capital is an increasingly important part of financing new and growing companies. Over the past few decades, VC investment has increased significantly. Part of the reason for this trend is the reluctance of industry and large corporations to take risks in funding new technologies. The amount of time and money required to focus on getting new technology to market is often too much for "corporate" America. For this and other reasons, venture capital's contribution to productivity and innovation will continue to be important in the years to come.

This chapter is intended to give an introduction to venture capital financing and some insight as to how the process works. VC investment is not suitable for all companies, but is an integral part of innovation and growth in the high-technology sector. Companies that offer a proprietary technology advantage in a large and growing market are contenders for venture funding. The companies that ultimately are chosen to receive investment dollars are only a select few that complement a strong market opportunity and technology position with a solid management team and vision. The companies that ultimately turn into "grand slams"—the Amgens and Cisco Systems of the world—are few and far between. But it is exactly that opportunity to invest in the next big success story that ultimately drives the venture capital market.

Notes

The author would like to extend his gratitude to Roger Ganser (founder and managing partner at Venture Investors LLC), John Neis (senior partner at Venture Investors LLC), Scott Button (partner at Venture Investors LLC), and George Arida (senior associate at Venture Investors LLC). My colleagues above provide me with daily guidance, intuition, motivation, wisdom, and education that allow me to continually improve my understanding of venture capital and strive for excellence every day, both inside and outside of work. I would also like to thank Bernie Issac and Kim Recker (Administrative Support at Venture Investors LLC) for taking the time to edit this chapter.

1. Silicon Valley history obtained from www.netvalley.com/.

2. Much of the historical information contained in this section is from the Web site www.indiainfoline.com/bisc/veca.

3. Much of the information on business plans contained in this section is from the Web site www.ventureinvestors.com.

References

Kwateng, David, ed. 2001. *Pratt's Guide to Venture Capital Sources*. New York: Thompson Financial.

Levin, Jack. 1998. *Structuring Venture Capital, Private Equity, and Entrepreneurial Transactions*. New York: Aspen.

National Venture Capital Association (NVCA). 2001a. Media Tool Kit (Summer). Arlington, VA: National Venture Capital Association.

———. 2001b. *Q3 Investment and Funding Report*. Arlington, VA: National Venture Capital Association.

———. 2001c. *2000–2001 Year in Review*. Arlington, VA: National Venture Capital Association.

Sjoquist, Mary J., and Phillip G. Feigen, eds. 2000. *Layman's Guide to the Legal Aspects of Venture Investments*, 1999–2000, 6th ed. Washington, DC: National Association of Small Business Capital Investments.

Smith, Richard L., and Janet K. Smith. 2000. *Entrepreneurial Finance*. New York: John Wiley.

About the Editors and Contributors

David E. Arnstein is an associate with Venture Investors LLC, an early-stage Venture Capital fund in Madison, Wisconsin. He focuses on the firm's information technology investments, with responsibilities including screening new investment opportunities and managing the due diligence process. Arnstein most recently served as an associate with radio station roll-up company Cumulus Media, Inc., where he was involved in the radio acquisition strategy and the management of the due diligence process. He holds a B.A. in accounting and an M.B.A. with concentrations in entrepreneurship and finance from the University of Wisconsin-Madison and is a certified public accountant.

Ziona Austrian holds a Ph.D. in economics from Case Western Reserve University. She is the director of the Center for Economic Development and a college fellow at the Maxine Goodman Levin College of Urban Affairs, Cleveland State University. Her areas of specialty include urban and regional economics, economic development, industrial clusters, and economic impact. She also directs a statewide network of urban and rural universities, which develops, maintains, and utilizes ES202 data. Prior to coming to Levin College, Dr. Austrian was the associate director for community analysis at the Center for Regional Economic Issues at the Weatherhead School of Management, Case Western Reserve University. Prior to that, she worked as an economic analyst in the research department of the Federal Reserve Bank of Cleveland.

James Bates is employed as a community builder with the U.S. Department of Housing and Urban Development (HUD) in Buffalo, New York. He serves as the initial point of contact for all HUD programs and services, and connects HUD's diverse constituencies to the agency's numerous community development resources for the Buffalo HUD office. He also provides technical expertise in community and economic development, urban problem solving, and comprehensive community planning to HUD constituents. Bates holds an M.S. from the University of Buffalo and is adjunct clinical assistant professor in the University of Buffalo's School of Social Work's Community Concentration.

Timothy Bates is distinguished professor of labor and urban affairs at Wayne State University. Dr. Bates received his Ph.D. in economics from the University of Wisconsin. Prior to his Wayne State appointment, he served as professor of urban policy analysis and chair of the graduate program in urban policy analysis at the New School for Social Research. His most recent book is *Race, Self-employment, and Upward Mobility: An Illusive American Dream*.

Richard D. Bingham is professor of public administration and urban studies at the Levin College of Urban Affairs and senior research scholar of the Urban Center, both at Cleveland State University. He teaches courses in industrial policy and research methods. His current research interests include the economies of urban neighborhoods and modeling of urban systems. Prof. Bingham has written widely in the fields of economic development and urban studies. His latest books include *Evaluation in Practice* (2002) with Claire Felbinger and *The Economies of Central City Neighborhoods* (2001) with Zhongcai Zhang. He is founding editor of the journal *Economic Development Quarterly* and is past president of the Urban Politics Section of the American Political Science Association.

Adam J. Bock is the research manager for Early Stage Research, LLC, an angel network in Wisconsin. He works with private investors to evaluate investment opportunities, primarily in the IT field. Mr. Bock is a co-founder of Stratatech, LLC, a biotechnology spinout of the University of Wisconsin-Madison. He has consulted to numerous other small businesses in Wisconsin. Bock received undergraduate degrees in both economics and aeronautical engineering from Stanford University. He completed an M.B.A. in entrepreneurship at the University of Wisconsin-Madison. He also serves on the board of advisers of the SEED Foundation, a nonprofit organization based in Washington, DC, that operates the nation's only public boarding school for inner-city children.

William M. Bowen is a professor of public administration and urban studies in the Maxine Goodman Levin College of Urban Affairs at Cleveland State University. His primary research interests are in computer-assisted decision making and problem solving in economic development, environmental affairs, and energy studies. His recent articles have appeared in *Public Administration Review*, *Environmental Management*, *Growth and Change*, the *Journal of Transport Geography,* and the *Journal of Real Estate Research*. Prof. Bowen is American editor of the *International Journal of Global Environmental Issues*.

Roger K. Dahlstrom has twenty-five years of professional city planning experience in both development and redevelopment work, including seventeen years as director of planning for the city of Elgin, Illinois. His areas of specialization include growth management, land use planning, capital improvement programming, community and fiscal impact analysis, development impact fee analysis and design, development agreements, and tax incremental financing. He has designed numerous computer applications for his noted areas of specialization, and he has authored published works on site and land capacity analysis, growth management, and local economic development planning.

Peter Fisher is a professor in the graduate program in Urban and Regional Planning at the University of Iowa, where he has taught since 1977. He holds a Ph.D. in economics from the University of Wisconsin-Madison. His research and teaching interests are centered on state and local government finance, economic development policy, and poverty and income inequality. Dr. Fisher is the coauthor, with Alan Peters, of *Industrial Incentives: Competition Among American States and Cities* (1998) and of a forthcoming book, also with Alan Peters, *State Enterprise Zones: Have They Worked?*

Edward W. (Ned) Hill is professor and Distinguished Scholar of Economic Development at the Maxine Goodman Levin College of Urban Affairs of Cleveland State University and nonresident senior fellow of The Brookings Institution, where he is affiliated with the Center of Urban and Metropolitan Policy. Prof. Hill writes on economic development and urban public policy and is an editor of *Economic Development Quarterly,* which is dedicated to publishing research on the development of the American economy. His most recent book was published in 2001: *Ohio's Competitive Advantage: Manufacturing Productivity.*

Rod Hissong is an associate professor in the School of Urban and Public Affairs at the University of Texas at Arlington. He earned his Ph.D. in economics from Rice University. He teaches courses in urban economic theory and policy, public finance, financial management, and research methods. His research interests include local economic development, tax incremental financing, and tax abatements. He is currently investigating the use and the efficacy of Texas's local economic development retail sales tax.

Larry Ledebur has been at the Levin College of Urban Affairs at Cleveland State University, where he currently serves as associate dean for Research and Public Service, since 1994. In addition to his academic appointments he has also served as senior research associate and director of the Urban Institute's Economic Development Program, senior economist of the White House Conference on Balanced National Growth and Economic Development, and as a visiting scholar and senior economist in the U.S. Economic Development Administration. Dr. Ledebur has written numerous books and articles on various aspects of urban economic development. His most recent book is *The New Regional Economies*, coauthored with William Barnes, research director at the National League of Cities.

John Magill is the assistant deputy director of the Office of Urban Development in the Ohio Department of Development. He is responsible for the design and administration of the Clean Ohio Revitalization Fund. Magill wrote portions of *Ohio's Urban Revitalization Policy Agenda and Task Force Report*. He was formerly the Revolving Loan Fund coordinator for the state of Ohio and developed Ohio's competitive Water and Sanitary Sewer program. He serves as an adjunct professor in the College of Engineering at the Ohio State University. He received his bachelors' degree from the University of Notre Dame, his master's in city and regional planning from the Ohio State University, and his M.B.A. from Ashland University.

Stephen Malpezzi is associate professor, and Wangard Faculty Scholar, in the Department of Real Estate and Urban Land Economics, as well as an associate member of the Department of Urban and Regional Planning, of the University of Wisconsin-Madison (www.bus.wisc.edu/realestate). Dr. Malpezzi's research includes work on economic development, the measurement and determinants of real estate prices, housing demand, and the effects of economic policies on real estate markets. He recently served on Wisconsin's Blue Ribbon Commission on State and Local Partnerships (www.lafollette. wisc.edu/reform).

Beverly McLean is currently a research associate with the School of Architecture and Planning, State University of New York at Buffalo. Her research interests are urban labor markets, community economic development, neighborhood crime prevention strategies, and community health planning. She holds a Ph.D. in urban studies from Portland State University School of Urban and Public Affairs.

Peter B. Meyer is professor of urban policy and economics at the University of Louisville, where he directs the Center for Environmental Policy and Management and the EPA Region 4 Environmental Finance Center. While at Pennsylvania State University, he was director of the Local Economic Development Assistance Center. He has conducted work on brownfield redevelopment and urban infill for the U.S. Environmental Protection Agency and U.S. Department of Housing and Urban Development, as well as the Economic Development Agency. Relevant recent publications include *Projecting Environmental Trends from Economic Forecasts* (2001), *Reclamation and Economic Regeneration of Brownfields* (2000), *Contaminated Land* (1995), and *Comparative Studies in Local Economic Development* (1993).

Michael T. Peddle is associate professor of public administration and a senior faculty associate at the Center for Governmental Studies at Northern Illinois University. An economist and accountant by training, his research focuses on local economic development, growth management, and education policy. He regularly assists local, regional, and state governments with formulating and refining economic development and growth management plans.

Alan Peters teaches in the graduate program in Urban and Regional Planning at the University of Iowa. He has written two books, both with Peter Fisher, and numerous articles on economic development issues in the United States. The focus of his economic development research is on measuring the size of incentives and estimating their likely impact on business and worker behavior. Dr. Peters also does research on the application of Geographic Information Systems (GIS) and related visualization technologies to urban planning practice. He has a Ph.D. from Rutgers University.

Kelly Robinson is senior research analyst at the Joseph C. Cornwall Center for Metropolitan Studies, Rutgers University (Newark). He has also served as an economist at the Economic Development Administration. Prior to that he taught in the Public Policy Department at Rutgers (New Brunswick). He received his Ph.D. from the Massachusetts Institute of Technology, Department of Urban Studies and Planning.

Mark S. Rosentraub is professor and dean at the Maxine Goodman Levin College of Urban Affairs at Cleveland State University. Dr. Rosentraub's research interests focus on the impacts on urban areas of professional sports teams and the facilities they use; the financing, organization, and delivery of urban services; tourism as a tool for economic development; and economic development issues. His book, *Major League Losers: The Real Costs of Sports and Who's Paying for It* was published in 1997 and 1999. His research has also appeared in *Public Administration Review, American Review of Public Administration, Economic Development Quarterly, Journal of Sports and*

Social Issues, Journal of Urban Affairs, Urban Affairs Review, Journal of the American Planning Association, Public Finance Review, and *State and Local Government Review,* as well as several other journals and numerous collections.

Ferdinand P. ("Andy") Schoettle is a professor of law at the University of Minnesota. Dr. Schoettle is a Harvard-trained Ph.D. economist and lawyer. He has worked for the U.S. Treasury Department, for three U.S. senators, and as law clerk to Judge Learned Hand. He has taught at Minnesota, Harvard, Uppsala University in Sweden, and William Mitchell Law School. Dr. Schoettle may be reached at andy-schoettle@msn.com or at schoe001@tc.umn.edu.

Donald L. Schunk is a research economist for the Division of Research and assistant professor of economics in the Moore School of Business at the University of South Carolina. Dr. Schunk teaches both graduate and undergraduate courses in money and banking and forecasting. His research interests include macro and monetary economics, and regional economics, with a focus on the nature of regional business cycles. He is responsible for the South Carolina Economic Forecasting Service in the Moore School of Business.

Robert A. Simons is a professor and director of the Master of Urban Planning, Design and Development Program at the Levin College of Urban Affairs at Cleveland State University in Cleveland, Ohio. Dr. Simons teaches courses in real estate development, market analysis and finance, public economics, and environmental finance. He has published over twenty-five articles on real estate, urban redevelopment, environmental damages, housing policy, and brownfields redevelopment. Dr. Simons recently wrote a book entitled *Turning Brownfields into Greenbacks,* published by the Urban Land Institute. He has an active consulting practice and has served as an expert witness in matters related to real estate and environmental damages.

Rachel Weber is an assistant professor in the Urban Planning and Policy Program of the University of Illinois at Chicago. Her current research focuses on the design and effectiveness of financial incentives to private businesses and developers. She is the author of the book *Swords into Dow Shares: Governing the Decline of the Military Industrial Complex* (2000), which explores the relationship between financial markets and corporate restructuring in the defense industry.

Sammis B. White is a professor of urban planning at the University of Wisconsin-Milwaukee. He was cofounder and for ten years, coeditor with Richard Bingham, of *Economic Development Quarterly*. He and Prof. Bingham also formed the organization known as the Great Lakes States Economic Development Researchers. Prof. White has researched numerous issues in economic development, including entrepreneurship, the sources of employment growth, and regional variations in growth. He has written over 120 articles and reports, the majority of which have been on economic development.

Kimberly Winson-Geideman is a Ph.D. candidate at Cleveland State University (CSU). She obtained her master's in Urban Studies from CSU in 1996 and spent the following five years in acquisitions and project management for Forest City Land Group. Her research interests include brownfield policy, brownfield development, and residential and office property valuation. Winson-Geideman has published in the *Appraisal Journal* and contributed chapters to books on toxic waste and retail development.

Douglas P. Woodward is the director of the Division of Research and associate professor of economics in the Moore School of Business at the University of South Carolina. His primary research interests are foreign direct investment and state and local economic development. Dr. Woodward is co-author of a book on foreign direct investment in the United States, *The New Competitors* (1989), which *Business Week* ranked as one of the top ten business and economics books and *Forbes* listed as one of the books that CEOs are reading.

Kristen R. Yount is associate professor and coordinator of the Sociology Program, and coordinates the Sustainable Future Program at Northern Kentucky University. She has applied her expertise in risk perception and ethnographic research skills to examining brownfield risk control, concentrating on public and private sector provision and utilization of environmental insurance. She has conducted brownfields studies for the U.S. Environmental Protection Agency, the U.S. Department of Housing and Urban Development, the Lincoln Institute, and state and local agencies. Relevant recent publications include: *Environmental Insurance and Public Sector Brownfield Programs* (2000), *Environmental Insurance Products Available for Brownfields Redevelopment, 1999* (2000), *Financing Small-Scale Urban Redevelopment Projects* (1997), and *Contaminated Land* (1995).

Index